FinTech 5.0

This book offers comprehensive knowledge, and the applications, of the rapidly evolving financial technology landscape. Authored by seasoned experts, it serves as a vital resource for both students and practitioners in the Fintech sector.

Covering the evolution of cryptocurrencies to the rise of Neobanks and Central Bank Digital Currencies (CBDCs), this volume delves into critical topics such as blockchain, PayTech, LendTech, WealthTech, InsurTech, RegTech and artificial intelligence in finance. It also provides insights into Neobanking and CBDC. Each chapter details the latest trends, challenges and regulatory frameworks shaping the industry, along with examples and illustrative case studies.

Students will benefit from the structured approach that facilitates understanding complex concepts, while practitioners will find real-world applications, case studies and strategic insights to enhance their professional practices. With a focus on innovation and technology, this book not only prepares readers for the future of finance but also equips them with the tools to navigate and thrive in this dynamic environment. This unique volume is an essential guide to understanding and leveraging Fintech advancements, for beginners and experts alike.

Jayanta Chakraborti holds the position of Dean and Principal at Global Institute of Business Studies, Bangalore, India.

Shalini Aggarwal, alumni of IIM Ahmedabad, is Professor of Finance at Chandigarh University, India, and has 20 years of industry and teaching experience.

Pardeep Kumar is Associate Professor of Finance at Chandigarh University, India.

FinTech 5.0

The Journey from Cryptocurrency to Neobanking

Jayanta Chakraborti, Shalini Aggarwal and Pardeep Kumar

Routledge
Taylor & Francis Group
LONDON AND NEW YORK

Designed cover image: Getty images

First published 2025
by Routledge
4 Park Square, Milton Park, Abingdon, Oxon OX14 4RN

and by Routledge
605 Third Avenue, New York, NY 10158

Routledge is an imprint of the Taylor & Francis Group, an informa business

British Library Cataloguing-in-Publication Data
A catalogue record for this book is available from the British Library

ISBN: 978-1-032-63640-5 (hbk)
ISBN: 978-1-032-69940-0 (pbk)
ISBN: 978-1-032-69941-7 (ebk)

DOI: 10.4324/9781032699417

Typeset in Sabon
by Apex CoVantage, LLC

Contents

List of Figures — *vi*
List of Tables — *vii*
About the Authors — *viii*
Preface — *x*
Acknowledgments — *xiii*

1 Introduction to Fintech — 1

2 The Secret World of Cryptocurrencies — 10

3 Blockchain Demystified — 30

4 Digital Payments – The PayTech Model — 54

5 Digital Lending – The LendTech Model — 76

6 The WealthTech Model — 102

7 Risk Management – The InsurTech Model — 129

8 Financial Regulations and Compliances – The RegTech Model — 155

9 Neobanking – Bringing Convenience to Customers — 185

10 Central Bank Digital Currency (CBDC) — 206

11 Application of Artificial Intelligence in Fintech — 237

12 The Future of Fintech Industry — 253

Index — *264*

Figures

1.1	The Fintech Ecosystem	3
2.1	The Workflow of a Digital Currency Transaction	13
2.2	Application of Timestamping to Create Blocks	13
2.3	Application of Proof-of-Work (PoW) to Secure Blocks	14
2.4	The Mining Process of Bitcoins	16
2.5	Market Share of Cryptocurrencies	18
3.1	Blocks in a Blockchain	33
3.2	The Proof-of-Work (PoW)	41
4.1	The Digital Payment Ecosystem	56
4.2	The Payment Gateway	59
4.3	Quick Response (QR) Code	60
4.4	Application Program Interface (API)	61
5.1	Traditional Model of Lending	79
5.2	Different kinds of Debt Instruments	80
5.3	The LendTech Model	83
6.1	The Wealth Management Life	103
6.2	The WealthTech Ecosystem	105
6.3	Working Mechanism of Robo-Advisors	108
6.4	Algorithmic Trading Mechanism	110
6.5	Working Mechanism of Digital Portfolio Management System	112
7.1	The InsurTech Ecosystem	135
8.1	RegTech Process Flow	166
8.2	The RegTech Ecosystem	174
9.1	Neobanking Process Flow Diagram	194
9.2	Neobanking Architecture	195
9.3	Global Neobanking Market Size	196
10.1	Working Model of CBDC	213
11.1	Process of DevOps	244

Tables

2.1 The Reward for Creating Bitcoins 17
2.2 The Most Valued Cryptocurrencies (as of 10.03.2024) 18
3.1 Database versus Blockchain – The Main Differences 34
3.2 Proof-of-Work (PoW) and Proof-of-Stake (PoS) 41
6.1 The Robo-Advisory Firms 107
7.1 Traditional Insurance versus InsurTech Model 141
8.1 Different Phases of RegTech 162
9.1 Traditional Banks versus Neobanks 189
10.1 Cross-Border CBDC Transaction 216

About the Authors

Jayanta Chakraborti holds the position of Dean and Principal at Global Institute of Business Studies, Bangalore, India. He has done PhD in Business Analytics and Digital Marketing from NIT Agartala, an MBA from IMI Europe, an MA in Economics from Devi Ahilyabai University Indore and a Bachelor's Degree in Mechanical Engineering from NIT Agartala. He has worked at Symbiosis Pune as Director of School of BFSI and HOD at ICFAI University and Chandigarh University. He is SAP-certified ERP Consultant, IBM Certified Big Data Analyst and Google Certified AdWords Professional. He has also done certification in Data Mining from ISI Kolkata and ISI Bangalore, Certification in Data Analytics from IIT Madras and IIT Roorkee and Certification in E-Business from IIT Kharagpur. He has more than 30 years of experience in Steel, Education and IT Sector. He has jointly done workshops with eminent faculties from Harvard University, London Business School, INSEAD Paris and IMD Lausanne. He has trained more than 5,000 professionals in Asia and Europe in a career spanning more than 30 years. He is the author of books like *Digital Marketing 2.0*, *HR@Analytics*, *The Digital Entrepreneur* and *The Cinderella Jones Affair*.

Shalini Aggarwal, alumni of IIM Ahmedabad, is Professor of Finance at Chandigarh University, India, and has 20 years of industry and teaching experience. She has presented various papers at conferences including IIM Lucknow, IIM Bangalore, IIM Shillong and IIM Kashipur. She has published 35 papers and 5 case studies. Eight of her research papers including case studies have been published in the Scopus index and ABDC-listed journals. She has authored two edited books with Taylor & Francis (one completed and one under process). Further, she has contributed to two book chapters in Taylor & Francis books entitled *Crowdfunding in Financial Acumen* and *AI in Fashion – Present and Future Applications*. She has completed two funded research projects. One funded research project was done with IIM Ahmedabad, titled "Technology Upgradation at MICROSIGN Products" under the guidance of Prof. Vijay Sherry Chand of IIM Ahmedabad.

Pardeep Kumar is Associate Professor of Finance at Chandigarh University, India. He has over 20 years of experience in industry and leading academic institutions. He is an alumnus of the Army Institute of Management, Kolkata (MBA, Finance/Marketing), and Khalsa College, Amritsar (B.Sc. Non-Medical), and has received the Doctor of Philosophy (Management) degree from the prestigious IKG Punjab Technical University, Jalandhar, India. His teaching focus includes Project Finance and Financial Modeling, Business and Financial Analytics, Investment Management, International Finance; and other allied subject areas in the field of Finance. He has published three books and several research papers in various international and national journals of repute and has presented his research at several International conferences and seminars in the field of Management apart from guiding post-graduating students and supervising Ph.D. scholars. His areas of keen interest in research are Behavioral Finance, Investment Management and different areas of the field of Finance. He is a life member of the Indian Society of Technical Education and is associated with several social service works.

Preface

Circa 2008.

Banking has always been one of the most lucrative businesses in the world. The banker collects funds from both short-term and long-term depositors at relatively low interest rates and then provides loans to borrowers at comparatively high interest rates. The spread refers to the difference between the lending and borrowing rates. The greater the spread or margins, the higher the bank's profits. As the volume of loans increases, the growth rate also increases. Hence, banks always encourage customers to open zero-balance savings accounts or salary accounts and encourage the same customers to take credit cards at very low or zero annual fees. Deposits are taken at low rates; loans are given at high rates. The idea is to increase the spread and thus earn more profits. This strategy worked quite well till 2008 when the whole banking industry landed in the doldrums.

Over the years, the bankers had become too greedy. They started giving loans to people with high risk, low capability to repay and bad history of defaults. These loans were also called subprime loans. The idea was to bundle and package these loans and sell them off to other financial organizations to de-risk the balance sheet. But the big problem started when the end customer who was supposed to pay interest and equated monthly installments (EMIs) started to default. This was also called the subprime crisis.

The subprime crisis started with the collapse of Lehman Brothers and Bear Sterns in 2007 and soon spread like a financial contagion all across the world. As the banks struggled to survive and begged for financial stimulus, many bankers and financial professionals lost their jobs. The banking experts knew that they had to do something quick and fast; otherwise, their very existence would be in danger.

The problem with traditional banking was that it was over-regulated and tightly controlled by a few influential bankers and policymakers who could manipulate the system to maximize their own benefits. And it was quite difficult to dislodge this coterie or change their archaic practices. Hence, the practitioners of finance came out with disruptive technologies and systems that threatened the very fabric of the traditional and archaic banking and financial systems.

The disruption started with Bitcoins and blockchain, which we also call the wave of Fintech 1.0. Bitcoin is a type of cryptocurrency in which a record of transactions is maintained. The new units of cryptocurrency are generated by the computational solution of mathematical problems. The transactions with cryptocurrencies operate independently of a central bank. The father of Bitcoins is supposed to be a mysterious personality called Satoshi Nakamoto. He introduced "Bitcoin" to the world in the year 2008, exactly the year in which the subprime crisis happened. But very little is actually known about

Nakamoto. Nakamoto is also considered to be the founder of blockchain, which was invented to ensure a secure system of transactions with Bitcoins.

Fintech 1.0 was led by cryptocurrencies and blockchain in 2008 after the landmark innovations done by Satoshi Nakamoto. Cryptocurrencies and blockchains enable peer-to-peer (P2P) transactions without the direct control of any bank or financial institution. Initially, the governments and central bankers despised and created hurdles for P2P transactions but eventually accepted these systems by framing laws and regulations and giving them legal acceptance. The details of cryptocurrencies and blockchains are written in Chapters 2 and 3.

The next wave termed Fintech 2.0 came in 2015 with the rising popularity of smartphones. Smartphones and data access were getting cheaper and were within the reach of the common people. With the rise of smartphone and Internet usage, mobile banking took precedence over physical visits to a bank branch or going to the ATM to withdraw cash. But again, there was a problem. Many of the people had mobile phones but no access to credit cards, debit cards or net banking. This problem was resolved by e-wallets (electronic wallets).

PayPal launched an electronic wallet long back in 1998. Google launched Google Wallet in 2011. Apple launched Apple Pay in 2014. In India, electronic wallets such as Paytm, PhonePe, BharatPe and Freecharge were gaining popularity. In China Alipay run by Alibaba and WeChat run by Tencent were the most popular electronic wallets. This time, governments, instead of opposing the process, actually facilitated and encouraged the digital transformation with tools like unified payment interface (UPI) and Bharat Interface for Money (BHIM). This era was marked by innovations like PayTech, LendTech, WealthTech and InsurTech, which are covered in detail in Chapters 4, 5, 6 and 7.

With the rise of cryptocurrencies and P2P transactions came another big challenge. Bitcoins and the dark web were being used for many illicit activities like money laundering, drug trafficking, terror funding, collecting ransoms, gambling and betting activities. All these illegal and illicit activities needed to be controlled, and the traditional mechanisms were indeed too weak to check the onslaught. The regulators then turned to tech innovators and entrepreneurs, who came out with a new mechanism called RegTech. This can be called the period of Fintech 3.0. The details of RegTech are covered in detail in Chapter 8.

In the last three years, the pandemic caused by the COVID-19 virus pushed the world toward the brink of disaster. With more than 200 million cases and 5 million deaths, business activity went to a standstill. With people being confined to their home and doing remote transactions, everyone wanted a system where fast transactions could be done with a bare minimum of hassles. This decade is seeing the rising popularity of Neobanks, which have no physical presence. Neobanks operate completely in the electronic format and are now well accepted by common people and the business community. There are more than 200 Neobanks in different countries across the world, and the numbers are rising rapidly. Neobanks are all set to usher in Fintech 4.0. The details about Neobanks are given in Chapter 9.

Governments and regulators across the world were quite uneasy and uncomfortable in accepting the growing popularity of cryptocurrencies that heralded a parallel economy. Initially, they decided to ban cryptocurrencies, and then they imposed high taxes on cryptocurrencies but neither of these measures succeeded in dwindling the popularity of Bitcoins, Ethereum and other cryptos. Eventually, many governments across the world decided to launch their own version of digital currency, which is called Central Bank

Digital Currency (CBDC). Worldwide, all major countries in the developed world have made a foray into the process of introducing digital currency. China has already started the test run of digital currency called e-RMB, which has been created to counter the monopoly of the dollar. The Federal Reserve of the USA has released a research paper that explores a move to a Central Bank Digital Currency. Nine banks in India – State Bank of India, Bank of Baroda, Union Bank of India, HDFC Bank, ICICI Bank, Kotak Mahindra Bank, Yes Bank, IDFC First Bank and HSBC – are participating in a pilot project run by Reserve Bank of India to launch CBDC in India. The introduction of CBDC will usher in Fintech 5.0. The details of CBDC are covered in Chapter 10.

Artificial intelligence (AI) and machine learning (ML) are sweeping all industries, and the banking and financial services industry is no exception. In the present decade, AI is executing a key function. It is assisting Fintech companies in automating repetitive processes and enhancing results on a level that surpasses human intelligence. Early implementation of AI empowers Fintech organizations to detect risks, thwart fraudulent activities, automate routine processes and elevate service excellence. All of these factors contribute to enhanced efficiency and increased profitability. The details of how artificial intelligence and machine learning is playing a key role in the Fintech industry are covered in detail in Chapter – 11.

If Bitcoins, digital wallets and blockchain ushered in Fintech 1.0, the revolution of Fintech 5.0 is led by Neobanking, CBDC, AI, ML, big data, DevOps, chatbots and robotic process advisors (RPA). The dependence on human interface is reducing, and the automation process is gearing up to create a system of seamless 24 × 7 and 365 days of service delivery. Fintech has also spawned a new breed of entrepreneurs who are catering to the different financial needs of various types of customers. They are launching interesting and innovative products like Buy Now Pay Later (BNPL), smart contracts and non-fungible tokens that can be used for financial transactions in Metaverse. The future of Fintech and the financial industry has been discussed in Chapter 12.

This book starts with a journey of Fintech 1.0, takes you into the world of Fintech 2.0, 3.0 and 4.0 and ends with the description of tools and technologies of Fintech 5.0 that are all set to revolutionize and sweep the financial industry in the world. This book can be used as a textbook for students who are getting ready to take a course or enroll in a program on Fintech in a college or university. This book can be a guidebook for practitioners to understand how the Fintech business model can help their business. This book also has a lot of real-life case studies that help understand the business model and the business landscape in a better manner.

Fintech is the amalgamation of financial services and technological advancements. The challenge lies in the fact that those people who are proficient in finance often lack a strong expertise in technology. Individuals with a strong grasp of technology often struggle to comprehend finance. This book acts as a conduit for those proficient in finance and technology to comprehend the extent and implement optimal strategies that facilitate the creation of a smooth operation by amalgamating the finest aspects of both domains.

Technology is changing at a fast pace, and we have made our best endeavors to put together a tome of knowledge that is relevant and updated. However, we welcome all kinds of suggestions that can make this book a better one in subsequent editions.

Acknowledgments

I would like to express my heartfelt gratitude to all those who have contributed to the creation of this book *FinTech 5.0: The Journey from Cryptocurrency to Neobanking*.

First and foremost, I extend my deepest appreciation to my co-authors, Dr. Shalini and Dr. Pardeep, whose expertise and insights have been invaluable throughout this journey. Your collaboration has enriched the content and depth of this work.

I am profoundly grateful to my mentor, Dr. Raj Kapur, Chairman of the India Blockchain Alliance, for your guidance and encouragement. Your wisdom has been a beacon of inspiration for me.

A special thanks goes to Mr. Ritesh Goyal, MD of GIBS Business School Bangalore, for your unwavering support and leadership. Your belief in this project has motivated me immensely. I also wish to acknowledge my colleagues at GIBS, Mr. Bharat Gopalan and Mr. Guruprasad Rao, for your camaraderie and assistance during the writing process. I would also like to take this opportunity to thank my colleagues at Symbiosis Skills and Professional University – Dr. Ajeet Phanse, Dr. Smita Pachare, Dr. Pratibha Patil, Dr. Jiya Khatwani, Dr. Purushottam Petare, Dr. Raghavan Santhanam, Dr. Shailesh Kediya, Dr. Ravindra Kayande, Dr. Neetu Chouhan, Dr. Archana Ainapure and Dr. Prashant Chaudhuri – for giving their valuable inputs while writing this book.

To my beloved wife, Bhaswati, and our son, Biswajeet, your love and understanding have been my greatest strength. Thank you for your patience and support during the long hours I spent writing.

I would also like to thank Mr. Amit Kumar of Taylor & Francis for commissioning this book, as well as Ms. Srimoyee, who has expertly edited the manuscript. My appreciation extends to the entire editorial and publication team at Taylor & Francis/Routledge for their professionalism and dedication in bringing this book to life.

This work is a culmination of collective efforts, and I am grateful to everyone who played a role in its creation. Thank you all for your contributions!

Jayanta Chakraborti
Dean & Principal
GIBS Business School
Bengaluru, India

Fintech 5.0 has been a rewarding journey, one that would not have been possible without the guidance, support and encouragement of many individuals to whom I am deeply grateful.

First and foremost, I extend my heartfelt gratitude to my family for their unwavering belief in me. I would like to express my deepest gratitude to my father, Major Tilak Raj Sharma (retd.), whose love and guidance have been the cornerstone of my journey. His wisdom, patience and belief in my abilities have been a constant source of inspiration and strength. I am forever grateful for the sacrifices he has made and the values he has instilled in me. This work is a reflection of the lessons I have learned from him, and I dedicate this achievement to the incredible role he has played in shaping my life. Thank you, Dadha! For always being my biggest supporter and my greatest mentor. Tons of gratitude to my mother "Maa", beloved wife Dr. Charu and sweet son "Harshil". Their constant support, patience and love have been the bedrock of my endeavors.

I would like to extend my sincere gratitude to my co-author, Dr. Jayanta Chakraborti, whose collaboration, dedication and insightful contributions were instrumental in bringing this work to fruition. Big thanks to Dr. Shalini Agarwal, for greatly enriching this project. This work is a testament to our successful partnership, and I look forward to future collaborations.

I would also like to acknowledge the contributions of the wider Fintech community – academics, professionals and thought leaders – whose pioneering work laid the foundation upon which this book is built. Their innovative approaches continue to push the boundaries of what is possible in the world of finance and technology.

To the editorial and publishing teams who have worked tirelessly to bring this book to life, thank you for your professionalism, attention to detail and commitment to excellence.

Lastly, I extend my gratitude to the readers of Fintech 5.0. It is my hope that this book sparks new ideas, fosters understanding and serves as a catalyst for future innovation in this ever-evolving industry.

With sincere appreciation,

Pardeep Kumar
Associate Professor
Chandigarh University

1 Introduction to Fintech

After reading this chapter you will:

- Know what is Fintech
- Understand the Fintech Ecosystem
- Know about the different companies that are in the business of Fintech
- Understand the business model used by Fintech companies
- Know about the challenges faced by Fintech Companies
- Know about the future of the Fintech business

The transformation of paper currencies to digital currencies has been quite fascinating. This has been brought about by a series of innovations driven by the consumer need to make financial transactions in a fast and seamless manner. The use of paper money that was started in the seventh century by the Tang dynasty in China was backed by gold and silver, as it was quite inconvenient to carry the bulky metals.

From paper money evolved the fiat currency that had sovereign backing from the government and hence trust and confidence among the retail customers. We also witnessed the commencement of central banks which regulated the inflow and outflow of the fiat currency and formulation of monetary policy to maintain a balanced flow of money in the economy.

The technological advancements led to further innovations in the form of automated teller machine (ATM), credit cards and debit cards (also known as plastic money), electronic fund transfers (EFT), online banking and mobile banking. The physical currencies lost importance as more and more financial transactions started happening electronically.

The first decade of the twenty-first-century millennium witnessed a disruptive innovation called cryptocurrency, which heralded the era of decentralized finance (DeFi). This also heralded the popularity of P2P financial transactions that did not require the intervention of banks and financial institutions. The cryptocurrencies were mined and circulated using a technology called blockchain, which later found application in several other sectors like healthcare, supply chain and manufacturing.

The P2P mechanism of financial transactions at the popularity of DeFi applications brought about a lot of disruptive innovations like PayTech, LendTech, WealthTech, InsurTech and RegTech, which were developed with blockchain, big data analytics and artificial intelligence (AI) capabilities. Soon, startup companies with innovative Fintech applications were competing against the big banks and offering convenient and attractive options to customers. Some of the Fintech startup companies turned into unicorns (startups with a billion-dollar valuation).

DOI: 10.4324/9781032699417-1

The growing popularity of cryptocurrencies forced bankers to look for innovative solutions to counter the competition. One of the innovative solutions accepted by bankers was the Central Bank Digital Currency (CBDC). The CBDC is similar to the cryptocurrencies and is transacted through digital platforms. However, CBDC has higher conviction, trust and acceptability as it is backed by the central government.

The other innovation was Neobank, which is a virtual bank without a physical interface. This is completely run on an electronic interface with AI and technological tools providing operating and backend support. The transactions are faster and much easier to conduct in comparison to physical banks.

The growth of technology and mobile devices has been a great facilitator in the growth of Fintech business. Mobile phones have made financial transactions much easier, and now there are mobile apps for every kind of financial transaction. Technologies like near-field communication (NFC) and chatbots are helping Fintech companies to offer superior customer services in financial transactions. Financial inclusion, especially in rural and remote areas, has also been made possible by the application of Fintech.

The advance of the Fintech business has not been without challenges. There have been concerns raised about the safety and security of financial transactions carried out through Fintech. Although some instances of phishing, hacking and data breaches have been reported, the Fintech experts have created RegTech applications and cybersecurity measures to counter the threat.

Ultimately, the transition from physical currency to virtual currency signifies a profound transformation in our understanding, administration and exchange of worth. Although paper currency continues to play a crucial role in our monetary system, digital money presents unparalleled prospects for innovation, inclusivity and efficiency in the modern day.

Introduction to Fintech

Financial technology or Fintech is a sector based on the use of software to provide financial services. Fintech is technology-oriented and is quicker and more efficient than traditional financial service providers. Fintech has evolved from financial technology (Chishti & Barberis, 2016).

Previously, financial technology meant the backend digital technology that traditional services like banks used. However, now, it is totally different. It is gradually moving toward DeFi with the launch of decentralized applications (DApps). dApps are “digital applications or programs that run on a decentralized network, rather than a single computer or server. They are built on blockchain technology and use cryptocurrency as a means of exchange”. Fintech companies are now facilitating payments, lending, wealth management, insurance, financial transactions and risk management, which are being carried out in a faster and more streamlined manner through technology interfaces (Friesendorf, 2023).

Figure 1.1 illustrates the Fintech ecosystem. The Fintech ecosystem comprises PayTech, LendTech, WealthTech, InsurTech, RegTech and Neobanking. PayTech, short for “payment technology”, refers to the rapidly evolving landscape of technologies and solutions designed to facilitate and streamline the process of making payments. It encompasses a wide range of innovations that span digital, electronic and mobile payment methods, as well as the underlying infrastructure and systems that support these transactions. PayTech plays a crucial role in the modern economy, transforming the way businesses and

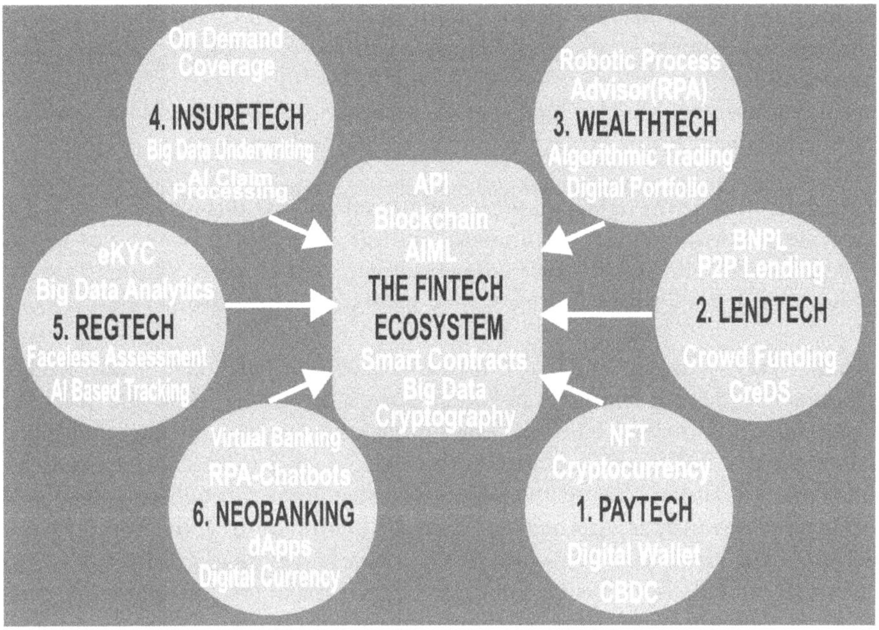

Figure 1.1 The Fintech Ecosystem

consumers make payments, from traditional cash and checks to digital and contactless options.

Companies like PayPal, Paytm, Alipay, WeChat, Razorpay, Stripe and Fiserv have created a business model by facilitating payments between vendors and customers. Many of them also provide payment gateways to e-commerce companies and facilitate bill payments and buying of movie tickets and bus, train and flight tickets, allowing customers to send and receive money around the world. PayPal helps customers link their bank account, credit card and debit card and make online payments in more than 200 countries across the world.

Stripe offers a range of tools and configurable APIs to make payments easier. Stripe makes it simple for platforms and marketplaces to handle payments while adhering to regulations, from confirming the vendors' identities to directing funds. Paytm is facilitating financial transactions of more than 20 million merchants in India and helps customers pay bills, book tickets for travel and movies and do P2P financial transactions with family and friends. There are several companies in China like Alipay that facilitate electronic payments and payments of bills. Alipay has an exclusive digital wallet that can be used for money transfers, purchases of products and services and payment through credit cards and debit cards.

A financial miracle that has happened in India is the unified payment interface (UPI). UPI was created by the National Payment Corporation of India (NPCI). This platform connects banks with merchants and customers and facilitates seamless money transfers and payments through mobile phones. All transactions in UPI are free and have contributed to exponential growth in SME business. Its user-friendly interface, real-time processing and secure authentication have contributed to its widespread adoption and success. The Government of India has also launched several other Fintech applications like Bharat Interface for Money (BHIM). Both BHIM and UPI have played a major role in the Indian Government's ambition to create a cashless economy fueled by digital monetary transactions.

The lending business has also seen several disruptions through LendTech, which is an important component of the Fintech ecosystem. LendTech refers to

> the integration of advanced technology and digital innovations into the lending and borrowing processes within the financial industry. LendTech companies leverage cutting-edge technologies to streamline, automate, and enhance various aspects of lending, making the process more efficient, accessible, and customer-centric.

The major players in the LendTech business are Revolut (UK), Chime and SoFi (USA). The prominent LendTech company in China is the Ant Group. There are several LendTech companies in India like Faircent, Loantap, Moneytap, Lendingkart and Fibe. Faircent has created a P2P lending platform through which people can lend and borrow from each other. Loantap offers personal loans to customers through an online platform. Moneytap provides instant approval for a credit line of up to INR 5,00,000 after the completion of the know-your-customer (KYC) process. Lendingkart gives easy business loans to small- and medium-business entrepreneurs. Fibe offers personal loans to people who work in companies and get a salary on a fixed date (Rubini, 2018).

There are different lending platforms that are used in Fintech. There are peer-to-peer (P2P) lenders who connect lenders and borrowers through a technology platform (e.g., Faircent). There are lending aggregators that bring all lenders into a common platform from where borrowers can evaluate, pick and choose as per their needs (e.g., BankBazaar). And then there are Fintech players who lend directly using their own proprietary technology platform (e.g., Dhani by Indiabulls). Almost all Fintech players use technology in the form of big data analytics, AI, machine learning and robotics to make the process of lending and borrowing much easier and accessible to common masses. There are also niche players like Avant, Zopa and Cabbage offering instant credit to small ticket borrowers (O'Hanlon & Chishti, 2021).

Wealth management is also being done by Fintech. WealthTech companies are helping individuals and companies manage their wealth using digital tools focused on the management of investments and savings. WealthTech companies leverage "data analytics to gain insights into market trends, investor sentiment, and portfolio performance". These insights guide investment decisions and enhance risk management. These companies offer innovative tools like robo-advisory services, quant advisory services, portfolio management services and algorithmic trading. WealthTech companies are combining AI, machine learning and big data to do investment management. Three prominent WealthTech businesses globally include Vanguard, Betterment and Wealthfront. In India, the top WealthTech companies are Groww, Zerodha, Scripbox and Upstox (Chishti & Puschmann, 2018).

The need for risk management has given the opportunity to a new type of companies that do InsurTech. InsurTech applies technology to identify risks, mitigate them and help in building portfolios with high returns and low risk. InsurTech also helps to maximize efficiency, leading to more savings. The traditional way of running an insurance business is to group a certain type of people with similar risk exposure and offer them long-term risk management and benefits. InsurTech utilizes advanced technologies such as big data analytics, blockchain, Internet of Things and AI to provide customers with customized insurance services that cater to their individual requirements. Acquiring life insurance and non-life insurance, such as vehicle insurance, house insurance, travel insurance and health insurance, is becoming more convenient and cost-effective due to the advancements in InsurTech. The top InsurTech companies in the world are Lemonade, Zego, Slice and Quantemplate. In India, the major InsurTech companies are Acko, Digit and Policybazaar (Wilamowicz, 2019).

The other rising segment in the Fintech industry is RegTech. The full form of RegTech is Regulatory Technology. RegTech is a specialized sector within the Fintech industry that specifically concentrates on utilizing cutting-edge technologies to assist financial institutions and organizations in meeting regulatory obligations and effectively managing risks associated with compliance. The primary goal of RegTech is to streamline and automate regulatory processes, reducing compliance costs and enhancing the overall regulatory compliance framework (Anagnostopoulos, 2018).

RegTech firms help companies manage new and complex regulations, litigation and regulatory issues. These are technology-based offerings which help companies to reduce the cost of compliance. RegTech companies operate to bring down the cost of compliance using cloud computing, AI, blockchain and big data. One of the major services offered by RegTech companies pertains to KYC. The top RegTech companies are Amareos, KyoLab, Reg-Room, Finchat and Enforcd (Knight, 2016).

The pandemic period has seen the rise of online transactions and the rising popularity of e-banking. Major banks across the world launched user-friendly apps to facilitate online financial transactions. The rise in the speed of the Internet, lower price of smartphones and lower access cost of the Internet have fueled the demand for online financial transactions. This has led to the rise of a new breed of financial institutions that operate primarily in the digital realm, offering banking services without physical branches. These banks leverage technology and innovative approaches to provide user-friendly, convenient and customer-centric banking experiences and are called Neobanks (Nurbaev, Au & Chou, 2022).

Neobanking is a disruptive force in the financial industry that challenges established banking practices by providing digital-first solutions specifically designed for the demands of modern consumers. Given the ongoing advancements in technology and changing consumer expectations, it is quite probable that Neobanks will have a substantial impact on the future of banking services. The top Neobanks in the USA are Chime (21.6 million), Varo (5.4 million), Current (4.6 million) and Aspiration (4.5 million). The top Neobanks in the UK are Monzo (6.6 million), Revolut (4.1 million), Starling (2.2 million) and Monese (1.6 million). The top Neobanks in India are Kotak 811, Razorpay, Fi Money, Jupiter and Fampay (Vaganova, Bykanova, Gordya & Evdokimov, 2021).

The digital push to Fintech business is also coming from governments across the world that have taken the initiative to introduce CBDC. The CBDC is actually virtual money backed and issued by a central bank. With the growing popularity of cryptocurrencies and stablecoins, central banks worldwide have come to the realization that they must offer an alternative. There are numerous reasons to investigate digital currencies, and the incentives behind each nation's issuing of CBDCs vary according to their respective economic circumstances (Tourpe, Lannquist & Soderberg, 2023).

The central governments launched the CBDC to introduce competition and resilience in the domestic payments market and incentivize cheaper and improved access to money. CBDC is also being introduced to create programmable money and enhance money flow transparency, promote financial inclusion for unbanked and underbanked populations and facilitate the smooth implementation of monetary and fiscal policy.

One hundred and thirty countries, representing 98% of global GDP, are exploring a CBDC at this moment. Following Russia's invasion of Ukraine and the subsequent imposition of G7 sanctions, the progress in wholesale CBDC initiatives has increased manifold. There are currently 12 cross-border wholesale CBDC projects. These projects are "Project mBridge, Dunbar, Sela, Icebreaker, Mariana, Jura, Onyx/Multiple wCBDC, Rosalind, Aurum, Helvetia, Jasper, Aber, Polaris, Nexus, Tourbillion and Cedar/Ubin".

The journey from cryptocurrencies to CBDC has been quite fascinating. It is important for students as well as business professionals to understand how the Fintech revolution is reshaping the way we do financial transactions. From Satoshi Nakamoto's proposition of a P2P financial system, we have actually come a long way in creating a truly decentralized financial (DeFi) system that is making the financial system more transparent, accountable, manageable and convenient for both customers and merchants.

The Future of Fintech

The rise of Fintech has not been a smooth one. Fintech has an intangibility aspect and hence has been viewed with skepticism right from the start. Governments across the world were wary of the creation of an alternative monetary system and have created roadblocks initially for cryptocurrencies and P2P transactions. However, blockchain technology has been received with open arms as this provides much higher security and ease of transaction than the current systems (Riemer, Hafermalz, Roosen, Boussand, El Aoufi, Mo & Kosheliev, 2017).

The spread of the usage of smartphones and the reduced cost of data access have contributed to the popularity of Fintech. The Fintech companies have democratized the process of financial transactions, and the common people are no longer at the mercy of complicated physical procedures like filling up forms, submitting documents and waiting endlessly for approvals. Fintech has paved the way for automation and accessibility and helped banking and financial professionals focus on creativity and innovation (Mahesh, 2021).

The Banking, Financial Services and Insurance (BFSI) business has traveled a long way from running physical branches, to introducing ATMs, Internet banking, mobile banking and now Neobanking with a P2P model. Cryptocurrencies and e-coins have started to replace physical currencies and plastic money in the form of debit and credit cards. Government regulators have found that it is actually easier to trace the money trail of Fintech operations using RegTech, which was not there in the case of physical currencies (King, 2018).

In the long run, the scope of Fintech looks quite promising with new companies emerging and the older ones getting the Unicorn status. Banks are also entering into Fintech space with their own dedicated apps. Multinational companies like Apple, Google, Amazon and Walmart are positioning their Fintech business in an aggressive manner. Mobile phone companies like Airtel, Jio and Vodafone are also promoting their digital wallets. The Government of India is very active in the Fintech space with NPCI, UPI and BHIM. The Chinese Government is leading the Fintech revolution with the introduction of e-CNY (digital yuan) CBDC. The customers are becoming digital savvy, and small ticket customers are also given equal importance.

The COVID-19 pandemic has made digital transactions an absolute compulsion. Customers in both urban and rural areas worldwide are readily embracing digital purchases. Following the implementation of demonetization, there has been an increased willingness among individuals in India to engage in digital transactions. The Fintech industry is currently seeing rapid expansion in various nations, and only those who are pioneering new ideas will thrive in the future. Technology will be pivotal in shaping the future of the Fintech industry.

Questions for Discussion

1. Explain what you understand by Fintech.
2. What are the different business models used in the Fintech business?
3. Explain the Fintech ecosystem.
4. What are the challenges faced by Fintech companies?
5. Explain how you foresee the future of the Fintech business.

Case Study – Paytm

The moment you say Fintech in India, the first name that comes to your mind is Paytm. Paytm was started by Vijay Sekhar Sharma in 2010. The full form of Paytm is pay-through-mobile. Paytm is the brand name and the name of the company is One97 Communications. It was started by Mr. Sharma with an initial investment of $2 million. Paytm has got investments from Alibaba of China, Softbank of Japan, SAIF Partners and Ratan Tata. Paytm is now valued at $16 billion and is coming up with a $2 billion initial public offer (IPO) in Indian stock markets.

Paytm started by providing a mobile wallet. It then forayed into bill payments, flight, train and bus ticket bookings, banking, finance and shopping. Paytm became very popular for providing "cashback" on shopping through Paytm. The mechanism of cashback ensured customers came back again and again to use the Paytm wallet and customer loyalty went up substantially with each transaction.

Paytm has changed the way we do financial transactions, facilitating more than a billion transactions per month. The Paytm app has been downloaded by more than 100 million users. Paytm is used by 20 million merchants in 250 cities and 19,000 pin codes. Paytm now empowers shopkeepers and customers in six lakh villages by facilitating financial transactions.

The word Paytm is now synonymous with the transfer of money. With UPI and QR (Quick Response) Codes, financial transactions through Paytm has become much easier than before. The payment market in India is estimated to be $1 trillion, as per figures released by Credit Suisse.

Paytm has come as a boon for customers who did not have credit cards and debit cards and shopkeepers who found the transaction charges of Mastercard and VISA Card too high and unacceptable. Paytm is now facing intense competition from PhonePe, Mobikwik, Google Pay, Amazon Pay and the government's own BHIM. It is not clear at this moment what new innovations and offerings Paytm and MobiKwik are going to bring after their IPO process is over, but it can safely be said that Paytm has been the harbinger of Fintech in India. Just like the way PayPal had created a revolution in the Western countries. And it is perhaps a sheer coincidence that the logos of Paytm and PayPal almost look similar!!!

However, the problems for Paytm started soon after it was listed in the Indian bourses – the Bombay Stock Exchange (BSE) and the National Stock Exchange (NSE). Paytm was valued at

$20 billion during the process of IPO, but it got listed at a 30% discount in BSE and NSE, thus eroding shareholder wealth. Paytm lost the confidence of shareholders as it could not provide clarity on how it could make up the losses and make profits in the long run. Since then, the share prices of Paytm have been rapidly falling and are now valued at only one-fourth of what it had been valued at the time of listing.

Paytm has also been facing headwinds because of regulatory issues. The Paytm payments bank subsidiary has been directed by the Reserve Bank of India (RBI) to cease taking new deposits in its wallets or accounts as of March 1. The RBI stated that after allowing the business enough time to address its non-compliance issues, the decision was reached to prohibit Paytm payments bank (PPBL) from taking fresh deposits. PPBL announced that Vijay Shekhar Sharma has resigned from his position as part-time non-executive chairman and board member. Additionally, the PPBL reorganized its board of directors by appointing two former officials and two former bankers.

The Paytm example shows that, although it might be beneficial to have an early start in the Fintech sector and get a competitive advantage, companies should not lose sight of compliance and regulatory guidelines. While being innovative has its own advantages, flouting regulatory norms has perils that the Fintech companies can ill afford.

Case Study Questions

1. Explain how Paytm managed to grow the Fintech business in India.
2. What were the enablers that helped Paytm to grow the Fintech business in India?
3. What are the hurdles now being faced by Paytm, and how are they strategizing to overcome the challenges?

Further Reading

1. "In the Game: Traditional Financial Institutions Embrace Fintech Disruption" – A Mastercard-Sponsored Report by Harvard Business Review Analytic Services.
2. "FinTech in India – Ready for breakout" A report by Deloitte

References

Anagnostopoulos, I. (2018). FinTech and RegTech: Impact on regulators and banks. *Journal of Economics and Business*, 100, 7–25.

Chishti, S., & Barberis, J. (2016). *The FinTech book: The financial technology handbook for investors, entrepreneurs and visionaries*. John Wiley & Sons.

Chishti, S., & Puschmann, T. (2018). *The WealthTech book: The FinTech handbook for investors, entrepreneurs and finance visionaries*. John Wiley & Sons.

Friesendorf, C. (2023). *Decentralized Finance (DeFi): How Decentralized Applications (dApps) disrupt banking*. Springer Nature.

King, B. (2018). *Bank 4.0: Banking everywhere, never at a bank*. John Wiley & Sons.

Knight, B. (2016). FinTech: *Who Regulates It and Why It Matters*. Milken Institute: Centre for Financial Markets.

Mahesh, A. (2021). Digital payment service in India – a case study of unified payment interface. *International Journal of Case Studies in Business, IT and Education (IJCSBE)*, 5(1), 256–265.

Nurbaev, V., Au, C. H. A., & Chou, C. Y. (2022). *Exploring the Critical Success Factors of Different Types of FinTech: A Beginning Case of Neobank*. Digit 2022 Proceedings.

O'Hanlon, S., & Chishti, S. (2021). *FinTech for dummies*. Wiley, 1st Edition.
Riemer, K., Hafermalz, E., Roosen, A., Boussand, N., El Aoufi, H., Mo, D., & Kosheliev, A. (2017). *The FinTech Advantage: Harnessing Digital Technology, Keeping the Customer in Focus*. Capgemini.
Rubini, A. (2018). *FinTech in a flash: Financial technology made easy*. Walter de Gruyter GmbH & Co KG.
Tourpe, H., Lannquist, A., & Soderberg, G. (2023). A guide to Central Bank Digital Currency product development. *FinTech Notes, 2023(007)*.
Vaganova, O., Bykanova, N., Gordya, D., & Evdokimov, D. (2021). Growth points of FinTech industry in the perception of financial market transformation. In *Finance, entrepreneurship and technologies in digital economy*, edited by N. Lomakin (Vol. 103, pp. 435–441). European Publisher. https://doi.org/10.15405/epsbs.2021.03.54
Wilamowicz, A. (2019). The great FinTech disruption: InsurTech. *Banking & Finance Law Review*, 34(2), 215–238.

2 The Secret World of Cryptocurrencies

After reading this chapter you will:

- Know what is cryptocurrency
- Know the history of cryptocurrency
- Get knowledge about Satoshi Nakamoto, the father of Bitcoins
- Know about the acceptance of Bitcoins and cryptocurrencies
- Understand how Bitcoins are mined

When the banks and financial institutions were reeling under the contagion effect of the subprime crisis in 2008, a mysterious person named Satoshi Nakamoto published a research paper titled "Bitcoin: A Peer-to-Peer Electronic Cash System". In this research paper, he argued that we can carry out financial transactions between two parties without the assistance of a third intermediary party like a bank or a financial institution. The challenge in these types of transactions was to resolve the issue of double spending.

Satoshi Nakamoto proposed a decentralized network that employs hashing to timestamp transactions and creates a continuous chain of proof-of-work (PoW) based on hashes, with the aim of addressing this issue. This establishes an immutable record that cannot be modified unless the PoW process is repeated. To ensure the smooth and safe execution of financial transactions, various cryptographic techniques like secure hash algorithm (SHA), PoW, proof-of-stake (PoS) and number used only once (nonce) are employed to mitigate any potential hacking risks.

He used this concept note to create Bitcoin, a cryptocurrency that is now widely accepted in more than 50 countries, albeit with some restrictions and a high amount of taxation. One Bitcoin is currently valued at $51,000, as of February 27, 2024. Nakamoto, in addition to implementing Bitcoin, created the initial blockchain database. Satoshi explicitly said that the objective of the peer-to-peer digital cash system was to eliminate the intermediaries often required for digital currency transactions.

Although Bitcoins and cryptocurrencies are not much popular among governments and financial regulators, the blockchain mechanism has found wide acceptance among them. Blockchain is also being used in other areas like supply chain, healthcare, media and entertainment. The mechanism of blockchain is also being actively used in the process of Central Bank Digital Currency (CBDT). Satoshi Nakamoto's dream of a decentralized financial (DeFi) system is now taking shape with the widespread use of cryptocurrencies, smart contracts and non-fungible tokens (NFTs).

DOI: 10.4324/9781032699417-2

What Is Cryptocurrency?

The word "cryptocurrency" comes from encryption and currency. Encryption is a process of using a password or key so that the data is not accessible to unintended persons. Cryptocurrency is digital in nature and intangible. They are mined and circulated using the blockchain technique. They are also finite and limited in number. Examples of cryptocurrencies are Bitcoin, Ethereum, Ripple, Tether and Dogecoin (Danial, 2023).

The primary characteristic of cryptocurrencies is that they are not issued by governments, and, therefore, they are not subject to government control. Cryptocurrencies operate without a central authority for issuing or regulating, relying instead on a decentralized mechanism to record transactions and create new units. Cryptocurrencies enjoy a high level of confidence due to their operation on an immutable blockchain, which prevents any form of manipulation.

Cryptocurrency, being a digital payment method, operates independently of banks for transaction validation. Peer-to-peer technology enables anyone from any location to engage in the exchange of funds. Cryptocurrency payments only rely on digital records in an online database to record individual transactions, rather than a physical currency that is physically transported and exchanged in the physical world. A public ledger records all cryptocurrency transactions that occur throughout the transfer of funds. Cryptocurrency wallets serve the purpose of securely storing digital currencies (Vigna & Casey, 2016).

The term "cryptocurrency" is derived from the use of encryption to verify transactions. The storage and transmission of Bitcoin data between wallets and public ledgers necessitate the use of advanced coding techniques. Encryption is employed to enhance the safety and security of items (Murry & Velasquez, 2023).

Bitcoin, being the inaugural cryptocurrency, is the most renowned and widely recognized in the present day. The launch occurred in the year 2009. The primary allure of cryptocurrencies is in their potential for financial gain through trading, as speculators may cause prices to skyrocket. The price of Bitcoin has fluctuated throughout time, with a low of $67.81 in July 2013 and a high of $69,044 in November 2021. On February 27, 2024, the price of one Bitcoin (BTC) is $51,000.

History of Cryptocurrency

Cryptocurrencies were born because of a mysterious person called Satoshi Nakamoto's frustration with the traditional financial system that crumbled under pressure when Lehman Brothers and Bear Sterns went bankrupt in 2008 due to the subprime crisis and the domino effect it created across the world.

From time immemorial, human beings have used clamshells, gold, silver, copper, nickel and various metallic coins and paper currencies for doing monetary transactions. The 1980s saw several experiments being done to create digital currency. A computer scientist called David Lee Chaum created the concept of digital cash in 1982. It took him almost 13 years of meticulous research to come out with Digicash in 1995, which was based on the cryptocurrency concept. However, this initiative was short-lived as the company that created Digicash went bankrupt in 1999.

There were several research papers published on how electronic currencies could be created. One such paper was "How to Make a Mint: The Cryptography of Anonymous Electronic Cash", published by the National Security Agency in 1996. This paper spoke about how to develop a cryptocurrency system (Law, Sabett & Solinas, 1996).

This was followed by several experts giving different versions of how electronic cash and currency systems could be developed. A computer scientist called Wei Dei gave the description of "an anonymous, distributed electronic cash system called B-Money" in 1998. Shortly thereafter, another computer scientist called Nick Szabo described a similar system called "Bit Gold" where gold would be used as a cryptographic currency. And then, it was Satoshi Nakamoto, in 2009, who gave the final shape to cryptocurrency and named it "Bitcoin". Despite resistance from government regulators across the world, the popularity of Bitcoins continued to grow and reached a value of $69,044 in November 2021.

Fearing for his life and imprisonment, Satoshi Nakamoto has kept his identity secret, just like the cryptocurrency he created. Another person like him attempted to create "Namecoin", which would also run on a decentralized domain name system (DNS) so that the regulators would not be able to trace the origin. Bitcoin and Namecoin were followed by the introduction of Litecoin in 2011 and Peercoin in 2014. Litecoin uses a password-based key derivation function called Scrypt as the hash function. Peercoin is based on a hybrid model comprising PoW and PoS.

In an effort to establish a decentralized DNS that would make Internet censorship extremely challenging, Namecoin was founded in April 2011. October 2011 saw the launching of Litecoin shortly after. Instead of using SHA-256 as its hash function, it used Scrypt, a PoW algorithm. Peercoin, another well-known cryptocurrency, employed a hybrid PoW/PoS system. Since 2018, Cardano has held the title of the largest PoS cryptocurrency (Kirillova, Pavlyuk, Mikhaylova, Zulfugarzade & Zenin, 2018).

The most popular protocol used for data encryption has been "SHA-256". This is used in some of the most popular authentication and encryption protocols, including "SSL, TLS, IPsec, SSH and PGP". Now, PoW and PoS and a hybrid of PoW and PoS are being used to create cryptocurrencies. The cryptocurrency Cardano has been created using the PoS protocol (Courtois, Grajek & Naik, 2014).

The Secret World of Satoshi Nakamoto

Satoshi Nakamoto is called the father of "Bitcoins" and is credited with giving shape to the cryptocurrency into a usable format. He is an enigmatic character, and nobody knows his real identity. Satoshi Nakamoto is a pseudonym, and it is not clear whether he is a Japanese, Chinese, American, European or Indian. He became famous for publishing a paper titled "Bitcoin: A Peer-to-Peer Electronic Cash System" that resolved the issues and challenges that had hitherto prevented the widespread adoption of cryptocurrencies (Nakamoto, 2008).

The problem with digital currencies was that of manipulation, hacking and double spending. The digital currencies always needed a third-party verification, like banks, to authenticate the transaction. A typical digital transaction is illustrated in Figure 2.1.

The problem was that digital currencies could be easily duplicated and hence stolen from the legal owner. This problem of double spending is not prevalent with physical currencies as each currency note has a unique number and security thread that cannot be duplicated. This peculiar stumbling block was preventing digital currencies from being used as a replacement for physical currencies.

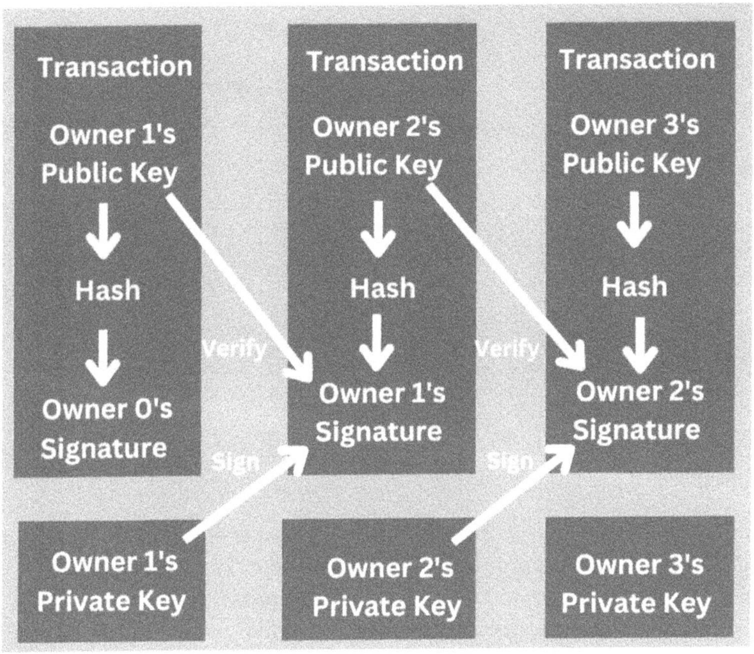

Figure 2.1 The Workflow of a Digital Currency Transaction

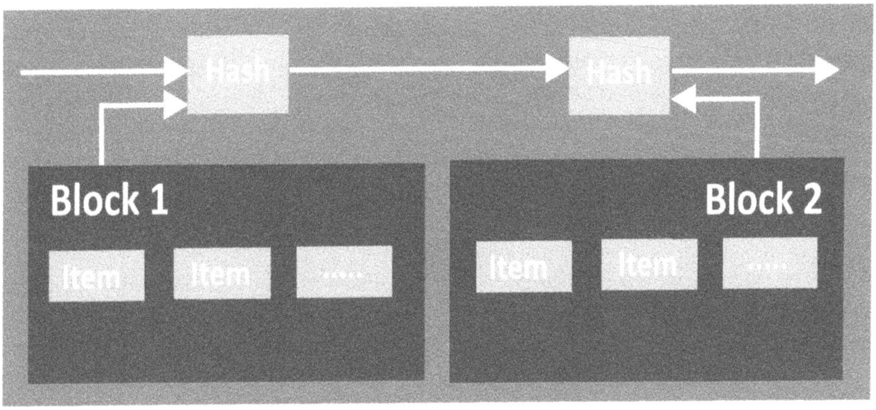

Figure 2.2 Application of Timestamping to Create Blocks

Nakamoto resolved this issue in a logical manner. He proposed a system of peer-to-peer networks to prevent the issue of duplication and malpractice. Blockchains will be used to power this peer-to-peer network. A blockchain creates an immutable historical record by appending a transaction's timestamp to the end of earlier timestamps using PoW.

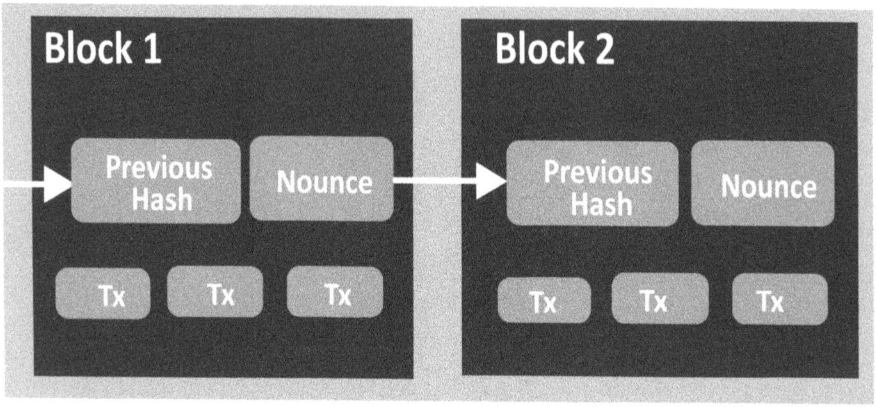

Figure 2.3 Application of Proof-of-Work (PoW) to Secure Blocks

Blockchain is a secure system because this is immutable and cannot be reversed or broken into due to the timestamping process. The blockchain records are kept secure using the PoW encryption protocol. The financial transactions done using blockchain cannot be reversed because the amount of computational power required to reverse them discourages small-scale attacks.

Nakamoto arrived on the cryptocurrency scene in 2009 as a mysterious person, resolved the issue of double spending and duplication, offering a secure system of DeFi transactions that doesn't need Government authorization or control, and disappeared without leaving a trace in 2010, exactly one year after he had published the research paper on cryptocurrencies and blockchain advocating the use of peer-to-peer systems. Though Nakamoto disappeared mysteriously, the Bitcoins that he created continued to grow in size and popularity. It is estimated that if Nakamoto is a real person, he would be currently having a wealth of $50 billion, based on the one million Bitcoins he kept in his possession. Satoshi Nakamoto will always be remembered in history as the "father of Bitcoins".

The Rise of Bitcoins

Bitcoins were created based on the peer-to-peer (P2P) protocols that run on blockchain technology, as envisaged by Satoshi Nakamoto in his research paper "Bitcoin: A Peer-to-Peer Electronic Cash System". Bitcoins were initially received with alarm by central bankers and government authorities. Their fear was that Bitcoins would create an alternate monetary system that could be used for criminal activities like money laundering, extortion, drug smuggling and terrorist activities. Their fear was not unsubstantiated as initially there were reports coming in about the misuse of Bitcoins. But, presently, that issue has also been resolved with the advent of RegTech (Ammous, 2018).

In the initial days, Satoshi Nakamoto mined close to one million Bitcoins and handed over the control of Bitcoins to Gavin Andresen. Gavin Andresen is a computer engineer who took up the responsibility of running the Bitcoin network and became the chief scientist of the Bitcoin Foundation in 2012.

Following the disappearance of Satoshi Nakamoto in 2010, Andresen assumed leadership of the Bitcoin core development team. Additionally, after the Bitcoin Foundation was established in 2012, Andresen served as its chief scientist. From 2012, Bitcoins started gaining acceptance as an alternative to physical currency. In 2013, the Bitcoin-based payment processor Coinbase sold one million Bitcoins at $22 per Bitcoin. The gaming company Zynga announced that it would accept Bitcoins as payments. Casinos in Las Vegas also started accepting Bitcoins for gambling.

The Bitcoin business suffered a jolt in 2014 when one of the biggest Bitcoin exchanges Mt Gox filed for bankruptcy. There were reports that around seven and a half lakhs of Bitcoins were stolen from Mt Gox (Rao, 2022). But the Bitcoin business was quick to bounce back within a year. The second most popular Bitcoin exchange Coinbase got a Series C funding of $75 million, and all was well with the Bitcoin business. The Switzerland Government gave legitimacy to Bitcoins by announcing that Swiss Railway Operator SBB (CFF) would accept Bitcoins as payments for railway tickets.

Very soon, one country after another started giving acceptance to Bitcoins. Japan and Russia passed legislation to give acceptance to Bitcoins. Other major countries like the USA, the United Kingdom, China, Russia, South Africa, India and Brazil have accepted Bitcoins for business transactions (Zharikov, 2023). The countries where Bitcoins are not used are Afghanistan, Zimbabwe, Mongolia, Guyana and Algeria. El Salvador has given recognition to Bitcoins as a legal tender. Central African Republic has also given recognition to Bitcoin as a legal tender. The objective of these two countries was to reduce their dependency on the US dollar.

The advent of user-friendly cryptocurrency exchanges facilitated the process for individuals to purchase, sell and engage in transactions involving Bitcoin. This ease of access had a significant role in its broader acceptance and use. The decentralized aspect of Bitcoin appealed to many who had skepticism toward conventional banking institutions. Its scarcity rendered it a viable safeguard against inflation. Its extreme volatility makes it a lucrative opportunity for traders to generate profit. The growing adoption of Bitcoin by merchants has enhanced its usability as a means of payment.

It's actually unclear at this moment where Bitcoin is headed. While some experts think it's a bubble that will eventually bust, others think it might become a common currency. Nonetheless, there's no denying that Bitcoin is a revolutionary technology with the power to alter the way we perceive money and conduct financial transactions.

How Bitcoins Are Mined

The Bitcoin mining process is illustrated in Figure 2.4.

The process of creating new Bitcoins and validating transactions is known as Bitcoin mining. To solve a cryptographic problem, add transactions to the blockchain and get paid in freshly produced Bitcoins and transaction fees, miners employ specialized technology. It's a fiercely competitive and resource-intensive procedure that's essential to the Bitcoin network's security and functionality (Kent & Bain, 2022).

The mining process, which is difficult, costly and time-consuming and requires a lot of electrical energy and sophisticated computer technology, puts new Bitcoins into circulation. Very advanced computers that can tackle incredibly difficult computational arithmetic problems are used for the mining.

Blockchain is a decentralized ledger technology that powers Bitcoin. A list of transactions is contained in each of the blocks that make up this blockchain. Miners are people or things that solve challenging mathematical riddles to validate transactions and safeguard the network. Miners receive transaction fees and freshly produced Bitcoins as payment for their labor.

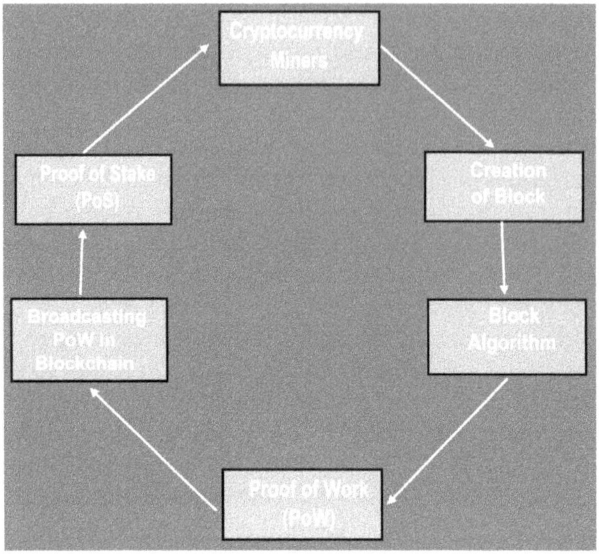

Figure 2.4 The Mining Process of Bitcoins

A transaction that a Bitcoin user starts is announced to the network. A collection of these transactions is known as the "mempool". Prioritizing transactions with larger transaction fees, miners choose which transactions from the mempool to include in the following block.

The PoW algorithm is a cryptographic problem that must be solved to mine Bitcoins. To construct a hash that begins with a specified amount of leading zeros, miners compete to find a specific 64-character hexadecimal number (referred to as a "nonce") that can be hashed with the data in the block.

The PoW computations are carried out by miners using specialized hardware. Initially, standard CPUs could be used for Bitcoin mining. However, as the network has expanded, the competition has increased, necessitating the use of application-specific integrated circuits (ASICs) created especially for mining. When it comes to carrying out the required computations, these gadgets are far more effective.

Due to the intense competition and the significant computational resources needed, individual miners frequently opt to join mining pools. A mining pool is a collaborative effort where numerous miners pool their computational capabilities, distribute the rewards and increase the probability of successfully mining a block. Compensation is allocated according to the miner's supplied computing capacity.

A transaction that is started by a Bitcoin user is announced to the network. These exchanges are gathered in a collection known as the "mempool". The transactions with the highest transaction fees are given priority when miners choose the ones from the mempool to include in the next block.

A cryptographic challenge called the PoW algorithm must be solved to mine Bitcoins. Miners compete to discover a unique 64-character hexadecimal number (referred to as a "nonce") that, when hashed with the data in the block, results in a hash that begins with a predetermined quantity of leading zeros. It takes a lot of computer power and resources to complete this procedure.

Table 2.1 The Reward for Creating Bitcoins

Period	*Reward per Block (Bitcoins)*
2008–2012	25
2012–2016	12.5
2016–2020	6.25
2020–2024	3.125

Source: Coinmarketcap.com

To carry out the PoW computations, miners employ specialized hardware. In the beginning, standard CPUs could mine Bitcoins. Nonetheless, as the network has expanded, competition has increased, and ASICs – specifically, application-specific integrated circuits – made for mining are now necessary. These gadgets are far more adept at carrying out the required computations.

The block reward is cut in half roughly every four years. The block rewards have progressively decreased every four years as given in Table 2.1.

Bitcoins have been created with an upper limit of 21 million coins to be allowed in circulation. Till now, already 18.638 million Bitcoins have been mined, which means only 2.362 million more Bitcoins can be introduced into circulation. After the 21 million upper limit is reached, the miners will no longer earn rewards for mining. Instead, they will be getting transaction fees from users who use Bitcoins for business transactions.

The PoW process serves two crucial purposes. First, it secures the network against fraudulent transactions and attacks. Second, it maintains the decentralized nature of the network by making it computationally expensive to gain control over 51% of the network's hashing power.

The Cryptocurrency Market

The market capitalization of cryptocurrencies is estimated to have crossed the $2 trillion mark (Source: Business Insider). The top cryptocurrencies are "Bitcoin, Ethereum, Binance Coin, Cardano, Dogecoin, Tether, XRP Polkadot, Solana and Ripple". Bitcoin alone commands 43.96% of the market share, while other cryptocurrencies are still niche players. Dogecoin was started as a joke. It shot up in fame when Elon Musk referred to himself as "Dogefather". This cryptocurrency appreciated by 14,000% in 2021, making it one of the top ten traded cryptocurrencies in the world (CoinMarketCap, 2024).

We have already discussed about Bitcoins and how they are mined. We have also outlined how Dogecoins saw a meteoric rise after the Elon Musk comment. The other prominent cryptocurrencies are Ethereum, Binance Coin, Cardano and Ripple. Let us understand these cryptocurrencies also in detail.

Ethereum

Ethereum (ETH) is the second-largest cryptocurrency in terms of market capitalization, following Bitcoins. It was developed in 2015 by computer scientists Vitalik Buterin and Gavin Wood, four years after the inception of Bitcoin. Ether, the inherent digital currency of the Ethereum platform, serves multiple purposes such as facilitating payments

Table 2.2 The Most Valued Cryptocurrencies (as of 10.03.2024)

Sl No	*Cryptocurrency*	*Symbol*	*Market Price ($)*	*Market Cap ($)*
1	Bitcoin	BTC	69,492.31	1,365.55 billion
2	Ethereum	ETH	3,917.16	470.47 billion
3	Binance Coin	BNB	529.12	79.12 billion
4	Cardano	ADA	0.73	25.93 billion
5	Tether	USDT	1.00	102.11billion
6	Ripple	XRP	0.61	33.46 billion
7	Dogecoin	DOGE	0.16	9.60 billion
8	Solana	SOL	144.33	3.24 billion
9	Polkadot	DOT	10.40	13.39 billion
10	Litecoin	LTC	87.76	6.52 billion

Source: Coinmarketcap.com

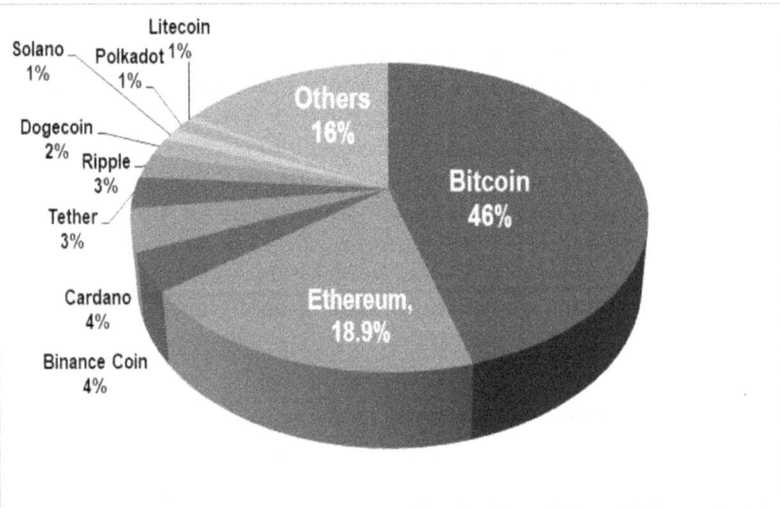

Figure 2.5 Market Share of Cryptocurrencies

for computational services and transaction fees, as well as functioning as a medium of exchange within the network. This coin utilizes a publicly accessible, distributed ledger that allows for the execution of programmable agreements (Solomon, 2019).

The increasing popularity of Ethereum can be ascribed to its capacity to generate and trade NFTs. Non-fungible refers to the quality of being unique and unable to be replicated. Presently, NFTs are employed to promote digital art, music and other forms of creative expression. They utilize blockchain technology to store supplementary data. Auction house Christie's recently sold an NFT artwork to an art enthusiast for a staggering $69 million.

The ability to construct and carry out smart contracts – self-executing contracts with the terms of the agreement explicitly put into code – is Ethereum's most important addition. These contracts do away with the necessity for middlemen by automatically enforcing the established guidelines.

On its blockchain, Ethereum enables developers to create DApps, offering a platform for a variety of uses, including supply chain management, gaming, digital identification solutions and protocols for DeFi. The Ethereum network can execute smart contracts thanks to the Ethereum Virtual Machine, a runtime environment. By running code inside a sandbox, it guarantees security and stability.

Ethereum and Bitcoin are decentralized cryptocurrencies that operate on blockchain technology. Bitcoin is mainly used for making payments, while Ethereum offers a platform to develop Fintech applications. The computational capabilities of Ethereum and the range of applications it offers are much higher compared to Bitcoin. Ethereum is mostly utilized for tamper-proof DeFi contracts and applications.

Binance Coin

Binance Coin (BNB) was founded by Changpeng Zhao, who is also known as CZ. He is listed as Singapore's 22nd richest person, as per data given by Forbes. Initially launched as a cryptocurrency exchange, Binance has expanded its offerings to create a comprehensive ecosystem that encompasses trading, investment, innovation and education.

Binance Coin initially debuted on the Ethereum blockchain. Later, it created the Binance Chain in 2017. Binance Coin has an upper limit of 200 million BNB coins. During an ICO (Initial Coin Offering), it offered 20 million BNB tokens to angel investors to raise, and 100 million coins were given to various public through the ICO process. The founding team retained 80 million coins. The BNB coins are used to make payments, take loans, offer gifts and also make donations to charity. The Binance Exchange is the most extensive platform used for trading digital currencies globally, with a capacity to handle over 1.4 million transactions per second (Source: Investopedia).

Binance acquired India's biggest cryptocurrency trading platform WazirX in 2019. WazirX was started by Nischal Shetty, who is a tech entrepreneur. In June 2019, WazirX became South Asia's first marketplace for NFTs. Binance is now one of the leading players who are trying to convert fiat money into cryptocurrencies. Fiat money is a currency that is not backed by commodities like gold. Examples of fiat money are dollar, pound and rupee.

Binance's evolution from a cryptocurrency exchange to a multifaceted ecosystem reflects its dedication to staying at the forefront of the industry. Its innovations have contributed to shaping the landscape of cryptocurrency trading, investment and technology.

Cardano

Cardano was founded in 2015 by Charles Hoskinson, who was the former CEO of Ethereum. He is a mathematician and a scientist. Cardano is the third-largest cryptocurrency in terms of market capitalization. Cardano is a PoS blockchain that has become a formidable rival to Ethereum and Solana. Cardano saw a sudden rise in price after the upcoming "Alonzo" upgrade was recently announced. The "Alonzo" upgrade would witness smart contracts being added to the blockchain run by Cardano.

PoS is a data encryption protocol where validators lock up their cryptocurrency to secure the network. Apart from Cardano, Polkadot and EOSIO cryptocurrencies use the PoS protocol of encryption. What sets Cardano apart is its strong emphasis on scientific research, peer-reviewed protocols and a layered architecture designed to address the limitations of existing blockchain platforms.

Cardano's commitment to scientific rigor, scalability and sustainability has attracted attention and interest from both the cryptocurrency community and traditional financial sectors. However, as with any ambitious project, Cardano faces challenges and competition within the rapidly evolving blockchain landscape. Its success will depend on its ability to deliver on its promises and overcome technological, regulatory and adoption hurdles.

Tether

Tether (USDT) is classified as a stablecoin, which is a specific sort of cryptocurrency. Stablecoins are specifically created to preserve a consistent value by linking their price to a reserve of assets, usually a fiat currency like the US dollar. Tether, specifically, is fixed to the US dollar at a 1:1 ratio, indicating that one USDT will always have a value equivalent to 1 US dollar.

Tether was created to address the price volatility inherent in most cryptocurrencies, such as Bitcoin or Ethereum. The price of Bitcoin, for instance, can fluctuate significantly over a short period, making it less suitable for everyday transactions and a less stable store of value. Tether aims to provide the advantages of cryptocurrencies (speed, security and borderless transactions) while maintaining a stable value.

Tether maintains its 1:1 peg to the US dollar through a reserve of assets. While the specifics of this reserve were a source of controversy and concern in the past, the company behind Tether, Tether Limited, claims that each USDT is backed by an equivalent amount of USD in its reserve. However, it's essential to note that audits or third-party verification of these reserves have been a contentious issue in the crypto community.

Tether is not the only stablecoin in the market. Other stablecoins, such as USD Coin, TrueUSD and DAI, also aim to provide price stability and have gained popularity as alternatives to Tether. Tether is a widely used stablecoin designed to maintain a 1:1 peg to the US dollar, providing stability in a cryptocurrency market known for its price volatility. Its use cases range from a safe haven during market turbulence to facilitating cross-border transactions. However, it has faced significant scrutiny and controversy, particularly regarding the transparency of its reserves and its regulatory compliance, making it a polarizing entity in the cryptocurrency space.

Ripple

With the goal of revolutionizing the global payments system and enabling faster, more affordable and more effective cross-border transactions, Ripple (XRP) is a blockchain-based platform and digital payment protocol. Ripple provides a diverse array of tools and technologies that facilitate the swift, secure and cost-effective transfer of funds across international borders.

XRP Ledger, a digital payment protocol developed by Ripple, makes cross-border transactions quick and easy. It seeks to do away with the excessive costs and delays that are sometimes connected to conventional international transfers.

Ripple's native cryptocurrency is XRP. While XRP can be used for transactions and payments, Ripple's primary focus is on its payment protocol rather than positioning XRP as a traditional cryptocurrency. XRP is a digital asset that serves as both a cryptocurrency and a key component of the Ripple ecosystem. Created by Ripple Labs in 2012, XRP is designed to be a bridge currency for facilitating fast, low-cost cross-border payments and settlements. While closely associated with Ripple, XRP also has its own distinct attributes and use cases. The decentralization strategy employed by Ripple has sparked controversy in the cryptocurrency world, as several detractors contend that it deviates from the principles followed by other blockchain initiatives.

XRP is a digital asset that operates on a decentralized blockchain called the XRP Ledger. It can be sent and received like other cryptocurrencies but is unique in its primary purpose of serving as a bridge currency for facilitating payments. One of XRP's key selling points is its speed. It is designed to enable almost instantaneous transactions, which makes it suitable for cross-border payments that require quick settlement times. XRP transactions typically have very low fees, especially when compared to traditional cross-border payment methods like SWIFT. Unlike some other cryptocurrencies, XRP has a fixed supply of 100 billion tokens. This supply is capped, and XRP transactions involve a small "burning" of XRP, which reduces the total supply over time. This deflationary mechanism is intended to help maintain value over the long term.

Despite its clear use case and technological innovation, XRP has faced challenges due to its association with Ripple's legal and regulatory battles. Regulatory uncertainty has led to fluctuations in its market value and adoption. However, its utility as a bridge currency for cross-border transactions and the ongoing development of the Ripple ecosystem continue to attract attention from financial institutions and payment providers seeking to enhance their international payment capabilities. As the regulatory landscape evolves, XRP's position within the broader cryptocurrency ecosystem remains an area of interest and speculation.

Ripple's efforts to improve the efficiency of cross-border payments have garnered significant attention from the financial industry and beyond. Its technology has the potential to reshape the way money is moved across borders, reducing costs and increasing accessibility. However, the company's journey has also been marked by regulatory challenges and debates about its decentralization model. As the payments landscape evolves, Ripple continues to be a noteworthy player in the ongoing transformation of the global financial system.

Dogecoin

Dogecoin (DOGE) is a cryptocurrency that originated as a meme before becoming well-known and widely used. Software programmers Jackson Palmer and Billy Markus first made it in December 2013 as a humorous parody of Bitcoin and other cryptocurrencies. Dogecoin is utilized for a variety of things and has a committed community despite its humble beginnings.

The "Doge" meme, which consists of a picture of a Shiba Inu dog with a certain text style – typically written in bad English – that represents the dog's inner monologue, is featured in Dogecoin's logo. Dogecoin's branding was inspired by this meme, which has also contributed to the cryptocurrency's unique approachability.

A public ledger comparable to Bitcoin is used by Dogecoin. But instead of using the SHA-256 method found in Bitcoin, it uses the Scrypt algorithm, which requires more RAM. This decision was taken to maintain Dogecoin's accessibility for individual miners and stop big mining companies from controlling the network.

Dogecoin initially had no supply restriction, in contrast to Bitcoin, which has a 21 million coin maximum. This implies that mining might continue forever. This was altered in 2014, though, when a "soft cap" was implemented, bringing the total amount of Dogecoin available annually to 5.2 billion coins.

One of the most vibrant and engaged communities in the cryptocurrency world is found on Dogecoin. This community raises money for charity causes on a regular basis. For instance, they have provided funding for clean water projects, sponsored athletes and assisted with disaster relief.

Because of its cheap transaction costs and quick confirmation times, Dogecoin is mostly utilized for microtransactions, contributions and tipping. It's well-liked on social media sites where consumers give content producers praise for their contributions. In addition to being traded on a number of cryptocurrency exchanges, Dogecoin is occasionally used as payment in online forums and tiny e-commerce transactions.

Celebrities like Elon Musk, Snoop Dogg and Mark Cuban have all endorsed and tweeted about Dogecoin, which has garnered a lot of attention over the years. Particularly, Musk's tweets have frequently caused notable changes in pricing. The price of Dogecoin has fluctuated greatly, experiencing sharp rises and falls. It's crucial to remember that, rather than being caused by underlying causes, these swings are frequently affected by social media trends and celebrity endorsements.

Solana

Designed for scalable and secure decentralized applications (DApps) and cryptocurrencies, Solana (SOL) is a high-performance, decentralized blockchain platform. It was developed to provide high throughput and cheap transaction fees to overcome some of the shortcomings of the current blockchain networks.

Former Qualcomm engineer Anatoly Yakovenko established Solana in March 2020. The Solana team set out to develop a quick, scalable, secure platform that could accommodate cryptocurrencies and decentralized apps to advance the state of blockchain technology.

With its astounding throughput of thousands of transactions per second, Solana is well-known for its performance. This is accomplished by combining a number of cutting-edge technologies and creative design decisions. Solana improves scalability through the usage of a special feature known as PoH. As an unreliable source of time, proof of history (PoH) is an authentic record of every event that has taken place on the Solana blockchain. This makes transaction validation and processing quick.

DPoS consensus is used by Solana, and it is speedier and more energy efficient than PoW blockchains. Additionally, block producers – who are in charge of verifying transactions – are introduced. With its native programming language, Rust, and a compatibility layer for Ethereum-based smart contracts, Solana facilitates the creation of decentralized applications. Because Solana has cheap transaction costs, it's a platform that appeals to both users and developers.

The Solana blockchain's native coin is called SOL. It fulfills a number of purposes. On the network, SOL is used to cover transaction fees. To protect the network and get benefits, SOL holders can stake their tokens. Voting on recommendations for network governance can be done via steered SOL. Storage and processing power are examples of network resources that are allocated using SOL.

By providing a scalable, high-performance blockchain platform that is ideal for DeFi, NFTs and other resource-intensive applications, Solana has carved out a position for itself in the Bitcoin ecosystem. Its creative application of PoH and DPoS technology may have an effect on the larger blockchain community.

The blockchain platform Solana has drawn notice due to its remarkable throughput, scalability and inexpensive transaction fees. With the goal of facilitating a broad spectrum of decentralized applications, it has drawn an expanding network of collaborations and projects. It does, however, confront difficulties, including worries about centralization and rivalry from other blockchain platforms. Its capacity to innovate going forward and to cultivate a strong developer and user base will determine its long-term viability.

Polkadot

A multi-chain blockchain platform called Polkadot (DOT) seeks to make different blockchains interoperable to improve the efficiency and connectivity of the ecosystem surrounding cryptocurrencies and decentralized applications (DApps). It was developed to solve the constraints and disarray in the blockchain industry.

Dr. Gavin Wood, a prominent person in the blockchain sector and one of the co-founders of Ethereum, designed and developed Polkadot. The project's official debut took place in May 2020, with the aim of encouraging creativity and cooperation within the blockchain industry.

Because Polkadot functions as a multi-chain network, it has the capacity to host numerous blockchains or "parachains". It is possible to modify these parachains to accommodate various use cases and applications. The relay chain, at the center of the Polkadot network, synchronizes communication among all linked parachains. It guarantees the safe transfer of assets and data between them. Polkadot uses a shared security paradigm in which the relay chain maintains the security of all parachains jointly. This lessens the requirement for each parachain to have a separate, sometimes resource-intensive, consensus method.

Because of Polkadot's smooth interoperability, parachains can communicate and share value with one another. Polkadot's cross-chain message-passing technology makes this possible. Due to Polkadot's on-chain governance structure, owners of DOT tokens can take part in decision-making procedures related to upgrades and parameter modifications. Nominated PoS, or NPoS, is Polkadot's consensus technique. To safeguard the network and receive incentives, holders of DOT tokens can nominate validators or stake their tokens.

The Polkadot network's native cryptocurrency is called the DOT token. It fulfills a number of purposes. To safeguard the network, cast votes on proposals for governance and get incentives, DOT holders can stake their tokens. To reserve a spot on the network, parachain developers must bond a specific number of DOT tokens. DOT holders have the ability to vote on proposals and referenda to take part in network governance.

In addition to supply chain management, identity verification, NFTs, DeFi and many other uses, Polkadot promises to be a flexible platform. It provides developers with a scalable and adaptable environment in which to create DApps and parachains. Acala, Moonbeam, Chainlink and many more projects and DApps have drawn attention to Polkadot and joined its ecosystem. These initiatives make use of Polkadot's skills to create and implement a range of blockchain-based solutions.

As the cornerstone of the blockchain ecosystem, Polkadot facilitates interoperability across many blockchains and offers a safe, scalable environment for decentralized apps. It is a crucial project for the cryptocurrency industry because of its capacity to promote creativity and cooperation in a variety of blockchain use cases.

A multi-chain blockchain platform called Polkadot (DOT) was created to facilitate communication across several blockchains. It provides a special remedy for the scalability and fragmentation issues facing the blockchain industry. Polkadot wants to be a major player in determining the direction that blockchain technology and decentralized apps take as its ecosystem develops and grows.

Litecoin

One of the first and most well-known cryptocurrencies is Litecoin (LTC), which was developed by Charlie Lee and launched in 2011 as a "lite" variant of Bitcoin. It has established its own niche for itself in the cryptocurrency market while having many similarities to Bitcoin.

Former Google developer Charlie Lee founded Litecoin in October 2011 to solve some of the alleged flaws with Bitcoin, namely, transaction speed and scalability, Lee created Litecoin. To balance out Bitcoin within the cryptocurrency ecosystem, he set out to construct a "lite" version of the platform.

The PoW method employed by Litecoin is Scrypt, which is intended to need more memory and withstand the ASICs needed to mine Bitcoin. This was done to keep the mining environment more decentralized and open to a larger group of miners. In comparison to Bitcoin, Litecoin has a faster block time. Litecoin has a block time of 2.5 minutes, whereas Bitcoin has a 10-minute block period. Faster transaction confirmations are the outcome of this. Like Bitcoin, the supply of Litecoin is capped. Only 84 million Litecoins will ever be produced, which is four times as many as there are Bitcoins (21 million).

Segregated Witness is a mechanism that improves transaction malleability and increases block size by separating transaction data from witness data. Litecoin was among the first to use this technology. The Lightning Network, a second-layer technology that facilitates quicker and less expensive off-chain transactions, has been deployed by Litecoin.

The native coin of the Litecoin network is called LTC. It accomplishes several goals. On the Litecoin network, LTC is used to pay transaction fees, which are mostly used for transaction processing and confirmation. Lithium is the digital gold. Like Bitcoin, some people view LTC as a store of value akin to gold or silver. Many people invest in LTC because they believe it will increase in value in the future. LTC is a payment method that certain establishments and Internet retailers accept for goods and services.

Litecoin is frequently applied to a variety of tasks. Because of its quicker block time and cheaper transaction costs compared to Bitcoin, it can be utilized for regular transactions like purchasing products and services. LTC is appropriate for applications that demand prompt and economical payments and can enable microtransactions. Like Bitcoin, a lot of people view LTC as a long-term investment with the possibility of future growth in value.

Litecoin has a devoted following and is generally recognized as a form of payment by both online and physical retailers. It has a significant presence in the cryptocurrency market and is listed on many cryptocurrency exchanges.

Litecoin, which has become one of the most well-known and enduring cryptocurrencies, is sometimes referred to as the "silver" to Bitcoin's "gold". It functions as a quicker and less expensive substitute for Bitcoin and is regarded as a significant resource and mode of payment inside the larger cryptocurrency market.

One of the first cryptocurrencies, Litecoin, is well-known for its quick confirmation of transactions, cheap transaction costs and limited supply of 84 million coins. Despite having many similarities to Bitcoin, it has established a unique identity and set of applications within the cryptocurrency market. Litecoin continues to have a notable and lasting influence in the cryptocurrency space.

The Cryptocurrency Exchanges

A cryptocurrency exchange is "a platform that lets clients swap cryptocurrencies or digital currencies for other assets, including traditional fiat money or other digital currencies". In exchange for digital currencies or cryptocurrencies, exchanges may take wire transfers, credit card payments or other payment methods. A cryptocurrency exchange can operate as a matching platform, charging fees or a market maker, earning transaction commissions on bid-ask spreads (Chan, Ding, Lin & Rossi, 2020).

Digital currency exchanges allow customers to buy and sell digital currency, which is then transferred into or out of the customer's depository account. While many of the exchanges are formally independent companies, some are subsidiaries of the depository. Money held in depository accounts might be either virtual or actual cash. A digital currency exchange might operate entirely online or as a brick-and-mortar store. It is a physical store that trades both digital currency and conventional payment methods. It is an Internet company that deals in digital currencies and electronically transferred funds.

Exchanges for cryptocurrencies are essential middlemen that make it easier to trade and invest in cryptocurrency. By bridging the divide between conventional banking and the cutting-edge realm of digital assets, they enable consumers to take part in the vibrant cryptocurrency market.

Exchanges for cryptocurrencies are essential parts of the ecosystem of digital assets since they give consumers a place to purchase, sell, trade and manage different cryptocurrencies. These platforms connect buyers and sellers and operate as middlemen in transactions, providing a variety of trading tools and services. Cryptocurrency exchanges serve as a vital link between the realm of cryptocurrencies and established financial institutions, facilitating the uptake and expansion of digital assets.

Users can trade different cryptocurrencies against one another or against conventional fiat currencies on cryptocurrency exchanges. Order books with real-time purchase and sell orders are provided. Exchanges list a wide variety of cryptocurrencies, ranging from obscure altcoins to well-known ones like Ethereum and Bitcoin. Users can diversify their assets thanks to the range of products. By enabling the exchange of assets between buyers and sellers, cryptocurrency exchanges give the market liquidity. Smoother trading experiences and more effective price discovery are typically the outcomes of increased liquidity.

Exchanges allow users to swap one cryptocurrency for another or for fiat money by providing a variety of trading pairs. More sophisticated trading methods are made possible by this versatility. Users can use limit orders to indicate the ideal price at which they wish to purchase or sell, or they can put market orders to execute trades at the current market price.

There are different types of cryptocurrency exchanges such as:

Centralized Exchanges (CEX): These are traditional exchanges where orders are matched by a central authority. They are user-friendly but require users to trust the exchange with their funds.

Decentralized Exchanges (DEX): Decentralized Exchanges do not have a central authority and facilitate peer-to-peer trading through smart contracts. Users maintain control of their funds during trading.

Hybrid Exchanges: Hybrid exchanges provide the benefits of both centralized and decentralized exchanges by combining their features.

Over-the-Counter (OTC) Exchanges: OTC exchanges facilitate large trades off the public order book, often providing personalized service for institutional and high-net-worth traders.

The well-known cryptocurrency exchanges Bitstamp, KuCoin, Coinbase, Binance and Kraken are just a few examples. The well-known cryptocurrency exchanges WazirX, CoinDCX, Coinswitch, Kuber and Zebpay are among a few operatives in India. With its P2P approach, WazirX makes it easier to deposit and withdraw fiat money by automatically connecting buyers and sellers and guaranteeing transaction speed and security. It works with Windows, Mac, iOS and Android platforms. With one lakh users, CoinDCX provides access to over 200 coins. While deposits and withdrawals are free, there is a small trading cost. With UnoCoin, users can top off wallets, recharge cell phones and DTH and use Bitcoins for these purposes. Additionally, it includes a merchant gateway technology that enables online retailers to take Bitcoin payments.

The Future of Cryptocurrency

The cryptocurrency market is presently on a roll. Cryptocurrencies are now accepted in most countries except Afghanistan, Algeria, Bolivia, Bangladesh, China and Nepal. Cryptocurrency adoption in India is on the rise, with Indians having invested $6.6 billion in cryptocurrencies in the past one year.

Although the future of cryptocurrencies is unknown, there are a lot of chances and difficulties that could arise. Cryptocurrencies have the ability to completely change how we use money, on the one hand. Since they are decentralized, neither the government nor financial institutions can control them. They are therefore a safer and more effective method of transferring wealth. Furthermore, using cryptocurrencies to make payments is frequently less expensive than using conventional payment methods, and it is possible to use them anywhere in the globe, independent of location or time zone.

On the other hand, cryptocurrencies are also volatile and risky investments. Their prices can fluctuate wildly, and there is always the potential for fraud or theft. Additionally, cryptocurrencies are not yet widely accepted by businesses, so they cannot be used to make everyday purchases in most places.

Notwithstanding these difficulties, there are plenty of reasons to think that the use of cryptocurrencies will only increase in the years to come. Cryptocurrency technology is always developing, and new uses are being created on a regular basis. Furthermore, an increasing number of establishments are starting to take cryptocurrency as payment. The value and stability of cryptocurrencies will probably rise as more companies and governments use them. As a result, they will draw in more investors and become a more generally used method of payment.

Cryptocurrencies are being used for a variety of applications beyond just payments. For example, they are being used to store value, provide loans and create decentralized applications. As these applications develop, the demand for cryptocurrencies is likely to grow.

Nations worldwide are currently grappling with the challenge of formulating regulations for cryptocurrencies. As rules become more defined, the utilization of cryptocurrencies will become more accessible for both enterprises and individuals.

Cryptocurrencies exhibit significant price volatility. This could render them a precarious investment for certain individuals. Nevertheless, once the market reaches a more developed stage, the level of unpredictability is expected to diminish.

The future of cryptocurrencies is unclear but there are a lot of possible advantages and difficulties ahead. The revolution started by Satoshi Nakamoto in 2009 has now come through a full circle. The general public across the world has started accepting cryptocurrencies like never before. Governments and central bankers across the world who had vehemently opposed cryptocurrencies are now discussing about introducing CBDC. The pandemic caused by COVID-19 has forced business transactions to go into a digital mode. And it looks like the financial transactions are also on the way to give a grand acceptance to digital currencies.

Questions for Discussion

1. Explain what you understand by cryptocurrency.
2. Explain how cryptocurrencies have evolved over the years.
3. How did Satoshi Nakamoto solve the double payment problem? Explain.
4. Explain the rise of Bitcoins over the years.
5. Explain how Bitcoins are mined.

Case Study – The Collapse of FTX Crypto Exchange

One of the biggest cryptocurrency exchange companies, FTX Trading Ltd., was well-known for its expertise in purchasing and vending cryptocurrency derivatives. Sam Bankman-Fried and Gary Wang, both alumni of the Massachusetts Institute of Technology, co-founded FTX in May 2019. FTX quickly established itself as a dominant player in the market by openly acquiring struggling competitors such as Blockfolio, LedgerX and Liquid Global. FTX utilized assertive marketing tactics such as Super Bowl advertisements, endorsements from celebrities and securing naming rights for the Miami Heat stadium. These commercials promised investors the opportunity to invest their money in these accounts and earn returns that exceeded those offered by traditional banks. FTX created the FTT digital token in May 2019. By staking FTT, users can additionally enjoy supplementary advantages from FTX, such as reduced prices and NFT rewards.

FTX was one of the numerous trading platforms that enabled investors to register for an account on a digital trading platform, purchase cryptocurrencies and engage in trading them until the end of 2022. People might also exchange cryptocurrencies for fiat money or cash via the FTX trading platform. To trade and purchase cryptocurrencies, users started creating accounts on FTX, and leading venture capital investors soon followed. The value of the corporation was $32 billion as of January 2022.

In November 2022, FTX had a collapse following the publication of a CoinDesk article that expressed concerns regarding the stability and potential use of leverage by Alameda Research, a trading firm associated with FTX. In November 2022, FTX encountered financial distress and sought financial assistance. Binance, a rival exchange, initially considered acquiring a share in the *company but subsequently reversed its decision. FTX's collapse had a significant impact on the volatile cryptocurrency market, causing it to lose billions and fall below a $1 trillion valuation.*

Upon closer examination, what initially appeared to be a mere accounting error was shown to be a substantial fraudulent scheme, resulting in the loss of billions of dollars for both investors and customers. Investigations revealed that consumer funds were diverted to accounts controlled by Alameda Research, a Hong Kong-based Bitcoin trading company, instead of being transferred to FTX. Subsequent to this revelation, FTX began to disintegrate.

The CEO of FTX tendered their resignation on November 11, 2022, and, subsequently, the company filed for bankruptcy. Subsequently, it is possible that FTX experienced a security breach, resulting in the unauthorized acquisition of a substantial number of tokens, amounting to hundreds of millions. In late December, Sam Bankman-Fried, the founder and former CEO of FTX, was apprehended in The Bahamas and subsequently deported to the USA. On January 3, 2023, he pleaded not guilty to all criminal charges.

The collapse of the FTX exchange in November 2022 was a significant event in the history of the cryptocurrency industry. The market was greatly impacted by the collapse of FTX, a prominent and well-regarded global exchange.

The initial report of the FTX debtors was released on April 9, 2023, providing a comprehensive account of the deficiencies in the management team, leading up to the bankruptcy of FTX Group. The study found that the FTX Group was deficient in terms of management, governance and organizational structure. The findings exposed security vulnerabilities, such as the utilization of unencrypted files to store private keys for transferring Bitcoin assets, as well as the lack of protection for online hot wallets containing cryptocurrency assets. The text mentions individuals who have access to substantial sums of money stored in Bitcoin wallets, as well as scenarios where multi-factor authentication was not employed in critical circumstances.

In addition, FTX lacked any financial or accounting controls. FTX was deficient in skilled personnel to oversee financial reporting, risk management, audits and accounting procedures. Based on the poll, most financial policies for a corporation that handles significant financial assets were either generic or nonexistent. Furthermore, there were no stipulations for intercompany transactions, allowing insiders and FTX Group entities to transfer assets and obligations without the need for documentation or protective measures.

Case Study Questions

1. Explain the business model of FTX Crypto Exchange?
2. What were the factors that led to the collapse of the FTX Crypto Exchange?
3. With FTX Crypto Exchange collapsing in such a dramatic manner, do you think that there is a future for decentralized finance and cryptocurrencies? Explain your viewpoint.

Further Reading

1. Nakamoto, S. (2008). Bitcoin: A peer-to-peer electronic cash system. *Decentralized Business Review*, 21260.
2. Global Blockchain and Cryptocurrency Market 2021 published by Researchandmarkets.com

References

Ammous, S. (2018). *The bitcoin standard: The decentralized alternative to central banking*. Wiley.

Chan, Q., Ding, W., Lin, C., & Rossi, A. G. (2020). *An Inside Look into Cryptocurrency Exchanges*. Available at SSRN 3759062.

CoinMarketCap. (2024). *Cryptocurrency Prices by Market Cap*. https://coinmarketcap.com

Courtois, N. T., Grajek, M., & Naik, R. (2014). Optimizing SHA256 in bitcoin mining. In *Cryptography and Security Systems: Third International Conference, CSS 2014, Lublin, Poland, September 22–24, 2014*. Proceedings 3 (pp. 131–144). Springer, Berlin and Heidelberg.

Danial, K. (2023). *Cryptocurrency investing for dummies*. John Wiley & Sons.

Murry, C., & Velasquez, V. (2023). *Cryptocurrency Explained with Pros and Cons for Investment*. Investopedia.com

Kent, P., & Bain, T. (2022). *Cryptocurrency mining for dummies*. John Wiley & Sons.

Kirillova, E. A., Pavlyuk, A. V., Mikhaylova, I. A., Zulfugarzade, T. E., & Zenin, S. S. (2018). Bitcoin, Litecoin, Namecoin: The legal nature of virtual currency. *Journal of Advanced Research in Law and Economics*, 9(1(31)), 119–126.

Law, L., Sabett, S., & Solinas, J. (1996). How to make a mint: The cryptography of anonymous electronic cash. *American University Law Review*, 46, 1131.

Nakamoto, S. (2008). *Bitcoin: A Peer-to-Peer Electronic Cash System*. www.bitcoin.org

Rao, S. (2022). Mt. Gox – the fall of a giant. In *Understanding cryptocurrency fraud: The challenges and headwinds to regulate digital currencies*, edited by S. Corbet (pp. 71–82). De Gruyter. https://doi.org/10.1515/9783110718485-006

Solomon, M. G. (2019). *Ethereum for dummies*. John Wiley & Sons.

Vigna, P., & Casey, M. J. (2016). *The age of cryptocurrency: How bitcoin and the blockchain are challenging the global economic order*. Picador.

Zharikov, M. V. (2023). Digital money options for the BRICS. *International Journal of Financial Studies*, 11(1), 42.

3 Blockchain Demystified

After reading this chapter you will:

- Know what is blockchain
- Know the history of blockchain
- Know the types of blockchain
- Know the working mechanism of blockchain
- Understand the applications of blockchain
- Understand the advantages and disadvantages of blockchain technology

ANZ is Australia's second-biggest bank, while in terms of market capitalization, it ranks fourth. ANZ faced the challenge of increasing operational efficiency, ensuring secure transactions and staying competitive in the rapidly evolving financial industry. To address these challenges, the bank initiated a strategic plan to explore and adopt blockchain technology. ANZ Bank recognized the potential benefits of blockchain, such as enhanced security, transparency and streamlined processes. The bank aimed to leverage blockchain to optimize its internal operations, improve customer services and explore innovative financial solutions.

To streamline its internal procedures, such as data management, record keeping and transaction settlement, ANZ Bank started by integrating blockchain. Blockchain technology's decentralized and unchangeable structure guaranteed a more transparent and safe infrastructure, lowering the possibility of mistakes and fraud.

With the objective of alleviating a problem faced by big landlords and the 11,500 shops in Australia and New Zealand that rely on bank guarantees rather than bonds or cash deposits, ANZ launched an initiative with an absolute bank guarantee that states, "You're good for the rent". This is required by the landlord when a shop wishes to lease space to build a store.

There are sometimes lengthy talks between the bank, the tenant and the landlord. The transaction may take many weeks to complete because the guarantee is a tangible document. Landlords are then required to maintain and keep the records, manually reconcile them with the leases and go through the same procedure again if any terms are altered. Furthermore, the bank will not honor a document altered by a tenant through fraud or error. If the tenant doesn't pay, the landlord will have to pay for it out of pocket.

ANZ teamed up with Westpac to establish a multi-bank experience and with Scentre Group to represent the landlords after understanding that a distributed ledger may revolutionize the procedure. ANZ also requested IBM to join the collaboration. They jointly

DOI: 10.4324/9781032699417-3

created a platform powered by the open-source Hyperledger Consortium framework. IBM assisted in gathering requirements and developing a solution that ANZ could adopt through the use of an agile strategy.

The proof-of-concept, which enables a renter to request a guarantee via an Internet platform, was finished in less than four months. The landlord can now modify the terms for the renter and bank to evaluate using drop-down choices. Once the document is approved by all parties, it is securely, irreversibly and publicly recorded in the blockchain ledger in a transaction that is transparent to all parties. Changes, including rent increases, can also be negotiated online.

The main advantage was speed; ANZ improved cycle time by 90% to 95%, going from weeks to hours. By validating the document, blockchain technology eliminated the chances of fraud. Landlords can now digitally reconcile rent rather than shuffle paperwork. Additionally, they value the uniform digital format. The benefits are so great that other banks and landlords want to get involved.

Financial and environmental guarantees are provided by ANZ to a wide range of industries, including government, construction, mining and natural resources. There is a short-term potential to digitize assurances for these and other products. In the long run, geographic expansion appears promising because the guarantee procedure is universally applicable. ANZ has the potential to open up a global market if it can settle on a standard, digitize the document and place it on a blockchain.

An analog process has been modified by the proof-of-concept to significantly enhance the client experience. This gives hope for the commercial applications of blockchain in the global economy. Although ANZ Bank saw several advantages from the implementation of blockchain, there were drawbacks as well, including the requirement for staff training, integration difficulties and regulatory uncertainty. The bank worked with regulatory agencies, formed strategic alliances and provided continuous training for staff members to handle these issues.

The strategic implementation of blockchain technology by ANZ Bank turned out to be a crucial step in overcoming the obstacles of the contemporary financial scene. By utilizing blockchain's benefits, the bank was able to improve customer service and internal operations, which helped it stay relevant and competitive in the constantly changing financial sector.

Introduction to Blockchain

The settlement of a bank transfer can take up to three days on average. Not only is this troublesome for the customers, but this is also logistically challenging for the banks. Nowadays a straightforward bank transfer goes straight to the recipient without going through a convoluted network of middlemen from bank to custodial service. This is facilitated by the blockchain technology.

Blockchain operates as a publicly accessible, easily understood and distributed system that keeps a record of transactions. This suggests that the transactions can be resolved on the public blockchain instead of relying on custodial services. Blockchain technologies in banking play a significant role in enabling expeditious and effortless transactions.

Trillions of dollars are made and lost every year as a result of late payments and additional fees. Public blockchains, where cryptocurrencies like Ether and Bitcoin are produced, allow anybody to send and receive money instantly and without incurring transaction fees. Additionally, because the payment is made on a decentralized network, there is no requirement for transaction verification, which speeds up and lowers the cost of payment transfers using blockchain in the banking and finance industry.

The banking industry is currently exploring and studying several business scenarios, such as vendor financing, customer loyalty programs and syndicated loans, and their connection to blockchain technology. Banks generally utilize blockchain technology for the purpose of maintaining backend utilities, facilitating registration processes and conducting fund transfers. This technology is accessible to all users on the network without any cost and operates in a manner that is comparable to a distributed ledger. Blockchain is inherently safe due to its high level of resistance to data alteration or manipulation once it has been recorded.

The worldwide blockchain market was projected by Statista to reach $5.85 billion in 2023. The forecast given by industry experts predicts that the industry will grow with a compound annual growth rate of 82.8% to reach $1.2 trillion by 2030.

Origin of Blockchain

The first cryptocurrency, Bitcoin, was created using blockchain technology as its foundation. In October 2008, a whitepaper titled "Bitcoin: A Peer-to-Peer Electronic Cash System" was released by an unidentified person going by the pseudonym Satoshi Nakamoto (Nakamoto, 2008).

The issue of trust in online transactions is the first topic covered in the whitepaper. Conventional financial systems rely on the facilitation and verification of transactions by centralized intermediaries, such as banks and payment processors. These middlemen may be costly, slow and susceptible to many types of fraud.

Nakamoto envisioned a decentralized system in which a network of nodes (computers) would keep track of transactions on a public ledger. The blockchain, a decentralized ledger, would replace the need for a central authority and offer an open, unchangeable record of all transactions.

Proof-of-work (PoW) is a consensus technique that Nakamoto created to preserve the integrity of the blockchain. A PoW system pits miners, or network nodes, against one another to solve challenging math problems; the first person to finish wins the privilege of appending a new block of transactions to the blockchain. This procedure guarantees the secure and trustless addition of transactions (Nakamoto, 2008).

On the blockchain, cryptography is essential for protecting user identities and transactional data. The purpose of public and private keys is to confirm ownership and approve transactions. Additionally, Nakamoto described how transactions are organized into blocks and how, because each block refers to the one before it (creating a chain), it is very difficult to change a transaction without also changing all of the blocks that come before it. This is how the word "blockchain" originated. The whitepaper explained the workings of the Bitcoin network, including how nodes exchange information and how transaction fees and freshly produced Bitcoins are used to reward miners. Peer-to-peer (P2P) networks of nodes are essential to the validation and dissemination of transactions in Bitcoin. In his work, Nakamoto described how nodes find each other and keep a consistent perspective of the blockchain (Nakamoto, 2008).

The development of blockchain technology began with the publication of this whitepaper, and, in January 2009, Bitcoin was introduced as an open-source software project. Since blockchain technology has developed throughout time, many more cryptocurrencies and blockchain platforms have been developed, each with special characteristics and applications. Beyond cryptocurrency, supply chain management, healthcare, government systems, educational institutions and more have discovered uses for blockchain technology.

What Is Blockchain?

Blockchain is an application that runs on the principle of distributed ledger technology (DLT). A P2P network is responsible for generating the blocks in a blockchain. Blockchain is a digitally encrypted form of database. A blockchain consists of chunks of information. Every transaction is documented in a block. Every block possesses a specific storage capacity. Once a block is completely completed, it is linked to the previously full block, creating a sequence of data called the blockchain (Tapscott & Tapscott, 2016).

According to the definition given by Iansiti and Lakhani, "Blockchain is an open distributed ledger that can record transactions between two parties efficiently and in a verifiable and permanent way" (Iansiti & Lakhani, 2017).

Blockchains work like a public ledger. Public ledger is a database of historical information that is available to general public and easily accessible. The main characteristics of blockchains are commitment, consensus, security, privacy and authenticity. They check the validity and ensure that every transaction is recorded within a finite time. They ensure the consistency of data in local files and get it updated in real time. They act as a check against any effort to tamper or manipulate the data. They also ensure the privacy and authenticity of the data (Tapscott, Iansiti & Lakhani, 2019).

The mechanism of block creation in a blockchain is given in Figure 3.1. The blockchain's transactions can be coded and tailored to computational logic due to the public ledger's digital nature. The database in a blockchain is open to all users on the network, permanently stored and arranged chronologically.

Time-stamped records are those that are added to the blockchain. It is thus tamper-proof and irreversible. By using timestamping, each block's data is uniquely identified by its serial number and is recorded at the precise moment the block is mined and approved by the blockchain network.

Nodes store the data blocks that make up a blockchain. Nodes are what build a blockchain's infrastructure. In essence, a node is a gadget such as a laptop, tablet, smartphone or desktop computer. A blockchain's nodes are connected to one another and exchange data. A device with a complete copy of the blockchain's transaction history is called a full node.

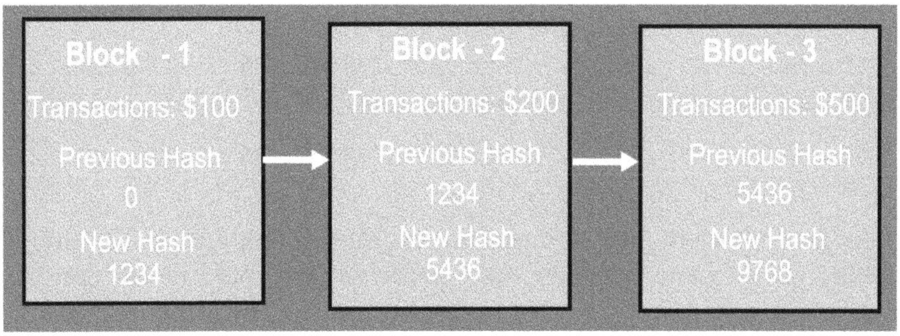

Figure 3.1 Blocks in a Blockchain

Database versus Blockchain – The Main Differences

Though a blockchain is similar to a database in many ways, there are cardinal differences between the two, which are illustrated in Table 3.1:

Table 3.1 Database versus Blockchain – The Main Differences

	Database	*Blockchain*
Type	Needs permission	Public access
Control	Centralized	Decentralized
Architecture	Client–server architecture	Peer-to-peer network
Data persistence	Non-persistent	Immutable
Chance of failure	High	Zero chance of failure
Performance	Depends on the system	Fast and real time

Source: Iansiti and Lakhani (2017).

While both databases and blockchains are tools for managing data, their architectures and purposes are distinct. Databases are centralized, mutable and controlled by a central authority, whereas blockchains are decentralized, immutable and rely on consensus mechanisms to maintain a secure and transparent ledger. Databases are well-suited for applications where a central authority needs to control and manage data efficiently. Common use cases include traditional business applications, content management systems and more. Blockchains are often used in scenarios where decentralization, transparency and security are critical, such as cryptocurrencies, supply chain management, smart contracts and decentralized applications (DApps).

Databases are often centralized systems in which a singular institution or a collective of entities have authority and oversight over the entire database. This central authority possesses the authority to effect modifications, add or eliminate data and regulate access. Blockchain is a system that operates without a central authority and allows for the distribution of a ledger. The system functions by utilizing a network of interconnected nodes, with each node containing a complete replica of the whole blockchain. Transactions are determined using a consensus procedure, and, once they are included in the blockchain, they cannot be changed (Chowdhury, Colman, Kabir, Han & Sarda, 2018).

Databases can employ diverse data models, such as relational, document-oriented, graph and others. The structure is tailored to meet the precise demands of the application. A blockchain consists of a sequential series of blocks, with each block containing a collection of transactions. The data is frequently structured in a manner that guarantees both integrity and security, employing cryptographic methods.

History of Blockchain

The greatest difficulty with digital transactions is duplication and falsification. In 1991, Stuart Haber and W. Scott Stornetta, two physicists, presented blockchain technology as a solution to this problem. They introduced the idea of digital papers that are time-stamped to prevent manipulation or backdating. The time-stamped papers were stored in an encrypted chain of blocks that was impenetrable to manipulation or breach.

With the advent of Merkle Trees, blockchain development advanced to a new level. Another name for Merkle Trees is "binary hash trees". A Merkle Tree creates a digital fingerprint of the complete set of transactions and saves them all in a block. It assists the user in deciding if a specific transaction belongs in a block. Hashing pairs of nodes are calculated repeatedly until only one hash remains, which is how Merkle Trees are made. With Merkle Trees, a "secured chain of blocks" can be made (Castellon, Roy, Kreidl, Dutta & Bölöni, 2021).

Expert in cryptography Hal Finney developed reusable proof-of-work (RPoW), a prototype for digital currency, to address the issue of double spending. By maintaining the ownership of tokens recorded in the IBM 4758 secure cryptographic coprocessor, which can safely validate the software's hash, the issue of double spending was fixed. Because RPoW tokens are constructed using a sophisticated security model, they are thought to be more reliable than money maintained in institutions. Asymmetric-key cryptography-based Rivest Shamir Adleman (RSA)-signed tokens and RPoW operated together (Feng, 2021).

The man known as the creator of Bitcoins, Satoshi Nakamoto, first appeared on the scene in 2008, just after the financial world was rocked by the subprime crisis. He employed the hash function's compression step to construct the notion of distributed blockchains and implemented the Merkle Tree concept in Bitcoins. According to his theoretical concept, blockchains are created using P2P networks that provide timestamping and verification. This signaled the start of the creation of public ledgers utilizing blockchains, which were made up of encrypted blocks that were timestamp-protected to make them safe from tampering. Bitcoins that were safe and unchangeable were made using the same technology and procedure (Nakamoto, 2008).

Block and chain were utilized independently by Satoshi Nakamoto in his research paper "Bitcoin: A Peer-to-Peer Electronic Cash System", but they are currently managed by a single organization that makes it easier to create cryptocurrencies and manages different kinds of Fintech businesses. Blockchain technology is currently being used by corporations including Walmart, Amazon, Unilever, Procter & Gamble, AIG and Siemens to optimize their processes. IBM is utilizing blockchain technology in a number of projects, such as the "Food Trust Blockchain", which tracks food from farm to table. Additionally, blockchain technology has been embraced by the Banking, Financial Services and Insurance (BFSI) sector to develop novel and inventive procedures that would provide them a competitive edge (Nakamoto, 2008).

Types of Blockchain

Generally, blockchains are either public or private. Public blockchains work on DLT. Examples of public blockchains are Bitcoins and Ethereum. Private blockchains operate on a smaller scale and have permission levels for accessibility and security with different levels of authorization. This is used by companies for supply chain management and asset ownership (Laurence, 2023).

Blockchains are classified into four types:

1. Public blockchains
2. Private blockchains
3. Hybrid blockchains
4. Consortium blockchains

Public Blockchains

A public blockchain is a decentralized system that permits unrestricted participation and accessibility to all individuals. DLT is the driving force behind public blockchains. DLT employs a decentralized approach by disseminating data over a P2P network instead of centralizing it in a singular location. Their networks can be accessed. Public domains are platforms where information is openly shared and accessible to the public. The data is determined by consensus and is not subject to the control of any single entity. These chains possess the characteristic of immutability and decentralization. Consequently, once an entry is recorded on the blockchain and verified, it becomes immutable and cannot be altered or deleted (Guegan, 2017).

Due to its decentralized nature, it is necessary to provide a mechanism for verifying the authenticity of the data. Through the utilization of a consensus mechanism, participants on the blockchain collectively agree on the current state of the ledger. The most often used consensus mechanisms are PoW and proof-of-stake (PoS).

The primary sectors that employ public blockchains are education and healthcare. Litecoin, Dogecoin, Ethereum, Bitcoin and other cryptocurrencies utilize public blockchain technology. Alternatively, it can also be utilized to establish an immutable record with a verifiable sequence of custody, such as public records of property ownership and electronic notarization of affidavits. For organizations such as non-governmental organizations or social assistance groups that rely on transparency and trust, this type of blockchain technology is ideal. Private firms do not prefer this type of blockchain because it is public in nature.

Private Blockchains

A private blockchain is a blockchain network that functions within a regulated environment, such as a restricted network. While operating on a smaller scale, this type of blockchain operates in a similar manner to a public blockchain network by utilizing P2P connectivity and decentralization. Private blockchains are often operated within a limited network controlled by a certain firm or group, as opposed to being accessible to anybody who wishes to participate and provide computational resources. They are also called "enterprise blockchains" or "permissioned blockchains" (Guegan, 2017).

Private blockchains operate on the idea of exclusivity, where access is limited to invited participants, and are overseen by a sole governing authority. Private blockchains offer many degrees of authorization to ensure both accessibility and security. Due to the multiple tiers of data access, this system offers a higher level of confidentiality. This is restricted to individuals who have been authorized and is not accessible to the general populace.

Private blockchains operate similarly to an intranet. The controlling organization establishes permission levels, security measures, authorizations and accessibility protocols. An entity that creates a private blockchain network has the authority to determine which nodes are allowed to view, contribute or alter data. Additionally, it has the potential to render certain information unattainable to external entities. Private blockchains are the optimal choice when there is a need for cryptographically secure blockchain technology, but the controlling institution wishes to restrict public access to the data due to their fast processing capabilities.

Private blockchains primarily facilitate business-to-business transactions. Financial institutions and governments are the primary users of this. Private blockchain technology can also be applied to internal voting, asset ownership and supply chain management.

Hybrid Blockchains

A hybrid blockchain is a system that integrates features from both public and private blockchains. These systems can be categorized as either permission-based or permission-less, depending on the type of information they choose to divulge, the domain in which they operate and the persons they allow access (Ge, Loghin, Ooi, Ruan & Wang, 2022).

On hybrid blockchains, users' identities are kept hidden and are only revealed when they engage in transactions. While the transactions remain confidential, they can be verified upon request. It allows organizations to establish both a public system that does not require permission and a private system that requires permission. This gives them the power to control which data is made available to the public and who can access specific data kept on the blockchain.

A hybrid blockchain often maintains the privacy of data and transactions, but allows for validation upon request, for as by providing access through a smart contract. Despite being safeguarded within the network, confidential information is susceptible to verification. The hybrid blockchain, albeit privately held, lacks the ability to alter transactions. Upon signing up for a hybrid blockchain, a user is granted full network access. Other users are unable to see the identity of a user unless they engage in a transaction. The other individual is thereafter informed of their identity.

The primary applications of these types of blockchains are in real estate enterprises and the management of medical history records. Medical records can be stored using a hybrid blockchain. Users have the ability to access personal information through a smart contract, but it is not available to random third parties. Hybrid blockchain technology provides governments with an additional choice for securely exchanging and storing citizen data among different organizations.

Consortium Blockchain

A consortium blockchain, also known as a federated blockchain, combines features of both private and public blockchains. However, it distinguishes itself by being a decentralized network where multiple members of the organization collaborate. A consortium blockchain mitigates the risks associated with a single company controlling the network on a private blockchain by limiting access to a certain group (Dib, Brousmiche, Durand, Thea & Hamida, 2018).

This type of blockchain is constructed on a decentralized network by the collaborative efforts of multiple individuals. Preset nodes control the consensus mechanisms in a consortium blockchain. The validator node is accountable for initiating, receiving and verifying transactions. Member nodes have the ability to initiate or receive transactions.

This type of blockchain is more efficient, scalable and secure when compared to a public blockchain network. It offers access controls similar to those found in private and hybrid blockchains. Federated blockchain is a synonym for this term.

These types of blockchains are utilized by banks and PayTech organizations. A consortium including multiple banks has the authority to determine which nodes will authenticate the transactions. It is very suitable for supply chains, particularly for applications related to food and medication.

The Ethereum Blockchain

After the Bitcoin network, the Ethereum blockchain is the second most widely used blockchain. Vitalik Buterin created this back in 2013. The process of creating Ethereum blockchain started when he released a whitepaper outlining the concept.

Ethereum is a blockchain-based open software platform that allows anybody to create and run decentralized apps or DApps. Ethereum's unique selling point is its use of the Ethereum Virtual Machine (EVM). To create smart contracts, utilize EVM. These contracts only come into effect when specific requirements are satisfied (Solomon, 2019).

The function of the decentralized network starts when a message is transmitted via decentralized applications (dApp) that reaches globally dispersed independent computers, called miners. They must download an application called Mist to connect to the network. Therefore, nobody has access to the entire communication. Using the Ethereum blockchain, the developer will produce a decentralized application. The transaction will be confirmed by the miners. After that, they will combine the transactions into a block. For their block to be added to the blockchain, the miners will compete. By resolving a mathematical puzzle, this will occur. A miner's fee will be paid to the victorious miner, and the new block will be appended to the network. Ether is the virtual money utilized on Ethereum. Blockchains based on Ethereum promise autonomy, transparency and accuracy.

Non-fungible tokens (NFTs) have made the Ethereum blockchain well-known. These coins, which store digital media (like music, paintings or videos), are based on blockchain technology. NFTs are becoming more and more well-liked because of their capacity to confirm the original authorship, authenticity and history of digital assets. This has made it possible for today's digital artists to purchase and market their works while receiving due credit and a just portion of the proceeds.

How Does a Blockchain Work?

A blockchain is a sequential series of blocks that store and preserve information. Each block consists of three distinct components: data, nonce and hash. The acronym "nonce" stands for "number used only once". When a block is created, a 32-bit integer called a nonce is randomly generated. A mathematical function called a hash can convert an input of arbitrary length into an encrypted output of a fixed length (Tapscott, Iansiti & Lakhani, 2019).

The cryptographic hash is produced by a nonce during the production of the initial block in a chain. A hash is analogous to an identification key. It provides identification for the contents of the block. Each hash is unique. Once the data in the block is extracted, it becomes permanently associated with the nonce and hash and is considered to be digitally signed.

Each block in the blockchain has its own hash as well as the hash of the preceding block. The genesis block, being the first block in the chain, does not contain the hash of the prior block. Any endeavor to modify the hash of any block will result in the entire blockchain becoming invalid.

Through the utilization of encrypted hashes and timestamps, the prevention of tampering is achieved. PoW is an extra process used to prevent tampering with the blockchain. PoW is commonly abbreviated as PoW. The PoW process appends a new block to the blockchain.

Blockchains utilize a DLT to establish a decentralized P2P network. A node refers to a recently added participant in the blockchain network. New members of the blockchain receive a full replica of the blockchain. Each node has the ability to observe a recently inserted block, and every node is required to grant its approval before the block can be included. This is commonly known as the consensus process.

Applications of Blockchain

The process of timestamping was invented long ago. But it was Satoshi Nakamoto who used the timestamping process to create a secure blockchain to mine and distribute Bitcoins. Although Bitcoins were met with suspicion and apprehension when it was initially introduced, the technology and process of blockchains were received with open arms, The blockchain was a distributed public ledger system and worked on P2P networks. It was secure as it used the timestamping process, hashtag encryption and the PoW protocol (Tapscott & Tapscott, 2016).

Very soon, the application of blockchains spread beyond the creation, distribution and management of cryptocurrencies and was adopted by other industries for supply chain management, public healthcare record keeping and also by the government for tax management. Blockchain is now used by the arts, music and film industry to create NFT-based products that can be digitally sold by creative people and digitally owned by connoisseurs.

The biggest user of blockchain technology has been the BFSI. Blockchain has helped financial institutions to start Neobanking, which operates digitally and functions 24 × 7 round a year. The blockchain technology helps to detect frauds without any human intervention. This is called RegTech. The processing of financial transactions happens in nanoseconds and can be processed in a smooth and comfortable manner using quick response codes and application program interface. PayTech companies like PayPal, Paytm, PhonePe and Google Pay use this system for smooth functioning. LendTech companies like Faircent, Lendingkart and LenDen are using this technology. InsurTech companies like Policybazaar and Acko are using blockchain to provide on-demand insurance services.

Research done by European bank Santander has shown that banks save $15 billion to $20 billion per year by running operations on blockchain technology. Research done by Capgemini has shown that consumers save up to $16 million per year in transaction fees because of blockchain technology. The work done by Satoshi Nakamoto and his peers after the subprime crisis of 2008 has proved to be a big boon for the BFSI industry.

Hash

A hash is "a mathematical function that converts an input of arbitrary length into an encrypted output of a fixed length". The hash is also a block identifier. It has a unique alphanumeric key (Di Pierro, 2017).

Bitcoins use the SHA 256 algorithm. The full form of SHA is the secure hashing algorithm. In the case of SHA256, the output will always be 256 bits in length irrespective of the length of the input. An example of hash is given here:

```
SHA3-256("hello") =
"3338be694f50c5f338814986cdf0686453a888b84f424d792af4b9202398f392"
```

The cryptographic hash functions are deterministic, capable of quick computation, resistant to pre-images, sensitive to changes in input and collision resistant. If there is a small change in the input data, the hash will change and the whole blockchain will become invalid. This property of hash makes the blockchain immutable and resistant to tampering.

The hash helps to track a particular transaction in a blockchain. The transaction can be tracked by copying the hash into the blockchain explorer.

Nonce

Nonce is a cryptographic number used to prevent the problem of tampering and double spending. There are randomly generated pseudo numbers. These are protocols that help to authenticate the transactions.

Nonce is the first number that a miner must discover to create a block in the blockchain. This is generated through mathematical computations. By introducing randomness and timestamping, the nonce makes it impossible for hackers to break into the system. Nonces are employed in many computer networking applications, such as two-factor authentication, account recovery and identification, as well as purchase authentication (Lewis, 2019).

PoW and PoS

For the smooth functioning of a blockchain, blocks have to be added to the chain using a secure mechanism. The blockchain also has to ensure that hackers do not enter the system and use the network for malicious purposes. To ensure this, the blockchain needs validators to certify and give permission for a block to be added to the chain. This is done by using cryptographic protocols. Two such protocols are PoW and PoS. Both PoW and PoS are called consensus mechanisms, as they operate based on the consensus of the stakeholders (Sriman, Ganesh Kumar & Shamili, 2021).

PoW is defined as

> a form of cryptographic zero-knowledge proof in which one party (the prover) proves to others (the verifiers) that a certain amount of a specific computational effort has been expended. This idea is also known as a CPU cost function, client puzzle, computational puzzle, or CPU pricing function.

There are two ways in which PoW works. One is called the "challenge-response protocol", and the other is called "solution-verification protocol". The challenge-response protocol works in a direct manner by linking the requester (client) with the provider (server). The solution provider protocol works in an indirect manner the provider must check both the problem choice and the found solution.

Let us understand this mechanism with a simple example. Suppose the miners are given a mathematical computational challenge to solve the problem: What is 8 + 7=?

Miner 1 gives the following answers:

8+7 = 11. Incorrect
8+7 = 12. Incorrect
8+7 = 13. Incorrect

Miner 2 gives the following answers:

8+7 = 14. Incorrect
8+7 = 15. Correct

Since Miner 2 has solved the mathematical puzzle, he or she will be rewarded for the effort and the blocks or coins that are mined will be added to the network.

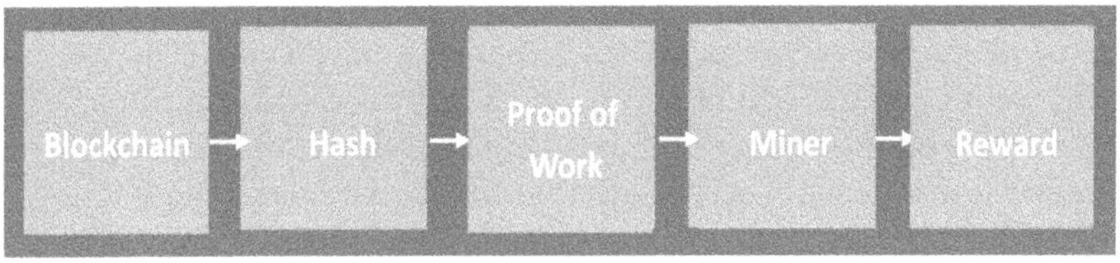

Figure 3.2 The Proof-of-Work (PoW)

Table 3.2 Proof-of-Work (PoW) and Proof-of-Stake (PoS)

PoW	*PoS*
PoW is a consensus mechanism that creates new blocks through a process that uses computing power to solve mathematical puzzles.	PoS is a cryptographic protocol used to determine how transactions are processed and new blocks are added to a blockchain in a cryptocurrency system.
PoW requires miners to engage in a competitive process of solving intricate mathematical problems to authenticate transaction blocks.	PoS employs a random selection process to designate validators responsible for validating transaction blocks.
The likelihood of successfully mining a block is determined by the amount of computational labor performed by a miner.	The likelihood of successfully validating a new block is contingent upon the magnitude of one's stake, which is determined by the number of coins they possess.
An incentive is granted to the initial miner who successfully solves the cryptographic problem associated with each block.	The incentive for the validator is the network validation fees that they can collect.
To append each block to the chain, miners must engage in a competitive process where they attempt to solve complex riddles utilizing their computational ability.	Miners must participate in a competitive procedure to add each block to the chain. This method involves solving intricate puzzles using their processing power.
To install a dangerous block to hack the blockchain, hackers would require a minimum of 51% of computational power.	For hackers to take control of the blockchain, they would require ownership of at least 51% of the whole blockchain network, which is logically impossible.
PoW systems need more energy, are highly expensive and are not environmentally friendly but show a higher level of accuracy.	PoS systems need less energy, are less expensive and are more environmentally friendly but show a lower level of accuracy.

Source: Tapscott, Iansiti and Lakhani (2019).

The problem with PoW is that it consumes a lot of electricity and the process is also quite slow. Hence, the cryptocurrency experts came out with a viable alternative, which was PoS. PoW was created by Satoshi Nakamoto in 2009. PoS was created by Scott Nadal and Sunny King in 2012. The first cryptocurrency to use PoS was Peercoin.

In the PoS Mechanism, the validator has to "stake" a certain percentage of his holdings in cryptocurrency to participate in the mining process. If the blockchain is hacked, the validator will lose his stake. If the mining process goes through successfully, the validator will get transaction fees. The chances of hacking in this case are very low because the hacker must have some cryptocurrency in his wallet to start the hacking process and will definitely lose the cryptocurrencies he has staked if the process is hacked. So, there is a high incentive for validation and there is a high disincentive for hacking.

The PoW decides on the winner based on the capability to solve complex mathematical computational problems. The PoS decides on the winner using a random process based on the percentage of cryptocurrencies they have staked. PoS is not very complicated like PoW, consumes less electricity and works in a faster manner. The criticism against PoS is that it discourages new players from entering the system and only helps the rich to become richer.

Several new cryptocurrencies like Dash and Neo are using PoS. Ethereum has also announced that they will be introducing PoS-based Beacon Chain which will be a part of Ethereum 2.0.

Smart Contracts

A smart contract, sometimes referred to as a crypto-contract, is computer software that autonomously and directly controls the transfer of digital assets between parties under specified situations. A smart contract not only functions similarly to a traditional contract but also incorporates automatic enforcement mechanisms. Smart contracts function exactly how their developers have specified, composed and designed them. Smart contracts are legally binding agreements that are enforced by code, similar to how traditional contracts are enforced through the law (Khan, Loukil, Ghedira-Guegan, Benkhelifa & Bani-Hani, 2021).

Characteristics of Smart Contracts

There are some special characteristics of smart contracts which are given here:

Distributed: The information on the network is equally distributed among all the nodes and everyone gets a similar copy of the smart contract. This cannot be altered or manipulated by anybody in the network.

Deterministic: Smart contracts work as per specifications agreed upon and will deliver a predetermined outcome, irrespective of any party that executes the smart contract.

Immutable: Immutable means the smart contract cannot be altered, tampered or manipulated by any party by changing or altering the contents.

Autonomy: Autonomy means that the smart contract is self-executable and does not need the intervention of a third party.

Transparent: This means that all participants will receive each and every piece of information about transactions in the blockchain, and nothing will be hidden from them.
Trustless: This means that there is no trust issue in the blockchain and hence no third party is required for verifying the transactions happening in the blockchain.
Self-enforcing: Smart contracts are automatically enforced as per the pre-decided and predetermined conditions and rules.

Capabilities of Smart Contract

The various capabilities of smart contracts are:

Accuracy: Smart contracts have a very high level of accuracy and can do impeccable execution.
Automation: Smart contracts perform the process in an automated mode.
Speed: By automating actions with software code, smart contracts minimize the amount of time required to move through every step associated with human interaction. The time it takes to complete all the work is the same as the time it takes for the smart contract's code to run because everything is coded.
Backup: The blockchain provides a backup of the shared ledger, which is available on demand and whenever needed.
Security: Cryptography can guarantee the security of the assets. The hacker will still need to change every block that comes after the altered block even if they manage to crack the encryption. Please be aware that a small or medium-sized business would not be able to complete this assignment due to its extreme difficulty and computational demands.
Savings: Smart contracts are economical to use as there are no third-party intermediaries and no paperwork is involved.

Use of Solidity Programming for Making Smart Contracts

Solidity Program was developed by Christian Reitwiessner in 2015. This runs on the Ethereum platform. The Solidity program is mostly used for writing and developing smart contracts. Solidity is also the main language used by systems that operate blockchains. It is an object-oriented (contract-oriented) language with statically typed syntax. The Python, C++ and JavaScript programs that operate on the EVM have a significant influence on Solidity. Solidity facilitates intricate user-defined programming, inheritance and libraries. Contracts like voting, crowdfunding, blind auctions and multi-signature wallets can be made with Solidity (Everts & Muller, 2018).

Hyperledger

Blockchain technology has emerged as a revolutionary power in the digital realm, providing enhanced effectiveness, robust security and clear visibility in various industries. Hyperledger is an open-source collaborative effort, overseen by the Linux Foundation, with the objective of advancing blockchain technologies across various industries. This distinguishes it from other blockchain platforms (Cachin, 2016).

Instead of being a single blockchain platform, Hyperledger is an open-source project that houses a number of frameworks, tools and libraries for creating blockchain solutions suitable for enterprise use. Since its 2016 debut by the Linux Foundation, it has grown significantly in popularity thanks to its industry-driven methodology, modular architecture and emphasis on interoperability.

A group of open-source initiatives called Hyperledger was developed to aid in the creation of distributed ledgers based on blockchain technology. Its goal is to develop the frameworks, standards, instruments and libraries required to construct blockchains and associated applications. These projects are hosted, maintained and supported by the Hyperledger Foundation.

One of the most popular Hyperledger frameworks for creating permissioned, modular blockchain networks is called Fabric. Because it has a strong permission architecture and allows smart contracts, sometimes referred to as "chaincode", it is appropriate for commercial use cases that demand secrecy and anonymity.

For several distributed ledger systems and libraries, Hyperledger serves as a central location. With this, a company could enhance the effectiveness, performance and transactions in their business processes by utilizing one of Hyperledger's frameworks, for instance.

The way Hyperledger operates is by offering the standards and infrastructure required to create blockchain apps and systems. The frameworks and tools that comprise Hyperledger, known as Hyperledger Greenhouse, are used by developers to create blockchain applications for businesses. Everybody in the network knows everyone else, and they can all take part in the procedures that lead to consensus.

Key Features of Hyperledger

Hyperledger frameworks are designed for permissioned blockchain networks, where participants are known and must be authenticated. This is crucial for enterprise applications where privacy, confidentiality and regulatory compliance are paramount.

The modular architecture of Hyperledger frameworks allows developers to choose and plug in components that best suit their specific use cases. This flexibility promotes interoperability and ease of integration with existing systems.

Hyperledger supports smart contracts, referred to as "chaincode", allowing developers to encode business logic into the blockchain. This enables the automation of complex processes, reducing the need for intermediaries.

Different Hyperledger frameworks offer various consensus mechanisms to suit different business requirements. Whether it's Practical Byzantine Fault Tolerance in Hyperledger Fabric or Proof of Elapsed Time in Hyperledger Sawtooth, these mechanisms ensure agreement among network participants.

Hyperledger has emerged as a pivotal player in the enterprise blockchain space, providing a diverse set of frameworks tailored to specific industry needs. Its open-source nature, modular architecture and commitment to interoperability make it a compelling choice for businesses looking to harness the power of blockchain technology for increased transparency, efficiency and security across various sectors. As Hyperledger continues to evolve, its impact on reshaping industries and driving innovation is likely to become even more pronounced in the years to come.

Applications of Hyperledger

Hyperledger frameworks are well-suited for creating transparent and traceable supply chain networks, ensuring the authenticity and integrity of goods throughout the entire supply chain.

In the financial sector, Hyperledger technologies are used for cross-border payments, trade finance and digital identity management, enhancing security, reducing costs and improving efficiency.

Hyperledger provides solutions for managing healthcare data securely, ensuring interoperability among different healthcare providers and enabling patients to have more control over their health records.

Non-Fungible Tokens

The majority of businesses and systems rely on the process of confirming the ownership of both digital and physical assets. In addition, people have amassed rare and priceless possessions like jewelry, art and land over time. These days, collectibles like trading cards and autographed souvenirs have followed suit. Traditionally, paper-based or centralized digital systems have been used to verify the ownership and legitimacy of these assets. These systems are frequently ineffective, cause obstacles to asset transfers and allow for fraud (Raman & Raj, 2021).

The decentralized Ethereum blockchain application CryptoKitties, developed by Dapper Labs in 2017, was the first real-world example of a digitally verified, transferable and NFT. These collectible gaming characters, known as NFTs, are CryptoKittys; each one has randomly given features that make it somewhat uncommon. Verifying the legitimacy of every CryptoKitty, together with its distinct characteristics and owner, is a straightforward process thanks to the blockchain's inbuilt digital signature mechanism. Additionally, there is a significant decrease in the likelihood of fraud and friction during the transfer of these assets to a new owner. The groundbreaking development of NFTs, popularized by CryptoKitties, is currently being utilized in a wide range of applications, ranging from digital identification credentials and land titling to digital art and in-game products.

A blockchain records a unique digital identity known as a NFT. It's employed to verify the legitimacy and ownership of a one-of-a-kind item, like media, digital content or artwork. NFTs cannot be divided, swapped out or cloned.

A novel use of blockchain technology, NFTs allow for the decentralized, safe ownership, trading and verification of distinct digital assets. As opposed to fungible and interchangeable cryptocurrencies like Bitcoin and Ethereum, NFTs are different and indivisible, making each token unique.

An artist, author or license holder can create an NFT using a process called minting. To activate a smart contract function that creates the token and assigns ownership, minters need to sign a blockchain transaction that specifies the crucial features of the token. Subsequently, this transaction is disseminated on the blockchain.

An NFT consists of a unique token ID, also known as a token ID, which is stored within a smart contract and associated with the identity of its owner. Confirming ownership and transferring a token to a new owner is a straightforward process when the current owner of a given token ID wishes to transfer it to another user.

It is possible to design NFTs that represent almost any kind of asset, digital, physical or metaphysical. Nonetheless, digital artwork, digital collectibles, audiovisual content and event passes are the most often used NFT assets.

Cartoons, music, movies, video clips, JPEGs, postcards, sports trading cards, virtual real estate and pets can all be utilized with NFTs. They may also stand in for tangible objects like shoes, a plane ticket, a diploma from college, real estate or in-game stuff from an online game.

Digital wallets that are specifically NFT-compatible are used to store NFTs. An NFT's ownership is documented in the blockchain and is transferable by the owner, enabling the selling and trading of NFTs.

The National Basketball Association (NBA) Top Shot is an NFT that has gained a lot of popularity recently. It is a collaboration between Dapper Labs and the NBA.

NFTs represent a paradigm shift in the digital economy, offering new possibilities for creators, collectors and industries alike. As blockchain technology continues to mature and address its challenges, NFTs have the potential to redefine ownership, authenticity and the value of digital assets. However, it is essential for stakeholders to navigate these developments responsibly, addressing environmental concerns, ensuring fair compensation for creators and maintaining the integrity of intellectual property rights in the digital realm. The evolution of NFTs is a dynamic and transformative journey that will shape the future of the digital landscape.

Commercial Applications of NFTs

NFTs gained initial popularity in the art world, allowing digital artists to tokenize their work and sell it directly to collectors. This has opened up new possibilities for artists to monetize their creations and for collectors to own digital art with provable scarcity.

NFTs are widely used in the gaming industry for creating unique in-game assets, characters and virtual real estate. Players can own, trade and sell these assets across different gaming platforms.

Musicians and content creators can tokenize their work as NFTs, enabling direct interaction with fans, fair compensation and proof of ownership for digital media.

Beyond the digital realm, NFTs have the potential to represent ownership of real-world assets such as real estate, luxury goods or even shares of physical businesses through the process of tokenization.

Future developments may focus on improving interoperability between different blockchain networks, enabling smoother movement of NFTs across platforms. Efforts are underway to address scalability issues, particularly in popular blockchain networks like Ethereum, to accommodate the growing demand for NFTs without compromising efficiency. NFTs are likely to continue influencing how we perceive and interact with digital ownership, fostering innovation in various industries, including finance, education and healthcare.

Advantages of Blockchain

Satoshi Nakamoto in his research paper in 2008 used the words "block" and "chain" separately. Blockchain technology was used by Satoshi Nakamoto to successfully create the cryptocurrency called "Bitcoins". Although Bitcoins were despised by bankers and financial regulators as they carried the threat of creating an alternate financial system, blockchain was heralded by everyone as the greatest invention of the twenty-first century that would radically change the way we carry out our business transactions.

There are several advantages offered by blockchains. Some of them are mentioned here.

Decentralization

In blockchain, there is no central database or ledger where the information is stored and other people have to seek access to the central database. Instead, it operates on the distributed ledger principle, where the information is copied and spread across a network of computers. The information is immediately updated on all the nodes. Nodes are the computers or devices connected to the blockchain network. This decentralization process makes it easier for all participants to access the information. It also makes it difficult for a hacker to hack the system as the information is not present in a single server.

Improved Accuracy

Blockchain is an automated function that operates with minimal human intervention. Because of the high degree of automation, blockchain offers greater user privacy, heightened security, lower processing fees and fewer errors. Ethereum has introduced the process of smart contracts that operate through synchronized execution of transactions between participants. The introduction of NFT using blockchain networks has further increased the accuracy and ease of access for the participants.

High Security

Blockchains operate on cryptic protocols like PoW and PoS that make it literally impossible to hack or break into the system. It operates on the principle of timestamping, which also makes it difficult to turn the clock back and hack the system. The process of identifying each block with a unique hash key also makes it more secure. It is possible to get an auditable trail of all transactions present on the blockchain, which is now facilitating the RegTech companies.

Alternative to Banking

As per information given by the World Bank, there are nearly two billion people in the world who do not have a bank account or access to banking and financial services. Blockchain offers an alternative system through the P2P networks. The third-party verification process is also not required in the case of P2P transactions and that saves a lot of time and money. Cryptocurrencies have much lower transaction fees in comparison to VISA, MasterCard and Internet banking charges. The unified payment interface (UPI) and Bharat Interface for Money (BHIM) are free services given by the Government of India and there are practically no charges for transactions done through them. Paytm, PhonePe and Google Pay also do not charge any transaction fees to the customer for making payment through them. Blockchain is a great boon for people doing transactions in rural areas where the banking network is poor and in countries where the banking network is weak.

The applications of blockchain are not limited to banking. Blockchain has now become very popular and highly acceptable and is being used in several areas like supply chain, manufacturing, education and healthcare. Various governments across the world are also using blockchain for maintaining taxation records, running welfare schemes and updating data on the activities of citizens.

Disadvantages of Blockchain

Cryptocurrencies and blockchain were initially met with suspicion because they also offer opportunities for money laundering, extortion, terrorist activities and peddling of illegal items like drugs and arms and ammunition. However, with the advancement of RegTech, there are companies that have developed tools to track the money trail and catch the culprits who are using blockchains for illicit activities.

Another concern about blockchain is the high cost associated with mining blocks and running the blockchain operations. To get a ballpark figure, we can say that the mining cost of a block would come to about ~$5,000–$7,000 per coin, if we assume electricity costs of ~$0.03–$0.05 per kilowatt-hour. Although this has been a major concern in the initial days, now, with the advancement of technology, the costs are significantly coming down.

Speed is also a concern when we talk about blockchains. It takes about ten minutes to add a block to the blockchain if we use the PoW protocol. In this way, we can manage only seven transactions per second (TPS) through a blockchain network. In comparison, the network used by VISA does 24,000 TPS. However, major research work is going on in this area and there are new blockchains which are capable of doing 30,000 TPS. The use of smart contracts and NFTs also adds to the speed and efficiency of the blockchain network.

Excessive regulation is also a matter of concern when it comes to the application of blockchain in various industries. Most governments across the world have given encouragement to innovation by using blockchains but with checks and balances in place. The regulations are also expected to ease as the application of blockchain becomes more pervasive across industries.

Implementation of Blockchain in India

Banks in India have, since a long time, grappling with challenging functions like issuing letter-of-credit (LoC), raising GST invoices and providing e-way bills. There has now been a ray of hope as the blockchain network started getting adopted in the BFSI industry. The public sector undertaking (PSU) banks in India like State Bank of India have partnered with private banks like HDFC Bank and ICICI Bank and international banks like Standard Chartered Bank to form the Indian Banks' Blockchain Infrastructure Company Private Limited (IBBIC). The IBBIC has 15 banks as members, out of which four are PSU banks and the rest are private banks. All the banks have an equal stake of 6.66% in this new venture (Jaikrishnan, 2021).

The prime objective of this consortium is to eliminate paperwork, reduce transaction processing time and offer a secure environment for banking and financial transactions. This will also help the small- and medium-scale enterprises (SME) in a big way by helping to issue LoC in a more efficient manner, smoothen the GST payment process and make it much simpler and help to generate e-way bills. All these transactions will be done using the blockchain network to make life easy for the SME sector.

LoC is an instrument that is issued by a bank which guarantees that the buyer will pay the correct amount to the seller and will also pay within the stipulated period. The present mechanism of issuing an LoC by a bank in India is quite complicated and tedious and has many inherent flaws that are successfully manipulated by fraudsters like Nirav

Modi. By shifting to the blockchain mechanism, the process of issuing LoC becomes much more simpler and the manipulation can be checked at every point. Blockchains operate on timestamping process and hence two LoCs cannot be raised on the same invoice, thus eliminating chances of fraud.

The process used by IBBIC to issue LoC is based on tokenization. The invoice will be converted into a token, which will be used to settle payments and conduct other transactions. The adoption of blockchain technology through tokenization will help the players in the SME sector to get quick approvals, faster disbursements and instantaneous settlements. The opportunity to commit fraud will also be reduced to a large extent.

IBBIC will operate like the National Payments Corporation of India (NPCI). NPCI was created by the Reserve Bank of India (RBI) and the Indian Bankers Association to facilitate interbank payments through the UPI. It also runs a mobile app called BHIM that helps in making payments through UPI. NPCI also created the Bharat Bill Payment System, BharatQR, Immediate Payment Service, Cheque Truncation System and National Automated Clearing House. NPCI has also played a major role in creating FastTag, which used radio frequency identification for national electronic toll collection.

The blockchain network operated by IBBIC will be based on Infosys' Finacle Connect. This is a blockchain-based platform that enables digitization and automation of trade-related finance processes. After the successful implementation of offering LoC through blockchain, IBBIC would be exploring other offerings like collateralized loan disbursal and credit rating. The tokenization of assets like stocks and bonds will help the owners to use them as collateral and get loans and also make it safer for lenders to verify their authenticity. The use of smart contracts and NFTs through blockchain platforms will increase the ease of use and efficiency of secure financial transactions.

Future Outlook of Blockchain Adoption

Banks will be unable to ignore the influence of blockchain technology for very long if they are still considering implementing it. The future of blockchain in Fintech is undoubtedly bright, as it offers a new degree of security and transparency in the financial services industry, drastically decreases complexity and gets rid of unnecessary components of the current infrastructure. Financial institutions are well-positioned to take advantage of blockchain's new transactional paradigm and cost-saving possibilities since they have a thorough awareness of end users' expectations (Tapscott, Iansiti & Lakhani, 2019).

However, there are a number of obstacles standing in the way of the banking and financial services industry's adoption of blockchain technology. Blockchain implementation in BFSI comes at a significant cost. This is due to the fact that it needs a lot of input regarding the hardware and software required for its debut. It could be an expensive issue for startups and small businesses at first because they often don't operate with big investments. Blockchain for finance will come at a high cost that not every organization is willing to pay for, in addition to the initial implementation costs.

Data alteration problems could also arise from integrating blockchain technology into BFSI. Data in the banking sector is frequently updated, particularly when a transaction is involved. Given the difficulties with ongoing changes, blockchain can end up becoming an issue rather than a solution for the business. It takes a lot of time to enter data. A lengthy procedure like this could delay transactions, since the finance industry deals with a lot of them every day.

Because blockchain technology is new and sophisticated, it demands computer literacy as well as expertise and skill. As a result, employees with little literacy will be unable to enter information into the system correctly. Because of this, businesses must engage teams of experts in blockchain and Fintech development services, which can be expensive. Finding the appropriate experts may also be difficult given the growing demand for blockchain expertise among businesses. Teaching motivated staff members is an additional choice, but it requires the same amount of work and doesn't always yield the desired outcomes.

The duration of recorded transactions is uncertain due to the obscure nature of the blockchain system's activities. The majority of financial transactions, however, require information about every prior transaction as well as the implications for the future. Therefore, this approach may lose its effectiveness in the financial sector when the duration of the data is unknown.

Not to mention, there are a lot of rules surrounding blockchain in banking. Any inexperienced organization will find it difficult to comply with these laws. This is due to the fact that inexperienced teams are typically terrified by the long list of rules that blockchain demands to guarantee a productive and secure user experience.

Computers are necessary for blockchain deployment, as you may have already surmised. Thus, issues with computers, such as power outages and malware, will have a significant impact on the blockchain system. Computers require a lot of power as well. Furthermore, if there are software issues or power outages, the systems become unreliable due to their reliance on computers and electricity.

Although the future of blockchain technology appears bright, issues including interoperability, scalability and regulatory uncertainty still need to be resolved before blockchain technology is widely used in the financial industry. To get over these obstacles, industry players and regulatory agencies must work together.

But despite all of these obstacles, blockchain technology adoption is picking up steam. Blockchain technology has a bright future in the banking and financial services sector, as it has the power to completely alter established procedures and organizational frameworks. Blockchain technology has the potential to be a key component of an increasingly safe, transparent and effective financial ecosystem as long as industry participants embrace innovation and technical advances. In the quickly changing financial landscape, companies that proactively adopt and incorporate blockchain technology will have an advantage over their competitors.

Questions for Discussion

1. Explain what you understand by blockchain.
2. Explain how blockchain technology has evolved over the years.
3. Explain the operational mechanism of blockchain.
4. Explain the different applications of blockchain
5. Explain the advantages and disadvantages of using blockchain technology.

Case Study – The Challenges of Adopting Blockchain Technology in Banking

Blockchain has been a major force behind the digital revolution. Many businesses from other industries, not just the financial services industry, are implementing the technology due to its substantial effects. It makes sense considering how universally accepted its core principles – immutability, consensus, openness, accuracy, accessibility, trust and security – are.

The banking industry can greatly benefit from blockchain technology. The technology reduces transaction costs and time while empowering end users, which leads to lower operating expenses. It does this by doing away with the need for institutions to oversee transactions.

Fintech startups are quickly surpassing their rivals and replacing the outdated banking system with their decentralized financial platforms. To stay competitive, banks are keen to collaborate with companies that have experience with blockchain technology, especially in the banking and finance services sector. United Bank of Switzerland (UBS), RBI, Bank of America, BNP Paribas, Commonwealth Bank of Australia, DBS Bank, Deutsche Bank, HDFC Bank, ICICI Bank, JPMorgan and Morgan Stanley are just a few of the financial institutions and banks that have jumped on the blockchain bandwagon.

Blockchain technology offers several benefits in addition to disadvantages. Among the risks and difficulties of implementing blockchain in banking include technological issues, issues with regulations and compliance and privacy concerns. The first challenge to blockchain adoption in the financial sector will be updating outdated technology and outdated systems. Inadequate technological infrastructure powers even the current digital banking systems. Banks will need to replace their outdated IT infrastructures with the newest blockchain systems and procedures to effectively utilize blockchain technology. Collaborating with companies that offer smooth integration of blockchain services is among the best ways to do that. One of the key characteristics of blockchain technology is its decentralization, but there are a variety of regulatory and compliance issues that might arise. Modern banking and financial institutions are driven by strict laws and reliable regulatory frameworks that thwart illegal activity.

P2P payments are safer than those made through traditional payment methods. However, they pose a lot of security and privacy risks for the banking sector. Because blockchain transactions are fully transparent, hackers, phishers, identity thieves, selfish miners and other illegal activity can be carried out with unprecedented security vulnerabilities. The only way for banks to overcome these shortcomings is to work toward gaining a comprehensive understanding of blockchain technology. Once they have figured out how to get beyond the security flaws, they can promote pseudonymity to get acceptance from the wider public.

Retail banks encounter difficulties in integrating blockchain-based know-your-customer (KYC) and anti-fraud solutions, despite multiple attempts and demonstrations of their feasibility. Initially, there are substantial financial expenses linked to transitioning from individual to communal institutions. Furthermore, banks need to adjust to a substantial culture transformation rooted in the imperative of data sharing. Within an industry that highly values confidentiality, this concept is peculiar and prompts inquiries about accountability: If Bank A conducts an individual's onboarding KYC process and shares the data on a blockchain, is Bank B liable for any mistakes or fraudulent activities that occur on its own account? Is Bank A sufficiently incentivized to submit its data? An inherent limitation of data sharing is its potential to impede banks in providing tailored services.

Additionally, there are pragmatic obstacles. Customers are required to provide consent for the uploading of digital fingerprints and completion of extra authentication procedures during the setup process. Retailers need to modernize authentication mechanisms at the point of sale and modify online checkout processes. To achieve significant advantages, banks must develop extensive networks that necessitate collaboration and the standardization of data.

The banking industry is already seeing the presence of blockchain technology, as demonstrated by the participation of prominent financial organizations like J.P. Morgan, Citi, Goldman Sachs, the Swedish Central Bank, HSBC, UBS and others in providing blockchain-related solutions. Nevertheless, the banking sector must enhance the existing digital experience for its clientele and make significant advancements in process automation to remain competitive.

Blockchain technology will be the foundation of modern banking systems. Financial institutions should consider adopting this emerging trend and seize the opportunity to establish themselves as early adopters. It is advisable for them to thoroughly evaluate the investment, as there are numerous risks and problems linked to the implementation of blockchain technology in the banking sector. The future holds numerous possible applications for blockchain technology; however, it is imperative to handle them with utmost security and caution.

Case Study Questions

1. Explain how banks are benefiting by adopting blockchain technology.
2. Describe the challenges faced by banks while adopting blockchain technology.
3. What are the recommendations and suggestions you would like to offer to help the banks adopt blockchain technology in a meaningful way?

Further Reading

1. "The Truth About Blockchain" by Marco Iansiti and Karim R. Lakhani, Harvard Business Review, January–February 2017.
2. "What Is Blockchain?" by David Rodeck and John Schmidt, Forbes, June 9, 2021.

References

Cachin, C. (2016). Architecture of the hyperledger blockchain fabric. *Workshop on Distributed Cryptocurrencies and Consensus Ledgers*, 310(4), 1–4.

Castellon, C., Roy, S., Kreidl, P., Dutta, A., & Bölöni, L. (2021, October). Energy efficient Merkle trees for blockchains. In *2021 IEEE 20th International Conference on Trust, Security and Privacy in Computing and Communications (TrustCom)* (pp. 1093–1099). IEEE.

Chowdhury, M. J. M., Colman, A., Kabir, M. A., Han, J., & Sarda, P. (2018, August). Blockchain versus database: A critical analysis. In *2018 17th IEEE International Conference on Trust, Security and Privacy in Computing and Communications/12th IEEE International Conference on Big Data Science and Engineering (TrustCom/BigDataSE)* (pp. 1348–1353). IEEE.

Dib, O., Brousmiche, K. L., Durand, A., Thea, E., & Hamida, E. B. (2018). Consortium blockchains: Overview, applications and challenges. *International Journal of Advanced Telecommunication*, 11(1), 51–64.

Di Pierro, M. (2017). What is the blockchain? *Computing in Science & Engineering*, 19(5), 92–95.

Everts, M. H., & Muller, F. (2018). *Will that smart contract really do what you expect it to do?* Groningen: TNO.

Feng, L. J. (2021). Cryptography and its role in blockchain. In *Financial management in the digital economy* (Vol. 6, p. 45).

Ge, Z., Loghin, D., Ooi, B. C., Ruan, P., & Wang, T. (2022). Hybrid blockchain database systems: Design and performance. *Proceedings of the VLDB Endowment*, 15(5), 1092–1104.

Guegan, D. (2017). Public blockchain versus private blockchain. *HAL SHS Sciences Humaines Et Sociales*. https://shs.hal.science/halshs-01524440

Iansiti, M., & Lakhani, K. R. (2017). The truth about blockchain. *Harvard Business Review*, 95(1), 118–127.

Jaikrishnan, G. (2021). IBBIC: Paving way for blockchain adoption by Indian banks. *Grant Thornton*. www.grantthornton.in/insights/blogs/ibbic-paving-way-for-blockchain-adoption-by-indian-banks/

Khan, S. N., Loukil, F., Ghedira-Guegan, C., Benkhelifa, E., & Bani-Hani, A. (2021). Blockchain smart contracts: Applications, challenges, and future trends. *Peer-to-Peer Networking and Applications*, 14, 2901–2925.

Laurence, T. (2023). *Blockchain for dummies*. John Wiley & Sons.

Lewis, A. (2019). *The basics of bitcoins and blockchains*. Two Rivers Distribution.

Nakamoto, S. (2008). *Bitcoin: A Peer-to-Peer Electronic Cash System*. www.bitcoin.org

Raman, R., & Raj, B. E. (2021). The world of NFTs (non-fungible tokens): The future of blockchain and asset ownership. In *Enabling blockchain technology for secure networking and communications* (pp. 89–108). IGI Global.

Solomon, M. G. (2019). *Ethereum for dummies*. John Wiley & Sons.

Sriman, B., Ganesh Kumar, S., & Shamili, P. (2021). Blockchain technology: Consensus protocol proof of work and proof of stake. In *Intelligent Computing and Applications: Proceedings of ICICA 2019* (pp. 395–406). Springer, Singapore.

Tapscott, D., Iansiti, M., & Lakhani, K. R. (2019). *Blockchain: The insights you need from Harvard Business Review*. Harvard Business Press.

Tapscott, D., & Tapscott, A. (2016). *Blockchain revolution: How the technology behind bitcoin and other cryptocurrencies is changing the world*. Penguin.

4 Digital Payments – The PayTech Model

After reading this chapter you will:

- Understand the concept of PayTech and the digital payment ecosystem
- Know about mobile banking, digital wallets and payment gateways
- Know about electronic fund transfer (EFT) and near-field communication (NFC)
- Know about the National Payment Council of India (NPCI), unified payment interface (UPI) and peer-to-peer (P2P) networks
- Understand how application program interface (API) is used in P2P network payments
- Know about companies who are leading the PayTech Revolution

PayPal was launched by Peter Thiel and Marx Levchin in 1998. The original name of the company was Confinity, and the company was formed to make security software. Later, the company created a digital wallet, merged with X.com led by Elon Musk, and changed the name of the company from Confinity to PayPal. PayPal was acquired by eBay for $1.5 billion in 2002. The company was later spun off as a separate entity in 2015.

PayPal became a successful company as it seamlessly integrated consumers (payers), merchants (payees) and banks for smooth online payment and financial transactions. It was known for providing a highly secure interface, and that further increased the popularity among consumers and merchants. PayPal also provided the digital interface for peer-to-peer (P2P) financial transactions. PayPal was mostly popular among small- and medium-sized merchants as they were mostly ignored by large banks and financial institutions. PayPal made a strategic alliance with VISA and Master Card and executed a series of acquisitions by acquiring companies like Venmo, Xoom, Hyperwallet and iZettle to become a $65 billion company. The total payment volume (TPV) done by PayPal in the pandemic period touched $936 billion. As of 2022, PayPal operates in 202 markets and has 426 million active, registered accounts.

In the post-pandemic period, PayPal has started facing stiff competition from the new age of Fintech companies. To gain a firm foothold in the financial markets, PayPal was providing a huge range of digital payment solutions and value-added services. However, the new age Fintech startup companies have created innovative offerings using application program interfaces (APIs) that are taking away market share from PayPal. PayPal is also facing intense competition from Big Tech Companies like Apple Pay, Google Pay, Amazon Pay, Microsoft Pay and Samsung Pay. PayPal is also facing intense competition from local payment companies like Paytm and BharatPe in India and Alipay and WeChat in China. Governments like India have created a unified payment interface (UPI) and launched their payment app called Bharat Interface for Money (BHIM).

DOI: 10.4324/9781032699417-4

How should PayPal react to this competition and develop a strategy to gain a competitive edge? That now seems to be the billion-dollar question to which PayPal is now seeking answers. . . .

The Evolution of Payment Business

Payments have evolved from a barter system, exchange of clam shells, coins and currencies to the use of automated teller machines (ATM), plastic money and digital currencies like Bitcoins. While the initial system of payment mechanism has been highly regulated by central banks, the new mechanism is shifting toward deregulation and faster and more secure transactions using Bitcoins and blockchains. The future will be payments through wearable items like watches and glasses, which will be facilitated through payment gateways and the Internet of Things (IoT) and is called PayTech of Things (Chishti, Craddock, Courtneidge & Zachariadis, 2020).

The credit card was invented by Ralph Schneider and Frank McNamara. They started the Diners Club, where a credit card holder had to pay the expenses incurred at the end of the month. However, it was American Express that allowed credit card holders to carry forward their balance. This facility popularized the use of credit cards. In the 1980s, magnetic stripes were inserted in credit cards which could read and store transactions in electronic format. Now, credit cards come with embedded computer chips, which are also called EMV. EMV stands for Europay, MasterCard and VISA (Patel, 2023).

The other major contribution of technology in banking was ATM. The ATM was invented by John Shepherd Barron in 1967. These machines helped customers to withdraw and deposit money during after-bank hours also using debit cards. The 1970s saw a boost in the usage of credit cards and debit cards as customers became less reliant on bank branches. Currently, there are more than five million ATMs installed across the world. The number of credit cards issued has risen to 2.8 billion, and the number of debit cards issued is 830 million. The debit cards and credit cards used to operate are based on personal identification number (PIN). Now, many of them operate through the use of one-time password (OTP) generated through mobile phones. Now, apart from magnetic card stripes, chips and readers, banks and financial institutions are using IoT, artificial intelligence (AI), machine learning and blockchain technology for various applications. Many countries have now adopted the tokenization of credit and debit cards to prevent their hacking (Abiew, Jnr & Banning, 2020).

The adoption of digital modes of financial transaction has ushered in and facilitated the rise of Fintech in financial transactions. During the demonetization process in India, it was Paytm and other digital wallets that came to the rescue of the buyers who were not getting access to cash and sellers who were unable to set up swipe machines for card transactions, because of the high costs involved.

Globally, it has been PayPal who has led the Fintech revolution. PayPal was started by Peter Theil and his associates in 1998 and was acquired by eBay in 2002 for $1.5 billion. PayPal currently has 361 million active users and is currently valued at $320 billion. PayPal mainly facilitates eBay and other e-commerce transactions and also helps in P2P payments and also transfers money from bank accounts to PayPal accounts (Berg, Burg, Keil & Puri, 2021).

In China, it is Alipay from Alibaba and WeChat from Tencent who are leading the Fintech revolution. Alipay currently has 400 million users, and WeChat has more than a billion users. Both Alipay and WeChat facilitate all kinds of financial transactions like doing shopping, paying bills, booking tickets and checking balances in bank accounts (Klein, 2020).

In India, the Fintech revolution was led by Paytm. Paytm started by Vijay Sekhar Sharma, scaled up their operations after getting investments from SAIF Partners, Softbank and Ant Group. Paytm became very popular for their "cashback" offers. The cashback mechanism ensured that they ensured a high level of customer loyalty. Paytm currently has 150 million monthly active users, processes 1.2 billion transactions per month and has a valuation of $15.3 billion.

After the super success of Paytm, we now also have other apps like PhonePe, Mobikwik, BharatPe and the Indian Government-owned BHIM, which are aggressively promoting and facilitating payments through quick response (QR) codes and UPI. Multinational companies like Google, Amazon and Apple are promoting their Google Pay, Amazon Pay and Apple Pay apps. Public sector banks like SBI have come up with an app called SBI YONO. Private sector banks like HDFC have come up with PayZapp. ICICI Bank is promoting Pockets. Axis Bank bought Freecharge from Snapdeal for $400 million in 2017 to get a pie of the Fintech business.

Overall, the Fintech space is looking very exciting in operations like payments, lending, wealth management and risk management.

The Digital Payment Ecosystem

The traditional payment ecosystem comprised banks, payment gateways, electronic clearing houses and credit card and debit card issuers. Customers deposit their money in banks and then use credit cards, debit cards, payment gateways and electronic payment systems such as NEFT (National Electronic Fund Transfer), RTGS (Real Time Gross Settlement) and IMPS (Immediate Payment Service) for making various types of payments (Mützel, 2021).

The introduction of Fintech has disrupted the digital payment ecosystem in a big way. Now, we have electronic wallets, P2P networks, mobile banking, UPI and payment gateways.

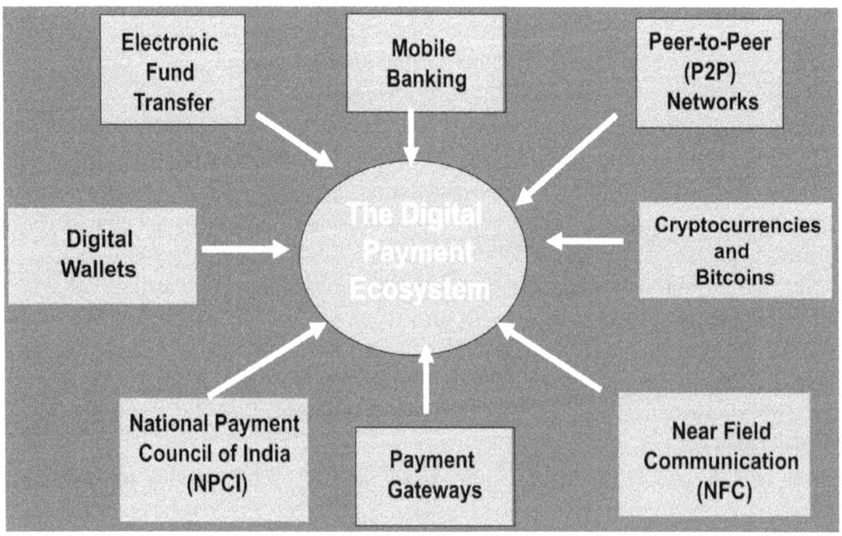

Figure 4.1 The Digital Payment Ecosystem

Electronic Fund Transfer

EFT refers to the process of transferring money from one bank account to another electronically, without the need for any physical exchange of cash or checks. It has become an integral part of modern banking and financial transactions, offering convenience, speed and security to both individuals and businesses. EFT encompasses various methods of electronic payments, including wire transfers, direct deposits, electronic bill payments and online banking transactions (Haralayya, 2021).

There are various types of EFTs like online bank transactions, wire transfers, direct deposits and electronic bill payments. Online banking allows individuals to transfer money between their own accounts or to others within the same bank or across different banks. Wire transfers involve transferring funds electronically from one financial institution to another. Wire transfers are typically used for large transactions and international transfers due to their speed and reliability. Employers use direct deposit to electronically transfer employees' salaries or wages directly into their bank accounts. Government agencies also use direct deposit for benefits payments like Social Security. Consumers can use EFT to pay bills online through their bank's website or a third-party payment service. This eliminates the need for writing and mailing physical checks. Online banking allows individuals to transfer money between their own accounts or to others within the same bank or across different banks.

The widespread adoption of smartphones has led to the growth of mobile payment platforms, allowing users to make EFT transactions using mobile apps and digital wallets. Emerging technologies like blockchain offer the potential to revolutionize EFT by providing decentralized, secure and transparent transaction networks. Real-time payment systems are being developed to enable instant fund transfers between individuals and businesses, further enhancing the speed and efficiency of EFT.

EFT has transformed the way money is transferred and managed, offering numerous benefits such as convenience, speed and security. As technology continues to advance, EFT will likely play an increasingly vital role in the global financial ecosystem, driving innovation and improving the efficiency of financial transactions. However, it's essential for individuals and organizations to remain vigilant against potential risks and challenges associated with electronic payments.

EFT has experienced significant growth and widespread adoption due to the numerous benefits it offers over traditional payment methods. The popularity of online banking has surged, with millions of consumers managing their finances, paying bills and transferring funds electronically through web-based platforms and mobile apps. Platforms like Venmo, PayPal and Cash app have gained widespread acceptance, allowing individuals to send and receive money electronically with ease.

Businesses increasingly use EFT to pay suppliers and vendors, streamlining the procurement process and reducing administrative costs associated with paper-based transactions. EFT has become the standard method for processing payroll, enabling employers to automate salary payments and comply with labor regulations efficiently. Subscription-based businesses, such as streaming platforms and software-as-a-service providers, rely on EFT to collect recurring payments from customers seamlessly.

Banks and financial institutions have invested heavily in upgrading their systems and infrastructure to support EFT capabilities, including real-time payment processing and enhanced security features. Financial institutions collaborate with Fintech companies and payment processors to offer innovative EFT solutions and expand their service offerings to customers.

Financial regulators continue to introduce measures to promote the adoption of electronic payments while ensuring the security and integrity of EFT systems. Compliance with regulations such as the EFT Act and Payment Card Industry Data Security Standard is paramount.

The globalization of trade and commerce has fueled the demand for cross-border EFT services, leading to the development of international payment networks and platforms like SWIFT and Ripple. Migrant workers and expatriates rely on EFT services to send money to their families and loved ones in their home countries, driving growth in the remittance market.

Emerging technologies like blockchain and cryptocurrencies offer new opportunities for EFT by providing decentralized and secure transaction networks, reducing costs and increasing transparency. Financial institutions leverage AI and machine learning algorithms to detect and prevent fraud in EFT transactions, enhancing security and trust among users.

The growth trajectory of EFT is expected to continue, driven by ongoing technological innovations, changing consumer preferences and regulatory developments. As digital transformation accelerates across industries, EFT will play a central role in shaping the future of finance, enabling faster, more efficient and more secure transactions globally.

In conclusion, EFT has become an indispensable part of the modern economy, facilitating seamless and secure money transfers for individuals, businesses and financial institutions worldwide. The widespread adoption and ongoing evolution of EFT underscore its importance in driving economic growth, efficiency and financial inclusion in the digital age.

Payment Gateways

Payment gateway is the crucial link between the payer and the payee. This facilitates the transfer of information between the browser and the merchant's web server to complete the transaction (Hassan, Shukur & Hasan, 2020). The information is encrypted to ensure privacy and security while transmitting the same to the bank. There are four main players who are mainly involved in an online financial transaction:

- The merchant who is selling a product or service.
- The customer who is buying a product or service.
- The issuer who has issued the debit or credit card. This is the bank where the customer has an account.
- The acquirer who accepts money on behalf of the merchant. This is the bank where the merchant has an account.

Payment gateway is defined as "the technology that captures and transfers payment data from the customer to the acquirer and then transfers the payment acceptance or decline back to the customer". The payment gateway acts as the intermediary between the customer and the merchant and also between the issuer and acquirer.

The payment gateway simplifies the process of shopping by transferring the money from the customer's bank account to the merchant's bank account through an authentication process like an OTP. The payment gateway ensures that the right money reaches the right person, the bank details are kept secure through the process of authentication and the payment process is made easy, fast and reliable.

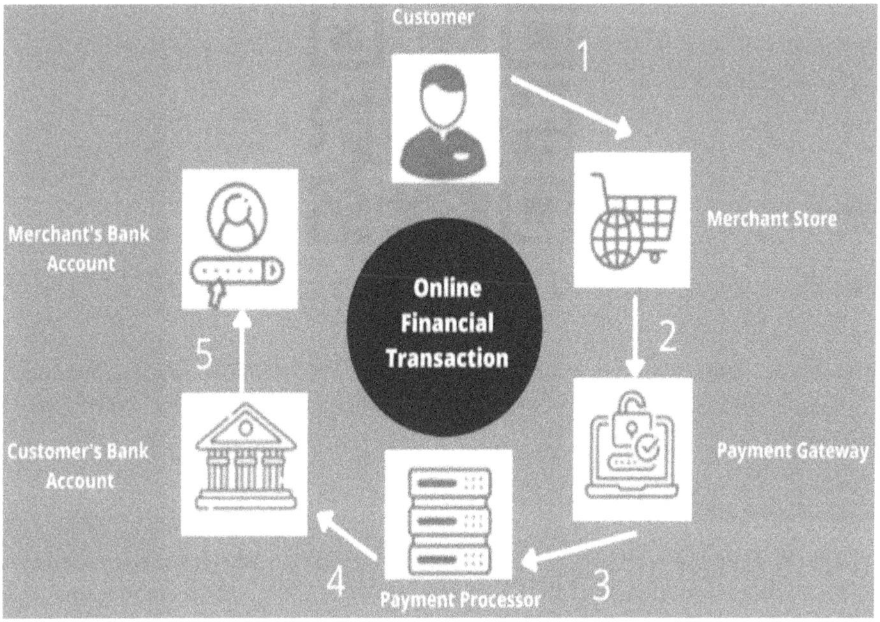

Figure 4.2 The Payment Gateway

QR Codes

"A quick response (QR) code is a type of barcode that can be read easily by a digital device and which stores information as a series of pixels in a square-shaped grid". QR codes were originally developed by a Toyota subsidiary called Denso Waves for use in the manufacturing process. But QR codes have now found wide acceptance in financial services.

QR codes comprise black squares arranged in a grid (matrix) on a white background which forms a matrix. They contain encrypted information that is stored in four types of formats: alphanumeric, numeric, binary and Kanji. They can be read by API software to extract data from the patterns. There are now several versions and variations of QR codes that are used for different purposes. Some of the variations are the Micro QR code, Model 1 QR code, Model 2 QR code, IQR Code, SQRC and Frame QR (Darshanbhai, 2023).

Micro QR codes are smaller versions of QR codes that are used where there are space constraints. Model 1 QR codes confirm to Version 1 to Version 14 registered with Automatic Identification Manufacturers International. Model 2 QR codes are better than Model 1 and have 40 versions. IQR has 64 formats and is shaped as squares or rectangles. SQRC has a restricted reading function to contain private information. Frame QR has a customizable frame that can contain larger data in formats such as graphics, illustrations or photos.

The best way to create QR codes is by using a QR code generator. There are QR code generators like Beaconstac, GOQR, Flowcode and Scanova. They have different processes ranging from $5 per month to $60 per year. You can also generate a free QR code from websites like www.qr-code-generator.com.

Figure 4.3 Quick Response (QR) Code

QR codes are now widely used in cryptocurrency, blockchain, storing product information, supply chain networks and augmented reality systems and for making payments through mobiles.

Near-Field Communication

NFC is a short-range wireless technology. NFC is based on radio frequency identification technology, which was invented by Charles Walton in 1983. More pioneering work on NFC was carried out by Sony and Philips, and it became one of the integral technologies along with Bluetooth that could help in the transmission of information from one device to another (Memiş, 2023).

NFC is now playing a key role in helping contactless pay by allowing smartphones, tablets, wearables and cards to share information and complete the payment process. This technology transmits data through electromagnetic radio fields to enable two devices to communicate with each other. This is possible when both devices have NFC-enabled chips. The devices also need to be in close proximity to each other.

NFC devices operate in three modes. They can connect with the mobile apps through a Tag Reader or Writer. They can help to do P2P transactions by connecting devices through physical proximity. They can also connect to a common infrastructure through card emulation. NFC-enabled card payments are safer than transactions done on swipe machines as the cards cannot be cloned, and NFC devices operate on the tokenization and encryption principle that makes them more secure.

Application Program Interface

The Fintech companies use both B2B and B2C interfaces for conducting business. The revenue model is based on fees or commissions. There are Fintech companies that charge both fees and commissions. A large number of Fintech companies also provide free services to customers.

Although Fintech companies are emerging as competitors to banks, many of them have built associations and partnerships with banks and non-banking financial companies to run their business. Some of them are reaching out to niche customers like self-employed professionals, students, housewives and first-time borrowers in the unorganized sector to offer financial services.

Banks are changing the way they do business. To make payments, a customer had to withdraw cash from a teller counter or an ATM and then make the payment. But not anymore. Today, the customer points her Paytm, PhonePe, Google Pay or Mobikwik app at the seller's QR code. The app scans the QR code and asks for the UPI PIN. Once the customer keys in the four-digit UPI PIN on her mobile, the Paytm app withdraws money from the customer's bank account and deposits the same in the seller's bank account. The financial transaction is completed. The whole operation takes 10 to 30 seconds depending on the processor speed of the smartphone and the strength of the Internet connection.

Banks are now collaborating with third-party application developers and third-party service providers to ease their workload and concentrate on core banking functions. And all these are facilitated through APIs.

The operations of Fintech are run using API. The full form of API is the API. APIs use a set of functions and syntax to access data and create links between different devices and operating systems. API helps in different functions like checking bank balances, making payments or submitting application forms. APIs help mobile apps and websites to conduct real-time interaction and execute real-time functions.

APIs are tools and software applications that the programmer's build to connect with the bank's technology. An API is a software intermediary that allows two unrelated applications to talk to each other. It acts as a bridge, taking a request or message from one program and then delivering it to another, translating the messages and performing protocols based on what the API is programmed to do. APIs are the hidden backbone that makes software systems in different devices work in perfect harmony with the use of plug-ins, digital interfacing and software communication. They connect everything together and make software systems work in harmony. APIs create a good user experience (UX) and make it easier for the customer to complete the transaction (Ünsal, Öztekin, Çavuş & Özdemir, 2020).

APIs have a "Sandbox Option". Through the sandbox option, application developers can incorporate the policies given by regulators so that the business operation is run in a legal way. The application of API has created an open marketplace and given a big boost to the Fintech business.

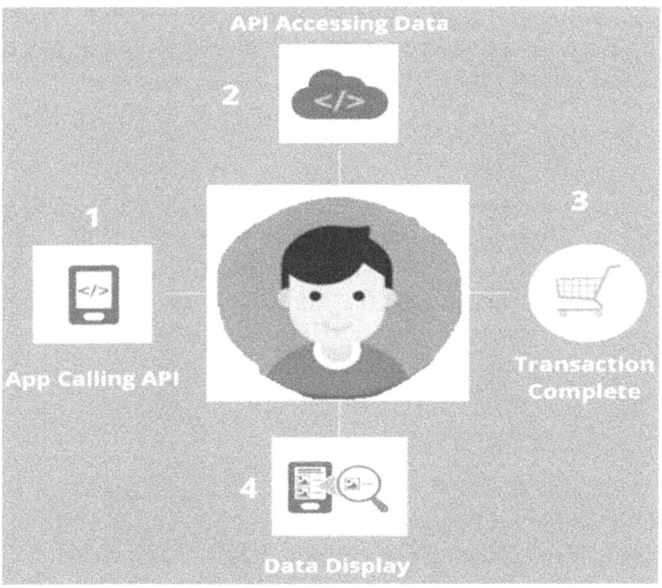

Figure 4.4 Application Program Interface (API)

APIs are not openly visible as they work in the backend of the systems. They work with the software's functionality and data in a controlled way. They help the developers access the different programs, different sets of hardware, different types of apps and data without needing access to the code for the entire system. This maintains the secrecy and security of the core banking system with optimum usage of particular data that are required to connect, verify and complete the transaction.

An API comprises a range of routines, tools and protocols to specify how different software components should act together. APIs are generally of two types – the public APIs and the private APIs. The public APIs work with consumer-facing applications and help customers connect a variety of apps, mobile devices and browsers. The private APIs mainly function in the back end to create tools, applications and operations to give a better UX to the customer.

APIs allow an organization to extend their own software and data usage to applications and data that they do not own. This allows a range of benefits such as increased functionality, cost savings, tech innovation and streamlined operations. APIs are mostly written in C, C++, JavaScript, Node.js and Python Languages. There are tools from Apache that help to adapt APIs from one computer programming language to another.

Benefits of Using API

APIs are the backbone of Fintech and PayTech and are growing in popularity because of their ease of use and offering of a great UX. APIs are rising in popularity and importance because of the following reasons.

Increased Functionality

APIs are offering increased and extended functionalities like identifying potential customers, identifying the needs of the customers, offering specific benefits customized as per the customer needs and making life easier for the banks, merchants and customers. For example, now we have unified QRs through which customers can pay through Paytm, PhonePe, Google Pay or any other apps they like.

Saving Money

Every banking transaction, whether it is withdrawing money from an ATM or depositing money in an account, has a cost associated with it. APIs are helping customers and merchants to cut down on these costs as they function seamlessly by integrating the software of different devices and synchronizing the same. The Indian Government is currently offering the usage of the UPI platform and BHIM app completely free of cost, and that is resulting in substantial savings for the customers and merchants.

Saving Time

There is also considerable wastage of time in going to a bank or ATM to deposit money or withdraw money to use for financial transactions. Now most of the financial transactions are done using mobile phones, QR codes and APIs that have made life comfortable and are saving a lot of time for the buyers and sellers. Also APIs have facilitated the payment of bills, school fees, buying movie tickets, bus and train tickets and also making payments to each very fast other within a fraction of a minute.

Encourage Innovation

APIs are also encouraging innovations and startups to come up with better business ideas. It is mostly young people, fresh out of IITs and engineering colleges, who are developing APIs and getting millions and billions of dollars of funding. Vijay Shekhar Sharma made a name for himself by developing an API to make payments through mobiles. He called it Paytm (Pay-through-mobiles). Rishabh Mehta has created an API called Gray-Quest, through which parents can pay school fees in equated monthly installments. Manish Khera created an API called FinoPaytech to help rural people get access to cash and funds. Government institutions, multinational companies, private companies and public companies are all encouraging the development of new and innovative APIs that could help customers make payments in a better way.

PayTech Companies

The PayTech innovation and payment revolution was started by PayPal. PayPal was founded by Peter Thiel and Max Levchin the year in 1998. Elon Musk came on board in 2000 when his company X.com merged with Confinity to rename the venture PayPal. Paypal reached the milestone of getting one million users within 15 months. EBay bought PayPal in 2002 for $15 billion, and all the founders of PayPal became billionaires.

In India, the Paytech revolution was led by Vijay Shekhar Sharma, who founded Paytm. He started Paytm with an initial investment of $2 million in 2010. The most attractive feature of using Paytm apps was "cashbacks". Every time a customer did a financial transaction using Paytm, they would receive a certain amount of money in their wallet as a cashback. This cashback feature encouraged the widespread use of Paytm wallets. Paytm became third-largest after Flipkart and Amazon seller during the Diwali festival of 2017 because of the cashback feature.

During the same time, Sandeep Tandon and Kunal Shah started a company called Freecharge. They were encouraging customers to use their app to recharge their mobile phones. In return, the customers would get an equivalent amount of discount coupons from McDonalds, Café Coffee Day and Domino's. It was a win–win proposition as Freecharge was getting a lot of customers and the food outlets were getting huge promotions. Freecharge was acquired by Snapdeal in 2015 for $400. However, they could not run the venture in a profitable manner and sold it to Axis Bank in 2017 for $60 million.

Today, the Paytech revolution in India is led by startups like Paytm, PhonePe (owned by Walmart), BharatPe and Mobikwik who have now become billion-dollar companies. The global revolution in PayTech is led by PayPal, Stripe, Apple Pay, Google Pay and Amazon Pay. Banks have also come out with their own PayTech Apps. SBI has YONO, HDFC Bank has PayZapp, ICICI Bank has Pockets and Axis Bank has got Freecharge. Mobile phone companies are also in the PayTech business. Airtel has got Airtel Money, Vodafone has got M-Pesa, Samsung has got Samsung Pay and Reliance has got Jio Money. Not to be left behind, the Government of India has come out with BHIM and Bharat Bill Payment System to join the PayTech revolution. This business certainly has room for a lot many startup companies.

Apple Pay

Launched in October 2014, Apple Pay is a mobile payment and digital wallet service developed by Apple Inc. It is designed to enable users to make secure, contactless payments using their Apple devices, including iPhones, iPads, Apple Watches and Macs. Apple Pay leverages NFC technology and is integrated into Apple's broader ecosystem, providing a seamless and secure payment experience.

Apple Pay enables users to make contactless payments at supported merchants by simply tapping their Apple devices on NFC-equipped terminals. This provides a convenient and swift transaction process. Apple Pay is deeply integrated into Apple devices, allowing users to add their credit or debit cards to the Wallet app. This integration extends to iPhones, Apple Watches, iPads and even Macs for online purchases.

Security is a paramount concern, and Apple Pay incorporates biometric authentication methods such as Face ID (on iPhones with Face ID) and Touch ID (on devices with fingerprint sensors). This ensures that only the authorized user can make payments. Apple Pay uses a dedicated chip called the secure element to store and encrypt payment information securely. This chip is isolated from the rest of the device's operating system, adding an extra layer of protection.

To enhance security, Apple Pay employs tokenization. Instead of transmitting actual card details during a transaction, a unique token is used, making it significantly more challenging for unauthorized parties to intercept sensitive information. Apple Pay seamlessly integrates with other Apple services, such as iMessage and Siri, allowing users to send and receive money through messages and use voice commands for transactions.

Apple Pay is not limited to physical transactions. Users can make secure in-app payments for goods and services, enhancing the overall versatility of the service.

Apple Pay has expanded its reach globally, making it available in numerous countries. It works with various banks and financial institutions, allowing users to link their accounts and make payments internationally. In different regions, Apple Pay adapts to local payment methods and preferences, providing a tailored experience for users worldwide.

Apple Pay users in the USA can access Apple Cash, a virtual debit card linked to the Wallet app. This allows for quick and secure cashless transactions. Users can send and receive money directly through the messages app using Apple Pay Cash. This feature simplifies splitting bills and reimbursing friends or family.

Apple emphasizes user privacy and limits the data it collects. Unlike some other payment platforms, Apple does not store transaction details, and user purchase history is kept on the device, not on Apple servers. Two-factor authentication adds an extra layer of security for setting up Apple Pay, ensuring that only the authorized user can add cards to the service.

Apple Pay is widely accepted at various merchants, including retail stores, restaurants, public transportation and online platforms. The growing acceptance encourages users to adopt the service for daily transactions. Many apps, in both the Apple App Store and third-party apps, integrate Apple Pay for in-app purchases, making it a convenient option for a broad range of transactions.

Apple Pay faces competition from other digital wallets and mobile payment solutions. Continuous innovation and enhancements will be crucial for maintaining a competitive edge. As wearable technology continues to evolve, Apple Pay is likely to see further integration with new devices, expanding its reach and functionality.

There have been speculations about Apple exploring the integration of cryptocurrency features into Apple Pay, although no official announcement has been made as of my last knowledge update.

Apple Pay has significantly influenced the digital payment landscape, offering a secure, convenient and widely accepted solution for users within the Apple ecosystem. As it continues to evolve with advancements in technology and user preferences, Apple Pay is poised to play a key role in shaping the future of digital payments, emphasizing both innovation and security in the ever-changing financial technology landscape.

Stripe

Stripe, founded in 2010 by Irish entrepreneurs John and Patrick Collison, is a technology company that provides a suite of payment processing and commerce infrastructure solutions. Stripe is renowned for its developer-friendly approach, offering tools and APIs that empower businesses to accept and manage online payments securely. Over the years, it has become a key player in the global Fintech and e-commerce landscape.

Stripe allows businesses to accept online payments by integrating its APIs into websites and applications. It supports various payment methods, including credit cards, digital wallets and localized payment options. Businesses can set up and manage subscription-based billing models using Stripe, automating recurring payments and invoicing for services like subscription boxes, SaaS products and memberships.

Stripe offers solutions for marketplaces and platforms, enabling businesses to facilitate payments between multiple parties. This includes features like split payments, allowing commissions to be automatically distributed. Stripe provides pre-built checkout components and customizable UI elements to streamline the payment process for businesses. This helps improve UX and conversion rates.

Stripe incorporates machine learning algorithms and customizable fraud prevention tools to help businesses detect and prevent fraudulent transactions, enhancing the security of online payments. Stripe Connect is a platform that enables businesses to create and manage multi-sided marketplaces. It handles identity verification, onboarding and payouts for platform users.

One of Stripe's distinctive features is its API-centric design, making it particularly appealing to developers. The APIs are well-documented and easy to integrate and provide flexibility for businesses to customize their payment flows. Stripe offers a range of developer tools, including software development kits for various programming languages, testing environments and resources to support developers in creating robust and efficient payment integrations.

Stripe supports payments in multiple currencies, allowing businesses to operate globally without the complexities of managing currency conversions. This feature is vital for companies with an international customer base.

To cater to different markets, Stripe integrates with various localized payment methods, such as Alipay, WeChat Pay and SEPA Direct Debit. Stripe Capital offers business loans to eligible users based on their Stripe transaction history. This service provides quick access to capital for business growth.

Stripe supports invoicing and billing functionalities, allowing businesses to create and manage invoices, set up payment schedules and automate invoicing processes. Stripe has built a robust ecosystem of third-party integrations. This includes partnerships with e-commerce platforms, accounting software and CRM systems, offering businesses a seamless experience with their existing tools.

Stripe collaborates with major technology companies, including partnerships with platforms like Shopify, providing a wide range of businesses with access to its payment processing capabilities. The online payment and Fintech space is highly competitive, with other players like PayPal and Square. Stripe needs to continue innovating to maintain its position and address evolving market demands.

Operating in multiple countries requires Stripe to navigate diverse regulatory frameworks. Compliance with financial regulations is crucial for the company's global operations. Given the evolving landscape, Stripe might explore further integration with blockchain technology and cryptocurrencies to offer additional payment options and services. Stripe may expand its financial services, potentially exploring offerings such as savings accounts, business credit cards or additional lending products.

Stripe has played a pivotal role in reshaping online commerce and payments, offering a suite of tools that empower businesses of all sizes. Its commitment to developer-friendly solutions, global reach and continuous innovation positions it as a leading force in the Fintech industry. As the online payments landscape evolves, Stripe is likely to remain a key enabler for businesses seeking efficient, secure and customizable payment solutions.

Google Pay

Google Pay is a digital wallet and online payment system developed by Google. It was launched in 2015 as a rebranding of Google Wallet and Android Pay, aiming to consolidate Google's various payment services under a unified platform. Google Pay is available in numerous countries and supports various payment methods, including contactless payments, online purchases and P2P transfers.

Google Pay allows users to make contactless payments by linking their credit or debit cards to the app. Users can tap their phones at NFC-enabled terminals for in-store purchases. Users can make payments within supported apps and websites using Google Pay. It simplifies the checkout process and offers a secure and convenient way to pay for online purchases.

Google Pay enables users to send and receive money directly to and from friends or family. This feature is particularly useful for splitting bills, repaying loans or sharing expenses. Google Pay integrates with various loyalty programs and allows users to collect and redeem rewards from participating merchants.

Users can use Google Pay to recharge mobile plans, pay utility bills and perform various financial transactions directly from the app. Google Pay offers solutions for businesses, allowing them to accept payments through the app. This includes the use of QR codes for in-store transactions.

Google Pay integrates seamlessly with other Google products, such as Gmail and Google Chrome, for a unified experience across different platforms. Google Pay incorporates several security features, including tokenization to protect card information, biometric authentication and the ability to remotely lock or erase data on a lost device.

Google Pay has established itself as a prominent player in the digital payments landscape, offering a user-friendly and versatile platform. Its success depends on adapting to evolving user needs, addressing regulatory challenges and staying competitive in a dynamic industry. As digital payments continue to evolve, Google Pay is likely to play a significant role in shaping the future of online transactions and financial services.

Alipay

Alipay is a leading digital payment platform developed by Ant Group, an affiliate of Alibaba Group. It was launched in 2004 as an escrow service to facilitate e-commerce transactions on Alibaba's platforms. Over the years, it has evolved into a comprehensive digital payment platform, providing a wide range of financial services beyond online payments.

Alipay is operated by Ant Group, formerly known as Ant Financial, an affiliate of Alibaba Group. Ant Group is a financial technology (Fintech) company that has expanded its services into various areas, including payments, banking and wealth management. Alipay serves as a digital wallet, allowing users to link their bank accounts or credit/debit cards to the app. Users can load money into their Alipay accounts for various transactions.

Alipay enables users to make payments for online and offline purchases. It supports QR code payments, allowing users to scan codes at merchant establishments for in-store transactions. Users can transfer money directly to other Alipay users, making P2P transactions convenient. This feature is often used for splitting bills or sending money to friends and family.

Alipay allows users to recharge mobile plans, pay utility bills and perform other financial transactions directly from the app. Alipay integrates with a wide range of third-party services, including food delivery, ride-hailing and entertainment platforms, providing users with a seamless experience within a single app.

Alipay offers users the option to invest in various financial products, including money market funds and wealth management products, allowing them to grow their savings. Alipay provides users with access to credit and financing options, including personal loans and installment plans for purchases.

Alipay generates revenue through transaction fees charged to merchants for processing payments. The fees vary depending on the type of transaction and the merchant's agreement with Alipay. Alipay offers various financial services, including wealth management and lending. Revenue is generated through fees, interest and other financial service-related charges. Like many digital payment platforms, Alipay may analyze user data to derive insights and trends, contributing to its broader data monetization strategy.

Ant Group, the operator of Alipay, has faced increased regulatory scrutiny in China, leading to the suspension of its initial public offering in 2020. Regulatory changes can impact the company's operations and future strategies.

Alipay has played a significant role in shaping the digital payment landscape, not only in China but also on the global stage. Its evolution from an escrow service for online transactions to a multifaceted financial services platform reflects the dynamic nature of the Fintech industry. Challenges such as regulatory scrutiny and competition are part of its landscape, but, as a leading player, Alipay continues to adapt, innovate and explore new opportunities in the rapidly evolving digital economy.

Paytm

Paytm started as a mobile wallet, allowing users to load money into the digital wallet and use it for various transactions, including mobile recharges, bill payments and online shopping. Paytm facilitated QR code-based payments, enabling users to make transactions by scanning QR codes at merchant establishments, providing a convenient and secure mode of payment.

Paytm expanded its offerings to become a one-stop shop for a wide range of products and services, including electronics, fashion and groceries. The platform acts as an intermediary between buyers and sellers, connecting consumers with a diverse range of products.

Paytm diversified into the banking sector by launching Paytm payments bank, offering savings accounts, fixed deposits and digital debit cards. Users can open savings accounts with minimal documentation and enjoy benefits such as cashback, interest on savings and seamless integration with the Paytm wallet.

Paytm provides users with the option to purchase insurance products, including health insurance and vehicle insurance. Paytm facilitates investment in mutual funds through its platform, allowing users to manage and monitor their investments.

Users can book tickets for various services, including flights, trains, buses and movies, directly through the Paytm app. This feature adds convenience for users, who can access multiple services within a single platform.

Paytm runs a loyalty program where users earn cashback and rewards for using the platform for various transactions. Cashback incentives encourage user engagement and promote the continued use of Paytm services.

Paytm monetizes its platform through targeted advertising and promotional activities. Businesses can leverage the platform to reach a large user base. Paytm may analyze user data to derive insights into consumer behavior and preferences. This data can be monetized through partnerships, targeted advertising or other means.

Paytm continues to explore new avenues and partnerships to enhance its offerings and expand its user base. The company has expressed interest in entering segments such as wealth management and financial advisory services.

Paytm's business model reflects its evolution from a mobile wallet to a comprehensive digital payments and financial services platform. By offering a diverse range of services, Paytm has positioned itself as a key player in India's digital economy. The success of its business model depends on continued innovation, regulatory compliance and the ability to meet the evolving needs of consumers and businesses in the digital landscape.

Bharat Interface for Money

BHIM is a mobile app developed by the NPCI to facilitate fast, secure and convenient digital payments. Launched in December 2016, BHIM is designed to promote financial inclusion and enable seamless transactions for users across India.

BHIM operates on the UPI framework, a real-time payment system that enables users to link multiple bank accounts to a single mobile application. This simplifies the process of money transfers and facilitates interoperability across banks. BHIM boasts a straightforward and user-friendly interface, making it accessible to users with varying levels of digital literacy. The app is available in multiple languages to cater to a diverse user base.

BHIM allows users to link accounts from various banks, providing flexibility and convenience. Users can choose their preferred bank for transactions within the app. BHIM supports QR code-based payments, allowing users to scan QR codes to make payments. This feature is widely used in merchant transactions, making it convenient for both consumers and businesses.

Users can request money from others or collect pending payments. This feature is useful for settling bills, splitting expenses or conducting business transactions. BHIM incorporates robust security measures, including multi-factor authentication and secure PIN-based access. This ensures the safety of users' financial information and transactions.

BHIM is available as a mobile app for smartphones, but it can also be accessed through feature phones by dialing an unstructured supplementary service data (USSD) code. This ensures that users with basic mobile phones can still participate in digital transactions. The USSD functionality of BHIM allows users to make transactions without the need for Internet connectivity, further extending its reach to users in remote areas.

BHIM is interoperable with other UPI-based apps, enabling users to transact seamlessly across different UPI platforms. This interoperability enhances the overall adoption and effectiveness of UPI-based digital payments.

BHIM has been actively promoted by the Indian Government as part of its push for a less-cash economy. Various awareness campaigns and incentives have been launched to encourage citizens to adopt BHIM for their digital transactions.

The government has introduced cashback and incentive programs to encourage BHIM usage. These programs aim to reward users for making digital transactions, contributing to the growth of the digital payments ecosystem.

BHIM faces competition from various other digital payment platforms and wallets. The challenge lies in continuously innovating and offering additional features to stay competitive in the market. To maximize its impact, BHIM needs to continue enhancing its acceptance among merchants, encouraging widespread adoption and usage for both P2P transactions and commercial transactions.

BHIM has played a crucial role in advancing India's digital payments ecosystem, leveraging the UPI framework to provide a user-friendly and secure platform. As technology continues to evolve, BHIM's success will depend on its ability to adapt, innovate and address the evolving needs of users. With ongoing government support and a commitment to financial inclusion, BHIM is expected to contribute significantly to India's journey toward a digital economy.

Vodafone M-Pesa

M-Pesa, originally launched by Vodafone in Kenya in 2007, has become a successful mobile money service that goes beyond the boundaries of any single telecom operator. M-Pesa, which stands for "mobile money" in Swahili, allows users to perform various financial transactions using their mobile phones.

M-Pesa was initially introduced in Kenya by Vodafone and Safaricom, Vodafone's affiliate in the region. The success of M-Pesa in Kenya prompted its expansion to other countries and regions, making it one of the most widely adopted mobile money platforms globally.

M-Pesa operates as a mobile wallet, allowing users to store money on their phones securely. Users can load funds into their M-Pesa accounts through agents and bank transfers or by linking their bank accounts.

One of the primary features of M-Pesa is the ability to transfer money to other M-Pesa users. This has been particularly impactful in regions with limited access to traditional banking services.

M-Pesa facilitates the payment of utility bills, school fees and other services directly through the mobile wallet. This reduces the need for physical cash and provides a convenient way to manage finances. Users can make payments at various merchants and retail outlets that accept M-Pesa, promoting a cashless economy.

M-Pesa agents, typically located at local shops or businesses, enable users to withdraw cash from their M-Pesa accounts or deposit physical cash into their mobile wallets.

M-Pesa allows users to receive international remittances, providing a reliable and efficient way for individuals to receive money from abroad.

M-Pesa has played a significant role in promoting financial inclusion, especially in regions with limited access to traditional banking services. It provides a simple and accessible platform for managing money. M-Pesa has empowered individuals who were previously unbanked by providing them with a secure and accessible way to store, send and receive money.

M-Pesa has formed partnerships with various financial institutions, mobile operators and other entities to expand its reach and offer cross-border financial services. Beyond Kenya, M-Pesa has expanded to several other countries, including Tanzania, Mozambique, Ghana, Egypt and India. The platform has adapted its services to the regulatory and market conditions of each region.

M-Pesa transactions are secured using encryption and authentication methods. PIN codes and biometric authentication may be employed to ensure the security of users' financial information. M-Pesa has evolved over the years, incorporating new technologies and features to enhance its capabilities and UX.

Operating in multiple countries requires compliance with various regulatory frameworks. M-Pesa has navigated different regulatory environments to offer its services globally. In some regions, M-Pesa faces competition from other mobile money services and digital payment platforms. Continuous innovation is necessary to stay competitive.

The integration of emerging technologies such as blockchain and digital identity could play a role in the future development of M-Pesa. M-Pesa may continue to diversify its services, potentially exploring partnerships or developing in-house solutions for areas like microfinance, insurance or investment products.

Vodafone M-Pesa stands as a transformative force in the realm of mobile money, promoting financial inclusion and offering convenient financial services to individuals globally. As it continues to adapt to changing technologies, regulations and user needs, M-Pesa is likely to remain a pivotal player in the digital financial services landscape.

Jio Money

Jio Money is a digital wallet and payment service offered by Reliance Jio Infocomm, a subsidiary of Reliance Industries Limited. It is a convenient and secure way to make online payments, pay bills and transfer money to other users. The Jio Money app is available for both Android and iOS devices and can be used across various platforms, including the JioPhone, JioTV and JioCinema. To use Jio Money, users need to have a Jio account and link their bank account or credit/debit card to the app. Once linked, users can add money to their Jio Money account using their bank account or credit/debit card and use it to make payments.

Jio Money offers various features, such as bill payments, mobile recharges, online shopping and money transfers. Users can also earn JioMoney cashback and rewards on their transactions. One of the advantages of using Jio Money is the convenience of making payments and transfers without the need for cash or physical cards. It also provides a secure and reliable way to make transactions online.

In addition, Jio Money is integrated with other Jio services, such as JioCinema and JioTV, allowing users to make payments for their subscriptions and other services within the app. Overall, Jio Money is a useful and convenient payment service for Jio users, offering a range of features and benefits for online transactions.

PhonePe

PhonePe is a leading digital payments platform in India that offers a wide range of financial services through its mobile app. Launched in 2015, PhonePe has quickly gained popularity and become one of the most widely used digital payment platforms in the country. It was founded by Sameer Nigam, Rahul Chari and Burzin Engineer as a UPI-based digital payments platform. In 2016, PhonePe was acquired by Flipkart, India's leading e-commerce marketplace, which helped accelerate its growth and integration into the Flipkart ecosystem.

One of the key features of PhonePe is its ability to allow users to make payments and transfers directly from their bank account, without the need for a physical debit or credit card. This makes it a convenient and fast way to make payments, especially for small purchases.

PhonePe also offers a range of other financial services, such as bill payments, recharges and investments. It has partnerships with a range of merchants and service providers, allowing users to easily pay for their purchases and services. In addition to its core financial services, PhonePe offers a range of other features, such as a virtual prepaid card, which allows users to make online purchases and bookings without the need to enter their bank details. It also has a feature called "PhonePe Pockets", which allows users to invest in mutual funds and other financial products.

The platform operates on the UPI, a real-time payment system developed by the NPCI, enabling users to transfer money instantly between bank accounts using their mobile phones.

PhonePe allows users to transfer money directly to friends, family or merchants using their phone numbers or UPI IDs. Users can recharge their mobile phones and pay utility bills, DTH bills and other expenses directly through the app. PhonePe offers a seamless shopping experience, allowing users to pay for purchases on various e-commerce platforms and apps using UPI or wallet balance. The platform provides investment options such as mutual funds, insurance and gold purchases, enabling users to grow their wealth conveniently. PhonePe has expanded its offerings to include banking services like savings accounts, credit cards and loans, partnering with various financial institutions to provide these services to users.

PhonePe has experienced rapid growth since its launch, surpassing 500 million registered users by 2023 and processing billions of transactions annually. The platform's user-friendly interface, seamless integration with UPI and innovative features have contributed to its widespread adoption among consumers across urban and rural areas in India. Strategic partnerships with merchants, banks and government agencies have helped PhonePe expand its reach and offer a comprehensive suite of financial services to users.

PhonePe's association with Flipkart has also played a crucial role in driving user acquisition and engagement, as it leverages Flipkart's extensive customer base and distribution network. PhonePe continually invests in technology and innovation to enhance its platform's security, reliability and performance. The app employs robust encryption and authentication mechanisms to protect users' financial data and transactions from unauthorized access and fraud.

PhonePe regularly updates its app with new features and improvements based on user feedback and market trends, ensuring a seamless and satisfying UX. PhonePe has played a significant role in driving the adoption of digital payments in India, particularly among individuals who were previously underserved by traditional banking channels.

The platform has contributed to the government's vision of a less-cash economy and financial inclusion by providing easy access to digital financial services to users across socio-economic segments. PhonePe's success has spurred competition in the digital payments space, leading to innovation, improved services and better customer experiences across the industry.

PhonePe is well-positioned to capitalize on the growing demand for digital financial services in India and expand its market share further. The platform is likely to introduce new features, partnerships and offerings to cater to the evolving needs of its diverse user base and maintain its competitive edge in the market. The company has emerged as a leading player in India's digital payments ecosystem, offering a comprehensive range of financial services through its user-friendly mobile app. Its rapid growth, technological innovation and strategic partnerships have made it a preferred choice for millions of users seeking convenient, secure and reliable digital payment solutions.

Future of PayTech

According to the latest Fintech report by Statista, the average transaction value per user in the digital payments segment is projected to amount to US$1,400 in 2020, and this is expected to increase by nearly 30% to reach US$1,800 in 2024. The technology giants are working on different mechanisms of electronic currency. Facebook is working on Libra cryptocurrency, and Amazon is working on palm payment technology, which lets shoppers at physical stores pay for their purchases by scanning the palm of their hand.

While older generations who are more comfortable with cash may be skeptical of a largely cashless economy with digital financial solutions, Millennials and Gen Z participants are known to be trusting of newer technologies. Additionally, their voices are now being heard in this space, as they begin to make up the majority of the workforce and consumer base all over the world (Bergemann, Brooks & Morris, 2015).

This is increasingly evident in the growth of cryptocurrencies because one of the most controversial points about them is that they are largely decentralized. This may seem like a detraction to older generations, who are comfortable with the idea that governments and central banks have some level of control. However, younger generations see this as a major advantage.

There are still many issues regarding a shift toward a largely cashless economy to iron out. These include, but are not limited to, technical difficulties surrounding digital infrastructure, cybersecurity, data collection/privacy regulation and marginalization of cash users. However, we see that the Fintech innovators around us are trying to solve every challenge with their tech (Polishchuk, 2023).

Though this will not replace traditional retail and commercial banking, in the long term, there is still plenty of room for new players. This can be achieved through collaboration between startups and major institutions, and it is clear that this is the direction we are moving in.

Questions for Discussion

1. Explain what you understand by the PayTech Model in Fintech.
2. Explain the ecosystem of PayTech Business.
3. What are the different modes of Electronic Fund Transfer (ETF)?
4. What do you understand by API? How does API work?
5. Write a short note on the companies who are spearheading the PayTech Revolution.

Case Study – Razorpay Payment Gateway 3.0

As per the Union Finance Ministry's latest monthly economic review, India is set to become the world's third-largest economy with a GDP of $7 trillion by 2030. With over 91 billion digital payment transactions in 2023, India is also the fastest-growing Fintech market in the world. The Digital India Stack is now a global benchmark for most countries, providing a competitive advantage for growing businesses.

Razorpay believes the digital person-to-merchant (P2M) payments market in India will continue to grow exponentially and reach $4 trillion by 2030! Recognizing the ever-expanding potential of startups, freelancers and enterprises, the company believes businesses today require an intelligent real-time financial infrastructure to scale with evolving payment and banking needs and diverse consumers and markets. In a mission to power the financial infrastructure of businesses so that they spend less time worrying about managing the entire money movement and more time creating new products, building on new ideas and thinking scale, Razorpay has launched Payment Gateway 3.0 and RAY – India's first AI assistant for payments and payroll.

Razorpay Payment Gateway 3.0 was born out of a profound understanding of the limitations inherent in payment gateways, aiming to offer businesses robust solutions tailored to navigate the dynamic digital landscape. These challenges included scalability, flexibility and security.

Payment gateways struggled to meet the growing demands of businesses, leading to operational bottlenecks and limitations in handling increasing transaction volumes. Traditional payment gateways were rigid, hindering merchants' ability to adapt to changing customer preferences and market trends and limiting their agility in responding to evolving business needs. Concerns about data security and fraud prevention were significant barriers for merchants, impacting customer trust and jeopardizing the integrity of online transactions.

To address these fundamental challenges head-on, Razorpay embarked on a mission to redefine the payment experience for businesses of all shapes and niches, culminating in the development of Razorpay Payment Gateway 3.0. This upgrade represents a substantial leap forward in payment solutions, leveraging cutting-edge technologies and user-centric design principles to empower businesses with unparalleled capabilities.

Razorpay has introduced Magic Checkout, a one-click checkout solution. This streamlines the customer's checkout journey with a one-click checkout solution, eliminating the hassle of spending 1.5 to 3 minutes navigating through multiple forms just to complete their orders. By simplifying transactions and minimizing frictions, e-commerce businesses can witness increased order conversions and reduced returns. Moreover, lower cart abandonment rates and greater prevalence of prepaid orders contribute to thwarting fraudulent transactions. Implementing Razorpay Magic Checkout, a one-click checkout solution, can result in a 40% uptick in conversion rates and a 50% reduction in return to origin (RTOs).

Razorpay has also introduced MagicX for Shopify. Razorpay MagicX for Shopify simplifies the checkout process, enriching the UX. It is built on top of Shopify's one-page checkout experience. It prefills contact, shipping and payment details for over 100 million online shoppers, facilitating faster transactions. With MagicX, businesses can experience a 40% boost in conversion rates and a 50% reduction in RTO rates. This solution offers full RTO protection and increases the share of prepaid orders by 20%. By addressing cart abandonment and RTO challenges, MagicX aligns with modern shoppers' expectations, driving conversions and mitigating risks effectively.

Razorpay has a product called "Loyalty Wallet" that promises to boost customer retention effortlessly. Loyalty Wallet is a customizable solution that nurtures brand loyalty through personalized rewards and simplified redemption. By aligning rewards with individual preferences, e-commerce stores can deepen customer engagement and stimulate repeat purchases organically. This can leverage personalized rewards, preferred by 55% of customers, and provide hassle-free reward redemption via wallets, a favored method by 61% of customers. With Loyalty Wallet, e-commerce stores can cultivate long-term relationships with their customers while driving sustainable business growth.

The sellers can enhance customer relationships with Razorpay Magic Konnect, a solution crafted to facilitate seamless customer engagement and support. The merchants can leverage the power of WhatsApp, the preferred communication platform for over 500 million monthly active users in India, to effectively connect with their target audience. By promptly addressing customer queries and needs, they can reduce customer acquisition costs by 40% and reduce cart abandonment rates by 60% – a significant advantage, considering that 70% of online shoppers abandon their virtual shopping carts at various stages.

With Razorpay Payment Gateway 3.0, payment solutions have advanced significantly and are now better equipped to meet the changing demands of modern enterprises operating in the digital world. Razorpay Payment Gateway 3.0's cutting-edge features promise to expedite your payment procedures and open up new business opportunities. With Razorpay, this can propel the company to new heights and set off a path of increased productivity and success.

AI forms the core of Razorpay's product stack. Razorpay AI-Nucleus, which is powered by the AI engine that drives the firm's payment infrastructure, is a crucial component of almost everything the company creates, making payments more reliable, secure and quick.

RAY is India's first AI assistant for e-commerce businesses that will handle all things related to payments, payouts, payroll, vendor payments and much more. Razorpay launched RAY by utilizing the AI-Nucleus powerhouse in addition to the company's dedication to providing unrivaled convenience and efficiency for businesses.

Razorpay has also introduced two new AI-powered products, the AI-Powered RTO Suite and Razorpay FraudShield, which will lower chargebacks and protect companies from potential fraud and RTOs.

Razorpay estimates that chargebacks can cost businesses up to 2–3% of their international revenue. Fraud chargebacks add cost and revenue pressure to the business. For a scaling business, this means fraud chargebacks can quickly balloon bringing a business' growth to a halt. To tackle this ongoing problem, Razorpay launched a chargeback protection program – FraudShield, and, if businesses opt-in, the company promises to reimburse businesses of any amount accounted toward fraudulent chargebacks.

Another common fraud for businesses in e-commerce marketplaces is RTO orders, causing them multi-crore losses every year. To stop RTO frauds much before they happen and protect businesses from fraudulent RTO orders, Razorpay launched an AI-powered RTO Suite. The company also boldly promises businesses RTO protection – that if businesses opt-in to this feature, and if they suffer a loss due to fraudulent RTO orders, Razorpay will take care of that cost.

The yearly TPV of Razorpay has touched a value of $150 billion. With this accomplishment, Razorpay has taken the lead in the Indian industry for digital payment processing, having amassed a majority market share.

Case Study Questions

1. Explain the business offering of Razorpay Payment Gateway 3.0.
2. Explain how Razorpay Payment Gateway 3.0 is different from the existing payment gateways.
3. Explain how Razorpay is using AI to resolve issues related to payments, payouts, payroll and vendor payments.

Further Reading

1. Chishti, S., Craddock, T., Courtneidge, R., & Zachariadis, M. (Eds.). (2020). *The PAYTECH Book: The Payment Technology Handbook for Investors, Entrepreneurs, and FinTech Visionaries*. John Wiley & Sons.
2. Fifteen Ways in Which Our Digital Future Will Be Shaped by PayTech by Tony Craddock, Wiley Online Library. https://onlinelibrary.wiley.com/doi/10.1002/9781119551973.ch67

References

Abiew, N. A. K., Jnr, M. D., & Banning, S. O. (2020). Design and implementation of cost effective multi-factor authentication framework for ATM systems. *Asian Journal of Research in Computer Science*, 5(3), 7–20.

Berg, T., Burg, V., Keil, J., & Puri, M. (2021). On the rise of payment firms. *Working Paper*.

Bergemann, D., Brooks, B., & Morris, S. (2015). The limits of price discrimination. *American Economic Review*, 105 (3), 921–957.

Chishti, S., Craddock, T., Courtneidge, R., & Zachariadis, M. (2020). *The PAYTECH book: The payment technology handbook for investors, entrepreneurs, and FinTech visionaries*. John Wiley & Sons.

Darshanbhai, P. N. (2023). FinTech as a driver of the financial market's creative growth. *International Journal of Law Management and Humanities*, 6, 396.

Haralayya, B. (2021). How digital banking has brought innovative products and services to India. *Journal of Advanced Research in Quality Control and Management*, 6(1), 16–18.

Hassan, M. A., Shukur, Z., & Hasan, M. K. (2020). An efficient secure electronic payment system for e-commerce. *Computers*, 9(3), 66.

Klein, A. (2020). *China's Digital Payments Revolution*. Brookings Institution, Washington.

Memiş, H. (2023). Payment facilitators' effects on the digital economy. *Journal of Digital Banking*, 7(4), 343–356.

Mützel, S. (2021). Unlocking the payment experience: Future imaginaries in the case of digital payments. *New Media & Society*, 23(2), 284–301.

Patel, K. (2023). Credit card analytics: A review of fraud detection and risk assessment techniques. *International Journal of Computer Trends and Technology*, 71(10), 69–79.

Polishchuk, Y. (2023). FinTech future trends. In *The European digital economy* (pp. 204–220). Taylor and Francis. https://doi.org/10.4324/9781003450160

Ünsal, E., Öztekin, B., Çavuş, M., & Özdemir, S. (2020, October). Building a FinTech ecosystem: Design and development of a FinTech API gateway. In *2020 International Symposium on Networks, Computers and Communications (ISNCC)* (pp. 1–5). IEEE.

5 Digital Lending – The LendTech Model

After reading this chapter you will:

- Understand the digital lending business
- Understand the peer-to-peer (P2P) model used in digital lending
- Know the different business models used in digital lending business
- Know about different companies who are operating digital lending business
- Understand the difference between traditional lending and digital lending

There are 1.4 billion adult people in the world who do not have bank accounts (Source: The Global Findex Database 2021 report). These people do not have access to banking products and services because of the lack of bank accounts. This has raised serious concerns about financial inclusion. The solution to this critical issue is now being provided by Open Banking and LendTech.

According to the World Bank, "Financial inclusion means that individuals and businesses have access to useful and affordable financial products and services that meet their needs – transactions, payments, savings, credit and insurance – delivered responsibly and sustainably". Access should be unrelated to the size or net worth of the company, to further clarify the term. It's about lowering entrance barriers for individuals and companies in the financial industry and leveraging these services to enhance people's quality of life.

A creditor lacks the tools necessary to conduct a risk assessment when individuals or companies have never used the financial system, particularly the credit system. This creates a number of issues because there is no credit history available for evaluation. How can banks be certain they will receive their money back? How can they research the organization to which they are going to lend the money?

Unconventional data is used in new lending technologies to create these profiles. Wallets, personality tests, mobile and web data and other sources can be used to create alternative credit scoring models without requiring a conventional financial footprint.

The technology underlying LendTech solutions, open banking, is what enables all of the previously mentioned. Real-time customer verification is powered by it. Paper-intensive procedures and the manual submission of paystubs are not necessary with open banking. Open banking technology facilitates the development of LendTech solutions by third-party suppliers and provides insights into non-financial data.

In India, the Aadhar database, permanent account number (PAN) card and CIBIL score are helping to expedite the Open Banking and LendTech processes. On behalf of the Indian Government, the Unique Identity Authority of India issues the 12-digit

DOI: 10.4324/9781032699417-5

Aadhar personal identity number. Anywhere in India, the number acts as documentation of identity and residence.

An application for a PAN must be submitted, or the Indian Income Tax Department may assign a ten-character alphanumeric identification foundational ID to anyone who requests one. The PAN is issued in the form of a laminated "PAN card" to those who do not need to apply. The PAN card is used to connect the financial transactions of an individual or company with their tax obligations. PANs are recognized as legitimate identity documents by many governmental and non-governmental organizations, and they are commonly accepted as proof of identity. The use of PAN Cards is not exclusive to India.

The Credit Information Bureau (India) Limited (CIBIL) is the most well-known of the four credit information companies that have been granted licenses by the Reserve Bank of India (RBI). Three more companies have been awarded licenses by the RBI to function as credit information companies. They are Experian, Equifax and Highmark. A person's CIBIL score is determined by a review of several factors, such as payment history, credit utilization, credit length, credit mix and current credit inquiries. A person's creditworthiness is established through the combined assessment of multiple criteria, each with a specific weight.

Microlending is one remedy that emerged from the use of open banking technology. The practice of providing modest loans to small- and medium-sized businesses (SMEs) is known as microlending. The modest sales volume of SMEs typically prevents them from receiving financing through traditional banks. Open banking enables loan solutions to be tailored based on the needs and profile of the consumer, doing away with the "one-size-fits-all" approach.

Because of the unique nature of their employment, digital nomads have difficulty opening bank accounts, reporting their income and ultimately getting loans. Nano loans provide a low-interest way to borrow small sums, filling a demand that is akin to the concept of microlending to SMEs. Furthermore, because open banking-driven LendTech solutions are not predicated on outdated frameworks and presumptions, they are capable of assimilating the constraints of remote labor. These products can reflect the needs of the end user since they can obtain real-time data.

Personal finance is another area that has benefited from the union of open finance and LendTech. With the help of personal finance management apps, anyone with a smartphone and Internet access can take control of their finances. People can receive loan recommendations tailored to their objectives, aspirations and risk tolerance by just clicking an app on their phone. Open banking cannot only pull data and information but also contextualize it. Open Banking and LendTech have revolutionized the lending and borrowing process and made credit accessible to every individual who owns a smartphone.

Who Wants a Loan?

Perhaps nobody better than Mark Twain understood the flaws in the banking system when he said that: "A banker is a fellow who lends you his umbrella when the sun is shining, but wants it back the minute it begins to rain". The other famous adage that has been applied to banking has been said by J Paul Getty: "If you owe the bank $100 that's your problem. If you owe the bank $100 million, that's the bank's problem".

Banks have been always accused, since time immemorial, of having denied loans to the people who genuinely needed them and showered largesse on people who were susceptible to defaults. On the one hand, we hear stories of poor farmers who were driven to suicide because they couldn't repay small amounts of loans due to crop failures. On the other hand, there are the famous instances of Vijay Mallya and Nirav Modi, who absconded to foreign destinations after diverting business loans into their personal accounts. Indian banks have written off business loans to the tune of INR 10.83 lakh crores in the last ten years. We also have seen multinational banking institutions like Bear Sterns and Lehman Brothers collapsing in 2008 because of giving subprime loans to people who had either no willingness or capability to repay. The subprime crisis shook the very foundation of banks and financial institutions across the world and led many of them toward insolvency and closure.

Bitcoins were created by Satoshi Nakamoto to create an alternative currency that was not at the mercy of any central bank and could not be manipulated by people occupying high positions in the banking and financial system. The distribution of wealth was democratized due to the creation of a blockchain system that was initially criticized by central bankers and governments across the world. Now, these same people are in a mad rush to create Central Bank Digital Currency, which is nothing but official currency in digital form.

The same innovation in borrowing and lending has been brought about by P2P lending. P2P lending platforms have connected people who want to lend and people who want to borrow. This has been done using digital platforms and has democratized the process of lending and opened up a viable alternative for people who would have otherwise not been entertained by banks.

History of P2P Networks

P2P networks were created by Shawn Fanning in 1999. He was a student studying at North Eastern University in the USA. It was in his college life that he got the idea of Napster. Napster is a music-sharing service that uses an application program interface to help users share music files with each other using the Internet. This was done through a centralized server, where users could search for a particular song or artist. This service was called Napster, and it became a hub for large-scale unauthorized distribution of copyrighted music. Napster was doing violation of intellectual property rights. The music companies filed a case against Napster and got it closed down in 2001 (Ohlendorf, 2023).

Napster closed down, but it popularized the P2P networks. Very soon, a flurry of companies rushed in to fill up the void left by Napster. They were also sharing music and video files using decentralized servers. And they were smarter than Napster. One of these applications, called "BitTorrent", uses the "swarm" model. Many of these applications use higher degrees of encryption making it impossible to detect them. As it is very difficult to detect the source, it becomes very difficult to sue these companies or get them closed down.

P2P networks have been used for a host of legal activities as well as illegal activities. These networks have been used for sharing copyrighted material like books, magazines, music, movies and other creative works with intellectual property rights. But perhaps the proper use of digital P2P networks has been done by companies like LendingClub, Lendermarket, SoFi, Zopa, Faircent and Finzy, who have connected borrowers with lenders so that both can meet their needs and objectives through financial transactions.

The Traditional Money Lending Model

The financial institutions operate with the system of flow of money from those who have it to those who need it. Before the banks were created, it was pawnbrokers who started this system. Pawnbrokers were present in ancient Greece as early as 300 BC. The system of pawn broking was to lend money against collaterals which reduced the risk of default. This could be against the exchange of goods also (Xu & Vadgama, 2022).

The lending process changed in the 1800s with the creation of society and savings fund. This led to the creation of property loans, where people could get loans by mortgaging their property. The modern system of lending evolved with the application of technology and institutions like banks and non-banking financial companies (NBFCs), being created for giving loans. Banks and NBFCs give loans to customers based on their requirements. The governments created regulatory authorities like the RBI in India, the Federal Reserve in the USA and the Monetary Authority of Singapore to monitor and regulate the functioning of the loan-giving institutions.

A number of procedures are involved in the conventional lending process that banks and other financial organizations use to evaluate potential borrowers' creditworthiness and control the overall lending risk. Figure 5.1 illustrates a general overview of the traditional lending procedure, however, specifics may differ throughout institutions.

The first step in the procedure is for borrowers to apply for a loan from a bank or other financial institution. Personal data, bank statements, credit history, business plans (for business loans) and the loan's intended use are usually included in the application. First, lenders evaluate the borrower to see if they satisfy the requirements for basic eligibility.

This stage aids in weeding out candidates who don't satisfy the minimal standards for creditworthiness. To assess the borrower's credit history and credit score, lenders run a comprehensive credit check. Getting a credit report from credit bureaus is required for this.

To evaluate the borrower's ability to repay the loan, financial statements, tax records and other pertinent financial papers are carefully examined. Lenders evaluate the worth and caliber of collateral that the borrower provides for secured loans. If the borrower doesn't make loan payments as agreed, this collateral will step in to cover the shortfall. It is possible to appraise goods, cars, real estate and other assets.

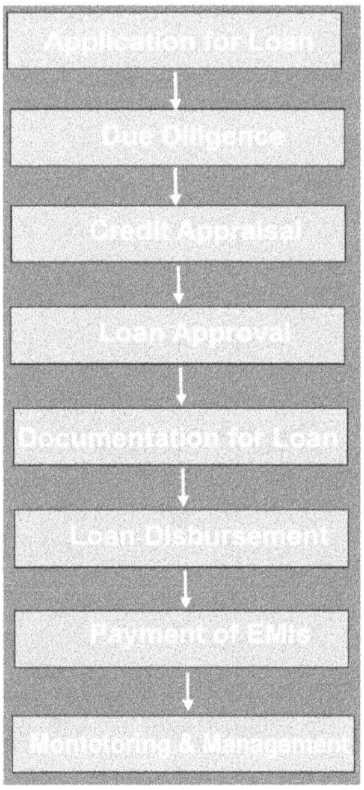

Figure 5.1 Traditional Model of Lending

Lenders examine a number of risk variables related to the loan and the borrower. This covers the borrower's financial stability, industry risk and prevailing economic conditions. Determining the interest rate and other loan terms is aided by risk assessment.

A credit committee or loan officer determines whether to approve or deny the loan application based on a thorough evaluation. The loan's terms and conditions, including the interest rate, repayment plan and any covenants, are set if it is authorized.

The required legal documents are prepared after approval. A promissory note, a loan agreement and other agreements defining the terms and conditions may be examples of this. To formally establish the loan agreement, both the borrower and the lender sign these documents. The borrower receives the money once the paperwork is completed. The loan type will determine whether the payment is made in one lump sum or over time in installments.

The borrower must adhere to the prearranged repayment schedule and make timely installments. Principal and interest are repaid together. Lenders keep a close eye on the borrower's financial situation and adherence to the terms of the loan. Lenders may collaborate with borrowers to find solutions in the event of financial hardship or other problems, or they may take required steps, such as modifying the loan or starting collection procedures.

The conventional lending procedure is intended to minimize risks, guarantee that banks and other financial organizations make well-informed judgments and safeguard the interests of lenders and borrowers alike. This procedure has long been a mainstay of the banking sector, but as technology advances, lending procedures are increasingly becoming more digital and automated.

Different Types of Loan Schemes

The different kinds of loans given by banks and financial institutions are:

- Secured loans
- Unsecured loans
- Demand loans
- Subsidized loans
- Concessional loans

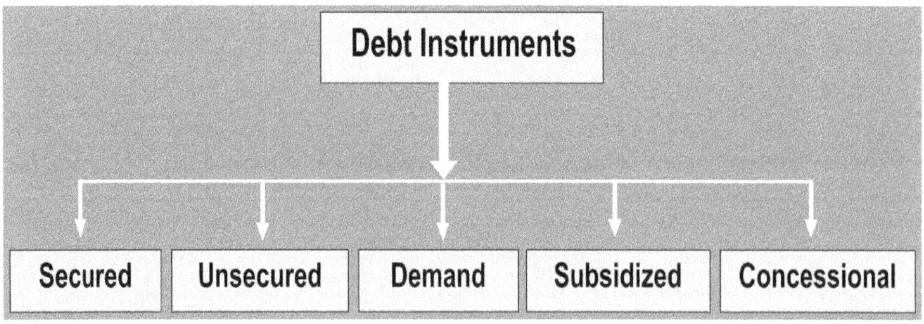

Figure 5.2 Different Kinds of Debt Instruments

Secured Loans

Secured loans are usually backed with collaterals. This means that the borrower is offering an asset as security for the loan, like a home or a vehicle. The lender may take possession of the asset to recoup the unpaid balance if the borrower defaults on the loan.

The fact that secured loans often have lower interest rates than unsecured loans is one of its key benefits. This is because the collateral provides the lender with an increased degree of security and lowers the default risk. The ability to borrow higher sums of money is another benefit of secured loans. For instance, a borrower may pledge their house as security to get a loan for a business startup or home remodeling.

Nonetheless, there are certain dangers connected to secured loans. The borrower may forfeit their asset in the event that they default on the loan. Furthermore, the procedure of taking possession of collateral can be time-consuming and costly, which could cost the lender a lot of money. The borrower must give the lender information about the asset they want to utilize as collateral when applying for a secured loan. After determining the maximum loan amount that can be given, the lender will evaluate the asset's value (Mann, 2022).

Unsecured Loans

Unsecured loans are those for which the borrower is not required to furnish any security or collateral. This implies that in the event that the borrower defaults on the loan, the lender will not be able to confiscate any assets. Unsecured loans can be taken out for a number of things, such as unforeseen costs, home upgrades and debt consolidation.

Unsecured loans are convenient, but, because they are not secured by collateral, they can be dangerous for borrowers. Lenders may therefore raise interest rates to make up for the added risk. Before taking out an unsecured loan, borrowers should carefully assess their financial status and ability to repay the amount (Tiwari & Somani, 2021).

Student loans, credit card loans and personal loans are a few popular categories of unsecured loans. Personal loans are usually paid back over a number of years and can be used for a number of purposes. One kind of unsecured loan that's utilized to cover credit card purchases is a credit card loan. Federal and private student loans are used to cover the expense of higher education.

Finding the best deal on an unsecured loan requires comparing conditions and rates offered by several lenders. Prior to signing, make sure you have read and comprehended the terms and conditions of the loan agreement.

Demand Loans

Demand loans are usually short-term in nature. Most of the time, these loans are determined by the borrower's creditworthiness and capacity for repayment. Demand loans are frequently utilized to satisfy short-term financial obligations, such as paying unexpected bills or making wages. Since demand loans don't require collateral, they are usually easier to obtain than secured loans. This is one of their key advantages. But because demand loans are viewed as a greater risk for the lender, they also typically have higher interest rates and costs than secured loans (Melitz & Pardue, 1973).

It's crucial to thoroughly assess the borrower's financial status and make sure they will be able to repay the loan on schedule before taking out a demand loan. To make sure that the borrowers are receiving the greatest deal possible, it's also critical to evaluate conditions and interest rates offered by different lenders. Having a strategy in place for the borrower's use of the loan and repayment of the principal is also a smart idea. By doing this, the borrowers may make sure they can meet their financial responsibilities and prevent taking on more debt than they can manage.

Subsidized Loans

Subsidized loans are the ones where a third party, usually a government body, picks up the responsibility of repaying a part of the loan, thus bringing down the actual interest rate charged to the borrower. One sort of financial aid that helps students pay for their higher education is subsidized education loans. These loans, which are intended to support students who exhibit financial need, are provided by the federal government and other organizations (Kayo, da Silva & Martelanc, 2023).

The fact that the federal government covers the loan's interest while the borrower is enrolled in classes, during the grace period and during any deferment periods is one of the primary advantages of subsidized loans. This implies that while pursuing their degree, students won't have to worry about incurring interest.

Furthermore, subsidized loans frequently have lower interest rates than unsubsidized loans, which can contribute to a low total cost of borrowing. For students who could be taking out big loans to pay for their tuition, books and other expenditures, this can be extremely crucial.

Students must complete the Free Application for Federal Student Aid (FAFSA) and show financial need to be eligible for a discounted loan. The student's estimated family contribution (EFC) is calculated by the FAFSA based on assets, family income and household size. The student might qualify for a subsidized loan if their EFC is less than the cost of attendance at their institution.

It's crucial to remember that a student's eligibility for subsidized loans is restricted. The loan amount is decided by the school and is based on the financial necessity of the student. Furthermore, the total amount of subsidized loans a student is eligible to obtain during their academic career is capped.

To sum up, subsidized loans are an excellent option for students who require assistance paying for their higher education. These loans can assist in lowering the total cost of borrowing because they have lower interest rates and the federal government pays the interest. If you're thinking about applying for a subsidized loan, be sure you know the rules for qualifying and that you only borrow the amount necessary to pay for your courses.

Concessional Loans

These are also known as "soft loans". They are given with zero interest rates or at very minimal interest rates. The borrower also gets a grace in the form of extended time to repay the loans. Usually, the World Bank or governments give such kinds of loans to other governments or institutions for social development projects. The major sources of concessional financing are multilateral development banks, bilateral aid agencies and development finance institutions. Many companies also give soft loans to employees as an incentive or to retain the employees for a longer period (Koeda, 2004).

Concessional loans are a vital instrument in international development finance, designed to provide financial assistance to countries and regions facing economic challenges or developmental needs. Unlike commercial loans, concessional loans are offered on more favorable terms, including lower interest rates, longer repayment periods and grace periods, making them more accessible and affordable for borrowers. These loans play a crucial role in promoting sustainable development, poverty reduction and economic growth in both developing and emerging economies.

Concessional loans typically carry interest rates significantly lower than prevailing market rates. These concessional interest rates help reduce the financial burden on borrowers and make the loans more affordable and sustainable over the repayment period. Concessional loans often include grace periods, during which borrowers are not required to make principal or interest payments. This grace period provides borrowers with time to implement development projects or reforms before repayment obligations begin, easing immediate financial pressures.

Concessional loans often feature longer repayment terms compared to commercial loans. Extended repayment periods allow borrowers to spread out repayment obligations over time, reducing the annual debt service burden and freeing up resources for other developmental priorities.

Concessional loans play a vital role in supporting sustainable development, poverty reduction and economic growth in countries and regions facing financial constraints and developmental challenges. By providing affordable financing on favorable terms, concessional loans help bridge the gap between development needs and financial resources, empowering countries to achieve their development objectives and build a better future for their citizens. However, careful planning, prudent debt management and effective governance are essential to ensure that concessional financing is used effectively and sustainably to maximize its impact on development outcomes.

The Digital Lending Model

With the advent of technology, the adoption of the Internet and the popularity of P2P networks, the money lending business has also moved toward digitization. Banks have also started to adopt the latest technologies to serve customers in a better way and offer loan products that are best suited to them. Most of the manual work has been automated and the whole process from identifying the customers who need loans, deciding on the principal and interest payables, tenure of the loan and finally the process of disbursal is now managed with artificial intelligence and machine learning (AIML). The adoption of online banking has benefited both the lender and the borrower in a big way (Cornelli, Frost, Gambacorta, Rau, Wardrop & Ziegler, 2023).

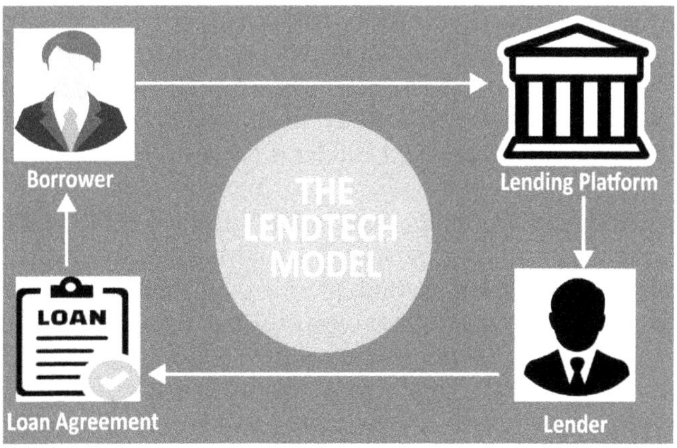

Figure 5.3 The LendTech Model

LendTech, or lending technology, refers to the use of technology to enhance and streamline the lending process. This can include everything from online loan applications to automated underwriting systems. LendTech businesses aim to improve the customer experience and make it easier and faster for individuals and businesses to access the funding they need. Some examples of LendTech companies include online marketplace lenders, P2P lenders and alternative lenders. These companies often use data-driven underwriting models to make lending decisions, which can result in faster approvals and lower interest rates for borrowers. Additionally, LendTech businesses often provide a more user-friendly and transparent borrowing experience compared to traditional lenders.

The LendTech ecosystem is now home to companies that are using blockchain, artificial intelligence (AI), machine learning and big data analytics to seamlessly run their operations with high efficiency, low error and minimal human intervention. This is making sure that the right product reaches the right customer. The user experience is better and customer satisfaction is also rising because of the application of the LendTech systems.

The New Mode of Lending – The Fintech Way

LendTech transforms the lending landscape by harnessing technology to automate processes, analyze data more effectively and create innovative financing solutions. By leveraging these advancements, LendTech companies aim to make borrowing more accessible, affordable and efficient for individuals and businesses alike. The new approaches that are used in the LendTech business are P2P lending, Invoice Financing, Trade Receivable Discounting System (TReDS), crowd funding, Loans on Salary, Student Loans and Buy Now Pay Later (BNPL).

P2P Lending

The creation of digital platforms, including websites or mobile apps, that act as a conduit between lenders and borrowers is the first step in the LendTech process. These platforms make it easy for lenders to handle loan applications and approvals as well as for borrowers to apply for loans.

P2P lending companies function through a technologically advanced platform that links lenders and borrowers, be they people or organizations, to provide loans at reasonable rates. P2P platforms typically serve as a middleman, easing transactions between these parties whether they take place online or offline (Basha, Elgammal & Abuzayed, 2021).

An important component of P2P lending is the use of Internet platforms as middlemen between investors and borrowers. These platforms offer an easy-to-use interface through which investors may peruse and choose which loans to support, and borrowers can post loan listings. Prosper, Funding Circle and LendingClub are a few well-known P2P lending websites.

Usually, borrowers begin by filling out an online application on the P2P network. The borrower's identification, creditworthiness, financial history and loan requirements are all gathered during the application. Certain platforms evaluate the borrower's credit risk and issue a credit grade or score based on sophisticated algorithms and data analytics.

Technology is used by P2P lending platforms to evaluate borrowers' creditworthiness. Credit scores, income levels, employment histories, debt-to-income ratios and occasionally other data sources like utility payments and social media activity are among the many data points they examine. Machine learning techniques are frequently used to detect possible default risks and increase the accuracy of credit assessments.

Borrowers are given an interest rate that represents their credit risk based on the results of the credit assessment. Risk-based pricing models are utilized by P2P lending platforms, wherein borrowers with lower risk profiles and higher credit scores are offered reduced interest rates, while riskier borrowers may be subject to higher rates. Dynamic pricing modifications based on current market conditions and risk assessments are made possible by technology.

Investors can use the site to search through loan listings and choose loans to fund according to their investment inclinations and risk tolerance. Investors have access to comprehensive loan data, which includes credit rating, interest rate, loan amount, borrower profiles and purpose of the loan. Certain platforms provide automated investment tools that let investors designate criteria and have loans that fit that criteria automatically invested in.

Technology is frequently used by P2P lending platforms to enable fractionalization and loan securitization, enabling investors to spread their bets over a number of loans. Investment products, such notes or funds, are created by grouping loans together and then offered for sale to investors. Investors can participate in loan portfolios with minimal capital contributions thanks to fractional ownership of loans, which lowers their exposure to individual risk.

P2P lending platforms use technology-driven methods to manage loan servicing and payment processing. Investors receive their portion of loan repayments when borrowers use automatic electronic funds transfers to make monthly payments. The platform uses automated processes and customer relationship management tools to manage loan servicing duties like debt collection, borrower interactions, delinquency management and payment collection.

P2P lending is made transparent and compliant by technology, which offers instant access to investor returns, platform metrics and loan performance data. P2P lending systems follow legal mandates, including investor accreditation procedures, borrower identification verification and anti-money laundering (AML) investigations. The platform is kept compliant with relevant laws and regulations through the use of compliance tools and reporting procedures.

To protect investor funds and reduce the danger of loan default, P2P lending platforms utilize sophisticated risk management strategies and fraud protection methods. To find fraudulent activity, questionable transactions and possible default signals, they employ pattern recognition, anomaly detection techniques and predictive analytics. Loan diversification, credit enhancement and loss provisioning are examples of automated risk mitigation techniques that reduce investor losses and preserve platform stability.

In conclusion, technology-driven P2P lending presents a disruptive substitute for conventional lending channels, giving investors the opportunity to generate profitable returns on their investments while giving borrowers access to reasonably priced loans. P2P lending platforms enable effective and transparent loan transactions while reducing risks for all stakeholders by utilizing data analytics, automation and risk management tools.

Established in February of 2005, Zopa was the UK's first P2P lending company. Established in August 2010, Funding Circle is the first notable example of a peer-to-business lender, providing small firms with loans from investors through its online platform. Funding Circle has arranged loans totaling more than £6.3 billion.

With the introduction of Prosper Marketplace in February 2006 and LendingClub shortly after, the P2P lending sector in the USA got underway. The main offices of LendingClub and Prosper are in San Francisco, California. Due to the lack of borrower eligibility constraints on early P2P platforms, there were issues with adverse selection and high borrower default rates. Furthermore, a few investors considered it unacceptable because these loans, the majority of which have a minimum three-year duration, lacked liquidity.

The P2P lending concept, which is essentially based on the crowdfunding model, has gained popularity in India because of companies like Faircent, Lendingkart and Lendbox. In India, the majority of P2P lending businesses are operated by NBFCs. This strategy, which uses the newest technologies, is becoming more and more popular with lenders and borrowers alike.

Lenders can find borrowers more easily thanks to the P2P lending business model and vice versa. The model uses an auction procedure to function. To give the borrowers competitive rates, the lenders must compete with one another, and the borrowers will choose the best offer. In addition, P2P lending platforms offer ancillary services including credit evaluation and loan recovery. The P2P platform facilitates seamless lending and borrowing transactions.

Invoice Financing

Invoice financing, facilitated by LendTech, is a form of short-term borrowing in which a business uses its outstanding invoices (accounts receivable) as collateral to obtain financing from a lender. This type of financing allows businesses to access cash quickly by selling their unpaid invoices at a discount.

LendTech companies offering invoice financing typically operate online platforms where businesses can apply for financing and submit their outstanding invoices for funding. These platforms provide a user-friendly interface for businesses to create accounts, upload invoices and manage their financing transactions (Guerar, Merlo, Migliardi, Palmieri & Verderame, 2020).

Businesses start by completing an online application on the LendTech platform, providing information about their company, financials and invoices they wish to finance. The application may also include consent for the lender to access the business's accounting or invoicing software to verify invoice details and creditworthiness.

Once the application is submitted, businesses upload their outstanding invoices to the platform. LendTech companies use technology to verify the authenticity and validity of the invoices, as well as to assess the creditworthiness of the business and its customers. This may involve analyzing historical payment data, credit scores and other financial metrics to determine the risk associated with financing the invoices.

Based on the verification and credit assessment, the LendTech platform provides financing offers to the business. These offers typically include the amount of financing available, the discount or fee charged by the lender and the terms of the financing arrangement (e.g., repayment schedule, recourse/non-recourse).

Upon acceptance of the financing offer, the business agrees to the terms and conditions outlined by the LendTech platform. The lender then advances a percentage of the invoice value to the business, usually ranging from 70% to 90%, depending on the risk profile of the invoices and the business. The remaining balance, minus the lender's fee, is held in reserve until the invoice is paid by the customer.

The lender takes responsibility for collecting payments from the business's customers on the financed invoices. When the customer pays the invoice, the payment is directed to a designated account managed by the lender. Once the payment is received, the lender deducts the amount advanced plus fees and interest and remits the remaining balance to the business.

LendTech companies leverage technology to automate and streamline the invoice financing process. This includes using algorithms and data analytics to assess credit risk, optimize pricing and expedite underwriting decisions. Automation tools are also used for invoice verification, payment processing and customer communication, reducing manual effort and improving efficiency.

LendTech platforms employ advanced risk management techniques and fraud prevention measures to mitigate risks associated with invoice financing. This may include monitoring payment behavior, implementing credit insurance or guarantees and conducting periodic reviews of the business's financial health. Technology-driven risk models help identify potential default risks and take proactive measures to mitigate them.

LendTech companies offering invoice financing must comply with applicable regulations governing lending, consumer protection and financial services. This may include licensing or registration requirements, adherence to AML and know-your-customer (KYC) regulations and disclosure of financing terms and fees. Regulatory compliance tools and protocols are integrated into the platform to ensure that all transactions meet legal and regulatory standards.

LendTech platforms provide ongoing customer support to businesses using their invoice financing services. This may include dedicated account managers, online chat support and educational resources to help businesses navigate the financing process and address any issues or concerns.

In summary, invoice financing through a LendTech Model offers businesses a flexible and efficient way to access working capital by leveraging their unpaid invoices. By combining technology-driven processes with advanced risk management and regulatory compliance, LendTech companies facilitate seamless and transparent financing transactions, enabling businesses to optimize cash flow and grow their operations.

Trade Receivable Discounting System

TReDS is "a technology-driven platform introduced in India to facilitate the financing of trade receivables of Micro, Small, and Medium Enterprises (MSMEs)". It provides a digital marketplace where MSMEs can discount their trade receivables from large buyers (such as corporates and government entities) to access working capital financing.

TReDS operates as an electronic platform that connects MSME sellers, large buyers and financiers (banks and financial institutions). The platform is built and managed by technology companies specializing in financial services (LendTech firms), ensuring robust infrastructure, security and compliance with regulatory standards (Raja, 2021).

MSME sellers register on the TReDS platform by providing the necessary documentation and undergoing a verification process. Once verified, sellers gain access to the platform's features and can start uploading their trade receivables for financing.

Sellers upload their invoices or trade receivables onto the TReDS platform, along with relevant details such as invoice amount, due date, buyer information and supporting documents. The platform uses technology-driven processes to verify the authenticity of invoices and ensure compliance with regulatory requirements.

Large buyers associated with the sellers on the TReDS platform are notified of the submitted invoices and required to validate them. Buyers confirm the authenticity of the invoices and approve them for financing, signaling their acknowledgment of the debt owed to the MSME seller.

Once invoices are approved by buyers, they become eligible for financing on the TReDS platform. LendTech firms operating the platform leverage technology to assess the creditworthiness of the MSME sellers and determine suitable financing offers. This may include evaluating factors such as the financial health of the seller, the creditworthiness of the buyer and the risk associated with the invoices.

Approved invoices are listed on the TReDS platform's marketplace, where financiers can view and bid to finance them. MSME sellers can choose from multiple financing offers based on factors such as discount rates, repayment terms and financier reputation. Upon acceptance of a financing offer, the MSME seller receives immediate funds, typically at a discounted rate, providing them with access to working capital to meet their business needs.

Financiers on the TReDS platform handle payment processing and collections from buyers on behalf of the MSME sellers. Payments made by buyers are directed to designated accounts managed by the platform, ensuring secure and timely settlement of transactions. Once payments are received, financiers deduct the discounted amount and remit the remaining balance to the MSME sellers.

TReDS platforms leverage technology to automate and streamline the entire trade receivables financing process. This includes using algorithms for credit assessment, auction mechanisms for financing offers, digital documentation and verification and real-time tracking and monitoring of transactions. Technology-driven operations enhance efficiency, transparency and accessibility, making trade receivables financing more accessible to MSMEs.

LendTech firms operating TReDS platforms implement robust risk management frameworks and compliance measures to mitigate risks associated with trade receivables financing. This may include credit risk assessment tools, fraud detection algorithms and adherence to regulatory guidelines issued by authorities such as the RBI. Compliance checks ensure that all transactions on the platform comply with legal and regulatory requirements, promoting trust and reliability among participants.

TReDS platforms provide ongoing customer support and educational resources to MSME sellers, buyers and financiers. This may include assistance with platform navigation, troubleshooting and guidance on best practices for trade receivables financing. Educational initiatives help raise awareness about the benefits of TReDS and empower participants to make informed decisions regarding their financing needs.

In summary, TReDS through LendTech enables MSMEs to unlock the value of their trade receivables and access working capital financing in a timely and efficient manner. By leveraging technology-driven platforms, MSMEs can improve cash flow management, optimize liquidity and fuel business growth, contributing to the overall development of the economy.

Buy Now Pay Later

BNPL schemes have gained significant popularity in recent years as a payment option for consumers, allowing them to make purchases upfront and pay for them over time in installments.

BNPL schemes work in a unique manner. When making a purchase online or in-store, customers are presented with the option to use a BNPL service at the checkout. They select this option and proceed with their purchase as usual. Instead of paying the full purchase amount upfront, customers agree to pay for their purchase in multiple installments.

These installments are typically spread out over a few weeks or months (Gerrans, Baur & Lavagna-Slater, 2022).

BNPL services often provide instant approval decisions, allowing customers to complete their purchases without delay. Approval is based on factors such as the customer's credit history, spending behavior and repayment capacity. Many BNPL services offer interest-free financing if customers make timely payments according to the agreed-upon schedule. However, late fees or interest charges may apply if payments are missed or delayed.

Customers are provided with a repayment schedule outlining the due dates and amounts of each installment. Some BNPL services automatically deduct payments from the customer's linked payment method on these dates, while others require manual payments. BNPL schemes offer customers flexibility and convenience by allowing them to spread out the cost of their purchases over time without incurring high interest charges or fees. This can be particularly appealing for consumers facing temporary cash flow constraints or seeking to manage their budget more effectively.

BNPL schemes streamline the payment process, making it quick and easy for customers to complete their purchases without the need for traditional credit checks or lengthy application processes. Many BNPL services offer interest-free financing options, allowing customers to make purchases without incurring interest charges as long as payments are made on time.

BNPL schemes provide customers with greater control over their finances by allowing them to split larger purchases into smaller, more manageable payments over time. Some BNPL services offer risk-free trial periods, allowing customers to try out products before committing to paying for them. If they decide to return the item, they may not be required to make any payments.

Although BNPL plans can provide temporary financial relief, they can also promote excessive spending and result in the accumulation of debt if customers fail to carefully handle their repayments. Customers who fail to make timely payments may be subject to late penalties or interest charges, which could result in an overall increase in the cost of their goods.

While BNPL services generally do not conduct conventional credit checks for approval, any missing or delayed payments may have an adverse effect on a customer's credit score, hence increasing the difficulty of obtaining credit in the future. BNPL programs are closely monitored by regulatory authorities in various countries to guarantee the safeguarding of consumers and the enforcement of equitable lending practices. Regulatory bodies have the authority to establish rules for the clarity of information, the sharing of relevant details, the evaluation of affordability and the methods for resolving conflicts.

BNPL providers may be obligated by regulatory authorities to offer upfront disclosure of essential terms and conditions, such as fees, interest rates, repayment schedules and penalties for missing payments. Regulators may require BNPL providers to perform affordability evaluations to guarantee that consumers have the financial means to repay their purchases without experiencing excessive financial difficulties.

BNPL providers must comply with data privacy and security regulations to protect customer information and transactions from unauthorized access, misuse or disclosure. Regulators may require BNPL providers to establish robust complaints handling and dispute resolution mechanisms to address customer grievances in a timely and fair manner.

In summary, BNPL schemes offer consumers flexibility and convenience when making purchases, but they also come with potential risks related to debt accumulation, late fees and credit score impact. Regulatory oversight is essential to ensure consumer protection, responsible lending practices and adherence to transparency and disclosure requirements in the BNPL industry.

Concerns and Debates Regarding LendTech

Payday loans' outrageous fees and rates, combined with how simple it is to obtain one, have long caused concern and issues for those who are already vulnerable in society. According to the Consumer Financial Protection Bureau (CFPB), the average payday borrower in the USA obtains approximately ten loans each year, typically in succession. Due to the accompanying expenses, a borrower will incur $458 in fees for a standard $350 loan with a duration of two weeks (Waliszewski, Cichowicz, Gębski, Kliber, Kubiczek, Niedziółka & Warchlewska, 2023).

These substantial fees might potentially have catastrophic ripple effects. As per the Financial Conduct Authority (FCA), 67% of individuals who borrow payday loans and 49% of individuals who borrow short-term installment loans in the UK are burdened with excessive debt, in contrast to only 15% of the general population in the UK. The inability to repay loans hinders borrowers from having sufficient funds to cover essential expenses, hence impacting the whole economy.

But individuals with low or inconsistent incomes are frequently the ones who want emergency payouts the most, and this need will never go away. Lenders justify their higher rates and fees by claiming that these borrowers carry a significantly higher chance of defaulting on a loan.

The Central Bank of China declared that it will progressively establish a framework of regulations governing Fintech and foster an atmosphere of policy that is conducive to Fintech growth. Draft revisions to regulations pertaining to financial instruments and payment services that will cap leverage in margin trading virtual currencies were approved by the Japanese cabinet. Acting pursuant to a recently passed Fintech legislation, the Mexican Central Bank last week suggested new rules that would restrict the number of cryptocurrency exchanges operating in the nation.

A consultation regarding the modification of federal law to accommodate advancements in distributed ledger technology has been launched by the Swiss Federal Council. Online banking licenses were initially issued by Hong Kong. The same oversight standards that apply to traditional banks will also apply to virtual banks throughout India. Businesses that offer BNPL services are enmeshed in a regulatory maze. The RBI has prohibited non-bank prepaid instruments (PPI) issuers from using credit lines to load their wallets or other PPI. Some BNPL players are afraid that this specific RBI move could be their last. Building transparency and adhering to regulations are demands made by Indian regulators. They want BNPL to operate under the regulatory framework while striking a balance between transparency and ease of use.

The RBI has also issued guidelines for the regulation of P2P lending platforms, which include requirements related to:

- Registration and licensing of P2P lending platforms
- Prudential norms for capital adequacy, leverage ratio and exposure limits
- Customer due diligence and KYC norms
- Fair practices code and transparency in operations
- Grievance redressal mechanism for borrowers and lenders
- Reporting and disclosure requirements to regulatory authorities

Future of the LendTech Sector

The future of the LendTech business looks promising as the industry continues to grow and evolve. With the rise of digital lending platforms, traditional financial institutions are facing increasing competition from Fintech companies that offer faster, more convenient and more accessible lending options.

One trend that is likely to continue is the shift toward online lending platforms. As more and more consumers turn to digital channels for their financial needs, lenders will need to adapt to this changing landscape by offering user-friendly, mobile-friendly and AI-driven platforms that can provide personalized and instant loan decisions.

Another trend that is likely to gain momentum is the use of alternative data sources for credit scoring. With the traditional credit scoring models becoming less relevant in the digital age, lenders are increasingly turning to alternative data sources such as social media activity, online shopping behavior and mobile phone usage to determine creditworthiness.

In addition, the use of machine learning and AI algorithms is becoming more prevalent in the lending industry. These technologies can help lenders automate their decision-making processes, reduce fraud risk and improve overall customer experience.

Overall, the LendTech business is poised for growth and innovation in the coming years, and companies that embrace these trends and technologies are likely to succeed in this competitive landscape (Pandey, 2022).

LendTech Companies

The digital lending business is growing exponentially across the world. In 2021, the LendTech market had a value of $8 billion. It is projected to increase at a compound annual growth rate of 23.2% from 2022 to 2031, reaching an estimated value of $61.9 billion (PR Newswire, 2023). This growth is mostly driven by the rising demand from the banking industry. Some of the prominent LendTech companies in the world follow.

LendingClub

LendingClub is a disruptive P2P lending platform that has transformed the borrowing and lending industry since its establishment in 2006. Established by Renaud Laplanche, it has emerged as one of the foremost and widely recognized organizations in the Fintech sector. LendingClub offers an Internet-based platform that links individuals seeking personal loans with investors interested in financing those loans, thereby eliminating conventional financial intermediaries such as banks.

The website is based on a straightforward principle: borrowers submit loan applications for many goals, such as consolidating debt, enhancing their homes, covering medical bills or obtaining capital for small businesses. LendingClub measures the creditworthiness of loan applicants by utilizing a unique credit scoring mechanism that is exclusive to their company. Once loans are approved, they are displayed on the site for investors to peruse and select which ones to finance. Investors have the opportunity to participate in fractional portions of loans, which enables them to diversify their investments over numerous borrowers and so decrease the risk associated with each particular borrower.

LendingClub offers borrowers the opportunity to obtain unsecured personal loans, which can range from a few thousand dollars to tens of thousands. These loans normally come with set interest rates and repayment periods that span from three to five years. The application process is conducted only through the Internet, ensuring convenience and accessibility for borrowers.

Investors on LendingClub can fund loans in increments as low as $25, enabling them to build a diversified portfolio of loans across different risk profiles. Investors earn returns through monthly principal and interest payments made by borrowers. The company offers an automated investing feature that allows investors to set specific criteria for loan selection, such as credit score, loan term and loan purpose. The platform then automatically invests in loans that meet these criteria on behalf of the investor.

LendingClub operates a secondary market where investors can buy and sell existing loan notes. This feature provides liquidity to investors who wish to exit their investments before the loan term expires. The company employs sophisticated risk assessment algorithms to evaluate borrower creditworthiness and assign appropriate interest rates to loans based on the risk level. This helps investors make informed decisions about which loans to fund.

As a financial services company, LendingClub is subject to various federal and state regulations governing consumer lending and securities offerings. The company adheres to strict regulatory standards, including those set forth by the Securities and Exchange Commission and the CFPB, to ensure compliance and protect the interests of both borrowers and investors.

LendingClub's innovative business model has had a significant impact on the lending industry, providing an alternative source of financing for borrowers and attractive investment opportunities for individuals and institutions. The company has facilitated billions of dollars in loans since its inception and continues to grow its user base and loan volume.

Despite its success, LendingClub has faced its share of challenges and controversies over the years. In 2016, the company's founder and CEO, Renaud Laplanche, resigned amid allegations of misconduct related to loan sales. Additionally, regulatory scrutiny and changes in the economic environment have posed challenges to LendingClub's operations and growth trajectory.

LendingClub has emerged as a trailblazer in the P2P lending space, leveraging technology to disrupt traditional lending models and democratize access to credit and investment opportunities. With its user-friendly platform, robust risk management practices and commitment to regulatory compliance, LendingClub continues to play a vital role in shaping the future of finance.

Lendermarket

Lendermarket is a rapidly growing P2P lending platform that specializes in providing investors with opportunities to invest in European consumer loans. Launched in 2019, Lendermarket has quickly gained traction in the Fintech industry by offering attractive returns and a user-friendly investment experience. The platform operates as an online marketplace, connecting investors with borrowers seeking personal loans across various European countries.

Lendermarket offers investors the opportunity to invest in short-term consumer loans originated by its parent company, Creditstar Group, which is a leading European digital consumer finance company. These loans are typically unsecured personal loans with durations ranging from one month to one year. Lendermarket boasts competitive interest rates, with annual returns for investors typically ranging from 12% to 14%, making it an attractive option for those seeking above-average returns on their investments.

Similar to other P2P lending platforms, Lendermarket provides investors with an auto-invest feature that allows them to set specific investment criteria, such as loan duration, interest rate and loan originator. The platform then automatically allocates funds to loans that match these criteria, streamlining the investment process.

Lendermarket offers a buyback guarantee on all loans, which means that in the event of borrower default, the loan originator repurchases the loan from the investor at the principal amount plus accrued interest. This feature provides investors with an added layer of protection against credit risk.

As a financial services provider, Lendermarket operates in compliance with European Union regulations governing P2P lending and consumer finance. The platform adheres to stringent regulatory standards to ensure investor protection and transparency. Lendermarket employs rigorous risk management practices to assess borrower creditworthiness and mitigate credit risk. The platform conducts thorough due diligence on loan originators and implements robust underwriting criteria to maintain loan quality and minimize defaults.

Lendermarket has emerged as a prominent player in the European P2P lending landscape, offering investors attractive returns and a diverse range of investment opportunities in consumer loans. With its emphasis on transparency, investor protection and user experience, Lendermarket continues to gain popularity among investors seeking alternative investment options outside of traditional financial markets. However, prospective investors should conduct thorough due diligence and carefully assess the associated risks before investing in P2P lending platforms like Lendermarket.

SoFi

SoFi, short for Social Finance, is a leading financial technology company that has transformed the landscape of financial services since its inception in 2011. Originally founded to provide student loan refinancing, SoFi has expanded its offerings to include a wide range of financial products and services, including personal loans, mortgages, investment management, insurance and banking solutions. The company's mission is to empower its members to achieve financial independence and success through innovative technology and personalized financial solutions.

SoFi gained early recognition for its student loan refinancing platform, which allows borrowers to consolidate and refinance their existing student loans into a single loan with lower interest rates and more favorable terms. This service has helped millions of borrowers reduce the burden of student loan debt and save money on interest payments.

SoFi offers unsecured personal loans with competitive interest rates and flexible repayment terms. Borrowers can use these loans for various purposes, such as debt consolidation, home improvement, travel or major purchases. It provides mortgage refinancing and home purchase loans, offering competitive rates and a streamlined application process. The company's digital platform simplifies the mortgage application and approval process, providing borrowers with a seamless experience.

SoFi offers investment management services through its automated investing platform, SoFi Invest. Investors can access a range of investment options, including stocks, exchange-traded funds and cryptocurrency, with no account minimums and low fees. It offers a range of insurance products, including life insurance, renters insurance and homeowners insurance, providing members with comprehensive coverage and peace of mind.

SoFi Money is a cash management account offered by SoFi that combines the features of a checking and savings account. Members can earn competitive interest rates on their deposits, access fee-free ATMs worldwide and enjoy other benefits such as mobile check deposits and bill pay.

SoFi provides members with access to financial education resources, including articles, guides, webinars and events, to help them make informed financial decisions. The company also fosters a sense of community among its members through networking events, social gatherings and online forums.

SoFi leverages cutting-edge technology and data analytics to deliver personalized financial solutions and enhance the overall customer experience. The company's digital platform incorporates AI, machine learning and automation into streamline processes; improves efficiency; and provides tailored recommendations to members based on their financial goals and preferences.

SoFi distinguishes itself from traditional financial institutions by fostering a strong sense of community among its members. Through networking events, social gatherings and online forums, SoFi creates opportunities for members to connect, share experiences and support each other on their financial journeys. Additionally, SoFi offers exclusive member benefits, such as discounts on financial products, career coaching services and invitations to special events and experiences.

Zopa

Zopa is a pioneering and highly visible P2P lending network, headquartered in the United Kingdom. Zopa, founded in 2005, has had a substantial impact on transforming the lending industry by directly linking borrowers with investors, thus circumventing conventional financial institutions. Zopa aims to offer easily accessible and reasonably priced loans, while also providing investors with appealing returns through its innovative platform.

Zopa provides borrowers with unsecured personal loans for a range of purposes, such as consolidating debt, making home improvements, funding trips and financing small businesses. Individuals have the option to request loans ranging from £1,000 to £25,000, and they can choose repayment terms that are adaptable to their financial situation.

Zopa provides investors with the opportunity to fund personal loans originated through its platform and earn returns on their investments. Investors can lend money across multiple loans, diversifying their portfolios to mitigate risk. Zopa offers different investment products, including Zopa Core, Zopa Plus and Zopa Access, each with varying risk profiles and potential returns.

Zopa offers an automated investment feature that allows investors to set specific criteria for loan selection, such as credit score, loan term and loan purpose. The platform then automatically allocates funds to loans that meet these criteria, simplifying the investment process.

Zopa operates in compliance with regulatory requirements set forth by the FCA in the UK, ensuring transparency, consumer protection and fair lending practices. The company adheres to strict regulatory standards to safeguard investor interests and maintain the integrity of its platform.

Since its inception, Zopa has facilitated billions of pounds in loans and has grown its customer base significantly. The platform has played a vital role in providing access to affordable credit for borrowers while offering attractive returns to investors. Zopa's innovative approach to lending has garnered recognition and accolades within the Fintech industry and has influenced the development of P2P lending globally.

Like other P2P lending platforms, Zopa faces challenges and controversies, including regulatory changes, economic downturns and credit risk. The platform must navigate regulatory requirements and adapt to evolving market conditions to ensure its long-term sustainability and success.

Zopa has established itself as a trailblazer in the P2P lending industry, pioneering a new model of lending that prioritizes transparency, efficiency and consumer empowerment. With its focus on providing accessible loans and attractive investment opportunities, Zopa continues to reshape the financial services landscape and drive innovation in the UK and beyond. As the company continues to grow and evolve, it remains committed to its mission of delivering fairer, smarter and more transparent financial services for all.

Auxmoney

Auxmoney is a prominent P2P loan network headquartered in Germany, established in 2007. The company has played a crucial role in revolutionizing the loan industry by directly linking borrowers with investors, offering an alternate means of funding that is not reliant on traditional banks. Auxmoney's platform facilitates individuals in obtaining cost-effective loans, while also providing investors with the chance to generate appealing returns by financing these loans.

Auxmoney provides unsecured personal loans to borrowers for a range of purposes, including consolidating debt, improving homes, financing vehicles and establishing small businesses. Applicants have the option to request loans ranging from a small sum of a few hundred euros to a substantial amount of tens of thousands, and they can choose from a variety of repayment arrangements that offer flexibility.

Auxmoney provides investors with the opportunity to fund personal loans originated through its platform and earn returns on their investments. Investors can diversify their portfolios by investing in fractions of loans across multiple borrowers, mitigating risk and maximizing potential returns.

Auxmoney utilizes proprietary credit scoring models and risk assessment algorithms to evaluate borrower creditworthiness and assign appropriate interest rates to loans based on the risk level. The platform conducts comprehensive credit checks, affordability assessments and fraud prevention measures to maintain loan quality and protect investor interests.

Auxmoney offers an automated investment feature that allows investors to set specific criteria for loan selection, such as credit score, loan term and loan purpose. The platform then automatically allocates funds to loans that meet these criteria, streamlining the investment process and maximizing efficiency.

Auxmoney operates a secondary market where investors can buy and sell existing loan holdings. This feature provides liquidity and flexibility for investors who wish to exit their investments before the loan term expires. It provides investors with transparent reporting and analytics tools to track their portfolio performance, monitor loan repayments and make informed investment decisions.

Auxmoney operates in compliance with regulatory requirements set forth by the German financial authorities, including the Federal Financial Supervisory Authority (BaFin). The company adheres to strict regulatory standards to ensure transparency, consumer protection and fair lending practices.

Auxmoney has played a significant role in providing access to affordable credit for individuals in Germany who may have difficulty obtaining loans through traditional banks. Since its inception, Auxmoney has facilitated billions of euros in loans and has grown its customer base significantly. The platform has garnered recognition within the Fintech industry and has contributed to the development of P2P lending in Germany and beyond.

Like other P2P lending platforms, Auxmoney faces challenges and controversies, including regulatory changes, economic uncertainties and credit risk. The company must navigate these challenges and adapt to evolving market conditions to ensure its long-term sustainability and success.

Auxmoney has emerged as a key player in the P2P lending industry, empowering borrowers and investors alike with its innovative platform and transparent approach to lending. With its focus on providing accessible loans and attractive investment opportunities, Auxmoney continues to reshape the financial services landscape in Germany and beyond. As the company continues to grow and evolve, it remains committed to its mission of delivering fairer, smarter and more inclusive financial services for all.

LendInvest

LendInvest is a prominent Fintech company specializing in property finance, particularly in the UK real estate market. Founded in 2008, LendInvest has established itself as a leading provider of bridging loans, development finance and buy-to-let mortgages. The company's innovative approach combines technology with real estate expertise to offer fast and flexible financing solutions to property professionals, investors and developers.

LendInvest provides short-term bridging loans to property investors and developers to finance the purchase of residential or commercial properties. These loans offer quick access to capital, typically with flexible terms and competitive interest rates. LendInvest offers development finance solutions to fund residential and commercial property development projects. The company provides tailored financing packages to support various stages of the development process, including land acquisition, construction and refinancing.

LendInvest offers buy-to-let mortgages for investors looking to purchase or refinance rental properties. The company provides financing options for individual properties as well as portfolio loans for investors with multiple properties. LendInvest's online platform provides borrowers with a streamlined application process, allowing them to submit loan applications quickly and track the progress of their loans in real time. The platform also offers investors access to a range of investment opportunities, including loan notes and investment funds.

LendInvest employs rigorous risk management practices to assess borrower creditworthiness and mitigate risk. The company conducts thorough due diligence on each loan application, including property valuations, borrower financials and market analysis.

LendInvest has played a significant role in providing access to property finance for individuals and businesses in the UK. Since its inception, the company has facilitated billions of pounds in loans, supporting thousands of property transactions and development projects. LendInvest's innovative approach to lending has earned it recognition within the Fintech industry and positioned it as a trusted partner for property professionals and investors.

As with any financial services company, LendInvest faces challenges such as regulatory changes, market fluctuations and credit risk. However, the company also has opportunities for growth, including expanding its product offerings, entering new markets and leveraging technology to enhance its platform and services.

In conclusion, LendInvest continues to play a vital role in the UK property finance market, providing innovative financing solutions to support property investment and development. With its focus on technology, expertise and customer service, LendInvest is well-positioned for continued success in the evolving landscape of real estate finance.

Faircent

Faircent was started by Rajat Gandhi in 2013 as a NBFC-P2P Company. This company is a pioneer in the field of P2P lending and ushered in a revolution in the lending industry long before RBI formulated laws to regulate the P2P lending business. This company was awarded by the *Economic Times* in 2018 for being the most promising Fintech startup. It has played a key role in delivering banking to the unbanked since its inception. It has more than 80,000 lenders registered in its P2P platform. These lenders have given more than INR 50 crores of loans to around five lakh borrowers.

The P2P lending platform offered by Faircent is technology-based and is available both as iOS and Android Apps. Loans can be availed through their user-friendly website. They have an innovative tool called AutoInvest, which is fully automated with AIML which helps to match the borrower's requirements and the lender's proposals.

On the Faircent P2P platform, different entities can get themselves registered as borrowers and lenders. Faircent follows a comprehensive background and verification check with KYC documents like Aadhar card, bank details and KYC. Once the information is verified, the different entities can get themselves registered as borrowers or lenders. The automated system of Faircent matches the borrower's requirement with the lender's proposals so that both parties can get the best rates and a fair deal.

A single lender can lend to multiple parties, and a borrower can borrow from multiple lenders. Once the offers are matched, a formal contract is signed between the borrower and lender. The repayment is also done through the same automated P2P platform. The repayments can be made through EMIs every month. The technology-enabled P2P platform of Faircent offers a smooth and user-friendly experience and helps the functions run in a seamless manner through an automated process.

Lendingkart

Lendingkart is a leading Fintech company in India that offers innovative and technology-driven solutions to meet the financing needs of SMEs. By leveraging data analytics, automation and digital platforms, Lendingkart provides quick, convenient and customized lending solutions that empower businesses to thrive and grow in today's competitive landscape.

It provides working capital loans to small- and medium-sized enterprises (SMEs) through its online platform. The company operates an online platform where SMEs can apply for working capital loans. The application process is streamlined and user-friendly, allowing businesses to submit their loan applications with minimal documentation and paperwork.

Lendingkart utilizes advanced data analytics and machine learning algorithms to assess the creditworthiness of borrowers. The platform analyzes various data points, including financial statements, bank transactions, GST filings, credit history and business performance metrics to evaluate the risk profile of applicants.

It offers instant approval decisions on loan applications, often within minutes. Once approved, funds are disbursed to the borrower's bank account quickly, allowing businesses to access working capital when they need it most. The company offers a range of loan products tailored to the needs of SMEs, including term loans, line of credit and invoice financing. Borrowers can choose the loan amount, repayment tenure and financing options that best suit their business requirements.

Lendingkart provides collateral-free loans, eliminating the need for businesses to pledge assets or provide security to obtain financing. This makes the lending process more accessible and less burdensome for SMEs, particularly those with limited tangible assets. It offers customized interest rates based on the risk profile of borrowers and the specific terms of the loan. Interest rates are determined using proprietary algorithms that factor in credit risk, market conditions and other relevant parameters.

Lendingkart leverages technology to automate and streamline its lending operations. This includes digital underwriting, document verification, loan processing and payment disbursal, resulting in a fast, efficient and paperless lending experience for borrowers. It provides personalized customer support to assist borrowers throughout the loan application and repayment process. Dedicated relationship managers are available to address queries, provide guidance and ensure a positive customer experience.

Lendingkart provides SMEs with access to working capital financing, enabling them to fund their day-to-day operations, manage cash flow and pursue growth opportunities. It offers a quick and convenient lending experience, with instant approval decisions and fast disbursal of funds. This allows businesses to seize opportunities and address financial challenges without delay. Lendingkart's collateral-free loans make financing more accessible to SMEs that may lack tangible assets or are hesitant to pledge collateral. This reduces barriers to entry and encourages entrepreneurship and business expansion.

Lendingkart provides personalized loan solutions specifically designed to meet the distinct requirements and situations of individual borrowers. This adaptability guarantees that firms can secure funding that is in line with their specific needs and financial goals. Data analytics and machine learning facilitate precise and efficient credit evaluation, leading to improved loan pricing, risk management and lending decisions. Lendingkart guarantees strict compliance with all regulatory obligations to uphold confidence, credibility and legal conformity, therefore protecting the interests of borrowers, investors and other stakeholders.

Questions for Discussion

1. Explain what you understand by P2P networks.
2. Explain how the P2P network is used in digital lending.
3. Explain the different business models used in digital lending.
4. What do you understand by crowdfunding? Explain with examples.
5. Explain how the Fintech Model of Lending is different from the traditional model of lending.

Case Study – How BNPL Created a Storm in the Indian Markets

One-third of the Indian population lies in the middle-class category whose annual income is between INR 10 lakhs to INR 30 lakhs ($12,000 to $35,000). Most of the middle-class population in India work in different companies and have a typical buying and spending behavior. They get a salary between the 1st and 7th of every month and spend generously till the 15th of the month. They are cash-strapped between the 25th and 31st of the month and mostly refrain from spending or buying any goods and services.

However, they do buy products from the local Kirana shop (Mom-n-Pop stores) where they get a short-term credit. The accounts are settled in the first week of the month when the salary comes into their account. Amazon and Flipkart, the leading e-commerce players in India, noticed this typical Indian middle class, which constitutes a population of 432 million people, and introduced the BNPL scheme to lure people into buying products and services from e-commerce sites throughout the month.

The BNPL market in India has witnessed remarkable growth. In 2022, it was estimated to be around INR 363.0 billion ($4.9 billion), reflecting a substantial increase of 125.8%. The major players in the Indian BNPL market are Amazon Pay Later, Flipkart Pay Later, ZestMoney and BharatPe.

The pay later service offered by Amazon is the rebranded form of Amazon Pay EMI, that can be used within the Amazon ecosystem. It offers instant credit, via a completely digital process, for purchases using EMI on Amazon.in. After signing in, customers need to go to Amazon Pay and register for the service to use it. They will see an option to begin registration for the Amazon Pay Later service on this webpage. The e-KYC process is pretty quick and easy for those who have already completed the KYC process for their Amazon Pay accounts. Others can still take advantage of it by simply uploading digital copies of their documents and verifying their PAN, Aadhar and phone number information.

Users of the Amazon Pay Later service will be able to pay off the entire balance due the next month. There will be no interest charged if they do this, and they will simply be repaying what they spent. If they spend more than INR 3,000 ($35), they will be automatically eligible to repay it in three months. An amount of interest will be levied in this scenario.

Launched in April 2020, it already boasts over 3.7 million registered users, leveraging Amazon's existing customer base. BNPL services have significantly impacted sales in India, driving growth in the e-commerce sector.

BNPL services have indeed created a significant impact in the Indian credit market, disrupting traditional lending practices and reshaping consumer behavior. BNPL has created a storm in the Indian credit market. BNPL services have democratized access to credit by providing an alternative financing option for consumers who may not qualify for traditional credit cards or loans. This has enabled a broader segment of the population, including young adults, students and individuals with limited credit history, to make purchases and manage their finances more flexibly.

BNPL services offer a seamless and convenient payment experience for consumers, allowing them to make purchases online or in-store with just a few clicks or taps. The simplicity of the BNPL process eliminates the need for lengthy credit checks, paperwork or complex application procedures, making it an attractive option for time-pressed consumers.

BNPL allows consumers to split their purchases into smaller, interest-free installments, often spanning several weeks or months. This deferred payment model provides consumers with greater financial flexibility and control, allowing them to spread out the cost of their purchases over time and manage their cash flow more effectively.

Many BNPL services offer interest-free financing if consumers make timely payments according to the agreed-upon schedule. Even when interest charges apply, they are often lower than those associated with traditional credit cards or personal loans, making BNPL a cost-effective financing option for consumers.

Unlike traditional lending products, BNPL services typically do not require consumers to undergo credit checks or provide collateral to qualify for financing. This makes BNPL more accessible to individuals with varying credit profiles and financial backgrounds, including those with limited credit history or subprime credit scores.

BNPL providers have formed partnerships with a wide range of merchants, including e-commerce platforms, retail chains and brick-and-mortar stores, to offer BNPL as a payment option at checkout. This widespread acceptance has accelerated the adoption of BNPL among consumers, driving transaction volumes and merchant revenues.

The BNPL market in India has witnessed rapid growth in recent years, fueled by increasing consumer demand for flexible payment options and the proliferation of digital platforms. Several domestic and international BNPL players have entered the Indian market, intensifying competition and innovation in the sector. Experts predict that the BNPL market in India will continue to grow rapidly. Redseer estimates that India's BNPL market could reach an impressive $45–50 billion by 2026, up from the current $3–3.5 billion.

BNPL has fundamentally changed consumer behavior and spending patterns, encouraging impulse purchases and driving higher transaction volumes. The convenience and immediacy of BNPL encourage consumers to make purchases they might otherwise have deferred or foregone, leading to increased consumption and economic activity.

The rapid growth of BNPL has attracted regulatory scrutiny from authorities such as the RBI and the Securities and Exchange Board of India. Regulators are concerned about consumer protection, fair lending practices, transparency and systemic risks associated with BNPL, prompting them to explore regulatory frameworks to govern the sector effectively.

In summary, BNPL services have revolutionized the way Indians shop online, providing a convenient and accessible payment option that fuels e-commerce sales and caters to the evolving needs of consumers. BNPL services have disrupted the Indian credit market by offering consumers an alternative financing option that is convenient, accessible and flexible. However, the rapid growth of BNPL has also raised concerns about consumer debt, regulatory oversight and systemic risks, underscoring the need for balanced regulation and responsible lending practices in the BNPL sector.

Case Study Questions

1. Explain the working mechanism of BNPL in India. Why is BNPL an attractive option for Indian buyers and customers?
2. What is the process followed by Amazon for offering BNPL services to customers?
3. Do a comparative analysis of BNPL services offered by Amazon and Flipkart and explain which one is better.

Further Reading

1. The power of digital lending, Gerald Chappell, McKinsey.com. www.mckinsey.com/industries/financial-services/our-insights/banking-matters/the-power-of-digital-lending
2. The rise of P2P lending in India by David Akizbir. Jupiter Capital. www.jupitercapital.in/blog/the-rise-of-p2p-lending-in-india/

References

Basha, S. A., Elgammal, M. M., & Abuzayed, B. M. (2021). Online peer-to-peer lending: A review of the literature. *Electronic Commerce Research and Applications*, 48, 101069.

Cornelli, G., Frost, J., Gambacorta, L., Rau, P. R., Wardrop, R., & Ziegler, T. (2023). FinTech and big tech credit: Drivers of the growth of digital lending. *Journal of Banking & Finance*, 148, 106742.

Gerrans, P., Baur, D. G., & Lavagna-Slater, S. (2022). FinTech and responsibility: Buy-now-pay-later arrangements. *Australian Journal of Management*, 47(3), 474–502.

Guerar, M., Merlo, A., Migliardi, M., Palmieri, F., & Verderame, L. (2020). A fraud-resilient blockchain-based solution for invoice financing. *IEEE Transactions on Engineering Management*, 67(4), 1086–1098.

Kayo, E. K., da Silva, W. E., & Martelanc, R. (2023). The two faces of subsidized loans. *Finance Research Letters*, 56, 104149.

Koeda, J. (2004). Grants or concessional loans? Aid to low-income countries with a participation constraint. *Job Market Paper* (pp. 1–37). University of California, Los Angeles.

Mann, R. J. (2022). Explaining the pattern of secured credit. In *The creation and interpretation of commercial law* (pp. 347–405). Routledge.

Melitz, J., & Pardue, M. (1973). The demand and supply of commercial bank loans. *Journal of Money, Credit and Banking*, 5(2), 669–692.

Ohlendorf, K. R. (2023). "No friends in the industry": The dominance of tech companies on digital music. In *Virtual identities and digital culture*, edited by V. Kannen & A. Langille. Taylor and Francis. https://www.routledge.com/Virtual-Identities-and-Digital-Culture/Kannen-Langille/p/book/9781032315089?srsltid=AfmBOopR4ryzYvXyxQJKSdzZQToxp6k0IyvLrFn-Awsf2P3jUssgJ5DU

Pandey, K. K. (2022). A study on role of FinTech in digital lending: Status quo and way forward. *International Journal on Research and Analytical Reviews*, 9(4), 83–91.

PR Newswire. (2023). Global $61.9 billion LendTech market opportunity analysis and industry forecasts, 2021–2022 & 2022–2031. *Yahoo Finance*. https://www.prnewswire.com/news-releases/global-61-9-billion-lendtech-market-opportunity-analysis-and-industry-forecasts-2021-2022--2022-2031--301846280.html

Raja, T. S. N. (2021). Trade Receivables Discount Scheme (TReDS). *The Management Accountant Journal*, 56(1), 72–75.

Tiwari, K. K., & Somani, R. (2021). Why unsecured loan having high loan delinquency. *International Business Management*, 15(6), 262–268.

Waliszewski, K., Cichowicz, E., Gębski, Ł., Kliber, F., Kubiczek, J., Niedziółka, P., & Warchlewska, A. (2023). The role of the LendTech sector in the consumer credit market in the context of household financial exclusion. *Oeconomia Copernicana*, 14(2), 609–643.

Xu, J., & Vadgama, N. (2022). From banks to defi: The evolution of the lending market. In *Future of business and finance* (pp. 53–66). Springer Nature Link.

6 The WealthTech Model

After reading this chapter you will:

- Get knowledge about the wealth management lifecycle
- Understand what are robo-advisors
- Get knowledge about micro-investment services (MISs)
- Know about digital portfolio management
- Understand the working mechanism of algorithmic trading
- Understand how digital brokerages work

Normally, for wealth management, people approach a personal financial advisor or wealth manager who designs a portfolio of investment assets based on the investment goals and risk appetite of their clients. However, being human beings, wealth managers are biased toward a particular asset class like equities, debt instruments, commodities or real estate. There are also chances of manipulation by wealth managers because of the commissions they receive from different entities. The portfolio construction may not be a foolproof exercise and might be vulnerable and susceptible to human errors that will lead to wealth erosion for the investors. The subprime crisis of 2008 proved beyond doubt that the bankers and fund managers had not followed the due diligence process of doing risk analysis while managing the money of the investors and depositors.

As the trust of the investors on human intelligence declined following the aftermath of the 2008 subprime crisis, some of the wealth management companies came out with a new process called WealthTech. The companies that led the WealthTech Revolution were Vanguard, Betterment, Charles Schwab and Wealthfront. Robo-advisors, algorithmic traders, digital wealth management platforms and online investment platforms are examples of WealthTech solutions. The global WealthTech market size was valued at US$ 9,788.46 million in 2022 and is expected to expand at a compound annual growth rate of 25.23% during the forecast period, reaching US$ 37,746.2 million by 2028.

A company that has created ripples in the Indian WealthTech market is Zerodha. Zerodha has taken the Indian wealth management markets by storm with its zero customer acquisition cost (CAC) strategy. With over 6.4 million clients, Zerodha has grown to become India's largest stock brokerage firm. In a market where brokerage commissions were fixed, Zerodha introduced India's first discount broking model with zero brokerage fees on equity delivery trades. This supported rapid customer acquisition while positioning Zerodha as an innovator. The bootstrapped startup's meteoric rise has disrupted traditional brokerages while ushering in greater investment participation across

DOI: 10.4324/9781032699417-6

the country. Behind this remarkable success lies a customer-centric marketing strategy focused on education, innovation and simplification.

Moreover, Zerodha has been at the forefront of leveraging technology to enhance the trading experience. The company has introduced initiatives such as "Varsity", an educational platform offering comprehensive resources on investing and trading, and "Coin", a platform for investing in direct mutual funds.

Zerodha has democratized investing for millions while cementing its brand as India's brokerage of choice for digital natives and savvy investors alike. The stage is set for even faster growth as more Indians discover the wealth-building power now accessible at their fingertips.

Wealth Management Life Cycle

Wealth management takes up different forms as a human being passes through different stages of life. The different stages of the wealth management lifecycle are wealth accumulation, wealth management, wealth preservation and wealth distribution (Kolkman, 2018). To manage the different needs at each stage of life, wealth must be optimally managed in each of these cycles.

Wealth Accumulation

This is the first phase in the lifecycle of wealth management. An individual needs to accumulate wealth before it can be managed optimally and there are several proven ways of accomplishing this target. What are the imperatives in this part of the wealth management lifecycle? Having a strong income base is the first step toward wealth accumulation. Individuals must ensure at least one or two steady sources of income if they wish to

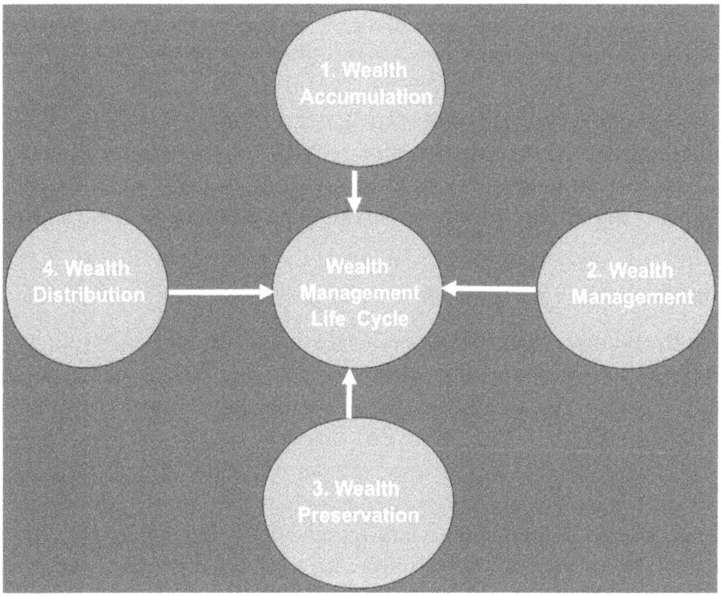

Figure 6.1 The Wealth Management Life

accumulate wealth sustainably. This can include anything from a well-paying occupation to a prosperous business.

Once the wealth begins to flow in, it is essential to divide it into segments – what people spend and what they save. The wealth saved must then be invested in appropriate avenues based on the risk profile and life goals. If a person is young and capable of withstanding high risk, the equity markets and equity mutual funds are strong avenues for high returns investment.

Wealth Management

While the wealth accumulation phase is likely to continue throughout life, depending on career and investments, it is now important to focus on managing the accumulated wealth appropriately. Life goals come at the forefront of the equation. Each person has certain goals in life – these could range from buying a house and creating an education fund for children to taking a long vacation or starting another business. Each of these goals requires a major outflow of wealth.

To accomplish life goals and create a robust investment portfolio, a person must create an asset allocation strategy that takes into consideration the time frame of their goals, the return requirements and their risk profile. Based on these parameters, a person can invest the accumulated wealth in short-, mid- and long-term wealth management avenues. Generally, if a person has a long-term investment horizon, he or she should look to grow their wealth through investments in equity and equity-related products. Due to the long-term horizon, the person becomes better positioned to withstand equity market volatility and benefit from its growth potential.

Wealth Preservation

The third stage is wealth preservation. Wealth preservation is as important as wealth accumulation. To adequately manage this part of the financial lifecycle, it is required to allocate a part of the corpus to investments that are secure and can still offer good returns. This is akin to creating a safety net. An ideal investment choice could be structured products that can potentially generate good returns with relatively lower risk than equities. While longer-term investments ensure wealth preservation for the future, there is also a need to create an emergency fund by investing in very low-risk and highly liquid instruments. This fund will go a long way in keeping a person solvent in times of crisis.

Wealth Distribution

The last part of the financial lifecycle is wealth distribution. This phase includes bequeathing the assets to the future generation while also securing resources for personal agendas like retirement, traveling or philanthropy. Also termed "legacy planning", this phase involves creating a will or a trust that can disperse the wealth and assets as per the requirement. This step ensures the proper transfer of everything, from property to other investments to the family members or beneficiaries in the event of disability or death.

This cycle of wealth management has traditionally been managed by experienced wealth managers. But now with the complexity of asset types and the growing importance of proper asset allocation, more and more people are shifting toward automated processes like robo-advisory services (RASs) and algorithmic trading. The growing use of automation in investments has also led to the democratization of the process, thus bringing in micro-investment services, where one can start investing with a small sum of as little as a hundred rupees. This whole new area of wealth management using technology is known as WealthTech.

Introduction to WealthTech

WealthTech is the application of technology in wealth management to maximize returns with minimum risk. The new breed of wealth management companies is using the latest technologies like robotics, artificial intelligence (AI), machine learning and big data analytics to analyze data and create effective portfolios for investment (Chishti & Puschmann, 2018).

Some of the applications of WealthTech are:

- RASs
- Algorithmic trading
- Digital portfolio management
- MISs

WealthTech is becoming popular because of the use of robo-advisors, algorithmic trading, technology-based portfolio services and micro-investment services that use big data and AI. Robo-advisors are automated platforms that operate on digital technologies and use algorithms to make decisions on investment analysis and portfolio management. Robo-advisors use online surveys to collect information about the financial objectives of the investors, set goals and then use technology-based algorithmic processes to meet the goals (Cull, 2022).

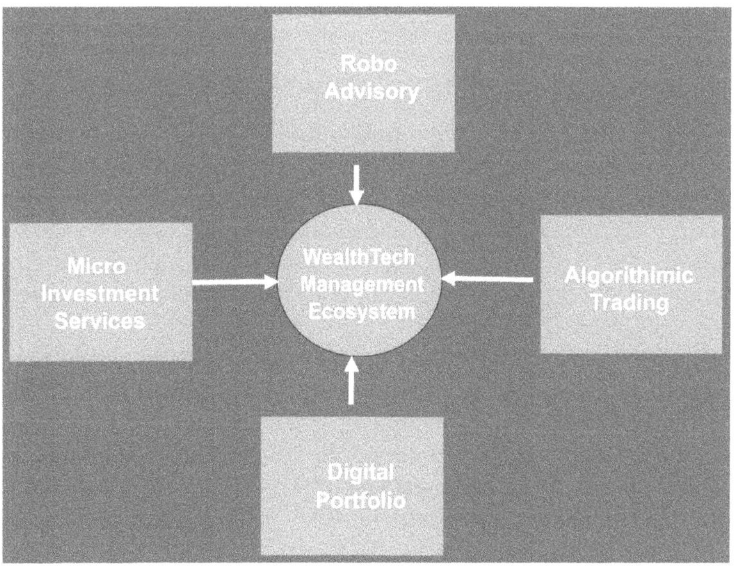

Figure 6.2 The WealthTech Ecosystem

Algorithmic trading is a type of trading that uses computer programs to execute trades automatically based on predefined rules and algorithms. These programs can analyze market data and make trades in fractions of a second, allowing traders to take advantage of even small market movements. Algorithmic trading can be used for a variety of financial instruments, including stocks, futures and currencies. One of the benefits of algorithmic trading is that it can help traders make more efficient and profitable trades by removing emotions and human biases from the decision-making process. Additionally, algorithmic trading can help traders diversify their portfolios and reduce risk by allowing them to trade a large number of instruments simultaneously. However, it's important to note that algorithmic trading also has its downsides, such as the potential for errors and the need for advanced technical expertise (Bao, Nekrasova, Neugebauer & Riyanto, 2022).

The digital portfolio and brokerage firms are also on the rise. They do not physically interact with their clients. They have websites and mobile apps and they use SMS and WhatsApp to interact with the clients. The services are also imparted using technology. One of the most popular services is algorithmic trading where there is no requirement for human intervention and the trading activities are carried out through predesigned technology-based algorithms (Moss, 2022).

MISs help small investors to enter the market with small amounts of money. This is made possible by applying technology to reduce transaction fees so that investors can afford the services and also use the services for making small investments. The transaction fees can be as low as $1 per month, as technology helps the micro-investment service companies play the volume game (Riitsalu & Uusberg, 2021).

Groww, started by Lalit Keshre, Harsh Jain, Neeraj Singh and Ishan Bansal has recently become the fastest-growing financial services company and a billion-dollar Unicorn. The company uses an automated technology platform to help investors invest in stocks, mutual funds, ETFs, IPOs and gold. Their automated platform currently has 1.5 crore registered users. They are right now among the top five investment companies in India, having the fifth-largest number of demat accounts.

Robo-Advisory Services

Planning the investments and creating a portfolio that can maximize returns and minimize risks is not an easy task. With people leading a fast-paced life, they hardly get time to choose investment products and track their investments. With too many investment advisors offering too many suggestions, understanding what could be the right decision is also a daunting task. Robo-advisors are now making life easy for investors by using analytics, automated processes and algorithms to help investors make the right investment decisions.

Immediately after the financial crisis of 2008, the first RASs were launched by Jon Stein, who launched a company called Betterment. A robo-advisor is a digital platform that provides algorithm-driven automated investing services. Investors started liking RASs for their digital interface, user-friendliness, accuracy, reliability and low fees. The popularity of RASs started growing very fast and by 2015, there were more than 100 companies offering this type of service. The RAS companies now manage more than $200 billion in assets under management (AUM).

Very soon, the top financial services companies like Charles Schwab, TD Ameritrade and Vanguard also jumped into the fray offering robo-advisory services. The RAS offered by Vanguard is called digital advisor. The minimum investment limit in the digital advisor is $3,000, and they charge net annual advisory fees of 0.15%. The RAS uses algorithms to create and manage portfolios of their clients. Most of the investment is done in exchange-traded funds (ETF) of Vanguard. This service is good for passive investors who are looking for personalized, automated investment portfolios.

One of the pioneers of WealthTech, Betterment provides a robotic process advisory platform that utilizes technology to provide automated and algorithm-driven financial advisory services. Betterment's approach to WealthTech involves the use of robotic process advisors (RPAs), commonly known as robo-advisors, which are algorithmic systems designed to provide financial advice and investment management services.

The use of RPAs by Betterment is a manifestation of WealthTech, which leverages technology to make financial services more efficient, accessible and personalized. By automating various aspects of investment management and financial planning, Betterment aims to provide a streamlined and cost-effective solution for individuals seeking professional financial advice without the high fees associated with traditional human advisors.

A robo-advisor is defined as "a digital financial advisor that provides financial advice or manages investments with moderate to minimal human intervention". Robo-advisors run on software that uses algorithms to understand the investor's goals and create a diverse portfolio based on the client's risk profile and objectives. The whole function is carried out in an automated manner. The software present in the robo-advisor takes up the execution of critical functions like asset allocation, asset management and risk-and-return optimization based on the client's needs (Bhatia, Chandani, Atiq, Mehta & Divekar, 2021).

Presently, there are more than a hundred robo-advisory firms across the world. There are two types of robo-advisors – simplistic robo-advisors (SRA) and comprehensive robo-advisors (CRA). The SRA sends a questionnaire to the investors and designs the investment portfolio based on the risk-return appetite. CRA is more sophisticated than SRA and does predictive analytics using AI to create a portfolio that will not only meet current needs but also take care of future requirements. The CRA does scenario planning using computerized simulation models that take care of different types of financial risks with optimization techniques. As an example, we can take the instance of a robo-advisory company called INDwealth. The company uses machine learning to provide users with hyper-personalized advice in real time.

The robo-advisory firms are currently managing more than $200 billion of AUM. The top robo-advisory firms in the world are given in Table 6.1.

Table 6.1 The Robo-Advisory Firms

Sl No	*Company*	*Country*	*Assets Under Management (AUM) ($)*
1	The Vanguard Company	USA	83 billion
2	Charles Schwab Corporation	USA	33 billion
3	TD Ameritrade	USA	20 billion
4	Nutmeg	Great Britain	1.9 billion
5	Wealthsimple	Canada	750 million
6	Kuvera	India	1.97 Billion

Source: Investopedia.com.

RASs have been permitted in different countries under strict Government supervision. The Securities and Exchange Commission regulates RASs in the USA while the Financial Conduct Authority regulates the business in the UK.

There are three types of robo-advisory firms in India. They are fund-based robo-advisory, equity-based robo-advisory and comprehensive robo-advisory. The fund-based

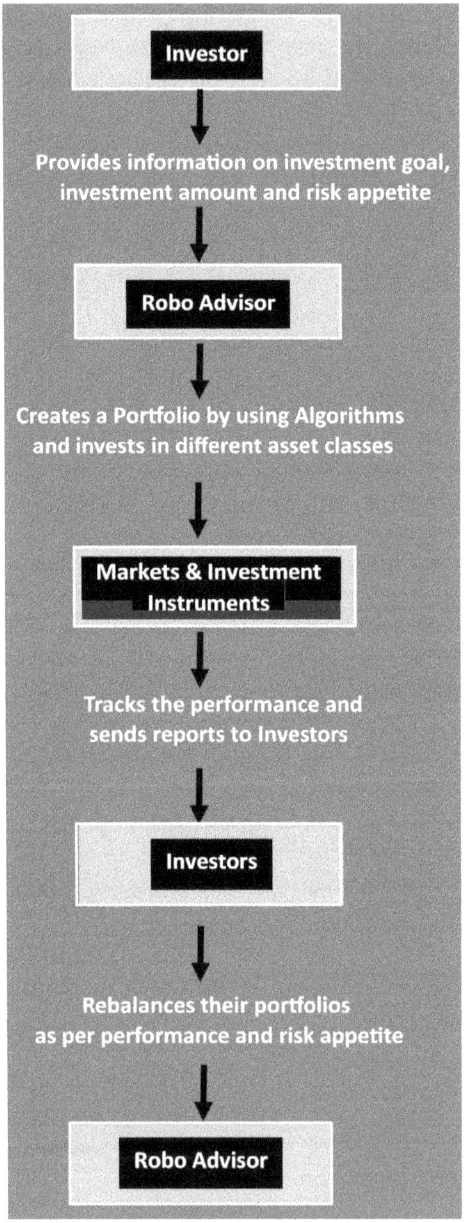

Figure 6.3 Working Mechanism of Robo-Advisors

robo-advisory is good for risk-averse investors. Here, there is no direct exposure to equity. This operates on the risk profiling method and gives goal-based suggestions.

The equity-based robo-advisory is offered to investors who have moderate to high-risk appetite. Here, the focus is only on the equity asset class. In this case, there are offerings based on sector-wise and thematic portfolios also.

In the comprehensive robo-advisory, the focus is on providing complete wealth management solutions. The various services offered are financial planning, portfolio management services, wealth management and estate planning. A fee is charged for a packaged combination of services.

The robo-advisory process starts with making a questionnaire to understand the investor's needs, goals and risk appetite. The questionnaire will have questions on demographic and psychographic profiling like age, gender, income, liabilities, willingness to take on risk and current asset allocation. Based on the requirement, the simplistic robo-advisory firms apply algorithms to build a portfolio that optimizes the risk and returns. The CRA applies machine learning and AI to deep dive into the data and create portfolios that are futuristic and risk-proof (Cull, 2022).

The main difference between normal wealth management firms and robo-advisors is in the use of distribution channels. Normal wealth management firms use offices and physical channels and do advisory and collection through human agents. The robo-advisory firms depend on electronic channels and apply the investment process through automated channels with a bare minimum of human intervention. RASs have helped wealth management firms to create new business opportunities. RASs are becoming the backbone and DNA of WealthTech.

There are two specialized services offered by robo-advisory firms. They are called robo-retirement and robo-tax-loss harvesting. In the case of robo-retirement, the firm creates and manages the retirement plan of the client using automated tools like analytics and algorithms. While most retirement fund managers would charge something between 1% and 2% for their services, robo-retirement firms charge between 0.14% and 0.15% of the AUM.

The robo-tax-loss harvesting is an automated service for investors who want to do tax planning using automated tools and platforms. In the case of tax-loss harvesting, a portion of the securities or assets is sold at a loss to avoid paying capital gains loss. This is a complicated mechanism that is made easy by RAS firms by applying algorithms and doing the trading on automated platforms. This kind of complicated advice is available at a low cost through robo-advisory firms.

Algorithmic Trading

Algorithmic trading uses automated built-in functions that are programmed to look for arbitrage opportunities and execute them. The software analyzes data like price and volume and chooses the precise timing when the returns can be maximized. The process utilizes complex formulas combined with mathematical models and human oversight, to make decisions to buy or sell financial securities on an exchange. Algorithmic trading can execute high volumes of trade in a flash of a second. This type of trading is used for various purposes like order execution, arbitrage and analyzing trends to create trading strategies (Chan, 2021).

Working Mechanism of Algorithmic Trading

The algorithmic trading process can be split into three major areas – pre-trade analysis, trading signal generation and trade order execution. In the pre-trade analysis, the financial data is collected to analyze the properties of an asset. Then the software and

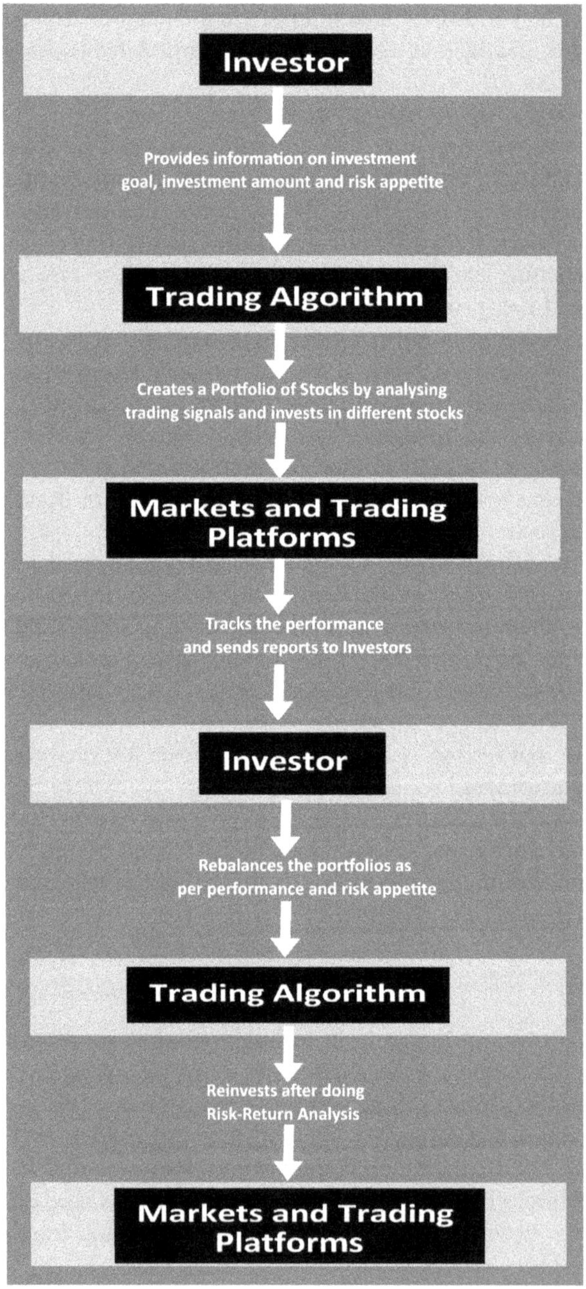

Figure 6.4 Algorithmic Trading Mechanism

algorithm are used to generate an actual trading signal. Finally, the trade orders are placed and executed through stock exchanges.

There are three components in pre-trade analysis – the alpha model, the risk model and the transaction cost model. The alpha model predicts the future behavior of the investment instrument. The risk model evaluates the level of risk the investment is exposed to. The transaction cost model calculates the potential cost that might be incurred in the transaction.

During the trading signal stage, the inputs from the alpha model, the risk model and the transaction cost model are taken to construct an effective portfolio that can do the risk-return optimization. The algorithm tries to bring down the risk as much as possible and maximize the returns to the highest possible extent. In the trade execution stage, the Execution Model completes the execution by placing orders on the stock exchange (Kissell, 2020).

Algorithmic trading right now is restricted only to big brokers, large fund houses and institutional investors. The costs and risks involved in algorithmic trading are justified only when the trading volumes are high. Algorithmic trading can both create liquidity and destroy liquidity. If the market movement and data analysis do not move in tandem, the trader may incur huge losses in algorithmic trading. The scalping trading strategy commonly employs algorithms because it involves rapid buying and selling of securities at small price increments.

Digital Portfolio Management

Portfolio Managers are the people who invest money on behalf of their clients into a basket of asset classes to reduce the risks and maximize the returns. The job of a portfolio manager is to optimize market risks and market returns to ensure that the client meets the goals of the investments. But, over the years, the cost of the services offered by portfolio managers has been rising steeply, while the performance has seen a sharp decline. To correct the anomaly, many investment advisory and portfolio management companies have started digital portfolio management services (Eckert & Hüsig, 2022).

Digital portfolio management services are typically offered through apps. The money is invested through apps and managed by automated algorithms. The apps use big data analytics to process the data and AI and machine learning to run simulations and build model portfolios. The apps keep the investors updated about the performance and help to make smart and better-informed decisions. Investors can even create a real-life portfolio or a watchlist of ideas to monitor.

The digital portfolios run by the apps are generally of two types – individual or institutional. Individual investments are done with shorter timelines and smaller amounts. Institutional investment is done with a larger portfolio, longer timelines and multiple clients.

The digital portfolio apps offer a myriad of free services along with paid options. Most of the advice is given for free. With payment, the investors can get complete access and additional services. Investment activities like buy, sell and trade involve fees.

The digital portfolio apps help digital brokerage firms leverage a foundational broker management system for the following advantages:

- Identifying investment opportunities
- Creating digital connections between clients and brokers
- Proper interaction with clients through mobiles and WhatsApp
- Offer services through the cloud

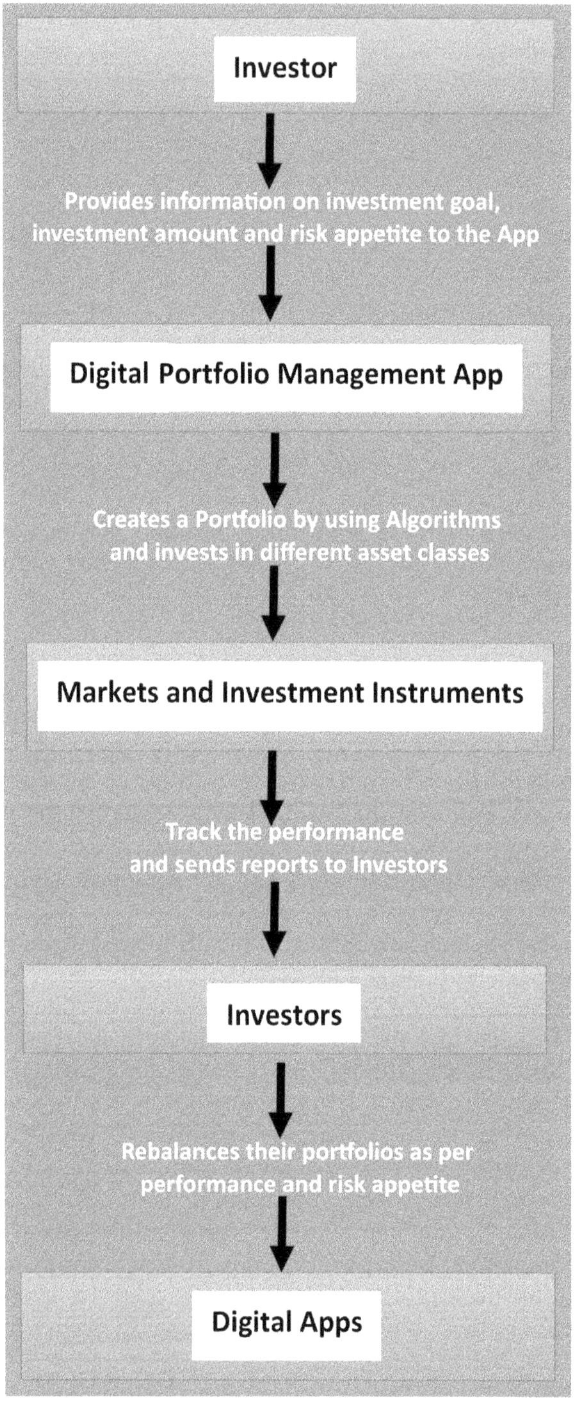

Figure 6.5 Working Mechanism of Digital Portfolio Management System

To thrive in current challenging scenarios, brokers must go for digital transformation and adopt digital. Consumers are expecting fast and user-friendly services and this is possible only through digital portfolio services. To become a digital brokerage, a business must have a digital transformation plan to support digital strategies.

Micro-Investment Services

One of the biggest beneficiaries of WealthTech is MISs. By employing technology in wealth management, investment advisory companies have been able to drastically cut down on operating costs and hence accept low deposits from investors. This has largely benefited the small-scale investors who till now could not avail of the services of specialist financial advisors. Investment in MIS platforms starts at as low as $1 and many of the services are given free of cost (Riitsalu & Uusberg, 2021).

Like RAS, MIS also depends on technology to run its operations. The investments are done only through the website or apps. The automated technology and algorithms analyze the data to decide on the securities and other asset classes where the money should be invested to build a portfolio. Human intervention in the whole process is kept to a bare minimum and hence the operating costs and infrastructure costs also come down in a big way. Because of the low costs incurred due to the widespread use of technology, micro-investment firms can give the opportunity to small investors to invest in their platforms.

Micro-investment services are a great way for individuals to start investing in the stock market with small amounts of money. These services allow users to invest in fractional shares of stocks, which means that they can invest in a company's stock without having to buy a whole share. This makes it easier for people to get started with investing, as they can start with a smaller amount of money and gradually build their portfolio over time.

One of the benefits of micro-investment services is that they often come with a user-friendly app that makes it easy to track investments and make trades. Some services also offer educational resources to help users learn more about investing and make informed decisions.

Another advantage of micro-investment services is that they often have low minimum investment requirements, making them accessible to a wider range of people. Some services even offer automatic investment options, which allow users to set up regular investments and build their portfolio over time without having to manually make trades.

However, it's important to keep in mind that investing always comes with some level of risk. While micro-investment services can be a great way to start investing, it's important to do your own research and understand the risks involved before making any investment decisions. It's also important to diversify your portfolio and not put all your eggs in one basket.

Overall, micro-investment services can be a great option for individuals who are looking to start investing in the stock market with small amounts of money. With their user-friendly apps, low minimum investment requirements and automatic investment options, they make it easy for anyone to get started with investing and build their portfolio over time. However, it's important to understand the risks involved and to make informed investment decisions.

WealthTech Companies

Betterment

One of the pioneers of WealthTech, Betterment provides a robotic process advisory platform that utilizes technology to provide automated and algorithm-driven financial advisory services. Betterment's approach to WealthTech involves the use of RPAs, commonly known as robo-advisors, which are algorithmic systems designed to provide financial advice and investment management services.

Betterment uses algorithms to create and manage investment portfolios based on the individual goals, risk tolerance and time horizon of each user. The platform automates the process of portfolio rebalancing to maintain the desired asset allocation over time. Users input their financial goals, such as saving for retirement, a home or education. Betterment's algorithms then create and manage a diversified portfolio tailored to help users achieve these specific financial objectives.

Betterment assesses users' risk tolerance through a series of questions and uses the data to recommend an appropriate investment strategy. The platform dynamically adjusts the portfolio's risk level based on market conditions and changes in the user's financial situation. Betterment employs tax-efficient investment strategies, such as tax-loss harvesting. Automated algorithms systematically sell investments that experience losses to offset gains, potentially reducing the investor's tax liability.

Betterment provides users with various financial planning tools and calculators to help them understand and plan for their financial future. These tools may include retirement planning calculators, savings goal trackers and other features aimed at improving financial literacy. Betterment typically invests in low-cost index funds and ETFs to keep investment costs down for users. The platform automates the selection and management of these funds to provide a cost-effective investment solution.

The Betterment platform offers a user-friendly interface, making it easy for users to set up accounts, monitor performance and access financial planning tools. Automation extends to account funding, withdrawals and other routine transactions. Betterment's algorithms continuously monitor the financial markets and economic conditions. The platform automatically adjusts investment portfolios in response to changes in the market environment to optimize performance.

The use of RPAs by Betterment is a manifestation of WealthTech, which leverages technology to make financial services more efficient, accessible and personalized. By automating various aspects of investment management and financial planning, Betterment aims to provide a streamlined and cost-effective solution for individuals seeking professional financial advice without the high fees associated with traditional human advisors.

Vanguard

Vanguard is a renowned investment management company that revolutionized the financial industry with its low-cost index funds and ETFs. Founded by John C. Bogle in 1975, Vanguard is unique in that it operates as a client-owned mutual fund company, meaning it's owned by its funds, which are in turn owned by the investors in those funds.

Vanguard is widely celebrated for its commitment to low fees, transparency and investor-friendly approach. By eschewing high-cost active management in favor of passive index tracking, Vanguard has consistently delivered strong returns to its investors over the long term.

The company offers a diverse range of investment products spanning various asset classes, including stocks, bonds and real estate. Its flagship product, the Vanguard 500 Index Fund, was the first index fund available to individual investors and remains one of the largest mutual funds globally.

Vanguard's philosophy emphasizes long-term investing, broad diversification and disciplined portfolio management. This approach has resonated with millions of investors seeking to build wealth steadily and reliably over time.

In addition to its investment products, Vanguard provides educational resources, retirement planning tools and personalized advice through its team of financial advisors. Overall, Vanguard's commitment to putting investors' interests first has made it a trusted partner for individuals, institutions and financial advisors worldwide.

The RAS tool of Vanguard also offers retirement planning and debt payoff calculators. But they do not provide tax-loss harvesting services. The RAS tool of Vanguard asks the investor several questions about their investment timelines, risk tolerance and financial goals. Based on the information given, the investors are classified into five categories: very conservative, conservative, moderate, aggressive and very aggressive. The information is processed and analyzed to design the personalized portfolio.

The RAS tool of Vanguard offers a great user interface based on the digital platform. It is quite simple to use and smooth to navigate. It shows the progression of the investment portfolio in reaching the desired financial goals and the time required to reach the preset milestones. The automated advisor also allows the investor to connect with other Vanguard and external accounts to generate more accurate goal growth projections. The RAS offering of Vanguard has been a big success of the strong distribution network of Vanguard.

The RAS market is growing at a very fast rate with a lot of startups offering these types of services. Wealthfront and Betterment are the biggest competitors of Vanguard apart from Morgan Stanley, Fidelity and Charles Schwab. The startups are trying to emulate the success story of the market leaders and offering innovative products like tax-loss harvesting. In tax-loss harvesting, certain assets are sold at a loss to avoid the capital gains tax. This can be done more accurately using RAS.

By using Vanguard as a model, startups can learn how to shape their company to compete in the digital wealth management market. Startups should adapt the company's successful choices to fit with their company. If done properly, the robo-advisor business will move from the startup stage and continue to grow.

Charles Schwab Corporation

Charles Schwab, a prominent financial services company, has expanded its operations into the burgeoning field of WealthTech, which encompasses the integration of technology and financial services to provide innovative solutions for wealth management. Schwab's WealthTech business focuses on leveraging cutting-edge technology to enhance the customer experience, streamline operations and offer a comprehensive suite of wealth management tools and services.

Charles Schwab has developed robust digital platforms that empower clients to manage their investments efficiently. These platforms offer user-friendly interfaces, allowing clients to access their accounts, perform transactions and monitor their portfolios from anywhere, at any time. Schwab's digital platforms include web-based applications, mobile apps and desktop software, providing a seamless and intuitive user experience across various devices.

An interesting offering from Charles Schwab is robo-advisors. Schwab Intelligent Portfolios is the company's flagship robo-advisor service, which utilizes advanced algorithms to provide automated investment management. Clients answer a series of questions to determine their risk tolerance, investment goals and time horizon, following which the platform creates and manages a diversified portfolio of ETFs on their behalf. Schwab's robo-advisor combines the benefits of automated portfolio management with low fees, making it an attractive option for investors seeking a hands-off approach to wealth management.

Charles Schwab harnesses the power of data analytics to gain insights into market trends, client behavior and investment preferences. By analyzing vast amounts of data, Schwab can identify patterns, detect opportunities and personalize recommendations for clients. These data-driven insights enable Schwab to offer tailored investment solutions that align with each client's unique financial objectives and risk profile.

Schwab integrates AI and machine learning technologies into its WealthTech offerings to improve decision-making processes and enhance portfolio performance. AI algorithms analyze historical market data, identify patterns and optimize investment strategies in real time. Moreover, machine learning algorithms continuously adapt and refine their models based on new information and market dynamics, enabling Schwab to deliver more accurate predictions and personalized recommendations to clients.

As cybersecurity threats continue to evolve, safeguarding client data and financial assets is paramount for WealthTech firms like Charles Schwab. Schwab invests in state-of-the-art cybersecurity measures to protect client information, prevent unauthorized access and mitigate cyber risks. These measures include encryption protocols, multi-factor authentication, intrusion detection systems and regular security audits to ensure compliance with industry regulations and best practices.

Schwab offers a wealth of educational resources and planning tools to empower clients to make informed financial decisions. These resources cover a wide range of topics, including retirement planning, tax strategies, estate planning and investment fundamentals. By providing access to educational content and interactive planning tools, Schwab aims to help clients build financial literacy, set realistic goals and create comprehensive wealth management strategies tailored to their individual needs.

Despite the increasing digitization of wealth management services, Schwab recognizes the importance of human interaction and personalized support. The company provides dedicated customer support channels staffed by knowledgeable professionals who assist clients with account inquiries, technical issues and investment guidance. Additionally, Schwab fosters customer engagement through personalized communications, educational webinars and interactive workshops, strengthening the client-advisor relationship and promoting long-term loyalty.

Charles Schwab's WealthTech business represents a strategic evolution of its traditional brokerage services, leveraging technology to deliver innovative solutions that meet the evolving needs of modern investors. By combining digital platforms, robo-advisors, data analytics, AI, cybersecurity, financial education and personalized support, Schwab aims to empower clients to achieve their financial goals with confidence and peace of mind.

TD Ameritrade

TD Ameritrade, a prominent brokerage firm, has also made significant strides in the WealthTech sector, leveraging technology to enhance the wealth management experience for its clients. TD Ameritrade offers robust digital platforms that enable clients to manage their investments conveniently. These platforms include web-based portals, mobile apps and desktop software, providing clients with seamless access to their accounts, investment research, market data and trading tools. The user-friendly interfaces make it easy for clients to execute trades, monitor their portfolios and stay informed about market developments in real time.

TD Ameritrade's robo-advisor offering, Essential Portfolios, provides automated investment management services to clients. Similar to other robo-advisors, Essential Portfolios uses algorithms to create and manage diversified portfolios of ETFs based on clients' risk tolerance, investment goals and time horizon. Clients benefit from automated portfolio rebalancing, tax-loss harvesting and low management fees, making it an attractive option for investors seeking a hands-off approach to wealth management.

TD Ameritrade offers a comprehensive suite of advanced trading tools and analytics designed for active traders and sophisticated investors. These tools include customizable trading platforms, advanced charting software, technical analysis tools and real-time market data feeds. Active traders can execute complex trading strategies, conduct in-depth market analysis and access a wide range of trading products, including stocks, options, futures and forex.

TD Ameritrade harnesses the power of data analytics and AI to provide personalized investment recommendations and insights to clients. By analyzing vast amounts of data, including market trends, economic indicators and client behavior, TD Ameritrade can identify investment opportunities, optimize portfolio allocations and mitigate risks. AI algorithms continuously learn and adapt to changing market conditions, enhancing the accuracy and relevance of investment advice provided to clients.

TD Ameritrade offers a variety of financial planning tools and resources to help clients achieve their long-term financial goals. These tools include retirement calculators, goal-setting modules, budgeting tools and investment planning guides. Clients can assess their current financial situation, set realistic goals and develop personalized investment strategies aligned with their objectives and risk tolerance.

TD Ameritrade provides extensive educational resources to empower clients with the knowledge and skills needed to make informed investment decisions. These resources include articles, videos, webinars and interactive courses covering topics such as investing basics, market analysis, trading strategies and retirement planning. Clients can enhance their financial literacy, deepen their understanding of investment concepts and stay updated on market trends and developments.

TD Ameritrade emphasizes client support and engagement, offering personalized assistance and guidance to clients whenever needed. The company provides multiple channels for client support, including phone, email, live chat and in-person consultations at local branches. Additionally, TD Ameritrade fosters client engagement through educational events, seminars and workshops, where clients can interact with experts, network with peers and deepen their understanding of investment topics.

TD Ameritrade's WealthTech business encompasses a wide range of digital tools, automated services, advanced analytics, educational resources and personalized support designed to empower clients to achieve their financial goals effectively. By leveraging technology and innovation, TD Ameritrade continues to enhance the wealth management experience for investors of all levels, from novice traders to seasoned professionals.

Robinhood

Robinhood was started by Vladimir Tenev and Baiju Bhatt in 2013. The company became famous for simplifying the process of investing and for charging zero commission to investors. Robinhood was the first company to charge zero commission for trading. Their technology-based platform and app made investment easier for the millennials, many of whom were first-time investors. They were the first company to use gamification in investment and also allow investment through Bitcoins. Robinhood provides real-time data to the investors and they can stay at the top of the market by analyzing data through the company's automated platform. Robinhood aimed to democratize finance by making investing more accessible to the masses, particularly younger and novice investors.

The platform initially gained popularity for its simplicity and user-friendly interface, allowing users to buy and sell stocks, options, ETFs and cryptocurrencies without paying traditional brokerage fees. This commission-free model disrupted the industry and attracted millions of users, particularly among millennials and Gen Z investors.

Robinhood's mission to "democratize finance for all" extended beyond commission-free trading. The platform introduced features like fractional shares, which allow investors to buy and own a fraction of a share of a stock, making it easier for users with limited funds to invest in high-priced stocks like Amazon or Google.

Since it operates on the zero-commission model, the big question is how Robinhood makes money to run its operations. They earn money through the "payment for order flow" mechanism. In the payment for order flow mechanism, the broker sends a commission-free retail trade to a wholesaler or market maker. It does this instead of sending trades to the traditional stock exchanges. The market maker pays a commission to the broker for getting high volumes of trade. Thus, the broker earns his commission from the market maker and not the investor.

Although other big players like Charles Schwab, E-Trade and TD Ameritrade tried to replicate the investment strategy of Robinhood, they met with little success. Robinhood has continued to be the fastest-growing micro-investment firm and currently has 21 million active users on its technology-based platform.

However, Robinhood has faced criticism and controversy, particularly regarding its business model and practices. Critics argue that the platform encourages excessive trading behavior and gamifies investing, potentially leading to irresponsible financial decisions among inexperienced investors. Additionally, Robinhood has faced scrutiny over its handling of regulatory issues and customer service challenges.

Despite these challenges, Robinhood remains a significant player in the financial technology space, continually evolving its platform and expanding its offerings. In addition to trading, Robinhood has introduced features like cash management accounts and cryptocurrency trading, aiming to provide a comprehensive suite of financial services to its user base.

Zerodha

Zerodha is India's largest stockbroker, boasting over 130 million clients and handling a significant portion of the country's daily retail trading volume. Founded in 2010, it has established itself as a leading player in the Indian financial market. It was founded by Nithin Kamath and Nikhil Kamath. It has emerged as one of the largest retail brokerage firms in India, known for its innovative approach, technological prowess and commitment to low-cost trading.

The company gained attention for introducing the concept of discount brokerage to the Indian market, offering significantly lower brokerage fees compared to traditional full-service brokerage firms. This disruptive model attracted a large number of retail investors, particularly young traders and investors seeking cost-effective trading solutions.

Zerodha's flagship platform, Kite, provides users with a sleek and intuitive interface for trading across various segments, including equities, commodities, currencies and derivatives. The platform is known for its speed, reliability and advanced charting tools, empowering traders to make informed decisions and execute trades efficiently.

One of Zerodha's notable innovations is its introduction of direct mutual funds, allowing investors to invest in mutual funds without paying any commission to distributors. This initiative aligns with Zerodha's mission to provide transparent and low-cost investment options to its customers.

Moreover, Zerodha has been at the forefront of leveraging technology to enhance the trading experience. The company has introduced initiatives such as "Varsity", an educational platform offering comprehensive resources on investing and trading, and "Coin", a platform for investing in direct mutual funds.

Overall, Zerodha has become a popular choice for both beginner and experienced investors in India, offering a combination of low costs, a user-friendly platform and educational resources. Zerodha's success underscores the growing demand for affordable and technology-driven brokerage services in India. By challenging traditional norms and focusing on customer-centric solutions, Zerodha has cemented its position as a leading brokerage firm in the country's rapidly evolving financial landscape.

Upstox

Upstox is an Indian financial technology company that has gained prominence in the country's brokerage industry. Founded in 2012 by Ravi Kumar and Raghu Kumar, Upstox offers online brokerage services, catering to the needs of retail investors and traders.

Upstox has made a name for itself by providing a user-friendly and technologically advanced trading platform. Its platform offers features such as real-time market data, advanced charting tools and customizable trading interfaces, empowering users to execute trades efficiently and make informed investment decisions.

One of Upstox's key differentiators is its competitive pricing structure, with low brokerage fees and no hidden charges. This has made it an attractive option for cost-conscious traders and investors in India's rapidly growing market.

In addition to its trading platform, Upstox has expanded its offerings to include investment products such as mutual funds and digital gold, providing users with a comprehensive suite of financial services.

Upstox's growth and success reflect the increasing demand for accessible and affordable brokerage services in India. By leveraging technology and prioritizing customer satisfaction, Upstox has emerged as a significant player in the country's evolving financial landscape, competing with established brokerage firms and contributing to the democratization of investing in India.

Groww

Groww is an Indian financial technology company that has quickly risen to prominence in the country's investment landscape since its inception in 2016. Founded by Lalit Keshre,

Harsh Jain, Neeraj Singh and Ishan Bansal, Groww aims to simplify investing and make it accessible to a wide range of individuals, particularly young and first-time investors.

At the core of Groww's offerings is its user-friendly mobile app, which provides a seamless and intuitive interface for investing in various financial instruments, including mutual funds, stocks, ETFs and gold. The app's simplicity and ease of use have resonated with users, empowering them to start their investment journey with confidence.

Groww's platform emphasizes education and guidance, offering users access to educational content, tutorials and tools to help them make informed investment decisions. Additionally, the app provides features such as goal-based investing, portfolio tracking and automated investment options to cater to the diverse needs of its user base.

One of Groww's key innovations is its focus on zero-commission investing, allowing users to invest in mutual funds and stocks without paying any brokerage fees. This transparent pricing model has helped Groww attract a large and loyal user base, particularly among millennials and young professionals.

As India's investment landscape continues to evolve, Groww remains at the forefront of empowering individuals to take control of their finances and build wealth for the future. With its commitment to simplicity, transparency and customer-centricity, Groww is poised to play a significant role in shaping the future of investing in India.

AlgoTrader

AlgoTrader is a Swiss-based company that provides algorithmic trading software and technology solutions for financial institutions, proprietary trading firms and individual traders. Founded in 2009 by Andy Flury, AlgoTrader aims to empower clients with advanced tools and infrastructure to develop, test and execute algorithmic trading strategies across various asset classes, including stocks, options, futures, forex and cryptocurrencies.

AlgoTrader's platform offers a comprehensive suite of features, including strategy development, backtesting and optimization, execution and connectivity, risk management and compliance, infrastructure and hosting. AlgoTrader provides a flexible framework and programming interface for designing and implementing custom trading algorithms. Traders can leverage popular programming languages like Java and Python to develop their strategies or choose from a library of pre-built strategies.

Traders can backtest their strategies using historical market data to assess performance and optimize parameters before deploying them in live trading environments. AlgoTrader's robust backtesting engine allows for thorough analysis and refinement of trading strategies.

AlgoTrader offers direct market access and connectivity to numerous exchanges, brokers and liquidity providers worldwide. The platform supports automated order execution, real-time market data feeds and advanced order types to facilitate efficient trading across multiple venues.

AlgoTrader includes risk management features to help traders monitor and control their exposure to market risks. Additionally, the platform enables compliance with regulatory requirements and internal trading policies through customizable risk controls and reporting capabilities.

AlgoTrader provides infrastructure solutions for hosting trading servers, data storage and connectivity infrastructure. Clients can choose from on-premises deployment or utilize cloud-based hosting services for increased scalability and reliability.

Overall, AlgoTrader empowers traders and financial institutions to leverage algorithmic trading strategies effectively, enabling them to capitalize on market opportunities, mitigate risks and achieve their trading objectives in dynamic and competitive financial markets.

Wealth Dynamix

Wealth Dynamix is a prominent provider of client lifecycle management (CLM) solutions specifically tailored for wealth management and private banking firms. Founded in 2012 and headquartered in London, Wealth Dynamix offers a comprehensive platform designed to streamline and optimize client engagement, relationship management and regulatory compliance processes within the wealth management sector.

The Wealth Dynamix platform integrates various functionalities, including client onboarding, data management, client profiling, relationship tracking and compliance monitoring, into a unified system. This enables wealth management firms to efficiently manage their client interactions and ensure adherence to regulatory requirements while enhancing client satisfaction and retention.

With a focus on innovation and technology, Wealth Dynamix leverages advanced features such as AI, machine learning and predictive analytics to deliver actionable insights and personalized experiences for both clients and advisors. By harnessing data-driven intelligence, Wealth Dynamix empowers wealth management firms to make informed decisions, anticipate client needs and drive business growth.

Overall, Wealth Dynamix plays a pivotal role in the digital transformation of the wealth management industry, helping firms navigate evolving market dynamics, regulatory challenges and client expectations. Its comprehensive CLM platform serves as a strategic enabler for wealth management firms seeking to achieve operational efficiency, regulatory compliance and client-centric excellence in today's competitive landscape.

Wealthfront

Wealthfront is a leading digital wealth management platform founded in 2008 by Andy Rachleff and Dan Carroll. Based in Palo Alto, California, Wealthfront has gained widespread recognition for its innovative approach to investing and financial planning, particularly among tech-savvy investors and young professionals.

The core offering of Wealthfront revolves around automated investment management, commonly referred to as robo-advising. Through its platform, Wealthfront provides users with access to a diversified portfolio of low-cost ETFs tailored to their risk tolerance, financial goals and time horizon. The platform utilizes algorithms and modern portfolio theory to optimize asset allocation and rebalance portfolios automatically, aiming to maximize returns while minimizing risk.

In addition to investment management, Wealthfront offers a range of financial planning tools and services to help users achieve their long-term financial objectives. These include features such as tax-loss harvesting, direct indexing, retirement planning, college savings planning and more. Wealthfront's emphasis on technology-driven solutions and data-driven insights enables users to make informed decisions and optimize their financial outcomes.

Wealthfront is known for its transparent fee structure, charging a competitive and straightforward annual advisory fee based on the AUM. The platform's low fees, coupled with its user-friendly interface and emphasis on passive investing, have attracted a significant user base, particularly among millennials and individuals seeking a hands-off approach to wealth management.

Overall, Wealthfront has emerged as a prominent player in the Fintech industry, disrupting traditional wealth management models and empowering individuals to take control of their financial futures through accessible, automated and cost-effective investment solutions.

Nutmeg

Nutmeg is a UK-based wealth management company that operates in the WealthTech sector, offering innovative digital investment solutions to its clients. Founded in 2011, Nutmeg has gained prominence as a leading robo-advisor in the UK, providing automated investment management services to investors of all levels.

Nutmeg's core offering is its robo-advisor platform, which leverages advanced algorithms and technology to create and manage diversified investment portfolios for clients. The platform utilizes a data-driven approach to assess clients' risk tolerance, investment goals and time horizon and then recommends a suitable portfolio allocation comprised a mix of asset classes, including stocks, bonds and alternative investments. Nutmeg's robo-advisor platform provides clients with a hassle-free way to invest, requiring minimal effort and expertise on their part.

Nutmeg's platform automatically rebalances clients' portfolios to maintain the desired asset allocation and risk profile over time. As market conditions change and asset values fluctuate, the platform periodically adjusts the portfolio holdings to ensure alignment with the client's investment objectives. This automated rebalancing feature helps clients stay on track toward their financial goals while minimizing the need for manual intervention.

While Nutmeg's robo-advisor platform offers pre-built investment portfolios based on clients' risk profiles, clients also have the option to customize their portfolios to align with their specific preferences and investment strategies. Nutmeg provides a range of portfolio options with varying levels of risk-and-return potential, allowing clients to select the portfolio that best suits their individual needs and preferences.

Nutmeg's WealthTech platform offers low-cost investing solutions compared to traditional wealth management services. By leveraging technology to automate investment processes and minimize overhead costs, Nutmeg is able to pass on the cost savings to clients in the form of lower fees and charges. This makes Nutmeg's services accessible to a broader range of investors, including those with smaller account sizes who may have been priced out of traditional wealth management services.

Nutmeg emphasizes goal-based investing, helping clients set and achieve their financial goals through personalized investment strategies. Whether clients are saving for retirement, a house deposit, education expenses or other financial objectives, Nutmeg's platform allows them to specify their goals and timeframes and then creates tailored investment plans to help them reach those goals efficiently.

In addition to its investment management services, Nutmeg provides clients with educational resources and guidance to help them make informed financial decisions. These resources cover topics such as investing basics, portfolio diversification, risk management and retirement planning. Nutmeg aims to empower clients with the knowledge and confidence they need to navigate the complexities of investing and achieve long-term financial success.

Nutmeg prioritizes transparency in its operations, providing clients with clear and comprehensive reporting on their investment portfolios' performance, fees and charges. Clients have access to online dashboards and statements that detail their portfolio holdings, asset allocation, historical returns and other relevant information. This transparency helps clients understand how their investments are performing and ensures they are fully informed about the costs associated with Nutmeg's services.

Nutmeg's WealthTech business offers a modern and user-friendly approach to wealth management, combining advanced technology, automated investing, customization options, low fees, goal-based strategies, financial education and transparent reporting. Through its innovative platform, Nutmeg aims to democratize investing, making it accessible, affordable and convenient for investors of all backgrounds and experience levels.

Wealthsimple

Wealthsimple is a Canadian-based financial technology company that specializes in providing automated investment management services, also known as robo-advising, within the WealthTech sector. Since its founding in 2014, Wealthsimple has rapidly grown to become one of the leading digital wealth management platforms in Canada, the USA and the United Kingdom.

Wealthsimple's core offering is its robo-advisor platform, which utilizes sophisticated algorithms and technology to create and manage diversified investment portfolios for clients. Clients begin by completing a questionnaire that assesses their risk tolerance, investment goals and time horizon. Based on this information, Wealthsimple recommends a personalized portfolio allocation comprised a mix of low-cost ETFs across various asset classes, such as stocks, bonds and real estate. The platform automates the investment process, including portfolio rebalancing and dividend reinvestment, to ensure that the client's portfolio remains aligned with their financial objectives.

Wealthsimple offers socially responsible investing (SRI) portfolios for clients who prioritize environmental, social and governance factors in their investment decisions. These SRI portfolios invest in companies that demonstrate positive environmental and social practices while excluding industries such as fossil fuels, tobacco and firearms. Wealthsimple's SRI portfolios allow clients to align their investment strategies with their values and contribute to positive social and environmental outcomes.

The company offers halal investing portfolios that adhere to Islamic principles, making them suitable for Muslim investors seeking Sharia-compliant investment options. These portfolios exclude investments in companies involved in activities such as alcohol, gambling and interest-based lending, in accordance with Islamic finance principles. Wealthsimple's halal investing portfolios provide Muslim investors with access to diversified investment opportunities while adhering to their religious beliefs and values.

Wealthsimple Crypto is a feature that allows clients to buy, sell and hold cryptocurrencies, such as Bitcoin and Ethereum, within their Wealthsimple accounts. While traditional robo-advisors focus on traditional asset classes like stocks and bonds, Wealthsimple Crypto caters to clients interested in digital assets. Wealthsimple Crypto provides a simple and user-friendly platform for clients to invest in cryptocurrencies alongside their traditional investment portfolios.

Wealthsimple offers a suite of financial planning tools and calculators to help clients set and achieve their financial goals. These tools cover various aspects of personal finance, including retirement planning, saving for education expenses, buying a home and debt repayment. Clients can input their financial information and goals to receive personalized recommendations and insights to help them make informed decisions about their finances.

The company offers features that help clients save and invest automatically. Clients can set up recurring deposits from their bank accounts into their Wealthsimple investment accounts on a regular basis. Additionally, Wealthsimple's Roundup feature allows clients to automatically invest spare change from their everyday purchases by rounding up their transactions to the nearest dollar and investing the difference. These features encourage consistent saving and investing habits and help clients grow their wealth over time.

The company also provides educational content and resources to help clients improve their financial literacy and understanding of investing concepts. These resources include articles, guides, videos and webinars on topics such as investing basics, retirement planning, tax strategies and market trends. Wealthsimple's educational content is designed to empower clients with the knowledge and confidence to make informed financial decisions that align with their goals and values.

In summary, Wealthsimple's WealthTech business offers a comprehensive suite of digital investment management solutions designed to make investing accessible, affordable and personalized for clients of all backgrounds and experience levels. Through its robo-advisor platform, socially responsible and halal investing options, cryptocurrency trading features, financial planning tools, automatic savings features and educational resources, Wealthsimple aims to empower clients to achieve their financial goals and build long-term wealth with ease and confidence.

Kuvera

Kuvera was started by Gaurav Rastogi, Neelabh Sanyal and Mayank Sharma in 2016. This company offers robo-advisory services for personal financial planning and investing. They have created a commission-free investing platform for investors for WealthTech. They are right now competing against big competitors like Paytm Money, Zerodha and Groww. The company now has more than three lakh investors and is currently managing INR 5,000 crores in AUM. The investment platform provided by Kuvera offers great benefits to investors in the form of an easy switch to direct plans, consolidation of different portfolios and opportunity for a family to invest and plan together.

The company is known for its innovative and user-friendly platform that helps investors make informed investment decisions. One of the key features of Kuvera Wealthtech Company is its focus on personalized investment advice. The company's proprietary algorithms analyze a client's investment goals, risk tolerance and financial situation to provide customized investment recommendations. This approach helps investors to achieve their financial objectives while minimizing risk.

Another important aspect of Kuvera WealthTech is its commitment to transparency and accountability. The company provides clear and concise information about its fees, investment strategies and performance track record. This transparency helps investors to make informed decisions about their investments and to hold the company accountable for its performance.

In addition to its investment management services, Kuvera WealthTech offers a range of educational resources and tools to help investors learn about investing and financial planning. The company's website and mobile app provide access to market news and analysis, investment research and educational content.

Overall, Kuvera WealthTech is a reputable and innovative financial technology company that provides a range of investment and wealth management solutions to its clients. Its focus on personalized investment advice, transparency and accountability and educational resources make it a popular choice for investors looking to achieve their financial goals.

Scripbox

Scripbox was started as a wealth advisory firm in 2012 by Atul Shinghal, Sanjiv Singhal and WS Ravishankar in Bengaluru. The company offers a digital platform that provides automated, algorithm-driven financial planning services with almost no human supervision. It uses algorithms and automated software to collect information from its clients. The future goals and current financial situation are analyzed using the automated software. Based on the information and analysis of data, the Scripbox platform invests the money of the clients into different assets to create a diversified portfolio with optimized risk and returns. The Scripbox platform manages funds and clients under different categories like long-term, short-term, tax saving and emergency funds. Scripbox is currently managing an AUM of INR 1,100 crore.

mProfit

mProfit was started by Kiran Shah, Pallav Bhatt and Manish Jain in 2009. The company was started with the objective of providing good portfolio management solutions in Indian markets. The services of mProfit are available on web, desktop and Android & iOS mobile devices. The software helps to track absolute gain and annualized returns of multiple asset classes. The software allows investors to manage multiple portfolios and create portfolio groups. One special feature of mProfit is that investors can download data on capital gains in Income-Tax-Return format for stocks, Mutual Funds & Bonds.

They have several versions of the product like mProfit Free, mProfit Investor+, mProfit Pro and mProfit Advisor. The base license price starts at INR 3,000 and goes up to INR 7,500. The investment software operates through web and mobile apps and can do auto import of transaction data from more than 5000 formats. mProfit helps to manage multi-asset investments in stocks, Mutual Funds, Bonds, F&O & other asset classes. The company has clients in more than 300 cities and counts big names like Barclays, JM Financial, Bharat Forge and Mangal Keshav as clients.

Questions for Discussion

1. Explain what you understand by WealthTech.
2. What do you understand by robo-advisors? Explain.
3. What do you understand by MIS? Explain.
4. What do you understand by digital portfolio management? Explain.
5. What do you understand by algorithmic trading? Explain.

Case Study – How Zerodha Created a Niche in the WealthTech Market with Zero CAC

Zerodha is a successful Indian Fintech company that has disrupted the WealthTech business in India through the zero brokerage and zero CAC strategy. This company was founded by Nithin Kamath and Nikhil Kamath in 2010 and has revolutionized the Indian stock brokerage industry with its innovative approach. The company has expanded its business by offering a range of products and services that meet the changing needs of its customers. The company has also focused on improving the customer experience through innovative technology and user-friendly interfaces.

Nithin Kamath was very clear on one thing – people don't get interested in trading or start investing by coming across ads about investing. Most likely, investors get interested in trading after having a conversation with a friend or a reliable/respected acquaintance or mentor. So, all marketing would've to be through word-of-mouth. It mainly had two ways of marketing its startup: Community Outreach and Offline Telemarketing.

During his trading days, Nithin was part of quite a few trading communities. These are your simple groups on platforms like Reddit and Yahoo! Messenger. In fact, he himself was running a few of the large communities. So, basically, he was quite well-known. He used this to his advantage by distributing the early version of Zerodha to these communities.

Nitin Kamath also used offline telemarketing. Nithin Kamath himself was going door to door dressed as "Sachin the salesman guy". He was working on getting prospective users & referrals signed up on the platform. With community outreach and offline door-to-door marketing, Zerodha gained its first 1000 customers.

The strongest pillars of Zerodha marketing now are the referral and affiliate programs. Rather than investing in ads, they came up with the idea of giving commissions to their referrals. Many bloggers and YouTubers promote the services through affiliate programs on their platforms, and, in return, they earn a commission on every purchase. The referral program has helped Zerodha to discover thousands of leads without zero upfront cost.

With digital marketing, they have kept their users engaged on the platform by offering to educate with blogs and much more. They offer content that educates users, and it brings a chunk load of traffic. It provides a subscriber base and improves their authority of the domain on Google,

Zerodha charges a sign-up fee of ₹200 per customer while onboarding partly contributes to its overall revenue. Zerodha makes money on customer acquisition, unlike competition which is losing money. Upstox spends a chunk of its money on acquiring users and has a very high CAC. 65% of Upstox's users join through referrals. Upstox pays INR 1200 per referrer.

Zerodha also has several interesting initiatives that have helped them to get a strong foothold in the Indian WealthTech market. They introduced "Coin", a platform enabling customers to invest in direct mutual funds. By bypassing distributors' commissions, Coin offers cost-effective options for long-term investors.

In addition to its core brokerage services, Zerodha has expanded into other areas of the financial industry, such as mutual funds and insurance. The company has also formed partnerships with other financial institutions to offer a more comprehensive suite of financial products and services.

Zerodha places a strong emphasis on technology. Their flagship platform, Kite, provides advanced trading tools and real-time market data. Security is paramount, with robust encryption and two-factor authentication (2FA) to protect customer data. The Kite Mobile app ensures traders stay connected and execute trades on the go.

Zerodha's reputation for low costs, reliable technology and exceptional customer service drives strong word-of-mouth referrals and organic growth. They produce high-quality educational content through blogs, videos and webinars, empowering investors through Zerodha Varsity.

In summary, Zerodha's focus on a niche market, disruptive technology, low-cost services and customer-centric approach has propelled it to success. Overall, Zerodha's success in expanding its business through innovation is a testament to the company's commitment to staying ahead of the curve and providing the best possible products and services to its customers.

Case Study Questions

1. Explain the zero brokerage and zero CAC model of Zerodha.
2. How was Zerodha able to get a strong foothold in the Indian WealthTech business? Explain how the company was using unique strategies in the stock broking and wealth management business.
3. Why were competitors like Upstox not able to match up to the competition with Zerodha? What are the constraints and challenges in the WealthTech business?

Further Reading

1. Marguerita Cheng, "The Future of WealthTech", Forbes, February 19, 2019, www.forbes.com/sites/margueritacheng/2019/02/19/the-future-of-wealthtech/#2ee2adfa35e6.
2. Boschke, H. (2018). Using Artificial Intelligence in Wealth Management. The WealthTech Book: The FinTech Handbook for Investors, Entrepreneurs and Finance Visionaries, 80–82.

References

Bao, T., Nekrasova, E., Neugebauer, T., & Riyanto, Y. E. (2022). Algorithmic trading in experimental markets with human traders: A literature survey. In *Handbook of experimental finance*, edited by S. Füllbrunn & E. Haruvy (pp. 302–322). Edward Elgar Publishing. http://dx.doi.org/10.2139/ssrn.3908065

Bhatia, A., Chandani, A., Atiq, R., Mehta, M., & Divekar, R. (2021). Artificial intelligence in financial services: Qualitative research to discover robo-advisory services. *Qualitative Research in Financial Markets*, 13(5), 632–654.

Chan, E. P. (2021). *Quantitative trading: How to build your own algorithmic trading business*. John Wiley & Sons.

Chishti, S., & Puschmann, T. (2018). *The WealthTech book: The FinTech handbook for investors, entrepreneurs and finance visionaries*. John Wiley & Sons.

Cull, M. (2022). The growing role of FinTech and robo-advisors. In *De Gruyter handbook of personal finance*, edited by J. E. Grable & S. Chatterjee (pp. 529–549). Walter de Gruyter. https://doi.org/10.1515/9783110727692-030

Eckert, T., & Hüsig, S. (2022). Innovation portfolio management: A systematic review and research agenda in regards to digital service innovations. *Management Review Quarterly*, 72(1), 187–230.

Kissell, R. (2020). *Algorithmic trading methods: Applications using advanced statistics, optimization, and machine learning techniques*. Academic Press.

Kolkman, A. (2018). *The life cycle of wealth: Decision-making through four phases of life*. WestBow Press.
Moss, A. (2022). *How Do Brokerages' Digital Engagement Practices Affect Retail Investor Information Processing and Trading?* Doctoral dissertation, The University of Iowa.
Riitsalu, L., & Uusberg, A. (2021). To double, quadruple, or keep? Semi-automated service increases micro-investments. *Journal of Behavioral and Experimental Economics*, 95, 101774.

7 Risk Management – The InsurTech Model

After reading this chapter you will:

- Know the different kinds of insurance policies
- Understand the business model of InsurTech
- Know how chatbots increase efficiency in the insurance industry
- Know about on-demand coverage
- Understand how big data is used in underwriting
- Know how the Internet of Things helps insurance companies to acquire and analyze data
- Know how artificial intelligence helps in claim processing

Insurance is a product that is not much desirable and a highly difficult item to sell. Compounded with the fact that a lot of mis-selling happens in the insurance industry, the level of mistrust is higher. While insurance agents are focused on the commission that they are going to earn, the customers are fixated on getting tax concessions. The main purpose of insurance is to get protection from unwanted mishaps or losses of life and property, which is completely lost among both the sellers and the buyers of insurance. And the fact that different insurance companies offer different types of protection and premium plans makes it more difficult for customers to understand what exactly they should buy. And the insurance claim processing is so complicated that the customers doubt whether the insurance companies have an honest intention to settle the claims. Many a time the policyholders have to file cases and approach the courts to get justice and settle the claims.

Among this mayhem, the insurance companies have taken several proactive steps to reach out to their target customers and explain the benefits of getting insured, easily buying insurance cover and settling insurance claims without much hassles. This approach comprises leveraging the prowess of technology to make life easy for insurance policy buyers and holders of insurance policies. Policy Bazaar has created an aggregator platform where customers interested in buying insurance coverage can compare different insurance policies to check the terms and conditions, premium to be paid and the benefits they offer. Companies like Acko and Digit are using big data analytics and artificial intelligence and machine learning (AIML) to offer both insurance cover and claim settlement within a few minutes. This has created a market for providing on-demand insurance services.

"The world is on-demand. Your insurance should be, too" is the claim of Slice, an on-demand insurance technology provider. Typically, the first on-demand insurance companies were startups like Trov, Slice, Cuvva or Lings. To deliver a completely digital service,

DOI: 10.4324/9781032699417-7

each of these market entrants uses some combination of digital technology, big data, computing power and data analytics – the components of the digital transformation. The risks that are addressed are related to activities like driving, traveling, taking on temporary jobs and sharing goods, housing or equipment.

Customers typically use their smartphones to activate coverage. They can choose to manually switch coverage on and off or accept some level of automation through data interchange. The flexibility and unbundling that underpin on-demand insurance's value proposition allow for the acquisition of insurance coverage for risks as needed, whenever needed and for as long as needed. A growing need for instantaneous, usage-based services and products related to lifestyle or changing work arrangements is driving the trend toward on-demand insurance. Practice-focused research contends that insurers must adapt to include on-demand insurance even though the phenomenon is now modest in terms of market share.

Introducing technology to insurance businesses acts as a catalyst for intermediaries to automate operations from start to finish. Intermediaries can create a seamless and efficient workflow with technology. Technology allows for automating product interfaces with customer onboarding, policy issuance and claims processing. Manual and time-consuming tasks that once hindered productivity can now be automated, allowing intermediaries to focus on building customer relationships and dedicating their time to selling policies.

Insurance business workflow automation is a game-changer in enhancing efficiency for intermediaries. Intermediaries can reclaim valuable time and redirect it toward revenue-generating activities by eliminating manual paperwork, redundant data entry and repetitive administrative tasks. Automating routine tasks reduces the risk of errors, ensuring greater accuracy and compliance in insurance processes and ultimately driving business growth.

The power of automation allows intermediaries to focus on what truly matters: building solid relationships with customers, product distribution and driving business growth. As the insurance industry evolves, intermediaries who embrace technological changes will be well-equipped to navigate the challenges and leverage opportunities, leaving their competitors in the dust.

Kotak Life Insurance was able to swiftly and efficiently introduce its sachet-sized life insurance policies into India's rural heartlands by utilizing the Briisk platform. The user interface was designed to be as basic as possible so that even inexperienced users could easily complete the online journey. Multiple partners and goods can be accommodated by the scalable platform. The ability to parameterize a lot of the features makes customization really simple. The outstanding platform is enhanced by a workforce that is quick to respond and knowledgeable about business and contributes to the solutions area.

The Insurance Business Model

Insurance is defined as "a contract, represented by a policy, in which an individual or entity receives financial protection or reimbursement against losses from an insurance company". An insurance company is able to pay for the losses of a client as it pools the risks of several clients so that it can offer policies to an individual client at low costs (Kagan, Rasure & Munichiello, 2024).

The insurance industry revolves around the principles of risk assumption and risk diversification. Insurance firms gather premiums from policyholders and utilize those funds to cover claims submitted by policyholders. Insurance firms' business strategy revolves around the accurate anticipation of risk and its effective management to mitigate potential financial losses. Insurance companies utilize actuarial science to create predictive models for assessing future risks and determining appropriate policy pricing. Insurance companies establish extensive portfolios to reallocate risks. Insurance companies generate money by collecting premiums from policyholders and investing these funds in various assets to generate income. Insurance firms allocate a significant portion of their funds toward advertising and supporting various activities (Mosig, Lehmann & Moeslein, 2021).

Underwriting is a crucial component of the insurance business model. The process of underwriting is evaluating a prospective policyholder's risk and figuring out how much to charge for coverage. Numerous factors, including the policyholder's age, health and claim history, are analyzed during this procedure (Toshmurzaevich, 2020).

Reinsurance is another component of the business model used by insurance companies. Insurance firms buy reinsurance as a kind of insurance to guard against significant losses. Insurance firms can lessen their own exposure to possible losses by assigning a portion of the risk to reinsurers (Cummins, Dionne, Gagné & Nouira, 2021).

Investment management is a key component of the insurance business model. The premiums that insurance firms receive from policyholders are invested in a range of assets, including bonds, equities and real estate. The money from these assets goes toward defraying the costs of expenditures and claims.

A major component of the insurance business model is customer service. Insurance businesses work hard to give policyholders and prospective clients outstanding customer care. This entails responding to inquiries and concerns, processing claims promptly and giving precise and understandable information regarding policies.

In conclusion, risk management, underwriting, investment management and customer service are the main focuses of the insurance business model. Insurance firms are able to make money for themselves while offering customers important protection by combining these factors.

Types of Insurance

There are basically two types of insurance – life and non-life. Non-life insurance is also commonly called general insurance. Beneficiaries of life insurance are financially protected in the case of the insured person's passing. Term, whole and universal life insurance are among the various varieties of life insurance. While whole life and universal life insurance offer coverage for the insured's whole life combined with an increasing cash value component, term life insurance only offers coverage for a predetermined term or length of time (Hodula, Janků, Časta & Kučera, 2021).

Non-life or general insurance comes in a variety of forms, including health, property, travel and auto insurance. Medical costs resulting from disease or injury are covered by health insurance. It assists people in covering the costs of medical services, including hospital stays, doctor visits, prescription drugs and preventive care. Plans for health insurance might differ greatly in terms of provider networks, costs and coverage (Hodula, Janků, Časta & Kučera, 2021).

Financial protection against losses brought on by collisions, theft or other vehicle damage is offered by auto insurance. Property damage, bodily injury liability, medical costs and uninsured/underinsured driver coverage are usually included. Many states have laws requiring auto insurance and lenders frequently ask for it to grant auto loans.

Commercial insurance, also referred to as business insurance, protects companies against a range of hazards, such as liability, income loss and property damage. Property insurance, general liability insurance, professional liability insurance and workers' compensation insurance are some examples of business insurance types.

Property insurance guards against covered risks including fire, theft, vandalism and natural catastrophes that may cause harm to a home, valuable property or its contents. It usually includes coverage for the house's structure, personal property, liability for injuries or damage to third parties' property and additional living costs in the event that the house becomes uninhabitable.

A type of business insurance known as general liability insurance covers a number of typical hazards that firms face, such as property damage, personal injury claims and bodily injury. This insurance shields companies from monetary damages brought about by third parties suing for carelessness or damages the company's activities, goods or services are said to have caused.

Legal expenditures, such as attorney fees, court costs and settlements or judgments granted to the injured party, are usually covered by general liability insurance. In the event that someone is hurt on company property or as a result of business operations, it also covers medical costs.

Professional liability insurance is a type of insurance coverage intended to shield professionals against responsibility resulting from negligence, errors or omissions in the performance of their professional services. It is often referred to as errors and omissions insurance or malpractice insurance. This insurance is especially important for professionals who advise, specialize or offer clients specialized services.

Professional liability insurance is beneficial for professionals including physicians, attorneys, accountants, consultants and financial advisors. It covers costs associated with defending against allegations of professional misconduct, carelessness or subpar performance of services relative to the expected standard of care, as well as settlements and judgments.

One important kind of insurance that helps employees who are sick or injured at work is workers' compensation insurance. It is intended to compensate workers who are hurt or ill at work for medical bills, rehabilitation expenditures and a percentage of lost income. In addition, dependents of workers who pass away from illnesses or injuries sustained at work usually receive death payments from workers' compensation insurance.

Most jurisdictions mandate this insurance, and it is usually legally necessary for companies to offer workers' compensation coverage to their employees. By offering a no-fault method of compensating injured workers, workers' compensation insurance primarily serves to safeguard both employers and employees. Stated differently, companies are shielded from litigation pertaining to workplace diseases or injuries, and employees do not need to demonstrate that their employer was at fault for their injuries to get compensation.

Travel insurance provides coverage for unforeseen circumstances, such as trip cancellations, medical crises, misplaced luggage or delays in transit. Assistance services and compensation for non-refundable costs can be obtained through it when traveling. The coverage provided by travel insurance policies varies and can include a number of benefits such as reimbursement for lost, stolen or damaged personal belongings during the trip; reimbursement for emergency medical expenses incurred due to illness or injury while traveling, including hospital stays, doctor visits and prescription medications; and compensation for additional costs incurred due to flight delays, missed connections or other travel disruptions, including lodging, meals and transportation. Emergency medical transportation coordination, medical referrals and access to a helpline for travel support are just a few of the 24/7 emergency assistance features included by many travel insurance policies. Certain travel insurance policies cover accidental death or dismemberment that happens while on the road.

The Evolution from Insurance to InsurTech

In the year 2020, the insurance industry had to deal with the nuances of COVID-19. Although the insurance industry suffered an initial setback due to high levels of claims, it recovered very fast and started investing in technology to make the insurance products easily accessible and the insurance business more profitable. A major shift happened in pivoting the business from "push-driven sales" to "on-demand insurance". The core systems of the insurance business started focusing on the digitization of manual and semi-automated processes (Wilamowicz, 2019).

There were some related shifts in insurer priorities, most notably toward more cloud computing and an increase in the importance of digital strategy – with digital covering both external channels and internal workflows. Insurers expect that these areas will continue to be prioritized in the post-pandemic era. Cloud and digital are two areas where the InsurTech companies are investing; in many cases, this has led to additional opportunities.

The pandemic has altered insurer approaches to InsurTech investments. With time horizons shortened to reflect uncertainty about the future, carriers appear to be focusing on tactical initiatives that can produce more immediate results than some of the more strategic R&D elements more prominent in the pre-pandemic era. This will continue to evolve and be influenced by the shape of the economic recovery.

Recent developments in customer behavior, regulations, technology breakthroughs and new trends have all had a major impact on the insurance sector. Numerous advances in the insurance value chain have resulted from the rise of InsurTech (insurance technology) startups. Technology is changing how insurers work, from digital distribution platforms to sophisticated underwriting algorithms and automated claims processing.

The terms "insurance" and "technology" are combined to form the term "InsurTech". "The use of technology innovations to bring in savings and efficiency to the insurance industry model" is the definition of InsurTech. Insurtech enterprises utilize digital innovation, artificial intelligence (AI), data analytics and other technology to enhance diverse facets of the insurance value chain.

One of the key elements of Fintech is InsurTech. Both large and small insurance players are benefiting from InsurTech's assistance in creating on-demand products, distributing those goods to the appropriate clientele, collecting premiums on time, resolving claims with the least amount of difficulty and efficiently running the insurance company. Smartphone apps, Internet of Things (IoT), artificial intelligence and machine learning (AIML), big data analytics, automated technologies and processes are what power the InsurTech industry. From the point of premium collection to the point of claim processing, these solutions are contributing to the improvement of the customer and insurance provider experience. The insurance sector is benefiting from InsurTech's assistance in increasing productivity, cutting expenses and providing better customer service (VanderLinden, Millie, Anderson & Chishti, 2018).

The distribution and consumption of insurance goods have been completely transformed by InsurTech. Customers can now study, compare and buy insurance products more easily thanks to digital platforms, online marketplaces and mobile apps, which improves the overall customer experience.

Large volumes of data from many sources are gathered and analyzed by InsurTech businesses using sophisticated data analytics. This makes it possible to price models based on individual behavior and traits, provide individualized underwriting and assess risk more accurately. Applications of AI and machine learning (ML) include fraud detection, underwriting, claims processing and customer support. With the use of these technologies, insurers may increase operational efficiency, automate repetitive procedures and make data-driven choices (Cappiello & Cappiello, 2018).

The insurance sector may benefit from increased efficiency, security and transparency thanks to blockchain technology. Blockchain-powered smart contracts allow for automated and self-executing provisions in contracts, eliminating the need for middlemen and lowering the possibility of disagreements.

IoT devices are used by InsurTech to gather data in real time and track many metrics. Whereas wearables in health insurance offer information into customers' health patterns, telematics devices in auto insurance track driving behavior. With the use of data, insurers are able to provide more specialized goods and services.

Within the InsurTech sector, usage-based insurance (UBI) is a prominent trend in vehicle insurance. Insurance companies are able to provide customized rates based on real usage patterns thanks to telematics devices and smartphone apps that track driving behavior.

The claims processing cycle is now more automated thanks to InsurTech, which also lowers the possibility of fraud. Certain InsurTech platforms provide comprehensive solutions by combining client communication, claims processing and policy administration into a streamlined online experience.

Using technology, peer-to-peer (P2P) insurance models establish communities of policyholders who pool their resources to insure one another against risk. P2P models have been investigated by InsurTech entrepreneurs as a substitute for conventional insurance arrangements.

With the increasing sophistication of cyber threats, InsurTech companies are creating customized cyber insurance solutions. These plans provide coverage for liability and financial damages resulting from ransomware attacks, data breaches and other cybersecurity catastrophes.

Insurtech firms employ regulatory technology (RegTech) solutions to guarantee adherence to constantly changing regulations. These solutions lower the risk of non-compliance and assist insurers in effectively managing regulatory requirements.

Microinsurance solutions, which are accessible and reasonably priced insurance products designed for those with lower incomes, are one of the services that InsurTech offers. By giving previously marginalized individuals access to insurance, this promotes financial inclusion.

To incorporate cutting-edge solutions into already-existing insurance ecosystems, InsurTech businesses frequently work with traditional insurers, tech companies and other stakeholders. These collaborations make it easier to share resources, technology and expertise.

The insurance industry is still changing as a result of InsurTech, which is encouraging innovation and opening doors for increased productivity, better customer service and new business models. The continued integration of technology in the insurance business guarantees a dynamic and changing environment for both insurers and policyholders, even though obstacles like regulatory compliance and industry-wide adoption still exist (Wilamowicz, 2019).

By bringing in the widespread use of technology in insurance, insurance providers have ushered in the era of InsurTech. By applying technology, insurance companies have managed to bring down the cost of marketing, cost of servicing and also the costs involved in claim processing. This has helped them to offer higher sum assured at lower premiums. The customer satisfaction has also gone up because of the online offerings and transactions.

The InsurTech Ecosystem

The InsurTech ecosystem is a dynamic and rapidly evolving network of companies, startups, technology providers, investors and other stakeholders that collaborate to bring innovation and technological advancements to the insurance industry. This ecosystem is characterized by the integration of digital technologies to disrupt traditional insurance models, enhance customer experiences and optimize operational efficiency. The various components of the InsurTech Ecosystem are startups, technology providers, investors and venture capitalists, insurance carriers, regulatory technologies or RegTech, insurance intermediaries, data providers, incubators and accelerators, academic and research institutions, professional service providers and consultancies, insurance associations and industry groups, customers and policyholders (Braun & Schreiber, 2017).

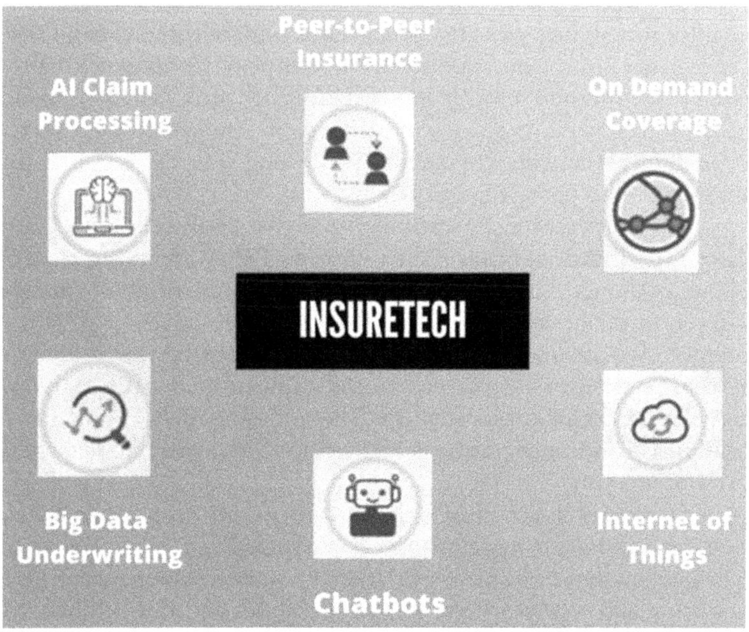

Figure 7.1 The InsurTech Ecosystem

InsurTech Startups

The leading forces behind innovation and change in the insurance sector are InsurTech startups. They are the center of the ecosystem that poses a threat to established insurance business models. These firms frequently concentrate on niche markets including innovative product development, data analytics, digital distribution and claims processing (Suryavanshi, 2022).

These firms are changing the way traditional insurance models are delivered and opening up new avenues for growth by utilizing technology to improve consumer experiences, expedite workflows and create innovative insurance solutions. By forming strategic alliances, entering new markets and utilizing cutting-edge technologies, InsurTech businesses are able to prosper in spite of obstacles like regulatory difficulties and trust barriers. InsurTech companies are positioned to be key players in determining how the insurance sector develops in the future. Examples of InsurTech startups include Lemonade (P2P insurance), Root Insurance (telematics-based auto insurance) and Hippo (digital homeowners' insurance).

Technology Providers

By providing a broad range of tools, platforms and services that are specifically designed to meet the requirements of the insurance business, technology providers contribute to the success and creativity of InsurTech startups. These companies use state-of-the-art technology to help startups improve client experiences, increase operational efficiency and spearhead digital change in the insurance industry. This covers blockchain technology, AI, data analytics and software development. To incorporate cutting-edge technologies into their offers, InsurTech frequently works with technology vendors.

Modern technologies including AI, ML, big data analytics, blockchain and the IoT are made available to InsurTech businesses by technology suppliers. These technologies enable companies to enhance risk assessment and underwriting capabilities, automate procedures and create novel insurance products (Cappiello & Cappiello, 2018).

Cloud-based platforms and scalable infrastructure are provided by technology providers, allowing InsurTech firms to quickly and affordably implement their solutions. These platforms offer the networking, storage and processing capacity required to enable the expansion and scalability of startup operations.

Technology companies create software solutions that are specifically designed to meet the demands and specifications of InsurTech startups. Policy administration, claims management, billing, customer relationship management and distribution channel optimization are just a few of the many features that these solutions cover.

Large volumes of structured and unstructured data can be transformed into usable insights for InsurTech businesses thanks to the sophisticated data analytics tools and solutions provided by technology suppliers. These insights help companies provide clients with customized insurance products and services, improve risk management tactics and guide decision-making processes.

Technology companies assist InsurTech startups in reducing cyber risks, protecting sensitive client data and assuring regulatory compliance by providing strong cybersecurity solutions and compliance frameworks. Identity and access management, encryption, security monitoring and regulatory reporting capabilities are some of these solutions.

Technology companies have had a significant impact on the insurance industry by enabling InsurTech businesses to challenge established insurance models with cutting-edge digital solutions that meet changing client demands and preferences. By taking on established players and conventional distribution methods, these alternatives promote competition and innovation in the insurance sector (Asmussen & Steffensen, 2020).

They provide the provision of smooth, customized and multichannel customer experiences by InsurTech startups across digital touchpoints. Startups can increase customer satisfaction and retention rates, provide customized insurance products and services and interact with clients in real time by utilizing cutting-edge technologies and data analytics.

Their assistance has resulted in increased operational efficiency and cost reduction for InsurTech businesses by streamlining operations, automating procedures and optimizing resource utilization. Startups can gain economies of scale and strengthen their competitive edge by utilizing software-as-a-service platforms, modular architectures and scalable cloud infrastructure.

Additionally, they have made it possible for InsurTech companies to enter new markets, concentrate on underrepresented groups and meet unmet insurance needs throughout the world. Startups have the potential to promote financial inclusion, raise insurance penetration rates and provide new growth prospects in emerging and developing countries by providing easily accessible, reasonably priced and adaptable insurance products.

Technology suppliers are crucial business partners for InsurTech companies because they offer the platforms, tools and services needed for these companies to grow, develop and thrive in the competitive insurance market. Technology providers empower startups to challenge established models, improve consumer experiences and propel digital transformation in the insurance sector by utilizing cutting-edge technologies, tailored solutions and industry knowledge. Technology providers are expected to have a significant impact on the future of the insurance sector, contributing to sustainable growth and value creation for all parties involved as InsurTech continues to transform the insurance environment (VanderLinden, Millie, Anderson & Chishti, 2018).

Investors and Venture Capital

Venture capital firms and investors support the development of InsurTech companies by contributing funds for R&D and market expansion. The potential for innovative technologies to transform the insurance sector and yield substantial returns is what draws these investors in. By offering startups and rising businesses financial resources, strategic advice and industry knowledge, they significantly influence the course of the InsurTech industry's growth. Their investments stimulate market growth, foster innovation and hasten the insurance industry's acceptance of innovative technologies (Chemmanur, Imerman, Rajaiya & Yu, 2020).

Venture capitalists and investors provide much-needed funding to InsurTech companies, allowing them to grow and scale their businesses, advance the creation of new products and reach a wider audience. InsurTech companies may attract top people, invest in R&D and construct strong technological infrastructure thanks to investor capital infusion, which paves the way for long-term success and sustainable growth.

Investors frequently enable strategic collaborations and alliances between InsurTech startups and well-established insurance companies, reinsurers and distribution partners by bringing important industry connections, networks and relationships to the table. Through these alliances, entrepreneurs can quickly penetrate new markets and get access to a larger consumer base by utilizing the experience, resources and distribution networks of established companies.

Venture capitalists' investments allow InsurTech companies to grow into new domestic and international markets by giving them the money, tools and strategic direction they need to deal with complex regulations and cultural quirks. Venture capitalists (VCs) are crucial in helping firms enter new markets, spot growth prospects and gain traction in their chosen sectors. They also propel the InsurTech industry's global expansion and market growth.

Investors and VCs are instrumental in driving the growth and evolution of the InsurTech industry by providing financial resources, strategic guidance and industry expertise to startups and emerging companies. Their investments fuel innovation, accelerate market expansion and foster collaboration between startups and incumbents, driving the adoption of disruptive technologies and reshaping traditional insurance models. As the InsurTech landscape continues to mature, the influence of investors and VCs will remain pivotal in shaping the future of the industry and driving sustainable growth and value creation for all stakeholders involved.

Insurance Intermediaries

InsurTech intermediaries, including online insurance brokers and comparison platforms, facilitate the purchase of insurance policies by providing digital marketplaces and streamlined user experiences. Examples include Compare the Market in the UK and Policybazaar in India.

Insurance intermediaries, including brokers, agents and other distribution channels, play a significant role in facilitating the growth and adoption of InsurTech solutions within the insurance industry. While InsurTech startups often aim to disrupt traditional distribution models, intermediaries serve as key stakeholders that can influence the adoption, implementation and success of InsurTech innovations (Stricker, Wagner & Zeier, 2023).

Insurance intermediaries play a crucial role in InsurTech businesses by bridging the gap between insurance providers and customers, leveraging technology to enhance the insurance process. They use digital platforms, websites and mobile apps to connect insurance companies with customers. They provide a user-friendly interface for customers to browse insurance products, compare quotes and purchase policies online. This connectivity increases the reach of insurance companies and makes their products accessible to a wider audience.

InsurTech intermediaries leverage technology to streamline the entire insurance process, from quote generation to claims processing. By automating various tasks and implementing intuitive interfaces, they make it easier for customers to understand their insurance options, customize policies according to their needs and complete transactions seamlessly.

InsurTech intermediaries collect and analyze vast amounts of data to gain insights into customer behavior, preferences and risks. This data-driven approach enables them to personalize insurance offerings and tailor recommendations and pricing based on individual needs and risk profiles. This level of personalization enhances customer satisfaction and improves the overall insurance experience.

InsurTech intermediaries offer innovative risk management solutions to both insurance providers and customers. They develop predictive analytics models, AI-driven underwriting tools and IoT-based monitoring devices to assess and mitigate risks effectively. By offering these solutions, they help insurance companies optimize their underwriting processes, reduce claim losses and offer more competitive premiums to customers.

Intermediaries in the InsurTech space frequently serve as bridges for collaborations and integrations between insurers and other technology companies. To make use of their experience and introduce cutting-edge technology into the insurance industry, they work with Fintech businesses, data analytics firms and InsurTech startups. These alliances and collaborations bring strategic collaborations and alliances between InsurTech startups and established insurance companies, reinsurers and distribution partners to the table, enabling insurers to improve their offerings, increase operational efficiency and stay ahead in a market that is changing quickly. Through these alliances, entrepreneurs can quickly penetrate new markets and get access to a larger consumer base by utilizing the experience, resources and distribution networks of established companies.

InsurTech intermediaries leverage digital channels such as social media, search engines and online marketplaces to reach potential customers more effectively. By utilizing targeted marketing strategies, search engine optimization (SEO) techniques and affiliate partnerships, they drive traffic to insurance products and increase conversion rates. This optimization of distribution channels enables insurers to expand their market reach and acquire new customers at a lower cost.

Overall, insurance intermediaries play a pivotal role in the InsurTech landscape by leveraging technology to enhance the insurance process, improve customer experiences and drive innovation across the industry. They act as enablers, bringing together insurers, customers and technology partners to create value and shape the future of insurance.

Data Providers

By providing the information and insights required to power many elements of the insurance industry, data providers play a critical role in supporting the InsurTech company. One of the key components of InsurTech is the availability of massive volumes of data. Data suppliers provide a contribution by offering insightful data for underwriting procedures, pricing models and risk evaluation. The data ecosystem includes wearables, IoT devices and other sources (Neale, Drake & Konstantopoulos, 2020).

Data providers offer enormous volumes of personal, real estate and business-related data. This data includes credit ratings, property attributes, past loss data, demographic data and more. These data are used by InsurTech companies to precisely evaluate risks and make well-informed underwriting decisions. They are able to set suitable premiums and more accurately estimate the possibility of claims by utilizing advanced analytics approaches and historical data analysis.

InsurTech organizations benefit from data providers' real-time data streams and historical records, which help to optimize the workflow of claims processing. This data contains, among other things, details from police investigations, medical records and prior claims. These data are utilized by InsurTech companies to speed up the settlement process, identify fraudulent activity and automate the processing of claims. Through the utilization of ML algorithms and predictive analytics, it is possible to detect dubious trends and mark possibly fraudulent claims for additional scrutiny.

Data providers give InsurTech companies access to demographic, market and consumer behavior data, which helps them understand the needs and preferences of their customers. InsurTech companies may customize insurance policies, make recommendations and launch focused marketing efforts by evaluating this data. They make it possible for more efficient client acquisition and retention tactics by being able to segment customers based on their risk profiles, preferences and purchase habits.

A plethora of real-time data from linked devices, including cars, wearables and smart home sensors, is made available by data providers thanks to the growth of IoT devices and telematics technology. Using this data, InsurTech firms provide UBI policies, in which the premiums are determined by the policyholders' actual usage patterns and behaviors. InsurTech companies may provide more accurate pricing and incentives for clients to adopt safer behaviors by incorporating IoT data into their underwriting algorithms.

To keep InsurTech companies updated about market trends and competitor plans, data providers provide industry benchmarks, competitive analysis and market intelligence reports. Through competitive analysis and industry monitoring, InsurTech companies can discern new market prospects, gauge consumer demand and enhance their product portfolio. They can remain competitive and adaptable in a market that is changing quickly thanks to this data-driven strategy.

Overall, by providing the data and insights that enable different parts of the insurance value chain, including risk assessment and underwriting, claims processing and customer engagement, data providers play a crucial role in supporting the InsurTech industry. Effective use of data by InsurTech businesses can boost operational effectiveness, strengthen risk management procedures and provide clients with more individualized and cutting-edge insurance options.

Customers and Policyholders

Ultimately, the end users of insurance products, the customers and policyholders, are an integral part of the InsurTech ecosystem. Insurtech aims to address their needs by offering more personalized, efficient and accessible insurance solutions.

The InsurTech ecosystem is characterized by collaboration and the convergence of diverse stakeholders with a shared goal of transforming the insurance industry. As the ecosystem continues to evolve, the synergy between InsurTech startups, established insurers, technology providers, investors and other participants will drive ongoing innovation and reshape the future of insurance.

Traditional Insurance versus InsurTech Model

Traditional insurance and InsurTech represent two distinct models within the insurance industry, each characterized by different approaches, methodologies and technological advancements.

Traditional insurance operates on long-established business models with a focus on risk assessment, underwriting and policy issuance. The approach is often characterized by manual processes, legacy systems and traditional distribution channels involving agents and brokers.

Traditional insurers typically rely on legacy systems and may have slower adoption rates for new technologies. Processes such as underwriting and claims management may involve manual paperwork and legacy systems that can be time-consuming.

Customer interactions in traditional insurance often involve face-to-face meetings with agents or brokers. Policy purchase, claims filing and customer service are usually conducted through traditional channels like phone calls or in-person visits.

Product development in traditional insurance can be a slower process due to bureaucratic structures and a focus on established products. There might be a limited range of insurance products and customization may be less prevalent.

Table 7.1 Traditional Insurance versus InsurTech Model

Factors	*Traditional Insurance*	*InsurTech Model*
Pricing	High operating cost	Low operating cost
Buying procedure	Multistep and complicated	Simple, easy and paperless. Done mostly through apps and websites
Communication	Complicated jargon makes it difficult to understand	Easy-to-understand explanations given on the website and mobile apps
Claims	Complicated and lengthy with a lot of paperwork and several levels of assessment and authentication	Made simple and user friendly with mobile apps and websites
Paperwork	Forms to be submitted for buying insurance, renewing policies and submitting claims	Digital process that is completely paperless

Source: Innov8tif Solution (2021).

While traditional insurers collect significant amounts of data, the utilization of data for decision-making and risk assessment may not be as advanced as in the InsurTech model. Data analysis and insights might be less dynamic.

Insurtech operates on innovative business models, leveraging technology to streamline processes and enhance customer experiences. Insurtech startups often focus on niche markets, introducing new products and challenging traditional insurance norms. Insurtech relies heavily on cutting-edge technologies such as AI, ML, blockchain and data analytics. Automation is a key feature, with the aim of reducing operational costs and improving efficiency.

InsurTech companies prioritize digital interactions, offering online platforms and mobile apps for policy purchase, claims filing and customer service. This digital-first approach caters to tech-savvy consumers who prefer seamless and convenient experiences.

Insurtech is known for its rapid product innovation. Startups are agile and can quickly introduce novel insurance products, such as microinsurance, P2P insurance and usage-based insurance (UBI), responding to emerging market needs and trends.

Data is a core asset in the InsurTech model. Startups leverage advanced data analytics to gain insights into customer behavior, assess risks more accurately and personalize insurance offerings. This data-driven approach enables dynamic pricing and risk management.

Both traditional insurers and InsurTech companies must navigate complex regulatory environments. However, InsurTech may face additional challenges as it introduces novel products and business models that regulators may need to adapt to. Traditional insurers often grapple with the limitations of legacy systems, making it challenging to integrate new technologies seamlessly. On the other hand, InsurTech startups can build their systems from the ground up, ensuring technological compatibility.

Traditional insurers may benefit from established brand trust, while InsurTech startups might need to work harder to build and establish trust, especially when introducing innovative models that deviate from the traditional norms.

Traditional insurers have an extensive market presence and customer base. However, InsurTech may initially struggle with market penetration and customer acquisition, particularly if they focus on niche markets or unconventional products.

In conclusion, while traditional insurance and the InsurTech model coexist, they represent different approaches to the insurance business. Traditional insurance brings stability, established market presence and a trusted brand, while InsurTech introduces agility, innovation and technology-driven solutions. The ongoing collaboration and competition between these models contribute to the dynamic evolution of the insurance industry.

P2P Insurance

One of the biggest innovations of Fintech has been the application of P2P networks. In insurance also P2P insurance systems have started gaining popularity. In the traditional mode of insurance, it is strangers from whom the money is pooled and they bear the risk of each other. The underwriter analyzes the risk profile of each individual and decides on the premium to be paid. In case, the policyholder is unable to pay the claims, the risk cover and the money paid both are gone. In the case of the traditional insurance model, the chances of conflict are high and the motivation to pay premium is less as one feels that they are covering the losses of someone that he or she does not know (Clemente & Marano, 2020).

The P2P Model of Insurance removes this bias. In P2P insurance, a group of people known to each other pool in the money and cover the risk of each other. The unclaimed money is refunded back to the members of the P2P insurance group. This ultimately reduces the cost of coverage and increases transparency in operations. This reduces the chances of conflict and increases the motivation to pay the premiums on time as there is social pressure. P2P insurance is also called "social insurance".

Lemonade in the USA was the first company to start the P2P insurance model. They started by offering life insurance and insurance for homeowners, renters and insurance for pets. Their monthly premiums start at as low as $5 per month to $25 per month. They extensively use technology like chatbots and AI to have a lower cost of operations. They have a chatbot called Maya that can answer queries and also help in paying premiums and processing claims. Their operations run on superfast mode. It takes 90 seconds to get insured and three minutes to get the claims on the automated platform of Lemonade. They charge a flat fee for running the operations and return the unclaimed money to policyholders.

On-Demand Coverage

Insurance has historically been a laborious procedure with a huge volume of complicated paperwork. Customers who wish to purchase insurance must complete extensive paperwork and send it, along with any necessary supporting documentation, to insurance agents or brokers. After carefully reviewing these forms and analyzing the data, the premiums and risk coverage are decided. It was a long, laborious and error-prone process. Underwriters were involved in some tiresome procedures as well. Customers in the insurance business asked that technology be used to deliver services more quickly and seamlessly, as the Fintech revolution swept across the banking and financial services sectors (Braun, Häusle & Thistle, 2023).

With the introduction of the digital model, insurance may now be purchased on demand straight from an insurance provider via their website or mobile application, negating the need for insurance brokers or agents to act as middlemen. Easy one-click purchasing, adjustable coverage and an appealing user interface and experience are the hallmarks of on-demand insurance. IoT, blockchain, AI and big data analytics are being used by on-demand insurance companies to remain ahead of the competition and provide clients with better goods and services at reduced rates. Additionally, they are using interactive procedures, mobile sensors and cognitive technology to provide near-instantaneous risk assessment, prompt policy issuance and easy management of claims. They provide adaptable choices such as preferential pricing for proactive safety measures performed by the insured or episodic coverage.

On-demand insurance can be stopped at any moment and can be purchased instantly from any location, depending on the needs. There is no long-term contract binding. Long form-filling or drawn-out conversations with insurance agents are not necessary. With a few taps on the smartphone, an easy procedure can be followed to purchase the coverage. Micro-duration policy premiums can be paid with mobile apps and claims can be submitted via a chat interface on a mobile device. Services are available around the clock.

On-demand insurance is provided by businesses like Slice Labs, Troy and Acko Insurance. Varun Dua founded Acko, which received a license to begin an insurance business from the Insurance Regulatory and Development Authority in 2017. It gained a lot of popularity by providing insurance products via websites and apps in an online format. The first totally digital insurance company in the nation is Acko. By utilizing the power of the Internet, the company is now providing insurance products directly to customers, doing away with the idea of insurance agents. Acko has simplified the process of purchasing, renewing and registering a claim by enabling paperless transactions. Funding was provided by SAIF Partners, Accel Partners and Catamaran Ventures.

Acko's policies have earned five stars, and the company has over five crore happy consumers as of right now. Over two lakh autos have been insured by the company. Additionally, the business offers microinsurance. Easypolicy, Digit and Policybazaar are Acko's primary rivals.

Trōv and Slice Labs are the other startups that provide an on-demand insurance approach. Troy provides an insurance-licensed app-based platform. Activating or deactivating coverage only requires one "swipe". To further automate the claims process, the software makes use of a chatbot. Another startup providing on-demand insurance coverage for renters, homeowners and small business owners is Slice Labs, Inc. Additionally, Slice and AXAXL have joined to provide small- and mid-sized enterprises with on-demand cyber insurance.

Internet of Things

IoT is very crucial for the functioning of the InsurTech business. InsurTech has helped to facilitate the established procedures and brought about a revolution in the sector. The insurance business is evolving quickly, and to maintain a competitive edge and withstand the influx of new competitors and client expectations for more affordable products and improved customer service, the industry is embracing InsurTech (Villamil, Hernández & Tarazona, 2020).

IoT is defined as "a network of smart devices (things) connected to the Internet, which can interact and communicate with each other". Smart appliances for cooking, refrigerators, air conditioners, televisions, watches and smartphones are all included in the IoT. Smart houses and driverless automobiles both use IoT. To put it briefly, IoT involves gathering and disseminating data about objects' surroundings and usage patterns. This can involve a wide range of items and technology, such as wearable fitness trackers, self-driving automobiles, smart houses and completely automated and networked production facilities.

The global count of devices with IoT capabilities has surpassed 30 billion. By 2025, this figure is projected to increase to 75 billion. Large volumes of data are being collected by these devices and big data analytics is being used to process and analyze the data to make conclusions. Prescriptive and predictive analytics are greatly aided by this. Furthermore, this has been crucial to the development of the InsurTech sector.

IoT is currently helping to understand the health condition of the customers, whose data is collected through smart devices. This helps to collect the data more accurately and also speeds up the claim settlement process. This helps to remove the data duplications and to optimize the processes. Customer satisfaction has also improved drastically after the application of IoT in InsurTech. This is because the needless paperwork has been removed and the waiting time for claim processing has been reduced. Customers are also able to track their data in a seamless manner through portals and apps.

One of the critical functions of the insurance business is the capability to assess risk. IoT helps in collecting accurate information in an automated manner and doing data modeling to analyze and predict risks. IoT also helps to identify the different types of risk groups, so as to classify them and determine how much premium they should pay.

IoT helps the InsurTech business in a big way by helping to prevent losses. Because of the availability of real-time data, the InsurTech Models can predict the risks and also prescribe strategies to mitigate them. This helps the insurer to reduce the number of claims that they need to pay and work on the principle: "An ounce of prevention is worth a pound of cure".

Big Data Underwriting

Underwriting is a process in insurance which determines how much coverage can be given to a customer and at what cost. An underwriter is a person who collects information about the present situation of the customer, the financial obligations and the future risks to determine what figure should be quoted to the customer for a particular sum insured.

There are two main components of the underwriting process. Financial underwriting is the process through which it is ascertained whether the needs of the customer are properly addressed. The financial net worth and the financial needs are taken into consideration for this process. Medical underwriting is the process that takes into account the mortality rate and the factors that affect the mortality rate. The lifestyle and the medical history are taken into account in this process. The whole process of underwriting is dependent on receiving authentic information, doing accurate analysis and making proper predictive analytics.

Today the underwriting process has become much simpler, accurate and much faster because of the application of big data analytics in underwriting. Banks and insurance companies can get data from social media and mobile phones easily to analyze and determine premium amounts. They can access real-time data on customer spending and payments to develop credit risk models. They can get data by using sensor-based technologies and telematics. Telematics is helping insurers collect real-time driver behavior and usage data to provide premium discounts and UBI. Unstructured data like satellite images, social media postings and geographical positioning systems also yield valuable data for insurers. These data are used for data mining, statistical modeling and ML to design better products for insurers (Kajwang, 2022).

The big advantages of using big data analytics in underwriting are:

- Collecting precise and accurate data
- Analyzing data with a higher level of precision
- Bringing more transparency to the process
- Developing better products for customers
- Improve customer experience by meeting their expectation
- Customize products as per customer needs
- Prevent fraud from happening in the system
- Improve solvency through the ability to more accurately assess risk

According to *Yes!* Magazine, "the implementation of big data in underwriting has resulted in 30% better access to insurance services, 40–70% cost savings and 60% higher fraud detection rates".

AI-Based Claims Processing

Claim processing is one of the biggest pain points of the insurance industry. The traditional companies in the insurance sector did deploy huge budgets in marketing and promotions and acquiring customers, but not much was done to streamline the claim processing activities. This has led to huge dissatisfaction among customers and given the insurance companies a bad name. Most customers have the perception that the insurance companies treat the customers well while collecting the premiums but do not offer the same level of satisfaction when they come to settle claims. There are innumerable delays and errors during claim processing causing customer dissatisfaction and frustration.

While automated data entry has provided some efficiencies, legacy technologies still struggle to accurately read the most challenging documents – which might contain handwriting or cursive, have been faxed, mailed or scanned or photographed by a smartphone and uploaded to a portal. In the absence of reliable results, organizations have continued to rely on people to check the outputs, fix errors and rekey data – an inadequate, short-term solution.

Fortunately, technologies are available today to address this challenge. Increasingly, innovative firms are turning to intelligent document processing (IDP) technology, which leverages AI and related technologies like ML, to automatically capture, classify and extract unstructured data from various documents. The right IDP solution can read messy, real-world documents with context and continues to learn and train itself in response to the data that it's exposed to. The result is a high level of accuracy, speed, efficiency and business value.

By implementing this type of AI-driven solution, claims processors can reduce clerical errors that can result in inaccurate customer data or slow the claims payment process and improve customer experience in the process. After all, when filing a claim – oftentimes a period of great stress – customers want their insurers to alleviate their worries and burdens, not add to them. With less manual and administrative work, insurers and their employees can focus on these higher-order initiatives, and more complete and accurate data lays the groundwork for greater downstream AI, analytics and strategic digitization initiatives (Brundage, Avin, Wang, Belfield, Krueger, Hadfield & Anderljung, 2020).

A 2019 Everest Group study reinforces the growing role of IDP across industries, estimating that IDP is expected to grow 70–80% in the next two years "and will rapidly accelerate as enterprises seek to harness the power of AI technologies to improve compliance and governance and reduce the overall cost of processing huge volumes of information".

Use of Chatbots

Insurance companies have deployed chatbots to understand customer needs and give proper advice to customers. Chatbots learn from real data and fully comprehend the services the insurance company provides using AI and ML to interact with customers and engage as a human would. The virtual assistant does the operations by integrating with the insurance company's back-office systems.

The prominent features of chatbots are:

- They are conversational.
- They are transactional.
- They are secure and reliable.
- They can be deployed across multiple channels.

Chatbots can be rule based or smart machine based. Chatbots which are rule based, use keywords to give predefined responses from a database to customers based on their queries. Chatbots which are smart machine-based use AIML to customize answers and become smarter with each interaction with the customer.

Smart machine-based chatbots are more efficient and effective but rule-based chatbots are cheaper. Rule-based chatbots are one-dimensional, whereas smart machine-based chatbots are multi-dimensional. Smart machine-based chatbots are more robust as they have AI capabilities.

The insurance companies need to choose the type of chatbots they want based on the business requirement, purpose and type of customers they are servicing. For simple tasks, the deployment of rule-based chatbots will be a wise decision. For complicated and multi-dimensional tasks, AI-based chatbots are better.

The use of chatbots in the insurance industry has gained significant traction in recent years, revolutionizing customer interactions, streamlining processes and enhancing overall efficiency. Chatbots, powered by AI and natural language processing, bring several advantages to the insurance sector (VanderLinden, Millie, Anderson & Chishti, 2018).

Chatbots provide round-the-clock assistance, allowing customers to interact with the insurance company at any time, regardless of business hours. Chatbots offer quick responses to customer queries, reducing waiting times and enhancing customer satisfaction.

Chatbots can guide customers through the claims process, collecting necessary information and documentation. This accelerates claims processing and reduces the burden on human agents. Chatbots can facilitate the submission of required documents, such as photos of damages, speeding up the claims assessment process.

Chatbots assist customers in understanding different insurance policies, coverage options and terms. They can provide personalized recommendations based on the customer's needs and preferences. Chatbots can notify customers about policy updates, renewals and any changes in coverage, ensuring that clients stay informed (Svetlana, 2016).

Chatbots can guide new customers through the onboarding process, collecting necessary information and ensuring a smooth start to their insurance journey. Customers can use chatbots to get quick answers to common questions about their policies, premiums and coverage details.

Chatbots are capable of analyzing data supplied by customers to evaluate risk profiles and choose the right insurance plan. By drawing attention to discrepancies in the supplied data, they can spot possible fraud. Chatbots are able to keep an eye on activities and transactions, quickly identifying any unusual conduct that might point to fraud. Chatbots improve operational efficiency by freeing up human agents to concentrate on more complicated problems by automating repetitive operations and inquiries. By processing a high number of inquiries at once, chatbots aid in resource optimization by lowering the demand for additional labor.

Chatbots are able to pick up on conversations and gradually refine their responses. They are able to adjust to shifting consumer preferences and market developments. Chatbots may gather and evaluate client input, giving insurers insightful information to improve their offerings.

A cohesive and consistent customer experience can be achieved by smoothly integrating chatbots across a variety of communication channels, such as websites, mobile apps and social media platforms.

The use of chatbots in the insurance sector is changing how companies handle claims, communicate with clients and run their operations. Chatbots will probably become more and more important as technology develops in the insurance industry in terms of improving client satisfaction and operational effectiveness.

The Future Outlook of the InsurTech Industry

The InsurTech industry is expected to face a volatile landscape in the future, influenced by developments in technology, changing client expectations and regulatory changes. The InsurTech industry is likely to be impacted by a number of trends and advancements in the future (Braun & Schreiber, 2017).

Predictive analytics will be used by InsurTech businesses more and more to better evaluate risk, which will improve underwriting procedures and pricing models. Through chatbots, virtual assistants and automated claims processing, AI will be helpful in streamlining repetitive activities, increasing operational efficiency and facilitating a more customized client experience.

The utilization of blockchain technology holds the capability to enhance both the security and transparency of transactions within the insurance industry. Smart contracts built on blockchain technology have the capability to automate the processing of claims, reducing instances of fraud and speeding up the settlement process. Blockchain technology can improve data integrity by providing a decentralized and tamper-proof ledger that ensures the accuracy and immutability of the recorded information (Sosa & Montes, 2022).

Insurance companies will increasingly leverage data from IoT devices, such as smart home appliances and connected autos, to assess risk. This could lead to customized premiums and rewards to motivate policyholders to engage in safer behaviors. IoT can assist insurers in reducing the occurrence and intensity of claims by offering preventive measures and services that rely on up-to-date data.

As cyber threats become more frequent and sophisticated, there will likely be a significant increase in demand for cyber insurance. The creation of creative solutions to deal with the changing terrain of cyber threats will be greatly aided by InsurTech enterprises.

The use of parametric insurance is growing in favor of traditional loss assessment since it pays out according to predetermined parameters. When it comes to risks related to natural disasters and other catastrophic events, this paradigm is very pertinent. The InsurTech sector will concentrate on developing more individualized insurance solutions that cater to specific requirements and preferences.

People will find it simpler to investigate, buy and maintain insurance plans because of the continued advancements in digital platforms and user-friendly interfaces. The insurance technology sector must adjust to changing legislative environments. To ensure consumer protection and monitor the use of technology in the insurance industry, governments and regulatory agencies are probably going to take a more proactive approach. Traditional insurers and InsurTech companies will increasingly collaborate to capitalize on one another's advantages. This kind of cooperation can result in new product development, better distribution systems and increased consumer outreach.

As technology continues to change the insurance market, the future of the InsurTech sector is full of exciting possibilities. The future success of the sector will largely depend on its capacity to adjust to new trends, work well with others and satisfy changing consumer demands. The InsurTech sector has the potential to significantly influence how the insurance industry develops in the future as new innovations continue to emerge.

Top InsurTech Companies in the World

Lemonade

Lemonade is a ten-year-old InsurTech company that was started in 2015 with the backing of Softbank. They sold over a million policies within three years and are now valued at $2 billion. It is an innovative InsurTech company that has disrupted the traditional insurance industry by leveraging technology, behavioral economics and a customer-centric approach. It has revolutionized insurance by making it faster, transparent and affordable. The mission of Lemonade is to provide insurance that is simple, delightful and driven by social good.

Lemonade has a user-friendly mobile app that makes it easy for customers to manage their policies and file claims. The app provides real-time updates and communication with Lemonade's customer service team, which helps to improve the overall customer experience. The app has earned 4.9 stars in the App Store and is highly rated by users. The insurance claims are disbursed within minutes, not days. Lemonade's customer service is exceptional, providing a refreshing change from traditional insurers.

One of the key features of Lemonade is its use of AI and ML algorithms to streamline the insurance process and provide personalized coverage to its customers. This allows Lemonade to offer faster and more accurate underwriting, as well as more affordable premiums for its customers.

Another unique aspect of Lemonade is its focus on social impact. The company donates a portion of its premiums to charitable causes selected by its customers, which helps to differentiate it from other insurance companies and appeal to socially conscious consumers.

Overall, Lemonade InsurTech Company is a disruptive player in the insurance industry, with a unique combination of technology, affordability and social impact that sets it apart from traditional insurance companies.

Root Insurance

Root is an InsurTech company that has made waves in the insurance industry with its innovative approach. It was founded in 2015 and the mission of the company is to empower insurers by providing an API-first platform for modern insurance strategies. They have won appreciation from customers for making insurance faster, transparent and affordable.

Root's platform is low-code and API-first, allowing insurers to launch and manage digital insurance solutions with ease. It covers the entire insurance value chain, from product creation to distribution. Root promises zero paperwork and instant policy issuance. Their sophisticated chat feature handles automated claims processing. Customers can customize their deductible amounts.

Root focuses on delivering first-class insurance experiences across all customer touchpoints. Insurers can embed insurance experiences and partner-distribution channels with just a few lines of code. Root streamlines insurance administration, compliance and reporting, allowing insurers to focus on growth. Insurers can unlock the power of their insurance data for data-driven products, operations and strategy.

Root provides secure and flexible access to all relevant data. Root collaborates with leading insurance companies and affinity brands to launch digital and embedded insurance experiences. They process millions of policies and thousands of claims across dozens of products. Root's APIs make integration easy, and their team offers exceptional support.

In summary, Root's platform simplifies insurance complexities, enables digital engagement and empowers insurers to create customer-centric products.

Insurify

Insurify is an online insurance marketplace that simplifies the process of comparing insurance quotes from multiple providers. While it is not an insurance company itself, it acts as a comparison site, allowing users to review quotes from various insurance companies in one convenient place.

The objective of Insurify's digital insurance platform is to give users an easy-to-use and convenient way to buy and manage insurance products. The platform provides a large selection of insurance products, such as health, travel and auto insurance. Using AI and ML algorithms to deliver customers individualized insurance recommendations based on their unique needs and risk profiles is one of Insurify's primary benefits.

Customers can evaluate various insurance plans and costs with ease using Insurify's user-friendly interface, which facilitates decision-making regarding insurance coverage. Customers may also maintain and modify their insurance policies online with this platform, saving them the trouble of getting in touch with their insurance companies directly.

Insurify enables users to compare insurance quotes from 75+ top companies. By entering their ZIP code and answering a few questions, users receive real-time quotes without any fees or spam. The platform has garnered positive reviews, with a 4.8 rating based on over 3,000 reviews. Users who compare insurance options through Insurify can save up to $717 on annual premiums. The platform empowers users to choose their preferred method of purchasing insurance – whether online or over the phone – with no hidden fees1.

Insurify provides accurate real-time quotes by considering individual circumstances. Users can easily find out which insurer offers the most competitive rates for their specific needs. Insurify unlocks exclusive rates and special discounts for users, ensuring they get the best deal available. Insurify streamlines the insurance shopping process, allowing users to compare quotes, find discounts and make well-informed decisions about their coverage needs. Whether the customer is looking for auto, home, pet, health or life insurance, Insurify aims to help you secure good, affordable coverage without any hassle or spam.

Insurify's editorial team consists of seasoned personal finance writers, insurance industry experts, former journalists, insurance agents and data scientists. They strive to provide readers with valuable information to make informed decisions about insurance coverage. Overall, Insurify represents a significant step forward in the insurance industry, providing customers with a more efficient and personalized way to manage their insurance needs.

Hippo Insurance

Hippo Insurance is an American property insurance company headquartered in Palo Alto, California. Established in 2015, it began offering insurance services in 2017. Hippo takes a modern and tech-friendly approach to homeowners' insurance. It leverages data analytics and AI to provide comprehensive coverage. Hippo Insurance combines technology, enhanced coverage and streamlined processes to offer a smarter and more efficient homeowners insurance experience for modern households.

Hippo offers coverage for homes and possessions, as well as liability protection for accidents occurring on the insured property. Hippo integrates smart home monitoring systems to detect issues like break-ins and water leaks. These systems help keep rates low and prevent small problems from becoming expensive ones.

Hippo provides higher coverage limits for computers, home office equipment, appliances and personal electronics compared to traditional policies. It provides service line coverage protection for gas, electric and sewer connections between the house and the street in case of accidents or wear and tear. Their free app assists homeowners in proactive maintenance and offers (Zeier Röschmann, Erny & Wagner, 2022).

Users can get an insurance quote in 60 seconds through the Hippo Home app. By eliminating commissioned agents, Hippo reduces costs and passes on the savings to customers. The company aims to save homeowners up to 25% by preventing problems before they occur.

Hippo Insurance also offers a variety of discounts to its customers, including a multi-policy discount for customers who bundle their home and auto insurance policies, a home security discount for customers who have a home security system installed and a safe driving discount for customers who have a clean driving record.

The company also has a user-friendly mobile app that allows customers to manage their policies, make payments and file claims. Hippo Insurance has received positive reviews from customers for its excellent customer service, including its fast and easy claims process.

Overall, Hippo Insurance is a promising insurance company that offers personalized coverage options and excellent customer service. Its use of technology and data analysis sets it apart from traditional insurance companies and makes it a great choice for customers who are tech-savvy and value personalized service.

Slice Labs

Slice Labs is a prominent player in the InsurTech space, known for its innovative approach to insurance through on-demand and UBI solutions. Slice Labs was founded in 2015 by

Tim Attia and Ernest Hursh. Headquartered in New York City, the company has gained recognition for its focus on providing insurance products tailored to the needs of the modern digital economy. Slice aims to revolutionize insurance by offering flexible, on-demand coverage that aligns with the evolving lifestyles and preferences of consumers.

Slice offers on-demand insurance solutions that allow customers to purchase coverage only when needed. This model contrasts with traditional insurance policies that typically require long-term commitments. On-demand insurance from Slice is particularly appealing to gig workers, freelancers and individuals with sporadic income streams who may require insurance coverage for specific periods or activities.

Slice provides UBI products that utilize data from IoT devices and other sources to customize premiums based on actual usage patterns. This approach enables fairer pricing and incentivizes safer behaviors. For example, Slice offers pay-as-you-go insurance for rideshare drivers, where premiums are based on the number of hours spent driving rather than a fixed monthly rate.

Slice's digital platform offers a user-friendly interface for customers to browse insurance products, obtain quotes and purchase coverage online. The platform leverages advanced technology to streamline the insurance process and enhance the customer experience. Through the platform, customers can access policy information, file claims and manage their coverage preferences conveniently from their computers or mobile devices.

Slice harnesses the power of data analytics and AI to assess risks, personalize insurance offerings and automate underwriting processes. By analyzing vast amounts of data, including customer behavior data and real-time IoT data, Slice can make more accurate risk assessments and tailor coverage to individual needs.

Slice collaborates with InsurTech startups, tech companies and industry partners to integrate innovative technologies into its insurance offerings. Through partnerships with IoT device manufacturers and data providers, Slice expands its capabilities in data collection and risk management, enabling more precise pricing and coverage customization.

Slice's on-demand and UBI models challenge the traditional insurance industry by offering more flexibility, transparency and affordability to consumers. The company's innovative approach resonates with a growing segment of the market seeking insurance solutions that align with their lifestyle and preferences.

Slice addresses emerging risks associated with the gig economy, sharing economy and digital platforms by providing insurance solutions tailored to the needs of workers and businesses in these sectors. By offering coverage for activities such as ridesharing, home-sharing and short-term rentals, Slice helps individuals and businesses mitigate risks in a rapidly changing environment.

Slice Labs continues to expand its presence in the InsurTech industry, driven by its commitment to innovation and customer-centric approach. The company's focus on on-demand and UBI models positions it well to capitalize on the evolving needs of consumers and businesses in the digital age. With ongoing advancements in technology and strategic partnerships, Slice is poised to play a significant role in shaping the future of insurance.

Questions for Discussion

1. Explain the model of P2P insurance.
2. Explain how on-demand coverage is being done in the insurance industry.
3. Explain how big data is being used for underwriting in the insurance industry.
4. Explain how IoT is helping the insurance industry in acquiring and processing data.

5. Explain how AI is being used in claims processing.
6. What are chatbots? How are they contributing to increasing the efficiency in the insurance industry?

Case Study – Policybazaar

Policybazaar was started by Yashish Dahiya, Alok Bansal and Avaneesh Nirjar in the year 2008. The business model of the company is that of an insurance aggregator. The company is based in Gurgaon and is the largest insurance aggregator in the country. Apart from India, Policybazaar runs operations in UAE.

Policybazaar is an Indian online insurance aggregator that provides a platform for users to compare and purchase insurance policies. Policybazaar operates on an aggregator model, serving as an online marketplace that allows customers to compare and buy various insurance products from multiple insurance providers. It provides a one-stop platform for users to explore policies across categories such as health insurance, life insurance, motor insurance and travel insurance.

Policybazaar earns revenue primarily through lead generation. When a user purchases an insurance policy through the platform, the respective insurance company pays Policybazaar a commission or fee for facilitating the sale. In addition to commissions from insurance companies, Policybazaar may earn affiliate commissions for referring customers to other financial products and services.

Policybazaar offers a wide range of insurance products, including health insurance, life insurance, motor insurance, travel insurance, home insurance and more. This diverse portfolio allows users to compare and choose policies based on their specific needs.

Policybazaar leverages technology to provide a user-friendly interface that allows customers to easily compare policies, understand terms and conditions and make informed decisions. The platform facilitates the entire insurance purchasing process online, from policy comparison to application and payment, streamlining the customer journey.

Policybazaar invests in creating informative content to educate users about different insurance products, coverage options and industry terms. This helps users make informed decisions and understand the value of insurance.

Policybazaar collaborates with various insurance companies, creating partnerships that allow it to feature a diverse range of policies on its platform. These partnerships are crucial for expanding the array of options available to users. Policybazaar heavily invests in digital marketing strategies to reach a wide audience. This includes online advertising, SEO and social media campaigns to increase brand visibility and attract potential customers. The platform may also implement referral programs to encourage existing customers to refer others to use Policybazaar's services.

Policybazaar provides customer support to assist users in navigating the platform, understanding policy details and addressing queries. Ensuring a positive customer experience is crucial for building trust and retaining users.

To stay competitive, Policybazaar continually invests in technological innovations. This includes updates to its website or mobile app, the integration of new features and the adoption of emerging technologies to enhance the overall user experience.

It collects all the detailed information on the different types of insurance policies offered by different companies and helps the insurance customer to make the right choice through comparative analysis. The business is run completely in a digital mode and the access to information in Policybazaar is only through an app or the website called www.policybazaar.com. It sells both life insurance and general insurance policies. The company promises to offer financial safety and a clutch of other benefits like instant quotes from different companies.

Policybazaar is currently doing brisk business. It gets more than 100 million visitors every year. They sell more than two lakh policies every year. There are more than three lakh transactions happening in the portal of Policybazaar every month.

It makes the process smooth and stress free. It also provides a repository of knowledge on insurance, simplifying the complicated terminology for the layman to understand the jargon in a better manner. Customers can buy insurance policies from the portal and also make claims through the portal. They can track their policy or download the policy with a single tap. They can store and share the policy in the portal of Policybazaar.

Policybazaar has brought about transparency and accountability in the insurance sector. After moving from being an information aggregator to an online insurance seller, Policybazaar has gained a market share of 25% of life insurance and 7% of health insurance business.

Policybazaar is now making innovations to get a pole position in the insurance market. It has launched both Android and iOS apps. It has developed a chatbot based on AI to increase customer satisfaction. Recently, the company has filed a draft red herring prospectus to raise $810 million through an initial public offering.

Case Study Questions

1. Explain the business model of Policybazaar.
2. How does Policybazaar facilitate the process of buying insurance?
3. What are the advantages of the online business model of Policybazaar over the offline business models?

Further Reading

1. Bisnoff, J. (2021, June 8). The Future of Insurance: Fintech 50 2021. Forbes. www.forbes.com/sites/jasonbisnoff/2021/06/08/the-future-of-insurance-fintech-50-2021/?sh=78e3e35774be
2. Bean, R. (2021, July 6). Transforming The Insurance Industry With Big Data, Machine Learning And AI. Forbes. www.forbes.com/sites/randybean/2021/07/06/transforming-the-insurance-industry-with-big-data-machine-learning-and-ai/?sh=103599e9f8a6

References

Asmussen, S., & Steffensen, M. (2020). *Risk and insurance*. Springer International Publishing.

Braun, A., Häusle, N. M., & Thistle, P. (2023). On-demand insurance. *Journal of Risk and Insurance*, 90(4), 975–990.

Braun, A., & Schreiber, F. (2017). *The current InsurTech landscape: Business models and disruptive potential* (No. 62). I. VW HSG Schriftenreihe.

Brundage, M., Avin, S., Wang, J., Belfield, H., Krueger, G., Hadfield, G., & Anderljung, M. (2020). *Toward Trustworthy AI Development: Mechanisms for Supporting Verifiable Claims*. arXiv preprint arXiv:2004.07213.

Cappiello, A., & Cappiello, A. (2018). Digital disruption and InsurTech start-ups: Risks and challenges. In *Technology and the insurance industry: Re-configuring the competitive landscape* (pp. 29–50). Palgrave Pivot.
Chemmanur, T. J., Imerman, M. B., Rajaiya, H., & Yu, Q. (2020). Recent developments in the FinTech industry. *Journal of Financial Management, Markets and Institutions*, 8(01), 2040002.
Clemente, G. P., & Marano, P. (2020). The broker model for peer-to-peer insurance: An analysis of its value. *The Geneva Papers on Risk and Insurance-Issues and Practice*, 45, 457–481.
Cummins, J. D., Dionne, G., Gagné, R., & Nouira, A. (2021). The costs and benefits of reinsurance. *The Geneva Papers on Risk and Insurance-Issues and Practice*, 46, 177–199.
Hodula, M., Janků, J., Časta, M., & Kučera, A. (2021). On the macrofinancial determinants of life and non-life insurance premiums. *The Geneva Papers on Risk and Insurance-Issues and Practice*, 1–39.
Innov8tif Solution. (2021). *Differences between InsurTech and conventional insurance?* https://innov8tif.com/differences-between-insurtech-and-conventional-insurance/
Kagan, J., Rasure, E., & Munichiello, K. (2024). Insurance: Definition, how it works, and main types of policies. *Investopedia*. www.investopedia.com/terms/i/insurance.asp
Kajwang, B. (2022). Implications for big data and analytics on underwriting practices in insurance sector. *American Journal of Data, Information and Knowledge Management*, 3(1), 1–11.
Mosig, T., Lehmann, C., & Moeslein, K. M. (2021). Business model innovation in the insurance industry: Barriers faced by incumbents. *International Journal of Entrepreneurship and Innovation Management*, 25(6), 391–419.
Neale, F. R., Drake, P. P., & Konstantopoulos, T. (2020). InsurTech and the disruption of the insurance industry. *Journal of Insurance Issues*, 43(2), 64–96.
Sosa, I., & Montes, Ó. (2022). Understanding the InsurTech dynamics in the transformation of the insurance sector. *Risk Management and Insurance Review*, 25(1), 35–68.
Stricker, L., Wagner, J., & Zeier Röschmann, A. (2023). The future of insurance intermediation in the age of the digital platform economy. *Journal of Risk and Financial Management*, 16(9), 381.
Suryavanshi, U. (2022). The InsurTech revolution in insurance industry: Emerging trends, challenges and opportunities. *International Journal of Management and Development Studies*, 11(08), 12–19.
Svetlana, V. (2016). InsurTech: Challenges and development perspectives. *International Journal of Innovative Technologies in Economy*, 3(5), 39–42.
Toshmurzaevich, Y. O. (2020). Developing the underwriting process in life insurance. *European Journal of Business and Management Research*, 5(6).
VanderLinden, S. L., Millie, S. M., Anderson, N., & Chishti, S. (2018). *The InsurTech book: The insurance technology handbook for investors, entrepreneurs and FinTech visionaries*. John Wiley & Sons.
Villamil, S., Hernández, C., & Tarazona, G. (2020). An overview of internet-of-things. *Telkomnika (Telecommunication Computing Electronics and Control)*, 18(5), 2320–2327.
Wilamowicz, A. (2019). The great FinTech disruption: InsurTech. *Banking & Finance Law Review*, 34(2), 215–238.
Zeier Röschmann, A., Erny, M., & Wagner, J. (2022). On the (future) role of on-demand insurance: Market landscape, business model and customer perception. *The Geneva Papers on Risk and Insurance-Issues and Practice*, 47(3), 603–642.

8 Financial Regulations and Compliances – The RegTech Model

After reading this chapter you will:

- Know what is RegTech
- Understand the role of artificial intelligence and machine learning (AIML) in RegTech
- Understand the role of big data analytics in RegTech
- Understand the role of robotic process automation (RPA) in RegTech
- Understand the role of blockchain in RegTech

Fund transfers between accounts that are started, cleared and settled almost instantly are known as real-time payments. This implies that the transaction's beneficiary has almost immediate access to the transferred monies. It also implies that once approved, real-time payments are irreversible.

Since real-time payments are initiated, processed and paid in a matter of seconds following a purchase, they eliminate payment friction for customers. The bank's backend system needs to be operational around the clock to process payments in real-time while safeguarding customers and the bank against fraud. RTPs make sure that clients can easily access their money whenever they need it, make quick payments and receive immediate settlements.

Nearly 100% of real-time payment systems in use today operate this way. This implies that you can use them to transmit money every day of the year, at any time of day. In many instances, that also applies to weekends and holidays!

There are numerous potential advantages to real-time payments for financial institutions, enterprises and consumers. They do, however, also provide difficulties in terms of preventing fraud using them.

In certain situations, real-time payments provide the advantage of almost instantaneous settlement and irreversibility once allowed. But they also make RTP systems attractive targets for scammers hoping to profit from rising RTP usage. Criminals find them appealing because they can't be undone once allowed and finish in a matter of seconds. Speedier payment methods typically translate into speedier payment fraud and con artists will do whatever it takes to take advantage of these systems for personal gain. It will be more crucial than ever for businesses to maintain payment compliance to stay safe.

One instance of this type of fraud is authorized push payment fraud, in which an attacker impersonates a genuine payee in real-time payments via social engineering techniques, or uses hacking techniques, such as account takeovers. The inability to revoke the payment makes it challenging for a victim to obtain their money back. Furthermore, the

DOI: 10.4324/9781032699417-8

instantaneous settlement of real-time payments allows the fraudster to swiftly launder the stolen funds through a variety of channels.

The increasing use of real-time payments emphasizes how critical it is for financial institutions to have cutting-edge AML and anti-fraud systems that can evaluate risk more quickly. For further context, Unit21's transaction monitoring solution examines a larger range of actions and data sources. Financial institutions might potentially prevent fraud before it even occurs by using this to identify activity patterns that often indicate fraud in addition to lowering their false positive rates. Governments and authorities are thinking about ways to strengthen their defenses against this type of fraud because of its possibility.

When transactions take only a few seconds to complete, real-time payment fraud detection becomes challenging. Thankfully, real-time payments are data-rich, and, since they process quickly, there will probably be a lot more of them in the future. Because of this, they are perfect for teaching machine learning (ML) models to search for patterns associated with fraud or anomalies that may indicate the emergence of new fraud schemes.

What Is RegTech?

RegTech is defined as "the management of regulatory processes within the financial industry through technology. The main functions of RegTech include regulatory monitoring, reporting, and compliance" (Estevez, 2020).

Regulatory technology, or RegTech for short, is a branch of financial technology that specializes in using technology to enhance regulatory compliance and operations. It entails assisting financial institutions in more effectively and efficiently meeting regulatory standards through the use of cutting-edge technology like artificial intelligence (AI), ML and data analytics.

RegTech is a more specific term coined

> to classify a group of companies that, by harnessing the capabilities enabled by new technologies such as cloud computing, big data, and blockchains, are devising solutions to help companies across all sectors of financial activity, ensure that they comply with regulatory requirements. In financial parlance. RegTech is deemed a subgroup of FinTech.
>
> (Charoenwong, Kowaleski, Kwan & Sutherland, 2023)

The main responsibilities of RegTech involve ensuring compliance, generating reports and monitoring regulatory activities. RegTech companies assist organizations in achieving more efficient and cost-effective compliance with regulations through the utilization of software-as-a-service and cloud computing technology. RegTech solutions have the objective of identifying issues or irregularities in the domain of digital payments through the ongoing surveillance of online transactions. Every deviation from the norm is promptly reported to the financial institution for the purpose of conducting an investigation and determining the presence of fraudulent activity. Institutions can mitigate the expenses and risks associated with financial losses and data breaches by promptly identifying potential threats to financial security (Chishti & Barberis, 2016).

Regulators and financial institutions are now utilizing RegTech extensively to address the increasing difficulty of managing complicated compliance procedures brought about by the use of the dark web, cryptocurrencies, blockchains, peer-to-peer (P2P) transactions and application program interface (APIs).

RegTech's ability to lower compliance costs for financial organizations is one of its primary advantages. RegTech facilitates time and resource savings for institutions by automating repetitive operations and offering real-time monitoring and reporting, allowing them to allocate resources to other aspects of their business.

Enhancing an institution's capacity for risk management is another advantage of RegTech. RegTech can assist organizations in identifying possible hazards and taking proactive measures to mitigate them by analyzing vast amounts of data. By doing this, organizations can safeguard themselves against expensive errors and financial losses.

Additionally, RegTech can assist organizations in enhancing the client experience. RegTech can assist institutions in offering their clients more individualized and effective service by automating repetitive operations and supplying real-time analytics.

To sum up, RegTech is an effective instrument for financial institutions seeking to enhance their client experience, risk management and regulatory compliance. It makes use of cutting-edge technology to boost productivity by automating repetitive processes and offering real-time information.

History of RegTech

RegTech's growth was spurred in part by the industry's reaction to the 2008 financial crisis. The advancement of technology and the use of data created concerns about the hazards that these activities opened up, such as cybercrime, data privacy and security. This did not just result in a rise in the complexity of legislation (Arner, Barberis & Buckey, 2016).

The rise of Fintech, which was mostly propelled by the IT industry, was not without risk. This made it clear that new regulatory actions were required to make sure these services and applications complied with all laws pertaining to the financial sector. Concerns were raised about the security and safety of online data storage against hackers.

Some of the early adopters of cryptocurrencies were money launderers, tax evaders, drug peddlers, terrorists and other criminals who were using the dark web and P2P networks to transfer and receive money. There were criminals who were releasing Trojan horses and other viruses and ransomware, seizing critical data of banks and financial institutions and asking to be paid in cryptocurrencies to let go of the data. There were kidnappers and contract killers who were demanding money in cryptocurrencies. The money trail in the case of all these nefarious activities needed to be tracked to nail down the criminals and bring them to justice. That was how the RegTech industry came into focus to help the cybercrime cells, anti-money laundering (AML) units and law enforcement authorities to track illicit activities, prevent them from happening and nail down the criminals (Knight, 2016).

In the present era, the Fintech sector is moving from the digitization of money to the monetization of data. Data sovereignty and algorithms are the prime focus and the systems have to create new frameworks to accommodate them. This called for a sequential approach to the development of the Fintech system within the RegTech framework.

If getting data was a challenge for the regulators in the previous century, the challenge in the new millennium is managing the data and analyzing them to make sense and draw incisive inferences. With the widespread use of mobiles and tablets, we are producing 2.5 quintillion of data every day. One quintillion is equal to 10^{18}. Regulators and cybercrime cells need competence to sift through and analyze this vast expanse of data. This is where RegTech comes into play to provide utility services.

The data centricity has also changed because of the prevalence of Fintech systems. We have now moved from know-your-customer (KYC) to know-your-data (KYD). With each passing day, the regulators are also understanding the importance of KYD and investing a substantial amount of their budget in RegTech systems that can facilitate the KYD approach.

Due to the aftermath of the 2008 subprime crisis, the regulators have made the rules, regulations and compliances more tough and banks and financial institutions have been made to pay heavy penalties for non-compliances and violations. In the last ten years, banks and financial institutions have paid more than $300 billion for non-compliance and violations. To prevent such hefty fines, banks and financial institutions have created electronic watchdogs and invested heavily in RegTech. JP Morgan itself has allocated more than $5 billion in RegTech. Smaller banks and financial institutions are also following suit. In the USA, the investment in RegTech is expected to cross $150 billion by 2025. In Europe, deals worth $1.5 billion were done in 2020 for setting up RegTech systems and processes (Buckley, Arner, Zetzsche & Weber, 2020).

In India, we have seen a major regulatory lapse when the billionaire diamantaire Nirav Modi siphoned off $2 billion (INR 14,000 crore) from the government-controlled Punjab National Banks using bogus letter-of-undertaking. This was done by manipulating the SWIFT code and not routing the release of funds through the core banking system (CBS). The alerts were not raised as the funds did not pass through CBS. It was too late by the time PNB officials realized that a fraud of such massive scale had taken place and Nirav Modi had fled to the UK. The Government of India has now started to invest in RegTech to ensure that such frauds are prevented in the future (Hanumantu, Worlikar & Narayanaswami, 2019).

Rules Governing Fintech Industries across the World

The Fintech sector is expanding quickly and has completely changed the way financial services are offered. But, just like any other sector, Fintech is likewise governed by a set of laws and guidelines. These regulations shield consumers from fraud and other financial crimes while also assisting in ensuring that the sector runs in a safe, secure and equitable manner (Knight, 2016).

The requirement that businesses seek licenses and permissions to function is one of the main regulations governing the Fintech sector. Depending on the kind of financial services being provided, these licenses and permits differ, and to get them, businesses must abide by all applicable rules and regulations. Fintech businesses must also abide by rules pertaining to AML, data security and privacy.

Transparency is a vital regulation that governs the Fintech sector as well. It is imperative for companies to exhibit transparency in their operations and to effectively convey the terms and circumstances governing their financial products and services. This makes it possible for customers to make well-informed decisions on their financial affairs and to be completely informed.

Lastly, rules protecting consumers also apply to the Fintech sector. These legal measures aid in guaranteeing that customers receive equitable treatment and that their financial interests are safeguarded. This covers guidelines for marketing and promotion as well as standards for fee and other charge disclosure for financial goods and services.

The general goals of the laws governing the Fintech sector are to further justice, safety and security. Fintech companies can contribute to the establishment of consumer trust and establish themselves as respectable and trustworthy suppliers of financial services by adhering to these regulations (Ozili, 2022).

Licensing and Registration

For legal compliance, the Fintech companies require certain licenses or registrations. Depending on the services provided – such as loan processing, investment advising or payment processing – different licenses may be needed. These companies also need to be registered with the respective regulators.

AML and KYC Compliance

Robust AML and KYC procedures are typically mandated for Fintech companies to prevent money laundering and guarantee the identification of their clients. This entails confirming users' identities and keeping an eye on transactions for questionable activity.

Data Protection and Privacy

Fintech businesses frequently deal with private and sensitive financial data. To protect consumer data, they must so abide by privacy and data protection laws. It is essential to abide by regulations such as the General Data Protection Regulation (GDPR) in the European Union.

Consumer Protection

Regulations aim to protect consumers by ensuring transparency, fair practices and clear disclosure of terms and conditions. Fintech companies must comply with rules that govern issues such as disclosure of fees, interest rates and terms of service.

Cybersecurity

Fintech organizations need to have strong cybersecurity measures in place because of their reliance on technology to guard against data breaches and unauthorized access. Regulation authorities frequently have policies in place to guarantee the protection of financial information.

Payment Services Regulations

If a Fintech company provides payment services, it may be subject to specific regulations governing payment processing, electronic funds transfers and other related activities. Compliance with the Payment Services Directive (PSD2) in the EU is an example.

Crowdfunding Regulations

Fintech platforms involved in crowdfunding or P2P lending may be subject to specific regulations designed to protect both investors and borrowers.

Capital Adequacy and Prudential Standards

Fintech companies involved in lending or other financial activities may be subject to capital adequacy requirements to ensure financial stability and protect customers in case of insolvency.

Cross-Border Regulations

Fintech companies operating across borders may need to navigate regulations in multiple jurisdictions. International cooperation and adherence to cross-border regulations become crucial in such cases.

It's important for Fintech companies to stay informed about regulatory developments and work closely with legal experts to ensure compliance with the specific regulations applicable to their operations. The regulatory landscape for Fintech is dynamic, with changes occurring as the industry evolves and authorities respond to emerging challenges.

Federal and state regulations govern the Fintech sector in the USA. Financial services and suppliers of financial services may be subject to the laws enacted by the federal government, all 50 states and individual states. The regulatory environment surrounding Fintech is always changing because different regulators have different ideas about how to create a framework that both complies with their mandates and encourages useful innovation. Some of the key regulations and regulatory approaches governing the Fintech industry in the USA include:

Gramm-Leach Bliley Act: This act requires "financial institutions to explain their information-sharing practices to their customers and to safeguard sensitive data".

Fair Credit Reporting Act: This act regulates "the collection, dissemination, and use of consumer credit information".

US Anti-Money Laundering regulations (AML): These regulations require "financial institutions to verify the identity of their customers and monitor their transactions for suspicious activity".

JOBS Act: This act allows startups and small businesses to raise capital through crowdfunding.

Fund Transfer Act and CFPB Regulation E: These regulations provide consumer protection for electronic fund transfers.

Securities Act and Exchange Act: These acts regulate the issuance and trading of securities.

CAN-SPAM: This act regulates "commercial email messages and gives recipients the right to have a business stop emailing them".

The particular combination of regulatory requirements and accountability to which a Fintech company must respond will vary based on the program's structure, the kinds of goods and services it provides and the regions in which it conducts business.

Both EU and national rules are in place to govern the Fintech sector in Europe. The European Union has implemented several rules, such as the GDPR, the Anti-Money Laundering Directive (AMLD) and the Payment Services Directive 2 (PSD2), with the aim of promoting innovation and protecting consumers. AMLD requires financial institutions to verify the identity of their customers and monitor their transactions for any suspicious activity, whereas PSD2 establishes uniform rules for payments made using mobile devices and the Internet. The GDPR regulates the collection, utilization and retention of personal data (Buckley, Arner, Zetzsche & Weber, 2020).

Apart from these requirements, Fintech companies operating in Europe are subject to additional legal frameworks. For instance, the Solvency II Directive governs insurance firms, whereas the Markets in Financial Instruments Directive II (MiFID II) regulates financial services.

It is important to note that the applicable regulations differ depending on the operations of the Fintech organization. This could result in a fragmented environment that hinders global enterprise growth, or it could create opportunities for taking advantage of price differences and an uneven competitive landscape, which may motivate corporations to seek permits in less regulated jurisdictions to reduce bureaucratic obstacles when doing business internationally.

In China, a combination of national laws and regulations govern the Fintech business. The main organizations in charge of executing laws and establishing Fintech rules in China are the "People's Bank of China (PBOC), China Banking and Insurance Regulatory Commission (CBIRC), and China Securities Regulatory Commission (CSRC)" (Zhou, Arner & Buckley, 2018).

The following are some of the main laws and regulatory strategies that control the Fintech sector in China:

- Prohibiting unlicensed Fintech businesses
- Strengthening Cyber Security Rules and Regulations
- Enhancing financial consumer protection
- Regulating online lending

In India, national laws and regulations work together to control the Fintech sector. Among the major regulatory agencies overseeing the Fintech sector in India are the "Reserve Bank of India (RBI), Securities and Exchange Board of India (SEBI), Insurance Regulatory and Development Authority of India (IRDAI), Ministry of Electronics and Informative Technology, and Ministry of Corporate Affairs" (Chugh, 2019).

Some of the key regulations and regulatory approaches governing the Fintech industry in India include:

- Payment and Settlement Systems Act (2007)
- Prevention of Money Laundering Act (2002)
- Foreign Exchange Management Act (1999)
- SEBI Regulations
- IRDAI Regulations

The Different Phases of RegTech

Businesses that are hindered by bureaucratic procedures and outdated infrastructure are resorting to RegTech solutions, which use software and automation to fill compliance gaps and handle other regulatory issues.

The regulatory environment has changed dramatically in recent years, which increases the potential for compliance lapses to occur in a variety of businesses, including the financial services sector. Regulators are levying unprecedented fines for non-compliance, and

Table 8.1 Different Phases of RegTech

Phase	*Process*	*Tools*
I	Manual Intervention	MS Excel, Google Sheets
II	Workflow Automation	Nintex, Appian, UiPath and IBM Robotic Process Automation
III	Continuous Monitoring	AcadiaSoft, Actimize, Thomson Reuters Regulatory Intelligence, AxiomSL, Compliance.ai and MetricStream
IV	Predictive Intervention	Statistical Analysis System (SAS), IBM SPSS Modeler, RapidMiner, Alteryx and Microsoft Azure ML

Source: Arner, Barberis and Buckley (2017).

businesses are rushing to develop compliant solutions in response to impending financial rules like GDPR, PSD2 and MiFIDII/MIFIR.

Because of this, financial institutions are using new regulatory technology (RegTech) more and more to close compliance gaps, reduce compliance costs, anticipate needs ahead of time and identify enterprise risk before regulators do.

The percentage of businesses using RegTech solutions is less than 17%. This can be broadly explained by a shifting regulatory environment, strained resources and legacy infrastructure. However, RegTech businesses that assist businesses in overcoming compliance-related challenges are becoming more and more popular; since 2013, they have raised over $6.2 billion through over 680 equity investments.

The application of RegTech comprises four stages which are manual, workflow automation, continuous monitoring and predictive analytics. The level of automation increases in each stage (CB Insights, 2018). The details of the processes and tools involved in each stage are given in Table 8.1.

Phase 1: Manual

The majority of regulatory and compliance teams begin with the first phase, which we refer to as manual and is determined by manual data collecting technologies. These systems offer a rudimentary audit trail and assist businesses in managing content and data centrally. Two of the earliest programs that compliance teams utilized to create manual data collection tools were Microsoft Excel and Google Sheets. The advantages have streamlined reporting and auditing processes and decreased the possibility of manual human error. A lot of businesses are still using antiquated manual procedures, and Google Sheets and Microsoft Excel are still essential tools for supporting risk and compliance operations.

Phase 2: Workflow Automation

The second stage of RegTech experienced workflow automation with software being specifically designed for regulatory and compliance applications. During this stage, banks began using software for a variety of purposes, including audit trail maintenance and regulatory reporting. This has facilitated firms in automating mundane compliance activities and reducing operational risks associated with meeting reporting and compliance obligations.

To guarantee regulatory conformance, increase productivity and streamline compliance procedures, workflow automation is crucial in the RegTech space. These needs are met by a number of tools in the RegTech space. Nintex, Appian, UiPath and IBM robotic process automation (RPA) are a few well-known solutions for process automation.

Organizations may automate business operations, such as compliance and regulatory procedures, with Nintex's workflow automation platform. With its visual drag-and-drop interface, users can easily design, automate and manage workflows without needing to know a lot of code. Nintex offers functionalities including task assignment, approval routing and workflow scheduling that enable financial institutions to efficiently automate processes related to regulatory compliance.

Regulatory compliance-related business process workflows can be designed, implemented and managed by enterprises using Appian, a low-code automation platform. It helps companies expedite the deployment of compliance procedures by providing pre-built templates and industry-specific solutions for risk management, audit tracking and regulatory compliance. In the RegTech space, Appian's features, which include document management, process monitoring and business rules management, enable the end-to-end automation of regulatory compliance procedures.

One of the best RPA platforms available is called UiPath. It helps businesses automate manual procedures and repetitive operations, including regulatory compliance. With its extensive automation features and visual workflow designer, users can effortlessly automate operations related to data entry, document processing and regulatory reporting. Financial organizations can automate compliance procedures and cut expenses by using UiPath's functionalities, which include workflow orchestration, data extraction and screen scraping.

Workflows related to regulatory compliance and other repetitive procedures can be automated by enterprises using IBM RPA technology. With the help of its RPA, AI and workflow orchestration features, customers can efficiently automate intricate compliance procedures and adjust to changing regulations. In the RegTech space, IBM RPA offers capabilities including task automation, process discovery and cognitive decision-making, which enable the end-to-end automation of regulatory compliance tasks.

In the dynamic and ever-evolving RegTech regulatory environment, these solutions enable financial institutions and regulatory bodies to automate regulatory compliance activities, enhance operational efficiency and reduce compliance risks. Organizations can select the workflow automation platform that best suits their needs and goals based on use cases and particular criteria.

Phase 3: Continuous Monitoring

Banks and financial institutions have switched in the third phase to implementing instruments for continuous monitoring. For the majority of businesses, traditional compliance control monitoring and revalidation are done on an as-needed or cyclical basis. This approach brings to light discrepancies and gaps that may have existed for years, depending on the review's cycle length.

Resolving the issue in a proactive rather than reactive manner can be accomplished by implementing a continuous monitoring method. Businesses that use this strategy are in a better position to deal with problems as they arise, preventing the company from taking unnecessary risks. Data science is used by continuous monitoring technology businesses to automate back-office activities and address various organizational risk issues. This covers information security standard (ISO) compliance, enterprise security and fraud prevention.

A crucial component of RegTech is continuous monitoring, which guarantees continued adherence to rules, identifies irregularities and immediately reduces risks. In RegTech, a variety of platforms and technologies that provide functions including data collection, analysis, alerting and reporting are used for continuous monitoring. Among the well-known RegTech tools for ongoing monitoring are MetricStream, AcadiaSoft, Actimize, Thomson Reuters Regulatory Intelligence, AxiomSL and Compliance.ai.

AcadiaSoft is among the first software companies to focus on continuous monitoring. A group of financial institutions and market utilities established the company in 2009 to comply with the recently enforced collateral requirements of the International Swaps and Derivatives Association (ISDA). Beyond its original goal of fulfilling the ISDA collateral criteria, Acadiasoft has expanded and is now essential to both banks and market utilities.

Actimize is a top financial crime and compliance management tool with continuous monitoring features, created by NICE Actimize. Financial institutions can keep an eye on trade compliance, market monitoring, fraud detection and AML in real-time thanks to the solutions it offers. Actimize alerts compliance teams for more inquiry by using advanced analytics, ML and anomaly detection algorithms to spot suspicious patterns and possible compliance violations.

A complete tool for regulatory compliance, Thomson Reuters Regulatory Intelligence offers real-time tracking of global regulatory developments, news and changes. Financial institutions may stay updated on regulatory changes and evaluate their impact on compliance duties using its real-time alerts, regulatory updates and analysis tools. Additionally, Thomson Reuters Regulatory Intelligence offers dashboards that can be customized and workflow tools that help firms successfully manage regulatory compliance tasks in the ever-changing regulatory landscape.

AxiomSL is a platform for regulatory reporting and risk management that provides financial institutions with continuous monitoring features. With the help of its data integration, validation and enrichment functions, businesses may combine and standardize data from many sources to monitor it continuously. Organizations can monitor regulatory compliance and evaluate risk exposure in real-time with the help of AxiomSL's prebuilt regulatory reporting templates, risk models and analytics tools.

A platform for regulatory compliance called Compliance.ai offers ongoing monitoring of regulatory content, such as legislation, rules and enforcement activities. With the help of its AI-powered search features, adaptable warning systems and carefully curated regulatory information libraries, businesses can keep tabs on changes and updates to regulations that are pertinent to their daily operations. Compliance teams may successfully manage regulatory change management processes and guarantee continuous compliance with the help of Compliance.ai's collaboration tools and workflow automation technologies.

MetricStream is a governance, risk and compliance (GRC) software that provides risk management and regulatory compliance with continuous monitoring features. Using its customizable dashboards, risk heat maps and compliance scorecards, businesses can keep an eye on compliance metrics, regulatory trends and key risk indicators in real time. With MetricStream's workflow automation, problem tracking and remediation management features, businesses can stay compliant with regulations and quickly address compliance issues.

In the dynamic RegTech regulatory environment, these solutions enable financial institutions and regulatory authorities to successfully execute strategies for continuous monitoring, improve regulatory compliance and limit compliance risks. Organizations can select the continuous monitoring tool that best suits their needs and goals based on use cases and specific criteria.

Phase 4: Predictive Analytics

The fourth phase of RegTech is driven by predictive analytics. This is a potent instrument that helps businesses make wise decisions and lower risks. To find trends and forecast future events, it entails examining vast volumes of data, including financial transactions and customer behavior. Predictive analytics is used in the regulatory technology space to identify possible compliance problems and regulatory risks, enabling businesses to take proactive measures to address them before they become an issue. Predictive analytics, for instance, can be used to spot possible fraud or money laundering schemes, enabling financial institutions to stop these kinds of operations. Furthermore, a corporation can utilize predictive analytics to evaluate the possible effects of regulatory changes on its operations and modify its strategy as necessary.

Predictive analytics is frequently employed in RegTech, and a number of solutions are available, each with special features and functionalities designed to meet the demands of regulatory agencies and financial institutions. The IBM SPSS Modeler, Alteryx, RapidMiner, IBM Statistical Analysis System (SAS) and Microsoft Azure Machine Learning are a few of the well-known technologies.

SAS is an all-inclusive analytics platform with many features for data mining, predictive modeling and statistical analysis. For the purpose of creating predictive models, evaluating data and producing reports, it offers an intuitive interface that is appropriate for both data scientists and business users operating in the RegTech sector. Additionally, SAS provides pre-built models and frameworks that are adjusted to meet regulatory standards for risk management, fraud detection and regulatory compliance.

Predictive analytics users may quickly and effectively develop, validate and implement predictive models with IBM SPSS Modeler. With its visual programming interface, users may analyze data, use different algorithms to build predictive models and evaluate the performance of the models without having to write complicated code. With capabilities including data preparation, model evaluation and deployment, the SPSS Modeler is appropriate for RegTech applications involving fraud detection, risk management and regulatory compliance.

A drag-and-drop interface is offered by the open-source predictive analytics platform RapidMiner for creating prediction models and carrying out sophisticated analytics operations. It is appropriate for intricate predictive modeling projects in the RegTech industry since it provides a broad selection of ML algorithms, data pretreatment tools and visualization capabilities. To facilitate users' access to and analysis of a variety of datasets for regulatory compliance, risk assessment and fraud detection, RapidMiner also facilitates integration with external data sources.

Alteryx is a self-service analytics platform that helps users make decisions by combining, analyzing and visualizing data from many sources. By providing a workflow-based interface, users may automate tasks related to data preparation, predictive modeling and reporting, which minimizes the time and effort needed for risk management and regulatory compliance. RegTech applications can benefit from Alteryx's strong predictive analytics capabilities, which include ML techniques and predictive model deployment choices.

With the help of these technologies, financial institutions and regulatory agencies may effectively use predictive analytics for risk management, fraud detection and regulatory compliance in the rapidly changing RegTech space. Organizations can select the predictive analytics technology that best suits their needs and goals by taking into account unique requirements and preferences.

RegTech Process Flow

The process of RegTech compliance involves several key steps, and Figure 8.1 illustrates the same.

A basic procedure of RegTech involves four steps. The first step is to sign up customers, which involves collecting customer information and verifying their identity. The second step is monitoring, which involves monitoring customer transactions and activities for suspicious behavior. The third step is detection, which involves detecting and investigating any suspicious activity that is identified during the monitoring process. The final step is reporting, which involves reporting any suspicious activity to the relevant regulatory authorities (CHI Software, 2021).

Data Collection

Regulatory data is collected from various sources, including government agencies, regulatory bodies and internal data sources. This data may include new regulations, updates and changes in compliance requirements.

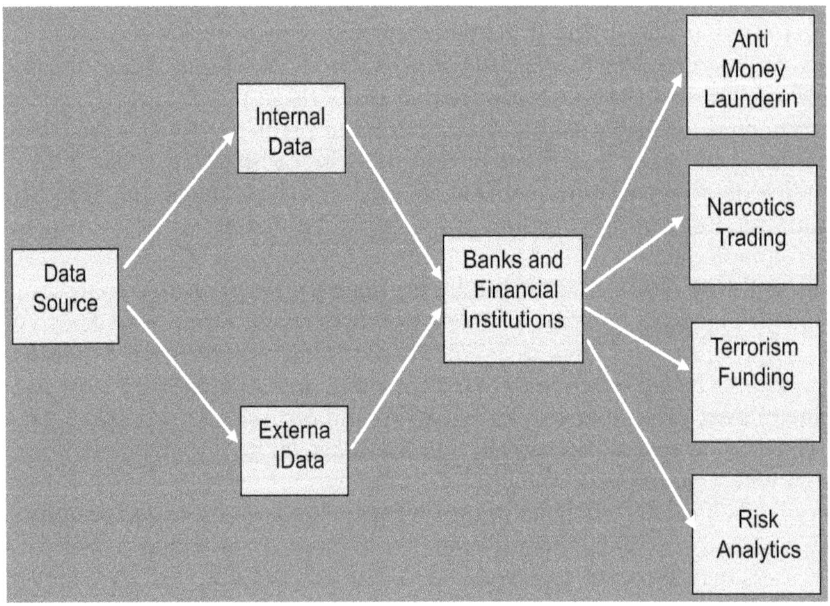

Figure 8.1 RegTech Process Flow

Monitoring and Reporting

Continuous monitoring of transactions, activities and relevant data to ensure ongoing compliance. Generation of real-time reports and alerts for any deviations or potential compliance risks.

Data Analysis

The collected data is analyzed to understand its implications on business operations. Advanced analytics, ML and natural language processing (NLP) may be employed to interpret complex regulatory language and identify relevant information.

Compliance Mapping and Reporting

A mapping process is conducted to align the regulatory requirements with the specific business processes, products and services. This helps in identifying areas of non-compliance and understanding the impact on the organization.

Technology Implementation

RegTech solutions are implemented to automate compliance processes. This may include the use of regulatory reporting tools, monitoring systems and other technologies that streamline compliance workflows.

Audit Trail and Documentation

Creating a detailed audit trail to demonstrate compliance efforts. Documentation of compliance processes and actions taken to address any issues.

RegTech compliance is an ongoing and dynamic process, and the use of technology helps organizations stay agile and responsive to evolving regulatory landscapes. The process of RegTech compliance involves several steps, including identifying regulatory requirements, implementing technology solutions, monitoring and reporting and continuously improving the process.

Identify regulatory requirements: The first step in RegTech compliance is to identify the regulatory requirements that apply to your business. This involves researching and understanding the laws and regulations that govern the industry, as well as any specific rules and regulations that apply to your business.

Implement technology solutions: Once the regulatory requirements have been identified, the next step is to implement technology solutions that can help to comply with those requirements. This may involve using software to monitor and track compliance, automating compliance-related tasks or implementing risk management systems.

Monitor and report: After implementing technology solutions, the need is to monitor and report on the compliance status. This involves regularly reviewing compliance data and reports, as well as conducting regular audits and assessments to ensure that the organizations are meeting regulatory requirements.

Continuously improve: Finally, it is important to continuously improve the RegTech compliance process. This involves regularly reviewing and updating your compliance policies and procedures, as well as staying up-to-date with changes in regulatory requirements and technology solutions.

Overall, RegTech compliance is an ongoing process that requires a commitment to identifying regulatory requirements, implementing technology solutions, monitoring and reporting and continuously improving the process.

Why RegTech Is Needed?

After the debacle of 2008, the financial regulatory authorities have made the processes stricter and more stringent by introducing a lot of new rules and regulations. The USA introduced the "Dodd-Frank Act" in 2010 to protect investors from malpractices and manipulations done by banks and financial institutions. The RBI issued detailed guidelines for KYC, AML and Combating of Financing of Terrorism (CFT). Banks and financial institutions have to comply with these directives and guidelines or pay hefty amounts in fines.

Two of the main concerns of the banking and financial services industry are KYC and AML operations. Both need very strong and meticulous compliances, and any lapse is heavily punished by regulatory authorities. RegTech helps in automating both KYC and AML operations.

KYC is a risk mitigation procedure that helps banks and financial institutions know their customers in a better way to offer them better products and services and also prevent any kind of malpractices like money laundering, doing illicit or illegal business or carrying out terrorist attacks. With banks and financial institutions having lakhs and millions of customers, KYC is a time-consuming and tedious process.

The KYC process is now becoming more systematic, structured, faster and convenient with the availability of data from the Aadhar database maintained by the Unique Identification Authority of India (UIDAI), the PAN database maintained by the Income Tax Department and the credit score database maintained by CIBIL, Equifax, HighMark and Experian. In the KYC process facilitated by RegTech, a customer is asked to submit a photograph, Aadhar Number, PAN number and bank statement, all in online mode through a website or mobile app. The RegTech software scans the data, captures the vital information, processes and analyzes the data and prepares the KYC in a fraction of a minute. The customer is saved from filling up lengthy forms and the banks and financial institutions are spared the rigmarole of sifting through tones of physical papers to comply with the regulatory processes (Yadav & Chandak, 2019).

In the case of AML compliances, banks and financial institutions are given a PEP list every year. PEP stands for "Politically Exposed Person". This could be ministers, councilors or a leader of the Opposition Party. They are strongly monitored as they could get involved in bribes or money laundering malpractices. Similarly, top business leaders of various companies could also come under the PEP list. Banks and financial institutions need to be very careful while maintaining their accounts in various banks (Singh & Lin, 2021).

RegTech helps in AML operations by automating the AML process through screening software and transaction monitoring software. A screening software helps banks and financial institutions segregate financial transactions that look suspicious and separate them from normal transactions. The bank accounts from where a large number of suspicious transactions are happening are then put under monitoring. Both the screening and the monitoring are done using automated software and without the need for human intervention. This is how RegTech plays a key role in preventing money laundering and generating alerts in real time to assist the AML process.

Using the most recent technological advancements, AML Screening and Monitoring Software fulfills financial institutions' AML requirements by keeping an eye on the entire transaction process. Companies can reduce false positives by creating scenarios and rules that are appropriate for their particular risk level by utilizing the dynamic rule development tool. Businesses can test the modifications they plan to make to their rules using their current transactions by utilizing the features of the Advanced Sandbox Test Environment. Dashboards for case management and real-time alert management help businesses streamline their control procedures.

RegTech is becoming more robust with applications of big data analytics, artificial intelligence and machine learning (AIML), the Internet of Things (IoT) and RPA. These tools aided by the latest technologies can capture huge data in all forms, structured and unstructured, analyze them smoothly and very fast without any need for human intervention and raise red alerts in real time wherever and whenever the compliance process is breached. RegTech has actually helped banks and financial institutions to save millions and billions of money that had to be paid in fines and also increased the reputation of being honest and ethical.

The main function of RegTech has been to facilitate the compliance processes and generate reports that need to be submitted to regulatory authorities. The main tools used in RegTech are for financial operations screening and financial institutions monitoring. Apart from that RegTech provides big support in the supervision of banking and financial activities, verification of customer identities, doing gap analysis and ensuring compliance with rules and regulations.

Apart from these activities, RegTech is supporting banks and financial institutions to do data management, employee surveillance, fraud prevention and audit trails. All these operations are run in an automated mode with RegTech. It helps banks and financial institutions to reduce the cost of compliance as well as free the manpower for other productive functions. It helps regulatory authorities to keep a tab on banks and financial institutions and their officials to understand if any illegal activities or breaches of compliance are happening.

One of the government departments that is mostly accused of corruption is the Income Tax Department. The IT officials are often accused of working hand-in-gloves with tax evaders and letting them slip away by accepting hefty bribes. The Government of India has introduced an interesting system called faceless scrutiny of income tax report (ITR) files. Under the faceless scheme, there is no human interface between the tax payer and the income tax officials. The scrutiny is done in an automated mode without any human intervention. The Government of India is also using big data analytics to detect trails of black money and unaccounted wealth and penalize the perpetrators of the crime.

The Enforcement Directorate, Central Bureau of Intelligence, Narcotics Control Board, Intelligence Bureau and others are also now seeking the help of RegTech to nail down the offenders. Apart from Income Tax Department and policing agencies, financial regulators like

RBI (Reserve Bank of India), SEBI (Securities and Exchange Board of India), IRDA (Insurance Regulatory and Development Authority) and Ministry of Finance are also getting great help from RegTech to ensure that banks and financial institutions comply with the rules and regulations in letter and in spirit.

RegTech has helped institutions to move from KYC to KYD. With proper processing of data using big data analytics, IoT, AIML and RPA, the banks, financial institutions and regulatory authorities are all now better placed to ensure a higher level of compliance and lower level of violations and malpractices.

RegTech Applications

The main applications of RegTech are as follows.

Banking and Financial Transactions

The unparalleled obstacles confronting the banking sector in 2020 have served as a reminder to all of us of the value of flexibility and accepting change. One improvement has been the rise in the application of regulatory technology ("RegTech"), which has been crucial in maintaining the availability of essential financial services under conditions that are changing quickly. Specifically, the difficult operating environment caused by COVID-19 has expedited the investigation and uptake of RegTech.

This is especially valid when it comes to the delivery of remote services. Approximately 90% of retail banks either have started or intend to start offering remote onboarding for individuals through RegTech solutions, while corporates' testing of these programs has increased significantly.

Just a few years ago, very few financial organizations were talking about how new technologies, including ML and graph database models, might be used to support AML/CFT activities. These days, it is hard to envisage discussing the future of AML/CFT procedures without at least taking into account the numerous concerns about the opportunities, dangers and difficulties presented by this cutting-edge technology.

However, while everyone understands the crucial role that data and technology play, not everyone is aware of how each institution should use and approach these new technologies.

Prevention of Money Laundering

Regulatory agencies and financial organizations worldwide are becoming increasingly concerned about money laundering. As criminals become more adept at money laundering, businesses must find new and creative ways to identify and stop financial crime.

RegTech, or regulatory technology, is useful in this situation. Through the use of cutting-edge and automated technological solutions, these aid in the prevention of financial crime, including money laundering. To help compliance specialists and identify questionable financial activity patterns, these technologies could involve data analytics, AI and ML. Regulatory technologies can also lower risk exposure in the fight against money laundering by streamlining data collection and analysis, increasing efficiency and increasing transparency in the regulatory compliance process.

AML compliance may be expensive and time-consuming to manually manage. Teams can spend hours reading through legislation and keeping an eye on their Fintech services for possible money laundering, diverting their focus from case management and enhancing their preventive tactics. Furthermore, shady activity may still go unnoticed.

The cost of AML compliance may be significantly decreased with the aid of the correct RegTech solution thanks to rule-based workflows that enable firms to automate numerous AML operations. With greater accuracy and efficiency, teams can better prioritize their time and stay ahead of money laundering thanks to the use of automation and customized rules in RegTech. To stay up, the majority of businesses will need to implement a risk and compliance solution; the question is when is the right time to do so.

Undoubtedly, the RegTech has served as a benefit to provide greater security when making any digital monetary transaction, so we can mention some of the advantages of these technological tools:

- Observation and verification of identity in a quick and simple manner in banking transactions to ensure compliance with legal regulations
- Increased control and detectability of customer information, which has an impact on customer relationships
- Improvement and reduction of administrative cycles through automated programs
- Expanded adaptability and versatility despite constant administrative changes
- Increased connection between the company and administrative bodies thanks to technological tools for reporting and data analysis

New technologies in monetary innovation will continue to develop, and with them will come more essential control guidelines in each country. RegTech will continue to help fight all types of crimes related to money laundering, helping to provide a more transparent and secure global financial system.

Risk-Based Authentication

A security technique called risk-based authentication (RBA) adjusts the amount of authentication needed in response to the perceived risk of a specific transaction or user activity. Regardless of the transaction's context, traditional authentication techniques frequently depend on immutable security features like passwords or two-factor authentication. In contrast, RBA modifies authentication requirements based on the assessment of the degree of risk involved in a given transaction, taking into consideration a number of different criteria.

Analyzing the historical behavior of a user, including login times, locations and devices used, can help establish a baseline. Deviations from this baseline might indicate potential risk. Unusual login locations or attempts from regions that are not typical for the user may trigger additional authentication measures.

Recognizing the device used for authentication and assessing its security posture (e.g., whether it's a recognized device or if it has security software installed) is crucial. Transaction Type and Amount: Different types of transactions may have varying risk levels. For example, a large fund transfer might trigger higher authentication requirements.

RBA is not a one-time event but an ongoing process. Continuous monitoring of user activities allows for real-time risk assessment. Unusual patterns or changes in behavior can be detected promptly, triggering appropriate authentication responses.

The authentication level can be dynamically adjusted based on the risk assessment. For low-risk transactions, minimal authentication may be required, while high-risk activities demand stronger measures. Adaptive authentication helps strike a balance between security and user convenience.

Advanced analytics, including ML algorithms, play a significant role in RBA. These technologies can analyze large datasets to identify patterns and anomalies, improving the accuracy of risk assessments.

Establishing a scoring system helps quantify the risk associated with each transaction or user activity. A higher score may prompt additional authentication steps. The scoring system is often based on predefined rules and ML models that evolve over time as they learn from new data.

Communicating the concept of RBA to users is essential. Users should understand why certain authentication measures are triggered and how these measures contribute to overall security. Depending on the industry and location, there may be regulatory requirements governing authentication practices. It's crucial to ensure that RBA complies with relevant regulations.

Despite its advantages, RBA is not without challenges. Balancing security and user experience, avoiding false positives/negatives and keeping the system up-to-date with emerging threats are ongoing concerns.

RBA is a dynamic and intelligent approach to security that adapts to the evolving landscape of threats. By considering various contextual factors, organizations can enhance security while minimizing friction for legitimate users. As technology advances, the effectiveness of RBA is likely to improve through the incorporation of more sophisticated analytics and ML techniques.

Combating Financial Terrorism

CFT involves the development and implementation of strategies, policies and measures aimed at preventing, detecting and disrupting financial activities that fund or support terrorist organizations. Financial terrorism refers to the use of financial systems and institutions to facilitate or enable acts of terrorism. Effectively addressing this threat requires a comprehensive and collaborative approach involving governments, financial institutions, intelligence agencies and international organizations.

Financial terrorism often transcends national borders, making international cooperation crucial. Countries need to share intelligence, coordinate efforts and harmonize regulations to prevent terrorists from exploiting differences in financial systems.

Governments should establish and enforce robust regulatory frameworks to monitor and control financial transactions. This includes implementing AML and counterterrorism financing (CTF) regulations that require financial institutions to identify and report suspicious activities.

Financial institutions should implement stringent KYC procedures to verify the identity of their customers. This helps prevent the use of fake identities or shell companies to move funds for illicit purposes.

Implementing sophisticated transaction monitoring systems enables financial institutions to detect unusual or suspicious patterns of financial activity. Unusual transactions, especially those involving large sums of money or frequent transfers, may indicate potential involvement in terrorism-related financing.

Adopting a risk-based approach to AML and CTF efforts allows organizations to allocate resources more efficiently. This involves assessing the risk associated with customers, transactions and geographic locations and applying enhanced due diligence measures accordingly.

Governments must have the legal authority to freeze and confiscate assets linked to terrorism. Quick and effective action in freezing assets prevents terrorists from accessing funds and disrupts their operations.

Intelligence agencies play a critical role in identifying and tracking financial flows associated with terrorism. Sharing intelligence among relevant agencies and across borders is essential for a comprehensive understanding of the financial networks supporting terrorist activities.

Collaboration between the public and private sectors is vital. Financial institutions, as key players in the financial system, should work closely with government agencies to share information and enhance collective efforts against financial terrorism.

Leveraging advanced technologies, such as data analytics and AI, enhances the ability to detect patterns and anomalies in financial transactions. These tools can help identify potential threats more efficiently than traditional methods.

Supporting capacity-building initiatives in countries vulnerable to financial terrorism helps strengthen their regulatory frameworks, law enforcement capabilities and overall resilience against illicit financial activities.

International sanctions can be an effective tool to isolate and pressure individuals, entities or countries involved in supporting terrorism. Enforcing and expanding sanctions regimes can be an integral part of CFT.

Promoting awareness and educating financial institutions, businesses and the public about the risks associated with financial terrorism is essential. This includes providing training on recognizing and reporting suspicious financial activities.

CFT is an ongoing and evolving challenge that requires a multifaceted and adaptive approach. By strengthening regulatory frameworks, fostering international cooperation and leveraging technology, countries can enhance their ability to identify and disrupt the financial networks that support terrorist activities.

Identity Management

Under identity management, the main function done by RegTech is KYC. There are important rules, regulations and directives given by central bankers and financial regulators that banks and financial institutions need to follow stringent KYC norms. The traditional KYC processes are cumbersome, time-consuming and complicated and cause irritation to both the bank officials and the customers. Many transactions get disrupted and banks and financial institutions end up losing customers because of non-conformance to KYC rules. RegTech has made life easy for customers and bank officials as the whole process is carried out through mobile apps or websites with minimum hassles.

Transaction Management

Under transaction management, two important tasks are done, which are monitoring and raising alarms whenever any deviation is noticed. The traditional processes had shortcomings as the violators would find some loopholes or processes to bypass the authorities so that alarms would not be raised. RegTech has offered effective solutions to plug the loopholes and ensure that compliances are observed in both letter and spirit.

Risk Management

With banking and financial operations having moved online, the risks arising from hackers, Trojan viruses, phishing agents and cloners have increased manifold. Credit cards, debit cards, online banking, online shopping and all kinds of online financial transactions are prone to such kinds of attacks. Data leakages are now threatening the privacy of customers and making them vulnerable to blackmailing and demands for ransom. To ensure a robust risk management system, RegTech has come out with applications that can act as a shield against all kinds of malware attacks.

Regulatory Reporting

After the aftermath of the 2008 subprime crisis, the regulatory authorities have tightened the controls and made stringent reporting systems. Any violation or non-compliance is punished with hefty fines. The banking and financial organizations had a tough time spending a lot of money and investment in man hours to ensure that proper reports were made and submitted within time. RegTech has made life easier for banks and financial institutions by monitoring the activities and generating reports through automated mode.

The RegTech Ecosystem

In today's technology-savvy world, criminals and law-breakers are using sophisticated tools like virtual private networks, cryptocurrencies, ransomware and dark web to carry out their illegal and illicit activities. Banks and financial institutions also need sophisticated tools to protect themselves from phishing, hacking and cloning. Regulatory and enforcement authorities need sophisticated tools to monitor and generate alerts whenever any breach or event of non-compliance has occurred. The RegTech Ecosystem is powered by "big data analytics, AIML, IoT and RPA". These are now coming to the rescue of the banks and financial institutions as well as aiding and supporting the regulatory and enforcement authorities (Jaradat, Al-Zeer & Areiqat, 2023).

The RegTech Ecosystem is illustrated in Figure 8.2.

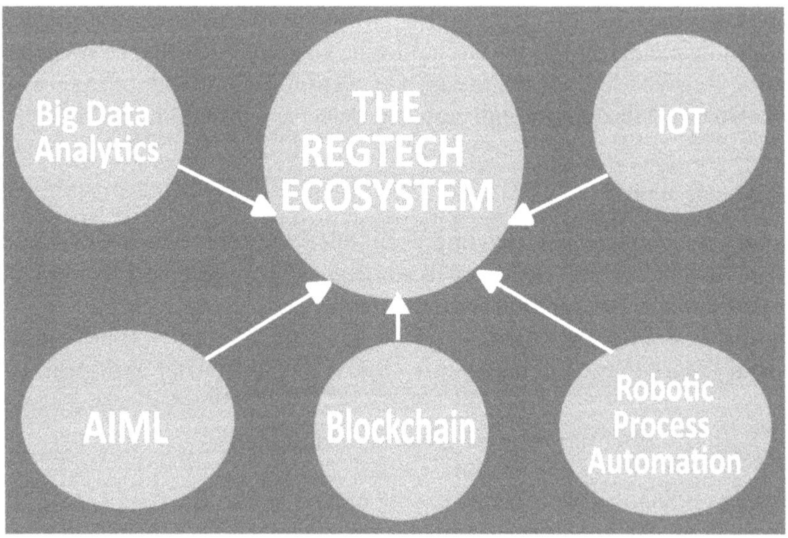

Figure 8.2 The RegTech Ecosystem

Application of Big Data Analytics in RegTech

Two of the main concerns for banks are asset liability management and liquidity risk. Banks need to analyze data pertaining to deposits, loans and derivatives to understand whether they are insufficiently funded or over-leveraged. Banks need a sophisticated process of analytics that can sift through millions and billions of data in various forms to understand the risk elements and take corrective actions before they are badly hit. The focus on granularity is increasing in the way banks identify and report risks to the regulatory authorities.

The reporting systems in banks and financial services organizations have also changed. The reporting is no longer once in a month, quarter, bi-annual or annual. Regulatory authorities are seeking real-time analytics and dashboards that can identify, alert and report anomalies as soon as they happen. And banks and financial institutions are also being forced to do innovations to ensure that compliances are done, risks are managed and the business process flow is also not affected.

The data that is now coming has the characteristics of 4V's. The 4V's are volume, variety, velocity and veracity. There are huge volumes of data running into quintillions (1 quintillion = 10^{15} bytes) that are getting generated every day. The data comes in the form of numbers, texts, images, audio and video formats. The data is coming at a phenomenal speed. And the question that is being raised is whether the system is equipped to segregate the original data from the spurious ones.

An important part of the RegTech process is big data analytics. RegTech big data software provider Hexanika has created the software platforms SmartJoin and SmartReg for financial institutions to help them with data sourcing and reporting issues related to regulatory compliance. Their array of novel and distinctive algorithms and rules engine helps business users to efficiently manage the data. By automatically updating regulatory reporting to match changing regulatory standards, the SmartReg Software effectively meets market demands (Grassi & Lanfranchi, 2022).

Application of AIML in RegTech

AIML is getting a lot of importance in RegTech as it resolves key issues like regulatory compliance, attacks from cyber criminals and fraudsters, opportunity to automate systems and reduce costs, time and manpower engagement. Intelligent algorithms are able to spot anomalies and fraudulent information in a matter of seconds.

According to research done by the United Nations, more than $5 trillion is siphoned off by money laundering organizations. Around $80–100 billion of money is siphoned off from insurance companies annually by making fraudulent claims. The regulatory authorities and enforcement agencies are able to freeze or seize only 1% of the illicit money flowing around the globe.

These issues are now being taken care of by AIML tools and processes. NLP is being used by insurance companies to analyze data and manage risks. This is also used in processes of underwriting and claims processing (Barde & Kulkarni, 2023).

Models for detecting fraud are getting more reliable and accurate thanks to cognitive analytics. MasterCard recently declared the launch of decision intelligence, an AIML product. With the use of ML technology, this AIML tool makes account-specific judgments based on data, including alert and decline levels that are predetermined. The technology is capable of stopping thefts and fraudulent transaction claims by identifying unusual spending patterns during shopping.

Application of Blockchain in RegTech

Cryptocurrencies were seen with apprehension by central bankers and financial regulators as they had little control over the process due to the P2P nature of operations. Many countries initially banned the use of cryptocurrencies as it was being extensively used by terrorists, drug peddlers and money launderers. But cryptocurrencies were based on blockchain technology, which is one of the robust and secure systems that cannot be tampered with or manipulated easily. Blockchain soon also became the backbone of RegTech helping banks and financial organizations to create secure online financial processes and block any kind of phishing, cloning or malware attacks by cyber criminals. Through cryptography and secure record keeping, banks and financial institutions have made their systems robust with strong firewalls.

The most common use of blockchain in RegTech is for AML and KYC compliance. Blockchain offers the facilities of better traceability and faster analysis wherever assets are digitalized. The use of smart contracts through blockchain has ensured that operations are smooth and secure and compliances are met. Tokenization is ensuring that systems are robust and cannot be hacked. While big data analytics helps by collecting massive data and analyzing them, blockchain helps by preventing the problems of attacks by cyber criminals. Blockchain operates through the distributed ledger system with a greater amount of transparency which makes data accessible for internal use, documented for audit purposes and protected against falling into the wrong hands (Fan, 2022).

Blockchain also has the potential to support cross-sector applications like trade finance. This helps in de-bureaucratization of the process and monitoring and making the compliance process easier and simpler with process automation.

Blockstream is a company started by Adam Back in 2014 with headquarters in Victoria, Canada. Blockstream offers two services, which are called Liquid Network and Lightning Network. Through the liquid network, all blockchain transactions are verified and customers can send or receive liquid assets like Bitcoins without any worries or fear of hacking and breach. The liquid note helps to peg in Bitcoins, issue new assets and fully verify blocks on the sidechain.

Lightning network is considered to be the innovative and disruptive company that changed the course of Bitcoin development. It is intended to reduce associated expenses of Bitcoin's blockchain and expedite transaction processing times. Establishing payment channels is aided by the Lightning Network. To enable network users to avoid problems and disagreements over transactions, as well as fraud, copies of the data are transmitted to them via the Lightning Network.

Application of RPA in RegTech

With compliances becoming stringent and strict and attacks by cyber criminals becoming more frequent, companies were forced to invest huge amounts of manpower, time and money to comply with regulations and also prevent cyberattacks. RPA has come as a blessing for companies that were struggling with compliance and cyber-attack issues.

Banks and financial institutions have migrated to automated workflow with RPA. The processes run through RPA are executed flawlessly without errors, thus mitigating the concerns raised regarding data transfer and migration like invoice processing and purchase order issuing. All actions are captured in the activity log thus making it easier to trace the origin and flow of transactions. Any illegal, illicit or non-compliant transaction is flagged off with automated alerts, thus preventing fraud and also the engagement of manpower in security and compliance. RPA enables firms to achieve exceptional levels of process accuracy, particularly when compared to the capabilities of human personnel (Charoenwong, Kowaleski, Kwan & Sutherland, 2023).

An example of the application of RPA is that of Landmark Group in the Middle East. Landmark has automated its process of applying value-added tax to transactions. The company can now process huge amounts of data and also adhere to strict compliances because of RPA. RPA has saved landmark hours of work, while simultaneously boosting internal efficiency.

Application of IoT in RegTech

Technology is getting smarter leading to the creation of smart devices. These days, we have smart lighting, refrigerators, televisions, watches, phones and homes. Additionally, fully autonomous smart cars are about to be released. Alexa from Amazon is one such application. All of the smart device ecosystem is powered by Alexa, Amazon's voice-activated AI digital assistant that can be used with simple speech commands. These smart devices can also conduct automated financial transactions and accept voice commands. Banks and other financial services firms have integrated chatbots, which use AIML to conduct conversations with consumers, into their mobile apps and websites. In the context of RegTech, IoT refers to the technology that allows devices to track, monitor and verify that compliances are upheld during transactions (Arner, Barberis & Buckley, 2017).

Quick response codes and sensors are also producing a lot of data. To collect this data and examine it for possible risks, a strong IoT system is needed. Another benefit of IoT is real-time compliance. To effectively anticipate risks and compliance failures, the risk and compliance operations of the future will be fueled by near real-time information and intelligent machines that can interpret complicated patterns in data. IoT application in RegTech aids in system and operation integration for improved security and compliance (Becker, Merz & Buchkremer, 2020).

IBM provides an IoT-based RegTech model for integrated GRC that is cognitively driven. The GRC Model identifies assets at risk, assesses vulnerabilities, compiles a library of regulations for compliance and implements procedures to manage the risks. IBM's cognitive fraud prevention solution is designed to assist fraud teams in recognizing and promptly responding to new threats related to payment fraud. It includes the analytics and simulation tools required to keep an ongoing eye on its business performance and modify the decision model in response to new and evolving fraud trends. IBM's cognitive approach to real-time fraud prevention was validated in 2019 when it was named "Financial Crime Product of the Year".

Benefits of RegTech

RegTech is "a disruptive invention that has gained traction in the financial sector in recent years". It alludes to the application of technology to improve financial services regulatory compliance and procedures.

RegTech's capacity to simplify compliance procedures and make it simpler for financial institutions to abide by complicated regulations is one of its main advantages. Financial institutions can use RegTech to automate repetitive compliance procedures, which eliminates the need for human intervention and frees up time for more strategic endeavors.

RegTech also has the advantage of assisting financial organizations in more efficiently identifying and reducing regulatory issues. RegTech detects any regulatory breaches before they happen by analyzing large volumes of data using ML algorithms and smart analytics. Financial organizations benefit from avoiding expensive fines and harm to their brand.

Furthermore, RegTech has the potential to improve accountability and transparency inside the financial industry. RegTech can aid financial institutions in demonstrating to regulators their commitment to regulatory compliance and their proactive approach to preventing regulatory violations. This is achieved through the automation of compliance processes and the provision of real-time insights into regulatory compliance.

RegTech can also help financial institutions reduce the costs associated with compliance. RegTech enables financial institutions to streamline operations and reduce costs by automating repeated compliance activities and minimizing the requirement for manual involvement. The time and money saved can be subsequently allocated to other parts of the firm, allowing for further investment.

RegTech is a powerful tool that has the potential to completely transform the way financial institutions manage regulatory compliance. RegTech is a technology-based method that assists financial institutions in meeting their regulatory obligations and operating with more effectiveness and efficiency. It achieves this by automating compliance activities, detecting regulatory risks and improving transparency and accountability.

RegTech Companies

There are several RegTech companies, which are currently offering products and services under several verticals like AML operations, CFT operations, compliance management, risk management, market and trade surveillance, digital identity and KYC, customer onboarding, regulatory change management and regulatory reporting.

Some of the top companies offering RegTech services across the world are given here.

BigID

Based in New York, BigID Inc. is an American software firm that develops tools for governance, compliance, privacy and data security. The business offers software for handling private and sensitive data. A platform for curated intelligence analytics on acquired sensitive data is hosted by BigID. The technologies of the company are focused on access management, classification and cloud-based data visualization for financial services, among other areas. Along with privacy automation, BigID boasts a system that complies with more than 20 data regulation rules. At the moment, 400 people are employed by them worldwide (Anagnostopoulos, 2018).

For a hybrid world, BigID provides technology and tools for data visibility and control. The program can automatically (and precisely) search for, locate and categorize the most important data at petabyte size, regardless of where it is stored or what kind of data it is. Additionally, it can detect high-risk data, unearth dark data and take appropriate action for privacy, security, compliance and governance in the context of contemporary data lifecycle management.

With an ML-driven data security platform to lower risk and correct data, this software helps to speed up data security and drive data security posture monitoring. Along with helping businesses comply with regulations, BigID also helps them manage their regulated data proactively and in accordance with security frameworks like NIST and HiTrust.

TruNomi

TruNomi is a London-based company that offers an enterprise data privacy platform that provides rules-based software for enterprise data privacy compliance. The platform enables businesses to understand what data they hold, under what regulation and why, allowing them to comply with current and future global regulations from a single platform. TruNomi's solutions are secure, easy to integrate and sit on top of any existing enterprise architecture. The company's board consists of some of the world's brightest minds, united by their vision for TruNomi.

TruNomi's platform is unique in that it requires zero Personally Identifiable Information to provide fully comprehensive compliance solutions. This means that TruNomi is the only privacy technology that can provide best-in-class business intelligence without compromising on privacy.

TruNomi offers a multi-award-winning Consent Management and Personal Data Rights Platform driving a new level of transparency and trust between businesses and consumers. With patented, bank-grade technology, companies can now demonstrate how they take care of their consumer data like never before. TruNomi's TruCert technology provides immutable proof of consent management and personal data rights. Data subject requests are fulfilled at the click of a button, and, for the first time, businesses can see the rights they have across their entire company from a single, easy-to-use dashboard, allowing them to make new and informed decisions around consumer data.

Hummingbird

Hummingbird is a software that helps financial institutions carry out quick and precise financial crime investigations with the help of the compliance and risk platform. Hummingbird's cutting-edge suite of investigative tools, which completely reimagines compliance operations, allows financial institutions to reduce costs and increase efficiency without compromising quality or taking on more risk. Hummingbird is the ideal compliance CRM, combining cutting-edge technology, careful product design and regulatory knowledge. The goal of Hummingbird is to leverage technology to make compliance processes more effective.

Ryan Gerard, Jesse Reiss and Joe Robinson lead Hummingbird. They have policymakers, heads of compliance for major banks and Fintechs, former regulators and the author of the American Bankers Association's Guide to Regulatory Compliance on their team.

Hummingbird supports those battling financial crimes. Their service is intended to improve investigations into counterterrorism financing and AML. It saves copious paperwork, offers intelligent analytics and facilitates communication between law enforcement and compliance specialists.

Everything required to oversee, look into and report on casework in the financial sector is available on the Hummingbird Platform. They are knowledgeable in testing, disputes, anti-fraud and AML. Using contemporary APIs, Hummingbird is able to track suspicious activity reports and validate files.

The Best Solution for Compliance and Risk winner of the 2021 Best of FinXTech Awards was declared to be Hummingbird. The victory of Hummingbird is a testament to a best-in-class evaluation procedure that incorporates input from financial institution partners as well as real results.

Chainalysis

Chainalysis was established in 2014 as a Bitcoin tracing service. In the battle against illegal cryptocurrency operations, Chainalysis is a leader in cryptocurrency research and compliance solutions, providing its services to numerous international law enforcement agencies, regulators and corporations.

Law enforcement has benefited from Chainalysis's assistance in recovering cryptocurrency from illicit businesses. In 2020, for example, Chainalysis helped law enforcement reclaim nearly $1 billion after the closure of the Silk Road dark web marketplace. It also helped identify the North Korean Lazarus Group as the culprit behind seven Bitcoin crimes that occurred in 2021. The company traced $100 million stolen from a California cryptocurrency company called Harmony to North Korean hackers who have taken billions of dollars from banks and cryptocurrency companies to fund their illicit missile program, working with US investigators and the South Korean National Intelligence Service. In April 2023, $1 million of the pilfered monies were found.

Now a well-known brand in the blockchain space, Chainalysis has over one billion addresses linked to actual organizations. Nine out of the ten largest cryptocurrency exchanges use the organization, which has a 4.7 Peer Insights grade from Gartner. Chainalysis is dedicated to producing original insights for its clients while demystifying the difficult.

ComplyAdvantage

Charles Delingpole established ComplyAdvantage in 2014 in London, United Kingdom. This RegTech business offers tools to help identify and control risks related to fraud and AML. The business assists regulated firms in managing risk requirements and preventing financial crime by utilizing AI, ML and NLP. Originally, the company was founded to provide RegTech solutions to help businesses meet the requirements of CFT and AML. The corporation maintains offices in Romania, Singapore and the USA.

With the use of its AI-enabled solutions, clients may increase the efficiency of their compliance effort, cut down on false positives by up to 70% and cut the onboarding cycle time by up to 50%. More than a thousand businesses currently work with ComplyAdvantage, and they all gain from the continuously updated data the RegTech offers regarding high-risk people, organizations and activities. ComplyAdvantage also has a group of professionals working with them who advise clients on current best practices and keep them ahead of constantly evolving regulatory standards.

ComplyAdvantage won Finovate's Best RegTech Solution award in 2019. The World Economic Forum designated the company as a Technology Pioneer in 2020. On the *Financial Times* list of the 1,000 fastest-growing firms in Europe, it came in at number 87. ComplyLaunch, a new product from ComplyAdvantage, allows Fintechs in their early stages to incorporate the company's AML and fraud detection technology into their businesses. The announcement was made in 2021. The company currently provides "payment screening, unfavorable media screening, PEPs screening, AML onboarding and monitoring, and AML transaction monitoring".

SymphonyAI

Leading ML company SymphonyAI (previously Ayasdi) is used by major banks and other financial organizations to analyze operational and market risks and spot possible money laundering trends. It offers generative and predictive AI applications to companies in many industries. SymphonyAI was first created for use by defense agencies, but it has now been shown to be beneficial to banks. It made Citigroup pass the US Federal Reserve's stress tests and helped cut HSBC's false positives in their money laundering surveillance by 20%.

Romesh Wadhwani launched SymphonyAI in 2017, with its headquarters located in Palo Alto, California. It provides bundled AI solutions with unparalleled outcomes that are customized for particular sectors and use cases. Applications from the company accelerate growth and productivity for companies in a variety of sectors, including corporate IT, retail, CPG, financial services, industrial and media.

Questions for Discussion

1. Explain what you understand by RegTech.
2. Explain how AIML is facilitating RegTech.
3. Explain how big data analytics is facilitating RegTech.
4. Explain how RPA is facilitating RegTech
5. Explain how blockchain is facilitating RegTech.
6. Explain how IoT is facilitating RegTech.

Case Study – The Hacking of Cryptocurrency Exchanges

The theft and hacking of cryptocurrency is currently the largest issue facing Fintech companies. Online hackers are a persistent danger to Bitcoin and Ethereum, whose valuations have reached stratospheric heights. North Korean hackers stole $395 million worth of cryptocurrencies last year through seven hacks into cryptocurrency exchanges and investment organizations, according to data supplied by the RegTech company Chainalysis. According to Chainalysis's data, hackers are now concentrating on Ethereum and the new cryptocurrency exchanges. The exchanges are more susceptible to hacking and incursions since they are new.

In the past five years, North Korean hackers have breached cryptocurrency accounts valued at about $1.5 billion. It is believed that the nation's severely sanctioned, isolated and failing economy is using this pilfered money to finance its weapons development. Chainalysis claims that Lazarus, a loose collective of hackers generally thought to be employed by the North Korean Government, was responsible for all of the crimes. However, other companies that track hackers have noted that Lazarus is made up of numerous different organizations. Nonetheless, security company Mandiant concurs with Chainalysis' findings, stating that almost all of the North Korean groups it monitors now prioritize Bitcoin theft in addition to any other objectives they may have.

The greater simplicity of laundering digital currency is undoubtedly one of the reasons hackers have turned their attention to cryptocurrencies rather than other financial crimes. Chainalysis discovered that gangs have many ways to disguise the cryptocurrency that has been stolen. They've profited from their profits by trading their cryptocurrencies for Chinese RMB on exchanges that don't strictly adhere to KYC laws. They've mostly taken advantage of Asian-based exchanges. To hide the source of the funds, the groups have frequently used "mixing" services. Furthermore, they have frequently made use of decentralized exchanges, which are frequently devoid of strict anti-money laundering regulations and are intended to link Bitcoin traders directly with one another.

An estimated $129 million was lost when a hacker targeted thousands of customers of Atomic Wallet, a non-custodial cryptocurrency wallet service, in June 2023. Subsequently, the FBI claimed that the Atomic Wallet breach was the first in a string of similar attacks, which also included the Alphapo and Coinspaid exploits later in the month and linked this attack to the hacking group TraderTraitor, which has ties to North Korea.

There were three stages to the hacking. The attacker moved assets from one blockchain to another, usually to conceal the flow of illicit funds, in the first phase of the operation before chain hopping to the Bitcoin blockchain. The stolen money was routed by the attacker to the OFAC-approved Sinbad in the second phase. North Korean money launderers have previously used Sinbad, a mixing service that hides on-chain transaction details. The attacker then took the money out of Sinbad and transferred it to Bitcoin consolidation addresses. The attacker's money laundering approach changed in the third phase, concentrating nearly entirely on the Tron blockchain as opposed to the Bitcoin network. After making a chain move to the Tron blockchain, the attacker hid their illicit gains.

The good news is that in 2023, there has been a decrease in cryptocurrency hacking and incursion. The reason for this is the involvement of RegTech businesses such as Chainalysis. In 2015, while looking into the Silk Road black web market, two rogue FBI agents stole Bitcoin. Chainalysis assisted in their capture, which made headlines. It repeated this process to track the movement of cryptocurrencies out of markets that exploit children, to find money launderers and to stop the funding of terrorism.

Every action you take on a public blockchain, such as purchasing, selling or exchanging cryptocurrencies, is publicly visible on the network. With 100 coins supported currently, accounting for over 90% of all cryptocurrency transactions, Chainalysis's tools can scrape this publicly available transaction data from blockchains to track down the money.

Despite the pseudonymous nature of blockchains, wallet owners are occasionally identifiable. Therefore, Chainalysis could detect the flow of transactions and notify the exchange that monies that have been stolen have entered it in the event that a known thief uses the exchange to launder money. Alternatively, Chainalysis can alert the authorities that the thief might be connected to the Facebook poster if the thief becomes careless and forwards it to a buddy who, without their knowledge, has disclosed their wallet address on Facebook. Financial institutions use Chainalysis Kryptos to determine the reliability of Bitcoin businesses, while cryptocurrency exchanges use another product, Chainalysis KYT, to track cryptocurrency transactions.

Case Study Questions

1. Explain why intrusions and hacking of cryptocurrencies are rising across the world.
2. Explain why the regulators and bankers are unable to detect fraud and collapse of crypto-currency exchanges.
3. Explain how RegTech can play a key role in preventing the hacking of cryptocurrency exchanges.

Further Reading

1. Dey, Aiyesha, Jonas Heese, and James Weber. "Regtech at HSBC". Harvard Business School Case 120–046, October 2019.
2. Arner, D. W., Barberis, J. N., & Buckley, R. P. (2016). The emergence of RegTech 2.0: From know-your-customer to know your data.

References

Anagnostopoulos, I. (2018). FinTech and RegTech: Impact on regulators and banks. *Journal of Economics and Business*, 100, 7–25.

Arner, D. W., Barberis, J., & Buckey, R. P. (2016). FinTech, RegTech, and the reconceptualization of financial regulation. *Journal of International Law & Business*, 37, 371.

Arner, D. W., Barberis, J., & Buckley, R. P. (2017). *FinTech and RegTech in a nutshell, and the future in a sandbox*. CFA Institute Research Foundation.

Barde, K., & Kulkarni, P. (2023). Applications of generative AI in FinTech. In *AIML' 23, September 21, 2023*. Bengaluru, India.

Becker, M., Merz, K., & Buchkremer, R. (2020). RegTech – the application of modern information technology in regulatory affairs: Areas of interest in research and practice. *Intelligent Systems in Accounting, Finance and Management*, 27(4), 161–167.

Buckley, R. P., Arner, D. W., Zetzsche, D. A., & Weber, R. H. (2020). The road to RegTech: The (astonishing) example of the European Union. *Journal of Banking Regulation*, 21, 26–36.

CB Insights. (2018). RegTech 102: The evolution of RegTech and the future of regulatory compliance. *CB Insights*. www.cbinsights.com/research/regtech-four-phases-expert-intelligence

Charoenwong, B., Kowaleski, Z. T., Kwan, A., & Sutherland, A. (2023). RegTech. *MIT Sloan Research Paper 6563-22*.

CHI Software. (2021). Banking RegTech: What is it, and why is it important? *CHI Software*. https://chisoftware.medium.com/what-is-banking-regtech-its-purpose-and-benefits-82cae081c1d9

Chishti, S., & Barberis, J. (2016). *The FinTech book: The financial technology handbook for investors, entrepreneurs and visionaries*. John Wiley & Sons.

Chugh, B. (2019). *Financial Regulation of Consumer-Facing FinTech in India: Status Quo and Emerging Concerns*. Available at SSRN 3520473.

Estevez, E. (2020). RegTech: Definition, who uses it and why. *Investopedia*. www.investopedia.com/terms/r/regtech.asp

Fan, Q. (2022). The application of blockchain in RegTech: A literature review. In *3rd International Conference on Computer Science and Intelligent Communication (CSIC 2022)*. Clausius Scientific Press.

Grassi, L., & Lanfranchi, D. (2022). RegTech in public and private sectors: The nexus between data, technology and regulation. *Journal of Industrial and Business Economics*, 49(3), 441–479.

Hanumantu, K. D., Worlikar, V., & Narayanaswami, S. (2019). The Punjab National Bank scam: Ethics versus robust processes. *Journal of Public Affairs*, 19(4), e1952.

Jaradat, N., Al-Zeer, I., & Areiqat, A. (2023). Transforming the financial ecosystem: The Synergy of FinTech, RegTech, and Artificial Intelligence. *Journal of Palestine Ahliya University for Research and Studies*, 2(3), 97–103.

Knight, B. (2016). *FinTech: Who Regulates It and Why It Matters*. Milken Institute: Centre for Financial Markets.

Ozili, P. K. (2022). Difficult issues in financial regulation for financial stability. In *The new digital era: Other emerging risks and opportunities* (pp. 55–67). Emerald Publishing Limited.

Singh, C., & Lin, W. (2021). Can Artificial Intelligence, RegTech and CharityTech provide effective solutions for anti-money laundering and counter-terror financing initiatives in charitable fundraising. *Journal of Money Laundering Control*, 24(3), 464–482.

Yadav, P., & Chandak, R. (2019, December). Transforming the know your customer (KYC) process using blockchain. In *2019 International Conference on Advances in Computing, Communication and Control (ICAC3)* (pp. 1–5). IEEE.

Zhou, W., Arner, D. W., & Buckley, R. P. (2018). Regulating FinTech in China: From permissive to balanced. In *Handbook of blockchain, digital finance, and inclusion* (Vol. 2, pp. 45–64). Academic Press.

9 Neobanking – Bringing Convenience to Customers

After reading this chapter you will:

- Know what is a Neobank
- Understand how Neobank works
- Understand the special features of Neobanks
- Know the difference between Neobanks and traditional banks
- Understand the future of Neobanking

The banking industry is undergoing fast change. Customers are holding more and more products and services that are developed on disruptive technologies and banks are changing how they behave when it comes to customer convenience, price, transparency and customer service. The business and operational models adapt along with the expectations and behavior of its customers.

Due to its technology expertise and adaptable, efficient business models, a non-banking service provider can now have access to all components of the banking value chain, including the banking services that clients anticipate and utilize. These models rely on the Internet or other electronic channels as the main method of providing banking services to small- and medium-sized businesses (SMEs) and the general public, instead of using physical branches. Neobanks are non-banking entities that are disrupting the existing landscape of traditional banks by offering very unique customer-focused experiences and cost-effective approaches. Neobanks, unlike traditional banks, are not constrained by outdated systems, complex networks of relationships, complicated administrative frameworks or strict regulatory demands. Neobanks in India utilize partnerships to offer banking services that require a bank license, although not possessing such licenses themselves.

Micro and small enterprises, underbanked or unbanked clients, freelancers and gig economy employees are attracted to certain advantages. These include the simplicity of opening and managing accounts, effortless payment processes, convenient transfer and remittance solutions and alternative ways to evaluate creditworthiness. Previously, these groups had restricted access to financial services and goods, due to either costly fees and restrictive conditions or limited availability. However, Neobanks have now provided them with access.

What Is a Neobank?

Neobanking emerged in the early 2010s as a response to the growing demand for convenient and accessible financial services. Traditional banks were often criticized for their

DOI: 10.4324/9781032699417-9

high fees, poor customer service and outdated technology. Neobanks were able to offer a more streamlined and user-friendly experience by leveraging the latest technology.

The definition of Neobank is:

> A Neobank is a bank that operates in complete digital mode. Rather than being physically present at a specific location, Neobanking is entirely online. Neobanks can be called fintech firms that provide digital and mobile-first financial solutions payments and money transfers, money lending, and more. Neobanks don't have a bank license of their own but count on bank partners to provide bank-licensed services.
>
> (Kasa, 2023)

Neobanks typically partner with traditional banks to provide their services. This allows them to offer Federal Deposit Insurance Corporation insurance on customer deposits and access to ATMs. When a customer opens an account with a Neobank, they are actually opening an account with a partner bank. The Neobank then acts as a front end for the partner bank, providing a mobile app and website that customers can use to manage their accounts.

Neobanks do not have brick-and-mortar branches. They exist entirely in the digital realm, allowing customers to access their services through mobile apps and web platforms. Neobanks prioritize user experience and often offer intuitive interfaces, personalized services and quick customer support. Their digital-first approach caters to the preferences of tech-savvy and mobile-centric users.

Neobanks are known for their agility and innovation. They can quickly adapt to changing technologies, regulations and customer demands, leading to faster implementation of new features and services. By eliminating the overhead costs associated with physical branches, Neobanks can operate at a lower cost. This cost efficiency often translates into better interest rates, lower fees and improved benefits for customers.

Fintech companies have immensely benefited from the partnership with Neobanks. The partnership has helped Fintech companies to offer an enhanced range of products and services. These collaborations enable them to incorporate state-of-the-art technology like artificial intelligence, blockchain and data analytics into their offerings. Certain Neobanks focus on specific demographics or niches, customizing their services to cater to the distinct requirements of particular consumer groupings. This targeted strategy allows them to develop specialized and highly customized products or services (Gust, 2021).

The advantages of using a Neobank are:

- Opening an instant account in a few minutes
- Very minimal paperwork
- Wide range of services offered
- Banking through the mobile app
- A free bank card and an ultra-competitive price list

The potential disadvantages of using the services of Neobanks are:

- **Limited services:** Neobanks may not offer the same range of financial services as traditional banks, such as investment advice or access to credit.

- **Limited access to funds:** Neobanks may not have a physical branch location, making it difficult to access your funds in person.
- **Security concerns:** Because Neobanks are entirely online, they may be more vulnerable to cybersecurity breaches.
- **Limited trust:** because they are new, less known and not regulated as traditional banks, it may be difficult for people to trust them with their money.
- **Uncertainty about the future:** Neobanks are relatively new and may not have a proven track record.
- **Dependence on technology:** Neobanks are dependent on Internet connectivity, which can be a problem in areas with poor Internet connectivity.

Most of the highly developed nations like the USA, the UK, Germany, France, Australia, Japan, China and India have Neobanks. Some of the well-known Neobanks are Chime, Revolut, N26, Kotak811 and WeBank.

Features of Neobank

Neobanks have a virtual presence and operate in online mode. This enables them to offer many specialized services to customers in a faster and better manner. They are also very high in creativity and innovation and offer many pathbreaking products and services which are beyond the realm of traditional banks. They do not have the legacy of maintaining a minimum balance and can offer a huge number of services at low or minimal cost. Neobanks are preferred by customers as they offer instant account opening, speedy credits and seamless cross-border payments (Larisa, Tetiana & Viktoriia, 2019).

Some of the special features of Neobanks are given here.

Instant Bank Account

Opening a bank account is the biggest hassle for many customers. There are a lot of rules, legalities and formalities and a lot of paperwork that needs to be completed before one can open an account. In earlier days, people had to take leave from offices for several days to open a bank account. With Neobanks, the whole process is carried out online through mobile apps or websites, and the whole process takes barely a few minutes. People can focus on their core job functions and students can focus on their studies instead of getting intimated by the process of account opening.

Remittances and International Payments

Remittance and international payments are a big challenge for businessmen who are into imports and exports and migrants who are working in foreign countries. The process has now been made easy by payment banks that offer easy procedures to open bank accounts and do remittances and international transactions in online mode. Neobanks often provide cost-effective and efficient solutions for international money transfers, challenging traditional banks that may impose higher fees and longer processing times. The users can set recurring payments, transfer money globally or send and receive money instantly. The charges are very reasonable, and the customers end up with delightful experiences because of hassle-free faster services at lower cost.

Mobile Banking

While mobile banking has been quite popular for the past few years, the advantage of Neobanking is that customers do not need to have a separate bank account for these operations. Customers can do funds transfers, instant notifications, savings and a lot more with Neobanking on mobile. The Neobanks are also offering a lot of free services and cashback to make their services more attractive. It can truly be said that Neobanks are mobile banks with no conditions applied.

Quick Credit, Loans and Mortgages

Applying for a loan in a traditional bank is a painful process which needs a lot of paperwork and a lot of follow-ups. Also, there is the issue of discretionary choice as traditional banks offer loans only to their most preferred customers. There is a long due diligence process and guarantors to be arranged. Neobanks excel in giving quick credit, loans and mortgages through online mode and offer a higher level of satisfaction to customers. This is especially good for startups and small and medium enterprises where getting guarantors and collaterals is a big challenge.

Some Neobanks offer investment options such as robo-advisors, allowing customers to invest in diversified portfolios based on their risk tolerance and financial goals. Neobanks may extend credit facilities, such as personal loans or credit cards, often with more transparent terms and competitive interest rates. Collaborating with insurance providers, Neobanks may offer insurance products, providing customers with a one-stop shop for their financial needs.

Spend Management and Account Aggregation

As Neobanks operate in the online mode, they have easy access to data and inbuilt analytics software. This software helps to do the account aggregation and analyze the spending, even if the customer has multiple bank accounts. There is also no requirement to take the services of a third-party analytics software. Many Neobanks offer advanced tools for personal finance management, helping users track expenses, set savings goals and receive insights into their spending habits.

Customized Financial Products

Neobanks provide core banking services, including savings and checking accounts, as well as the ability to make payments, transfer funds and manage accounts, all through their digital platforms. They operate on the online mode and hence they have access to real-time data about the customer. Taking the help of this data, they can actually design customized products and services for the customer. The cost of offering customized products is also very low as establishment costs and overheads are not there and most of the services are given in automated mode.

Difference between Traditional Banks and Neobanks

Neobanks and traditional banks differ significantly from one another in terms of operations, customer experience and structure, reflecting different approaches to banking. Traditional banks and Neobanks coexist in harmony. They depend on traditional banks for

Table 9.1 Traditional Banks versus Neobanks

Feature	*Traditional Banks*	*Neobanks*
Platform	Operates in the phygital mode, with physical branches, online banking and mobile banking.	They operate fully in digital mode.
Type of business	They are mostly set up by established financial institutions.	Most of the Neobanks are set up in the startup mode.
Customer relationship	Not much focus on customer relationship management (CRM).	CRM is a top priority.
Fees	Lack of transparency in fees charged.	There is a high level of transparency in the fees charged.
Opening/managing account	Usually involves a set of complex procedures that take time.	Operations are very fast and done in digital mode.
Extra offerings	Not much of rewards and extra offerings.	There are plenty of rewards and innovative offerings.

Source: Bradford (2020).

their licensed services, but they also rely on traditional banks for their digital solutions for certain consumer categories (Bradford, 2020).

When it comes to providing digital solutions for a specific clientele, traditional banks are limited by a number of factors, ranging from banking rules to technological infrastructure. If they want to target particular markets, it might be simpler for them to work with these Neobanks as partners and split the revenue rather than developing and investing in more front-end infrastructure and technology specifically for that purpose.

Traditional banks operate through a network of physical branches. Customers can visit branches for various services, including account opening, deposits, withdrawals and consultations with bank representatives. Physical ATMs are available for cash transactions. Neobanks operate exclusively online without physical branches. They provide services through web platforms and mobile apps. They may not have physical ATMs or rely on partnerships with existing ATM networks.

Traditional banks incur higher operating costs due to maintaining physical branches, staff and associated infrastructure. These costs can impact the fees and interest rates offered to customers. Neobanks have lower operating costs as they do not maintain physical branches. This cost advantage can lead to more competitive rates and lower fees for customers.

Traditional banks are historically slower to adopt cutting-edge technologies. Legacy systems may limit the speed of innovation and the introduction of new features. Neobanks embrace technology and innovation, leveraging modern infrastructure. They are quick to adopt the latest Fintech solutions and offer innovative features such as real-time notifications, budgeting tools and personalized financial insights.

Traditional banks offer traditional customer service through in-person interactions and telephone support. Their processes can be more bureaucratic, potentially leading to longer wait times for services. Neobanks focus on digital-first customer experiences. They provide intuitive mobile apps, quick account setup and often faster and more efficient customer support through online channels.

Traditional banks offer a wide range of financial products, including "savings accounts, checking accounts, loans, mortgages, and investment services". They may have more diverse and complex product portfolios. Neobanks initially focused on core banking products, such as savings and checking accounts. Some Neobanks expanded their offerings over time, often through partnerships with Fintech providers.

Traditional banks are subject to extensive and well-established banking regulations. Compliance often involves navigating complex regulatory frameworks. Neobanks must also comply with financial regulations, but the regulatory landscape may be evolving, and there may be variations in regulatory scrutiny depending on the jurisdiction.

Traditional banks generally target a broad customer base, including individuals, businesses and institutions. They may have a long history and established reputation. Neobanks initially targeted tech-savvy individuals and millennials. Some Neobanks are expanding to cater to a broader audience.

Traditional banks face challenges in implementing changes quickly due to complex decision-making processes and legacy systems. Neobanks are more agile and can implement changes rapidly, responding to customer needs and market trends quickly.

In summary, Neobanks and traditional banks differ in their physical presence, cost structures, approach to technology, customer experience, product offerings, regulatory environment, target markets and speed of implementation. Neobanks, with their digital-first focus, streamlined operations and emphasis on innovation, represent a modern alternative to the more traditional banking model.

The advantages that Neobanks enjoy over traditional banks are given here.

Banking-as-a-Service

Working with current banking products is essential to Neobanks' goal of streamlining the financial management process for their customers through digital banking. In essence, they create the application layer for the products and services on top of the payment infrastructure and fundamental banking products that are supplied by banking partners. Neobanks can also cross-sell value-added products through partnerships with other parties. They may now concentrate on the component of their products that affects the consumer experience (King, 2018).

New Age, Flexible and Scalable Tech Platforms

Neobanks are significantly more tech-focused than traditional banks, frequently characterizing themselves as tech businesses first and banks second. Examining the system's internal workings reveals that Neobanks' front and back ends are entirely digital and unrestricted by larger, more antiquated tech platforms. Additionally, because they are mostly app-driven, you should be able to do the majority of basic tasks, like creating an account, transferring funds and contacting customer service, with a few finger taps. Neobanks allows customers rapid, paperless virtual account opening and financial management from the comfort of their homes.

Marketing as a Strategic Differentiator

The marketing strategy is one of the main areas of interest in Neobanking. Neobanks more than make up for any inherent lack of history and customer trust – given that many of them are really startups – with a plethora of consumer engagement initiatives. This is where digital banking and Neobanking diverge totally. Neobanks frequently use digital and social media to promote their campaigns, with an emphasis on community building, influencer marketing and the publication of uplifting testimonies. A major asset for any Neobank is customer referrals, which are frequently modeled after the models of prosperous platform economy behemoths like Uber and Netflix.

Hassle-Free Account Creation

In the case of Neobanks, the whole operation is run in an online mode. The details of the customers are submitted online and the know-your-customer (KYC) documents like Aadhar card, PAN card, income tax returns (ITR) and photograph can all be submitted through a mobile app or website. Digital signatures are used to open the account, and there is no physical interface. It usually takes only a few minutes to open a Neobanking account.

Seamless International Payments

Normally a bank customer needs to have a debit card or credit card and activate it for international transactions. In the case of Neobanking, there is no such procedure involved and customers can make international payments through Neobanking at prevailing exchange rates.

User-Friendly Interface

Neobanking is known for its great user interface (UI) and user experience (UX). There are very few glitches, and the banking operations go through smoothly at a faster rate than traditional banks. The mobile applications offered by Neobanks are highly polished, streamlined and intuitive for users. These products are extremely responsive and expertly created to meet the specific requirements of customers. The app's popularity among its clients can be attributed to its user-friendly interface.

Smart Reporting

Neobanking operates in an online mode. Data is collected online and stored in repositories. The data is analyzed by inbuilt software, and smart reports are generated. All the information regarding payments and transactions can be accessed through the mobile app or website. Customers can also generate smart reports using artificial intelligence (AI) tools embedded in the software.

The Neobanking app offers customers a comprehensive summary of their expenditures, as well as a customizable savings objective tailored to their specific requirements. Neobanking customers can effectively and knowledgeably manage their funds using this feature.

Difference between Digital Banks and Neobanks

The terms "Neobanks" and "digital banks" are often used interchangeably, but there are subtle differences in their meanings. The distinctions are not always clear-cut, as the financial industry and regulatory environments can vary, leading to different interpretations. However, there are some general differences that are often associated with Neobanks and digital banks (Bradford, 2020).

Neobanks are typically digital-only entities that operate exclusively through online channels. They have no physical branches, and their primary interface is through mobile apps and web platforms. Neobanks often collaborate with Fintech companies to enhance their service offerings. They may partner with third-party providers for services like payments, lending, investment and insurance, leveraging APIs for seamless integration.

Neobanks place a strong emphasis on user-friendly interfaces and a positive customer experience. They strive to simplify the banking process, making it more intuitive and accessible to users who may be less familiar with traditional banking. Some Neobanks target specific niche markets or demographics, offering specialized services tailored to the needs of particular customer segments. This targeted approach allows them to differentiate themselves in the market.

Neobanks often introduce innovative features and services that go beyond digital banking. These may include budgeting tools, real-time spending notifications and other value-added services designed to improve financial management.

Digital banks, while primarily operating online, may have a hybrid approach that includes some physical touchpoints. This could involve the presence of a few physical branches or partnering with existing brick-and-mortar institutions for certain services. Digital banks offer a full range of banking services, including savings accounts, checking accounts, loans and other traditional financial products. They aim to provide a complete suite of services comparable to traditional banks but with a greater emphasis on digital accessibility.

Digital banks may or may not collaborate extensively with Fintech partners. Some operate independently, relying on their technology infrastructure to deliver a comprehensive set of banking services without relying heavily on external partnerships. Digital banks often target a broader customer base and may not focus on specific niche markets. They aim to appeal to a wide range of customers seeking a digital alternative to traditional banking.

Both Neobanks and digital banks must comply with financial regulations, but the degree of regulatory scrutiny may vary. Digital banks may face more regulatory oversight due to their broader range of services and, in some cases, their physical presence.

In summary, while there is considerable overlap between the terms "Neobanks" and "digital banks", Neobanks are often associated with a more exclusive focus on digital channels, Fintech collaborations and a strong emphasis on user experience. Digital banks, on the other hand, may have a broader range of services, potentially including some physical touchpoints, and may operate with a more traditional banking structure. The distinctions can vary, and the terms are used differently in different regions and contexts within the financial industry.

The Operating Model of a Neobank

Neobanks have been popular due to their intuitive interfaces, openness and ability to quickly address consumer requirements. These alternatives to traditional banks are excellent options since they provide reduced costs, increased interest rates on savings accounts and a smooth digital banking experience.

In contrast to traditional banks, Neobank app development is not bound by legacy systems and infrastructure, allowing them to innovate rapidly and tailor their services to the evolving demands of clients. Building a digital bank or Neobanking startup also means being strategically focused on rapid expansion. The main advantage lies in allocating resources toward aggressive marketing campaigns, both online and offline, to attract new users. Additionally, the Neobanks are always coming up with new ideas, for example, offering attractive pricing packages for new customers, since that can help them be on top of the competition (Rocchi, 2022).

The Neobanks come with an easy-to-access and easy-to-navigate onboarding process that helps the users easily navigate the app, find features, execute transactions and so on. The authorization feature enables users to access the bank or utilize its services. The time users spend creating an account or logging into a Neobanking app should be minimal.

The KYC system protects clients from scams, corruption, illegal gains and funding for terrorism. Personal account management lets users access their account management controls, where they can change their profile and settings to fit their needs.

Customer support should be reachable whenever users have a query or run across an issue. Messaging is a great solution. Card issuing schemes may vary, such as by printing them off or using virtual debit cards, obtaining a unique bank identification number (BIN) or even sharing one. The provider should suit the region and terms and have suitable price policies.

The transaction history in a Neobank helps track customers' spending and process their payments. The Internet limits allow customers to control the maximum amount they may commit to an online purchase and make informed decisions about their budgets.

The payment templates are a great way to streamline the user experience of the Neobank. The contact database synchronization enables the use of phone numbers instead of card information. A notification and reminder system must inform customers about account activity, payment receipts and app updates.

In terms of operating models, Neobanks may follow one of three approaches (Niyo, 2024):

- Non-licensed Fintechs that collaborate with traditional banks and provide a mobile/web interface and wrapper around the products of their partner banks
- Traditional banks with their own digital initiatives
- Licensed Neobanks that exist as their own entity without tying up with a traditional bank

Although a number of Neobanks hold banking licenses, most of them collaborate with conventional banks rather than securing their own banking licenses. The banking partner offers the overall infrastructure for managing client accounts, retaining customer cash and providing the framework for interbank payments and settlements under this operating model. Neobank is in charge of overseeing the entire customer journey, from customer acquisition to servicing, as well as product distribution.

Online data processing systems power Neobanks. Neobanks find it simpler to obtain data and process it to have up-to-date consumer information because they are solely online. Instead of only focusing on one or two datapoints, they use these insights to form cohorts of clients depending on their behavior. The KYC process can be completed quickly by submitting documents online. In India, Neobanks employ the unified payments interface (UPI), introduced by the National Payment Council of India, and e-KYC provided by the Unique Identification Authority of India. Neobanks are able to provide consumers with quick and individualized services as a result. Neobanks have rather good UIs and UXs when compared to traditional banks.

Neobanks are location agnostic, and the cost of servicing customers is very minimal as they do not have physical branches and infrastructure costs. They also do not

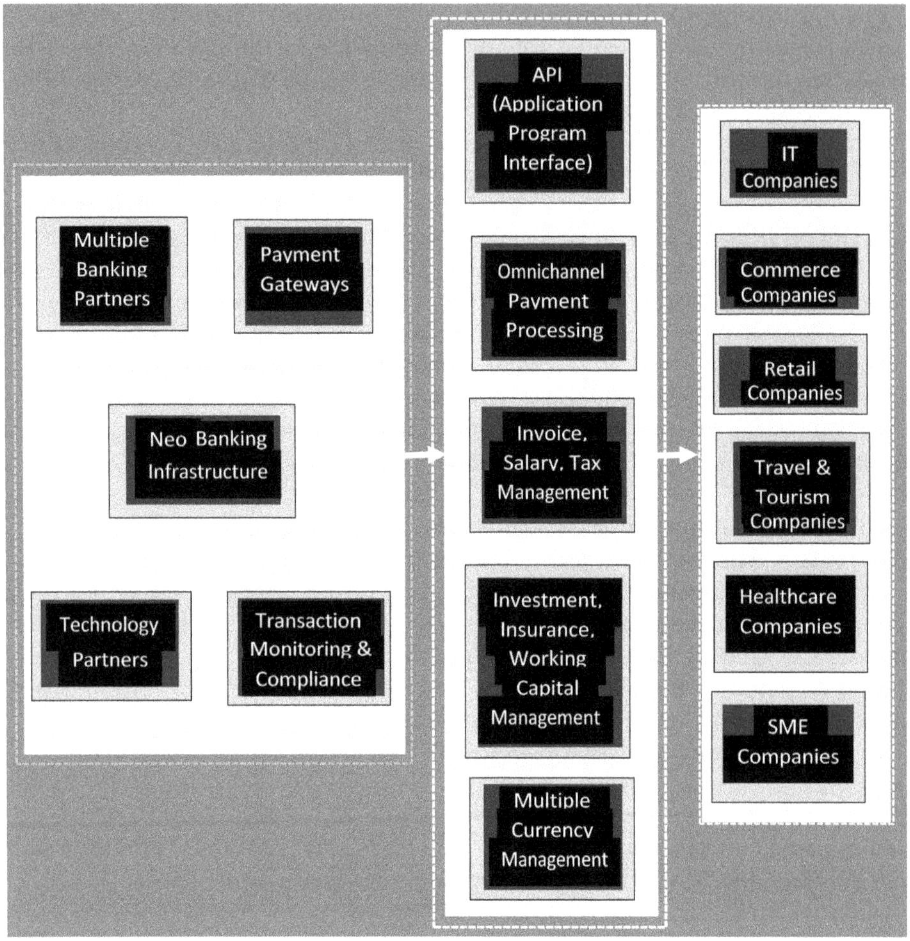

Figure 9.1 Neobanking Process Flow Diagram

have overheads and most of the operations are run in automated mode. This helps the Neobanks to offer high-quality service at the lowest cost. The self-explanatory workflow diagram of a Neobank is given in Figure 9.1 (Sitech, 2024).

Neobanks operate in virtual space and do not have any physical existence. They use the core infrastructure or the core banking system (CBS) of the parent banking institution or partner bank to offer their products and services. The payment gateways, transaction systems and compliance networks are all provided by the parent bank. The Neobank builds an application program interface (API) on the Neobanking layer and offers innovative products and services to the customers.

The offerings by Neobanks can be in B2B(Business-to-Business) or B2C(Business-to-Customer) mode. Neobanks can service multiple accounts and can also build APIs on multiple partner banks. The level of flexibility is very high in the case of Neobanks. They can also be a tool for Omnichannel Marketing as they are platform and physical location agnostic. The APIs can be customized to offer various services like raising invoices, paying salaries, expense management and tax compliance. Because of their flexibility, they are becoming very popular among e-commerce players and small-and-medium enterprises (SMEs).

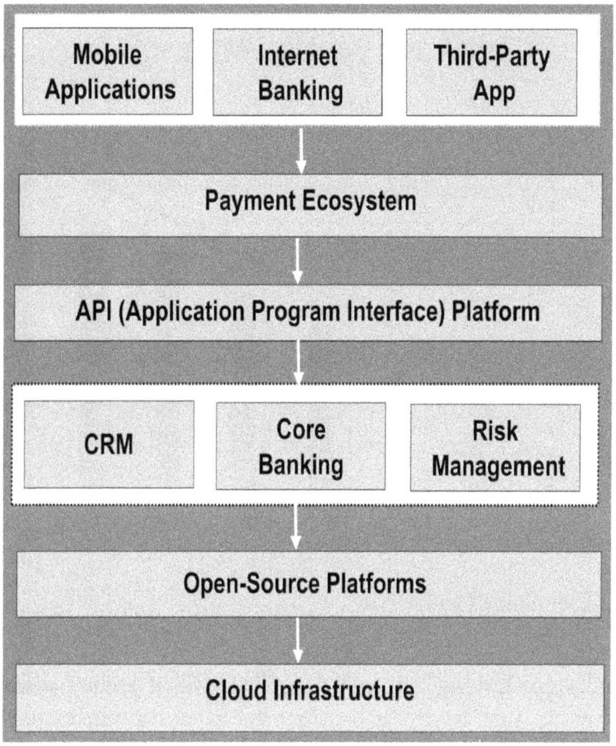

Figure 9.2 Neobanking Architecture

Different types of Neobanks are operating with different business models. Monzo in the UK, Xinja in Australia and N26 in Europe are operating like normal banks. Starling, a UK-based Neobank offers low and no-fee accounts and services. Some Neobanks are offering "Banking-as-a-Service (BaaS)".

Neobank technology begins with the product's architecture, as any banking application comprises a number of different parts, platforms, services and data sources. A Neobank's design consists of three main components: the front end of the application, the core platform and the hosting infrastructure (Morozko, 2024).

The Neobanking Architecture is given in Figure 9.2.

Also, Neobanks are automating security measures with AI and bots that recognize any suspicious activity within the system. The smart algorithms can detect data breaches and act accordingly to stop the malware.

The Rising Importance of Neobanks

With the rapid rise in the number of tech-savvy customers, a gap has been created between what the banks are offering and what the customers expect from banks. The popularity of mobile banking has been on the rise, and many customers have stopped physically going to banks. Neobanks have been created to bridge the gap and offer banking services to customers in a completely electronic mode (Corander, 2021).

The global Neobanking market size is given in Figure 9.3.

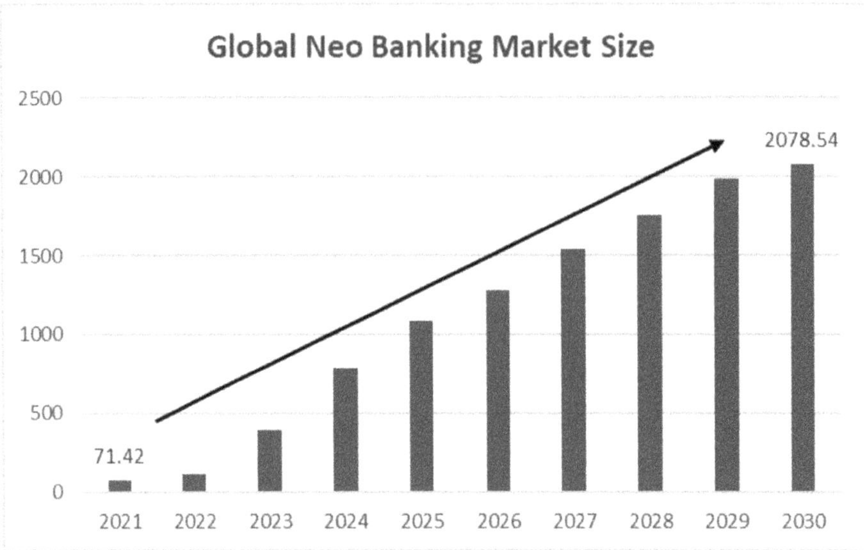

Figure 9.3 Global Neobanking Market Size

Traditional banks are having a tough time because of legacy systems. They have a shortage of manpower; they are bogged down due to compliance rules and they do not have access to critical information that is required for doing due diligence. They are still issuing chequebooks and debit cards to depositors and asking borrowers to physically fill up forms for taking loans along with attested photocopies for various types of proof. The stringent KYC norms required for banking and financial transactions have taken the wind out of the sail of traditional banks.

The new-age banks on the other hand are operating with innovative and disruptive tools, technology and models to lure away customers. The new-age banks are asking customers to use mobile banking, quick response (QR) codes and UPI to make payments. They are asked to send SMS to know the account balance and use interactive voice response (IVR) to register complaints. They are asked to give missed calls to avail of various kinds of services. For KYC, the new-age banks are asking customers to submit scanned copies of their Aadhar card, PAN card, ITR form and photograph through mobile phone app or website from the comfort of their phone. Traditional banks take 15 days to a month to sanction or disburse a loan, while the new-age banks do it in 15 minutes. No doubt, the popularity of new-age banks like Kotak Mahindra Bank, IndusInd Bank, Yes Bank and IDFC Bank are on the rise.

The banks are now getting challenged by brands like Paytm, PhonePe, BharatPe, Google Pay, Mobikwik and Bharat Interface for Money-offering digital wallets and QR code-based PayTech systems. Then there are payment banks run by Airtel, Jio, Paytm, India Post and Fino who offers convenient banking and financial services. Multinational companies like Google Pay, Amazon Pay, Apple Pay and Samsung Pay are giving stiff competition to banks. Digital payments are growing in popularity with over 2,500 Fintech companies creating exciting platforms for transactions. Customers are moving away from physical banks and physical cash and more toward online banking and wallets.

India is currently transitioning into a period of increasing financial technology. Indian consumers are increasingly engaging in digital transactions, and the figures are rapidly increasing. An increasing number of individuals are becoming at ease with doing online transactions using platforms such as Google Pay, Paytm, PhonePe and others, particularly in the present time.

This opens up a huge scope of opportunity for Neobanks. India has more than 50 million SMEs, and only 47% of them have access to traditional banking products. Less than 25% of the SMEs use ERP and CRM software. This poses a huge market opportunity for Neobanks.

There are also more than 15 million contract workers and freelancers, many of whom are working in the unorganized sector. Many of the people in this segment do not have access to banking products and services. There are approximately 900 million people living in rural areas. Many of them do not have banks in their nearby areas but have electricity, Internet and good bandwidth. This represents a large chunk of potential customers for Neobanking.

To address the needs of individuals who do not have access to traditional banking services, a number of Neobanks have commenced their operations. The most notable options include 811 by Kotak, Yono by SBI, RazorpayX and NiYo. Neobanks have made a significant impact on the banking and finance business and are being well-received by people who do not have access to traditional banking services. The preliminary reports indicate a rather high level of client satisfaction. Over the past three years, Neobanks have effectively assisted small- and medium-sized firms, major corporations and the gig economy in various financial tasks such as billing, cashflow management, disbursals and vendor management. Given the increasing interest in Neobanks, it is reasonable to assert that they embody the future of modern banking.

Neobanks leverage cutting-edge technology to offer seamless and user-friendly digital banking experiences. The use of mobile apps, intuitive interfaces and AI distinguishes them from traditional banks. Advanced technology enables faster account opening, real-time transaction tracking and personalized financial insights, meeting the evolving expectations of tech-savvy consumers.

Neobanks typically have lower operating costs compared to traditional banks due to their lack of physical infrastructure and streamlined operations. This allows them to offer competitive or even no-fee services, attracting cost-conscious consumers. Many Neobanks operate without geographical restrictions, allowing customers to access their accounts and conduct transactions from anywhere in the world. This global accessibility is particularly advantageous for individuals who travel frequently or live in different countries.

Neobanks often pioneer innovative financial products and services. They may introduce features such as budgeting tools, automated savings, investment options and cryptocurrency support, providing customers with a diverse range of choices beyond traditional banking offerings. User-centric design is a hallmark of Neobanks. By prioritizing customer experience, these institutions strive to make banking more intuitive, transparent and enjoyable. This focus on user satisfaction can lead to increased customer loyalty and word-of-mouth referrals.

Neobanks have the potential to enhance financial inclusion by reaching underserved populations. Traditional banking services may be inaccessible or impractical for certain demographics, but Neobanks, with their digital-first approach, can cater to a broader range of customers. Unlike traditional banks burdened by legacy systems and bureaucratic processes, Neobanks are more agile and adaptable. This allows them to respond quickly to market trends, regulatory changes and customer feedback, fostering a culture of continuous improvement.

A multitude of Neobanks embrace an open banking strategy by establishing alliances with Fintech firms and seamlessly incorporating a wide range of financial services. This ecosystem integration allows users to conveniently access a diverse range of financial goods and services through a unified platform. Neobanks utilize customer data and analytics to get knowledge about user behavior, preferences and financial habits. By utilizing a data-driven strategy, they are able to provide individualized advice, focused advertising and a customized banking experience.

Regulatory bodies in several regions are increasingly supportive of innovative financial models, fostering a conducive environment for Neobanks to thrive. As regulations evolve to accommodate digital banking, it provides Neobanks with opportunities for growth and expansion.

Neobanks in the World

Globally, there are 272 Neobanks. This covers Neobanks for youth, individuals and corporations (Monis & Pai, 2023). Chime is the greatest Neobank. Chime is a US-based Neobank that offers one service for professionals and two offers for individuals. Here, people get to enjoy free and limitless withdrawals within the Eurozone with MasterCard bank cards that work anywhere in the world. Additionally, there are no fees or limits for international payments, which are handled via an easy-to-use smartphone app. Other noteworthy benefits for individuals at Revolut include the cashback bonus, referral programs and free and limitless payments in both euros and other currencies. If you're searching for a simple and easy way to manage your finances, Monzo is a terrific choice. Monzo is renowned for its open and honest approach to banking, emphasizing the need to empower clients to comprehend their financial situation and make wise choices. The following are the specifics of a few chosen Neobanks from various geographic regions.

Chime (USA)

The American Neobank called Chime provides a variety of financial services, such as debit cards, mobile banking and checking and savings accounts. The emphasis Chime places on offering a more accessible and user-friendly banking experience is one of its main advantages. Customers may handle their accounts, transfer money and pay bills while on the road with its user-friendly and straightforward mobile app (Agnihotri & Bhattacharya, 2023).

Chime's inexpensive fees and absence of minimum balance requirements are further advantages. This makes it a desirable choice for people searching for a more cost-effective way to handle their money or who might not have access to standard banking services. A variety of financial services and products are also provided by Chime, including financial coaching, automatic savings and early direct deposit. These can assist clients in achieving their financial objectives, establishing credit and saving money.

All things considered, Chime is a fantastic choice for anyone searching for a simple, affordable and convenient banking experience. Chime's emphasis on financial inclusion and empowerment contributes to lowering the cost of banking and increasing accessibility for all.

Revolut (UK/Europe)

Revolut was started by Vlad Yatsenko and Nikolay Storonsky in 2015. Revolut offers financial products and services like current accounts, debit cards, virtual cards, interest-bearing vaults, stock trading, cryptocurrency and commodities trading. The company has 18 million customers and is clocking an annual revenue of more than $1 billion annually.

In 2020, Revolut increased its workforce from 1,500 to 6,000 employees and entered the USA and Japan1. With a valuation of £4.2 billion, it emerged as the most valuable Fintech business in the UK. Revolut became the most valuable digital startup in the United Kingdom at the moment when it raised $800 million in funding in July 2021, increasing the company's valuation to $33 billion. In December 2023, the anticipated value was $18 billion.

Revolut allows users to open and maintain multiple currency accounts, make free international purchases and receive real-time transaction notifications. They are ideal for international businesses and vacationers as they can convert currencies at the interbank rate without any markup. They can effortlessly and swiftly transfer and receive money overseas, all with affordable fees and favorable exchange rates. With fractional shares, they can also invest as little as $1 in stocks, ETFs and cryptocurrency.

Customers of Revolut can also create savings objectives and vaults to automatically save money and earn interest on their balance. Through the app, they may instantly obtain insurance for their phone, trip and other possessions.

Revolut distinguishes itself from other Neobanks with unique features including fee-free banking, ease and inventiveness. Many of Revolut's fundamental functions, like creating an account, storing various currencies and making international purchases, are free to use. All financial information is managed centrally with the user-friendly Revolut app. Revolut is a pioneer in the Neobanking industry since it is continuously introducing innovative features and services.

All things considered, Revolut is a fantastic choice for those seeking an easy and reasonably priced solution to handle their money. Before utilizing the Neobanks' services, it's crucial to understand their restrictions. Revolut does not compensate victims of authorized push payment fraud in the UK because it does not currently hold a banking license in that nation.

Monzo (UK)

The UK-based Neobank Monzo provides its clients with a variety of financial services. Since its founding in 2013, it has expanded to rank among the biggest and most well-known Neobanks worldwide. A current account, savings account, loans and other financial products are among the services offered by Monzo. The mobile app offered by Monzo, which enables users to handle their money while on the go, is one of its primary benefits. Monzo just offers its app for banking transactions; it does not have any physical branches. In addition, Monzo provides a number of features and tools, such as savings targets and budgeting, to assist users in managing their finances.

Monzo is not yet accessible outside of the UK, but plans to expand are in the works. All things considered, Monzo is a welcome change in the banking industry, providing a pleasant blend of entertaining features, astute tools and straightforward banking. For banking consumers searching for an easy, entertaining and reasonably priced way to handle their money, Monzo provides an excellent experience.

N26 (Germany/Europe)

The German Neobank N26 offers financial services like checking, savings and investment accounts. It is a fully licensed bank with up to €100,000 in deposit protection programs. Forbes has named N26 the "Best Bank in the World" for the year 2023. They provide a mobile-first, surprisingly straightforward banking experience. They are entirely mobile. The user-friendly software allows users to manage their finances, open accounts and make payments.

N26's mobile app, which enables customers to manage their funds while on the road, is one of its best features. N26 also provides a number of advantages, including budgeting tools, early access to direct transfers and simple account freezing and unfreezing. In addition, N26 provides a range of financial services and goods, including investing and insurance alternatives, to assist customers in reaching their financial objectives. In general, N26 is a fantastic choice for anyone searching for a practical and easy-to-use financial management solution.

Customers have the option of premium N26 Smart/Metal plans with extra features including travel insurance and Spaces (sub-accounts for savings objectives) or the free N26 You plan. There are explicit payments for certain services only – no hidden costs. With the use of automated budgeting tools, classified transaction histories and real-time spending data, customers can keep tabs on their spending patterns. Up to ten virtual sub-accounts can be made by them to divide up particular savings objectives, such as bills or vacations. They can easily observe their savings increase by rounding up to the closest euro on their purchases. All things considered, N26 is a serious competitor for anybody looking for a clear, easy and modern banking experience with astute money management features.

Starling Bank (UK)

Starling Bank, also known as Neobank or a challenger bank, has revolutionized the UK financial landscape with its creative strategy and emphasis on the customer experience. Customers of this Neobank can choose from a variety of financial services. It was established in the UK in 2014 and has since grown to operate in other nations. With no physical locations, the bank conducts all of its operations online and provides personal and business banking services.

Starling Neobank's user-friendly mobile app, which enables users to manage their funds while on the go, is one of its primary benefits. A number of features are available in the app, such as real-time transaction alerts, savings objectives and budgeting tools. A variety of financial products are also available from Starling Neobank, such as credit cards, loans, savings accounts and current accounts.

The emphasis that Starling Neobank places on security is another benefit. The bank protects the financial information of its clients using cutting-edge security features like biometric login and two-factor authentication. In addition, Starling Neobank is subject to UK Financial Conduct Authority regulation, guaranteeing the bank's impartial and open operations.

All things considered, Starling Bank is a strong competitor for people looking for a convenient, feature-rich and easy-to-use banking experience. Starling is ideally positioned to continue its rise in the world of digital banking thanks to its concentration on clever tools, cutting-edge features and a focus on financial well-being.

Niyo Neo (India)

Niyo Solutions was founded in 2015 by Vinay Bagri and Virender Bisht. The company initially started with solutions aimed at simplifying payroll and benefits for employees. Over time, it expanded its offerings to include Neobanking services with the launch of Niyo Neo (Lindström & Nilsson, 2023).

Niyo Neo was developed with the goal of offering a comprehensive suite of banking services entirely through a mobile application. The aim was to cater to the needs of digitally savvy customers who prefer the convenience and efficiency of managing their finances via their smartphones. Niyo Neo provides its users with a range of financial products and services, such as savings accounts, fixed deposits and personal loans, all within the same platform.

Niyo Neo has forged partnerships with various financial institutions and service providers to enhance its offerings. For instance, it collaborates with banks to provide savings accounts and forex services and with mutual fund companies for investment options. One of the standout features of Niyo Neo is its multi-currency forex card. Users can load multiple currencies onto the card and use it for international transactions while enjoying competitive exchange rates.

Niyo Neo has now evolved into a digital wallet and payment gateway that offers a range of features and benefits to its users. One of its key advantages is its seamless integration with various e-commerce platforms, allowing users to make payments and transfer funds with ease. Additionally, Niyo Neo offers a user-friendly interface and 24/7 customer support, ensuring a hassle-free experience for its users. Overall, Niyo Neo is a practical and comprehensive digital wallet solution that provides users with a range of benefits and features (Niyo, 2024).

Niyo Neo represents a modern approach to banking, leveraging technology to offer a range of financial services that are convenient, efficient and tailored to the needs of digital consumers. With its user-friendly interface, innovative features and commitment to security and compliance, Niyo Neo is well-positioned to make a significant impact in the Indian Fintech landscape.

WeBank (China)

WeBank is the premier digital bank in the world and the first digital bank in China. This Neobank is using technology to propel its expansion. It has been actively developing cutting-edge technologies, such as AI, blockchain, cloud computing and big data, to achieve this goal.

China's WeBank is a digital-only bank that opened for business in 2014. It is dedicated to serving the various financial requirements of SMEs and retail clients. Wealth management, corporate banking, microcredit and blockchain technology are just a few of the financial services and goods that WeBank offers. It is the top digital bank in the world, always coming up with new ideas to make life better.

Tencent, Baiyeyuan, Liye Group and other businesses support WeBank. With an estimated 30% ownership percentage, Tencent is by far the largest shareholder. WeBank was valued at an estimated US$21 billion in 2019.

WeBank provides financial services like loans, deposits and investments to unbanked and underbanked people as well as SMEs. WeBank took the initiative and introduced "Weiyedai", the first online unsecured corporate working capital loan product in China, to address the financing challenges that the majority of MSMEs experience. This product successfully lowers the costs and constraints associated with financial services. WeBank is dedicated to building an ecosystem of whole-chain commercial services for MSMEs, and we are always pushing inclusive financing to guarantee broad reach, profound penetration and simple fund accessibility.

WeBank is a technology and innovation-driven company. It has made investments in the development and use of important technologies like big data, blockchain, cloud computing and AI. WeBank develops a CBS with a strong support system for economically sustainable financial inclusion, all while meeting the financial demands of hundreds of millions of consumers using a safe and controllable distributed architecture. WeBank supports the global comprehensive open-source policy of important technical accomplishments to facilitate the sharing of scientific research findings.

WeBank is dedicated to achieving its goal of "Better Banking for Everyone". It has continuously investigated a cutting-edge financial services model supported by Fintech solutions over the years. WeBank seeks to enhance coverage, accessibility and customer happiness in the financial services industry by offering safe, effective and inclusive financial services that cater to the various financing needs of retail clients in a tailored way. WeBank proactively upholds the rights of customers and attends to the financial requirements of specific groups. It supports social welfare initiatives, protects the environment and gives back to the community.

Future of Neobanking

There are more than 100 Neobanks across the world at this moment and the number is rising. Various market research reports have predicted immense growth in the Neobanking sector. Neobanks are very popular among millennials and SME owners as there is no hassle of minimum account balance and providing collaterals and guarantors for loans. This is also gaining popularity among students and migrant workers for the ease of transactions and doing remittances and international transactions (Sardar & Anjaria, 2023).

The Neobanks do not have the burden of legacy systems and have the potential of reaching out to a high number of customers in the online mode. For countries like India and China where the number of unbanked people is high, Neobanks have a great customer base to tap into.

While Neobanks are coming out with innovative and creative offerings, the traditional banks are also launching Neobanks to keep up the pace of growth and address the needs of the customers. Thus, we have 811 by Kotak Mahindra Bank and Yono by State Bank of India, which are Neobanks. It will be indeed very interesting to see what shape Neobanking takes and what impact it makes in the coming days.

The Neobanks are going to face several challenges in the coming days like building trust, regulatory compliance, monetizing the business and seeking profitability, Building trust without a physical presence can be a challenge. Regulatory compliance is crucial, and Neobanks must navigate a complex regulatory landscape to ensure the security and privacy of customer data.

Achieving profitability without traditional revenue streams like branch-based services can be challenging. Neobanks often explore alternative revenue models such as subscription fees or partnerships.

Neobanks will likely continue integrating emerging technologies to enhance security, efficiency and customer experience. This may include the use of blockchain, biometrics and advanced AI. Neobanks may evolve into financial ecosystems, collaborating with various Fintech and non-financial entities to offer a comprehensive suite of services beyond traditional banking. Some of the Neobanks aim for global expansion, leveraging their digital infrastructure to serve customers across borders.

In conclusion, Neobanks represent a disruptive force in the financial industry, challenging traditional banking models with their digital-first approach, innovative services and customer-centric focus. As technology continues to advance, Neobanks are likely to play an increasingly prominent role in shaping the future of banking.

Questions for Discussion

1. Explain what you understand by Neobanks.
2. Explain the working mechanism of Neobanks.
3. What are the special features of Neobanks? Explain.
4. What is the difference between Neobanks and traditional banks?
5. What do you think is the future of Neobanking? Explain.

Case Study: Kotak 811 – The Neobank from Kotak Mahindra

Kotak 811 is a Neobanking service launched by Kotak Mahindra Bank (KMB) in the month of March 2017. 811 is a totally digitalized Neobank that operates online to provide retail goods and services. Promoting the usage of Internet transactions over cash transactions was the primary goal of the Neobank's launch.

Customers must register for the opening of an account and finish the KYC procedure online to use the Neobanking service of 811. In KMB's Neobank, opening an account simply takes five minutes. The value proposition comprises quick, customer-focused onboarding as well as straightforward, reasonably priced and accessible products. KMB believed that by offering simple, quick and inexpensive procedures, they would be able to attract a larger clientele.

Kotak 811's primary unique selling proposition was its focused marketing, real-time, fully digital customer onboarding experience, free digital transactions and payment processing and competitive interest rates on deposits over the industry average. This was also about embracing the newest banking trends and attaining organic growth for KMB.

Clients of KMB's Neobank are analyzed, and the majority either are first-time bank clients or come from lower-middle-class or middle-class backgrounds. A considerable portion of SME owners utilize KMB Neobank's services. The account is inexpensive for low-income users because there are no usage costs. Customers of KMB are currently switching to traditional services as well.

This ease of use assists clients in overcoming the obstacles that are physical while visiting banks and may help lower the amount of time that low-income clients – especially women – must spend traveling to and from branches. This is especially important for the vast majority of 811's clientele, who don't have a steady source of income and include students and the unemployed.

811 operates using the backend infrastructure and core banking of KMB. Clients can complete the onboarding process via the 811 mobile app. In 811, every procedure is entirely digital. In addition to utilizing KMB's whole technological stack, 811 has included value-added capabilities that make remote onboarding for online operations easier. Customers who wish to utilize KMB's other banking services are guided into KMB's regular flow after they are on board.

The majority of 811's services are free, and there is no minimum balance requirement. The primary sources of income for Neobank are net interest income, cross-selling commissions from different financial products and special fees from some non-free transactions.

Customers embraced KMB's recent launch, and, in just 18 months, the number of account holders more than doubled from 8 million to 16 million.

Case Study Questions

1. Explain the business model of Kotak 811, a Neobank launched by Kotak Mahindra.
2. How is Kotak 811 different from the traditional KMB?
3. Explain the reasons for the success of the Kotak811Neobank.

Further Reading

1. Growth In Neo Banking, S Ravi, www.businessworld.in/article/Growth-In-Neo-Banking/15-02-2021-377698
2. "Neobanks" May Not Be New, or Banks, but They Are Hot Stocks, Telis Demos, WallStreet-Journal, www.wsj.com/articles/neobanks-may-not-be-new-or-banks-but-they-are-hot-stocks-11628847006

References

Agnihotri, A., & Bhattacharya, S. (2023). *Chime Neobank: A new business model in the banking sector*. SAGE Publications: SAGE Business Cases Originals.

Bradford, T. (2020, August 12). Neobanks: Banks by any other name. *Federal Reserve Bank of Kansas City* (pp. 1–6). Payments System Research Briefing.

Corander, B. (2021). Neobanks: Challenges, risks and opportunities. *Theseus*. www.theseus.fi/handle/10024/498077

Gust, M. (2021). Traditional banking and disruption FinTech. evolutions, causes, typologies. *Revista Economia Contemporană*, 6(1), 57–72.

Kasa, R. (2023). What is a Neobank? Everything you should know. *Razorpay*. https://razorpay.com/blog/business-banking/what-is-a-neobank/#:~:text=Neobanks%20are%20new%2Dage%20banks,transfers%2C%20lending%2C%20and%20more.

King, B. (2018). *Bank 4.0: Banking everywhere, never at a bank*. John Wiley & Sons.

Larisa, G., Tetiana, N., & Viktoriia, V. (2019, October). Neobanks operations and security features. In *2019 IEEE International Scientific-Practical Conference Problems of Infocommunications, Science and Technology (PIC S&T)* (pp. 839–842). IEEE.

Lindström, V., & Nilsson, O. (2023). The sudden rise of neobanks and the threat it poses upon the traditional banking system. *Digitala Vetenskapliga Arkivet*. www.diva-portal.org/smash/record.jsf?pid=diva2%3A1763436&dswid=-9664

Monis, E., & Pai, R. (2023). Neo banks: A paradigm shift in banking. *International Journal of Case Studies in Business, IT and Education (IJCSBE)*, 7(2), 318–332.

Morozko, Y. (2024). Neobank technology: Architecture, integrations, and tools for building a banking app. *Jatapp*. https://jatapp.co/blog/neobank-technology/

Niyo. (2024). Neo Bank – how does a Neobank work. *Niyo Global*. https://goniyo.com/blog/how-does-a-neo-bank-work-2/

Rocchi, J. M. (2022). How to build a leading so-called Neobank and pursue its growth?: The case of the FinTech nickel in Europe. In *Cases on digital strategies and management issues in modern organizations* (pp. 177–199). IGI Global.

Sardar, S., & Anjaria, K. (2023). The future of banking: How neo banks are changing the industry. *International Journal of Management, Public Policy and Research*, 2(2), 32–41.

Sitech. (2024). How to build a Neobank: Mobile banking development process. *Sitech*. www.sitech.me/blog/how-to-build-a-neobank-mobile-banking-development-process

10 Central Bank Digital Currency (CBDC)

After reading this chapter you will:

- Know what is Central Bank Digital Currency (CBDC)
- Know the different forms of CBDC
- Understand how CBDC works
- Know the difference between CBDC and digital currency
- Know about cross-border CBDC

The global economies rely on fiat currencies such as the US dollar, euro, British pound sterling, Chinese yuan and Indian rupee. The US Federal Reserve printed three trillion dollars in 2020. The European Commercial Bank (ECB) printed 156 billion euros in 2023. The Bank of England printed 4.6 billion pound sterling in 2023. The People's Bank of China issued 9.62 trillion yuan in 2022. The Reserve Bank of India printed 31 billion of INR (Indian national rupees) in the period 2021–2022.

Although a huge volume of currency notes is currently in circulation, the transaction volume is shrinking by the day. Modern technologies like the use of QR codes for payments through e-wallets (electronic wallets), mobile banking and Internet banking have reduced the importance of physical currencies. On the other hand, people have shown their proclivity for instruments of decentralized finance (DeFi) like cryptocurrencies and non-fungible tokens (NFT). Decentralized finance poses a big threat to governments across the world as cryptocurrencies and non-fungible tokens can be used for nefarious activities like money laundering, drug peddling and terrorism.

Central banks are contemplating the use of Central Bank Digital Currency (CBDC) as an alternative form of payment for their citizens, instead of cryptocurrencies and non-fungible tokens. CBDC refers to a form of digital or electronic currency that is created and issued by a country's central bank. Unlike cryptocurrencies such as Bitcoin and Ethereum, a government-backed digital currency, known as a CBDC, is often centralized. In recent years, there has been a significant surge in interest in the concept of CBDC as central banks seek ways to modernize their monetary systems and adapt to the quickly changing landscape of digital finance.

Based on a recent survey conducted by the Bank for International Settlements in 2021, it was found that 86% of the 65 central banks included in the poll are actively engaged in the development of a digital currency. Based on a poll done by the Bank for International Settlements, it is anticipated that central banks represents around 20% of the world's population will introduce their own digital currency within the next three years. While 60% of the banks were in the process of testing at the proof-of-concept

DOI: 10.4324/9781032699417-10

stage, 14% of them asserted that they were actively carrying out pilot programs. Cryptocurrency-backed digital currencies have already been approved in Nigeria, Jamaica and The Bahamas. The term "sand dollar", as it is commonly referred to in The Bahamas, is already being utilized. Furthermore, nearly 100 nations are currently in the preliminary stage of exploration. Taking the lead are central bankers from Brazil, China, the Eurozone, India and the UK.

When it started pilots in 2014 to establish a digital currency called the digital yuan – also known as e-yuan, e-CNY, digital renminbi or digital RMB – China was the first big economy to test a CBDC. Shenzhen, Suzhou, Xiongan and Chengdu were the first four cities in which the government introduced the currency. Afterward, 23 cities and 15 provinces made up the entire number of pilot locations, as announced by the People's Bank of China (PBOC). A report released in January 2022 by the PBOC said that 261 million individuals have created digital yuan wallets. When e-CNY was widely utilized in November 2022 during the Beijing Winter Olympics, it received a huge boost.

The CBDC is being implemented by the US Federal Reserve in a methodical manner. The digital or electronic version of the US dollar that is issued by the Federal Reserve will be known as the CBDC in the USA. The main distinction between cryptocurrencies, and this digital fiat money will be that a CBDC will function as legal cash and be supported, controlled and governed by the Federal Reserve. In a similar vein, the goal of the ECB is to introduce CBDC by 2025. On October 18, 2023, the ECB made a significant move toward the introduction of a digital euro that would enable secure, cost-free electronic transfers between residents of the 20 member nations that share the single currency. According to the ECB, a two-year "preparation phase" for the digital euro would begin on November 1st. During this time, regulations would be finalized, partners in the private sector would be selected and "testing and experimentation" would be conducted. Although the decision made on Wednesday is merely the first in a long-term effort, it puts the ECB ahead of other wealthy nations in the Group of Seven (G7) and could serve as a model for others to follow. In most ways, the digital euro will resemble any online wallet or bank account, with the exception that it will be safer because it will be guaranteed by the ECB and be available for free.

The Reserve Bank of India (RBI) introduced the CBDC in 2022. The digital iteration of India's official currency is referred to as the CBDC. The banks that participated in the RBI pilot effort were State Bank of India, ICICI Bank, Yes Bank, IDFC First Bank, Bank of Baroda, Union Bank of India, HDFC Bank, Kotak Mahindra Bank and HSBC. The RBI released two versions of CBDC known as CBDC-Wholesale (CBDC-W) and CBDC-Retail (CBDC-R). CBDC-R is accessible to a broader spectrum of users, encompassing private sector entities, non-financial clients and firms of varying scales. In contrast, CBDC-W is specifically created for limited access and is primarily intended for select financial institutions.

The RBI, the central bank's digital currency, is actively collaborating with financial institutions to introduce innovative functionalities aimed at enhancing the appeal of the e-rupee. These activities are part of a comprehensive strategy aimed at promoting the adoption and integration of digital money inside the Indian banking industry.

The retail e-rupee is available in many values, including 50 paise, 1, 2, 5, 10, 20, 50, 100, 200, 500 and 200. Conversely, the annual report of the central bank for the fiscal year 2022–2023 specifies that the wholesale e-Rupee does not own any designated denominations. These many denominations respond to the diverse financial demands and preferences of users in the digital currency ecosystem.

In simple terms, CBDCs are the digital form of cash, representing the physical money issued by central banks. The primary contrast between their design and that of existing online payment platforms in most parts of the world is that funds held on a CBDC application or website would operate in a manner akin to bank deposits.

The central banks are primarily motivated by the objective of mitigating the risks connected with the worldwide shift toward cashless payment systems. Their responsibility is to uphold the integrity of the financial system, beginning with verifying the permissibility of cash transactions. In a scenario where Apple Pay and Alipay dominate, everyday transactions would rely on private enterprises rather than central banks. Bitcoin and other cryptocurrencies, along with "stablecoins" such as Diem (formerly known as Libra) supported by Facebook, which peg its worth to the US dollar or other assets, present a risk and might potentially undermine governmental authority over time. The increased adoption of CBDCs will lead to a greater presence of central banks in online payment systems. Consequently, relying solely on private payment networks would decrease the danger to financial stability.

Introduction to CBDC

CBDC stands for Central Bank Digital Currency, which is a new form of money that is issued and regulated by a central bank. The fiat money of a central bank is represented digitally by CBDC. It is a digital payment method issued by a central bank that has the same legal tender status as actual cash and is valued in the nation's official currency. To provide a more safe, practical and effective method of making payments, CBDCs are intended to supplement, if not completely replace, hard currency. CBDC seeks to preserve the central bank's authority over the money supply while offering a safe, effective and universal method of payment (Tourpe, Lannquist & Soderberg, 2023).

In contrast to cryptocurrencies like Bitcoin and Ethereum, a digital currency supported by the government is usually centralized and known as CBDC. Depending on the policy objectives and use cases of each nation, CBDCs can have a variety of design options and technological features. The idea of a CBDC has drawn a lot of interest lately as central banks look for methods to update their monetary systems and adjust to the rapidly evolving world of digital finance.

The main goal of CBDC is to give users in the digital economy a digital currency substitute that makes transactions quicker and more effective. The central bank issues and regulates CBDC, which is intended to be a digital equivalent of a nation's official currency (such as the dollar, euro or yuan).

CBDCs differ from current fiat currencies in several key ways. First, CBDCs can be stored digitally in electronic wallets rather than in traditional bank accounts. Second, CBDCs can be recorded on synchronized record-keeping platforms such as DLTs, rather than separate and isolated bank sub-ledgers. Lastly, CBDCs can be programmed and executed automatically through the use of smart contracts, eliminating the need for manual paper-based processes.

The use, storing and transfer of money could all be revolutionized by CBDCs, which also provide advantages including greater efficiency, security and privacy. But putting them into practice will mean carefully weighing the difficulties and ramifications for privacy, monetary policy and the financial system.

Some of the important features of CBDC are:

Type of CBDC: CBDCs can be either wholesale or retail. Wholesale CBDCs are used for interbank transactions and settlement, while retail CBDCs are used for general public transactions and payments. Some countries may choose to issue both types of CBDCs or only one of them.

Issuance of CBDC: CBDC can be issued and managed by the central banks directly or through intermediaries such as commercial banks or payment service providers. The direct model gives the central bank full control and responsibility over the CBDC system, while the indirect model relies on existing financial infrastructure and intermediaries. A hybrid model can combine elements of both models.

Form of CBDC: CBDCs can be either token-based or account-based. Token-based CBDCs are similar to cash, as they do not require the identification of the sender or receiver and can be transferred offline. Account-based CBDCs are similar to bank deposits, as they require the verification of the identity and account balance of the parties involved and can only be transferred online.

Design of CBDC: CBDCs can be either remunerated or non-remunerated. Remunerated CBDCs pay interest to the holders, while non-remunerated CBDCs do not. Remunerated CBDCs can be used as a monetary policy tool to influence the demand and supply of money, while non-remunerated CBDCs can be used as a simple medium of exchange.

Privacy Controls: CBDCs can have different levels of privacy and transparency, depending on the trade-offs between user protection and regulatory compliance. CBDCs can use various cryptographic techniques, such as zero-knowledge proofs, to ensure the confidentiality and integrity of transactions, while allowing selective disclosure of information to authorized parties, such as law enforcement or tax authorities.

These are some of the main technical aspects of CBDC construction. However, there are many other factors and challenges that need to be considered, such as scalability, security, interoperability, usability and legal implications. CBDCs are still an evolving and experimental technology, and different countries may adopt different approaches and solutions to suit their specific needs and circumstances.

Types of CBDC

There are various types of CBDC. The CBDC could be token based or account based, wholesale CBDC or retail CBDC.

Token-Based CBDC

Token-based CBDC is a digital currency that is controlled and issued by a central bank and functions as a claim on the issuing bank. It is intended to function on a blockchain network, facilitating the safe and effective exchange of value between people and companies. The basis for this is a token system. Within this framework, every token is backed by the central bank and signifies a specific value of the CBDC (Soderberg, Kiff, Tourpe, Bechara, Forte, Kao & Yoshinaga, 2023).

Token-based CBDCs can be transmitted offline and do not require sender or recipient identity, making them comparable to cash. Although a token-based CBDC can provide a high level of anonymity, it also presents difficulties in terms of confirming the token's legitimacy and avoiding fraud or double spending. Token-based CBDCs are distinct from account-based CBDCs, which are kept at the central bank in separate accounts.

A token-based CBDC has a number of benefits. The ability to enable programmable money, which offers more control and flexibility over the currency's use, is one of the key advantages of token-based CBDCs. For instance, a central bank might designate a CBDC to be used exclusively for paying small companies or covering educational costs.

Anyone with the token, which could be a password or a public-private key pair, could access and utilize it. This can lessen reliance on middlemen and boost financial inclusion. It does not require a network connection or a central authority to be transferred peer-to-peer. This can lower transaction costs while improving the payment system's robustness and efficiency. Because users do not have to divulge their identity or personal information to transact, it can offer a high degree of privacy and confidentiality for them. Additionally, it can shield users against fraud, censorship and identity theft. It may be programmable, which allows for the incorporation of criteria or rules to control how it is used or transferred. This may make it possible for creative applications, autonomous execution and smart contracts (McKinsey, 2023).

Because token-based CBDCs record transactions on a public blockchain that is impenetrable and immune to fraud, they also provide improved privacy and security features. Financial crimes like money laundering and financing of terrorism can be avoided in part by doing this. Nevertheless, there are dangers and difficulties associated with implementing token-based CBDCs. For instance, there could need to be a substantial overhaul of the current financial system and rules, and there might be issues with the centralization of currency control.

Token-based CBDC is not without its difficulties. The token's integrity and authenticity can be hard to verify because it can be stolen, copied or changed. This may result in money loss, double spending or counterfeiting. Because the transactions and users are decentralized and anonymous, it might be challenging to track and keep an eye on them. This may cause issues with tax compliance, law enforcement, anti-money laundering and the fight against terrorism financing. Designing and implementing a token-based CBDC can be challenging since it calls for sophisticated cryptographic methods to balance the trade-offs between privacy and openness, like zero-knowledge proofs. Compatibility and interoperability with current payment systems and standards are also necessary.

The digital currency issued by the Bank of Canada in 2020 that is denominated in Canadian dollars is an illustration of a token-based CBDC. The digital currency of the Bank of Canada is based on a token system, in which a specific value in Canadian dollars is represented by each token. The tokens can be used for peer-to-peer transactions and for the purchase of products and services. They are kept in a digital wallet.

The digital yuan, which is being created by the PBOC, is another instance of a token-based CBDC. A token system underpins the digital yuan as well; each token is equivalent to a specific amount of Chinese cash. The tokens can be used for peer-to-peer transactions and for the purchase of products and services. They are kept in a digital wallet (Kshetri, 2023).

All things considered, a token-based CBDC gives increased efficiency and security in financial transactions by combining the advantages of digital and traditional fiat currencies. The field of developing token-based CBDCs is fast developing, and it is unclear how they will be embraced and put to use in the future.

Account-Based CBDC

Token-based CBDC and account-based CBDC are different. CBDC units in an account-based system are associated with particular person accounts. Usually, these accounts are kept through commercial banks or directly with the central bank. Like regular bank accounts, people need to have a verified identity to access CBDC. The identification of the account holder determines whether a transaction is permitted. The central bank debits the sender's and the beneficiary's CBDC accounts when transferring money. Since not everyone has a bank account, account-based CBDC may be inaccessible to some people. It also requires a banking relationship. Strong security protocols are essential for preventing fraud and illegal transactions (Armelius, Claussen & Hull, 2021).

DCash is one instance of an account-based CBDC that is being used in the Eastern Caribbean. The Eastern Caribbean Central Bank (ECCB) has created a new digital currency called DCash. Through the provision of a quicker, safer and more affordable method for sending and receiving Eastern Caribbean (EC) money, it seeks to completely transform financial transactions inside the Eastern Caribbean Currency Union (ECCU). DCash is intended to function as an electronic equivalent of the EC. It is distributed through ECCU-licensed banks and non-bank financial institutions and is issued by the ECCB. The objective is to enable different kinds of transactions, such as cross-border payments, people-to-people and consumer-to-merchant transactions. DCash is user-friendly because it runs on smart devices (McKinsey, 2023).

With DCash, transactions may be completed instantly and concurrently, greatly cutting down on wait times. Since DCash is digital money, handling actual cash carries fewer hazards. Because DCash transactions are free, businesses may be able to save money. Digital EC money can be sent and received both domestically and internationally by users. The DCash Wallet allows users to handle cash-in and cash-out, send and receive digital EC money and make both domestic and international purchases. Companies can submit live invoices for instant payments, accept payments in digital EC currency and take advantage of instant settlement.

Wholesale CBDC and Retail CBDC

Wholesale CBDC is a digital form of a country's fiat currency. The wholesale CBDC is designed for use by financial institutions and other large-scale financial intermediaries. It is meant to offer a more effective and safer substitute for the current system of settling payments and transactions between banks. It is generally used for interbank transactions and settlements (Athanassiou, 2021).

The high liquidity and potential to be used as collateral for other financial transactions are two important aspects of wholesale CBDC. Because of this, it's a helpful tool for controlling financial risks and promoting the smooth operation of the financial markets.

A nation's digital version of fiat money, known as retail CBDC, is intended for usage by private citizens and small enterprises. It is meant to offer a more accessible and convenient substitute for cash and is generally used for routine activities like paying for products and services (Morales-Resendiz, Ponce, Picardo, Velasco, Chen & Hodge, 2021).

The ease with which retail CBDC can be transported and kept on digital devices like cell phones is one of its main advantages. Because of this, it can be an effective instrument for advancing financial inclusion, especially in nations with limited access to traditional banking services.

All things considered, there are several potential advantages to both wholesale and retail CBDCs, such as improved accessibility, security and efficiency within the financial system. But they also bring up a lot of issues and concerns, like how to protect privacy, stop fraud and handle any possible effects on the established banking system.

The Development of CBDC

As CBDC projects progress worldwide, patterns have started to emerge. One is the tendency for wholesale CBDCs to be token-based, whereas the foundational layer of retail CBDCs is often account-based. There's a need for a bridge between the two to avoid operating two entirely separate CBDC systems.

The distinction between token-based and account-based systems is often made, but it can be problematic. Many digital currencies, including Bitcoin, exhibit features of both. Account-based CBDCs offer familiarity (similar to traditional banking) but must address challenges related to access and security. In the case of token-based CBDC, the validity of the payment object matters (e.g., a valid bill). Account-based CBDC requires identity verification (e.g., bank deposits). Some CBDCs may combine elements of both, allowing flexibility and security. In summary, As CBDCs evolve, we'll likely see innovative solutions that blend the best of both worlds (McKinsey, 2023).

Average users do not care about differentiating between an account or token-based CBDCs, as they focus on the CBDC's utility rather than the backend. However, two features related to token-based platforms make them undesirable for retail CBDCs. The first limitation is associated with offline functionalities. If a token-based CBDC uses a distributed ledger to prevent double spending, offline functionality is usually a significant challenge. However, token-based CBDCs don't have to use distributed ledger technology (DLT) and account-based can use a DLT. Many jurisdictions, including the EU require offline functionality, which tilts the scales toward an account-based retail CBDC offering. The second barrier concerns scalability, as any DLT would need to be highly scalable to log every single retail CBDC transaction. This is currently not the case, so an account-based CBDC is preferable for the retail option (at least at the base level).

Conversely, the approach for a wholesale CBDC is different because most banks already have accounts at the central bank. Instead, wholesale CBDCs will likely involve blockchains and tokens to allow for the adoption of DLTs in financial market infrastructures. This would enable more manageable on-chain payments to power things such as tokenized securities settlements, which is what countries like France and Switzerland have been testing, and the ECB is about to unveil a formal pilot.

But central banks don't have to provide a wholesale CBDC for DLT securities settlement. On-chain settlement could be done using tokenized commercial bank money, privately issued synthetic CBDCs or trigger payments from real-time gross settlement systems.

Working Model of CBDC

The working model of CBDC is given in Figure 10.1.

Central banks issue and oversee CBDCs, which are digital renditions of a nation's fiat currency. They can be used for peer-to-peer transactions without the use of middlemen like banks and run on DLTs like blockchain (Tsai, Zhao, Zhang, Yu & Deng, 2018).

A central bank oversees the issuance and management of CBDCs and is in charge of the supply, circulation and general integrity of the virtual currency. As with traditional

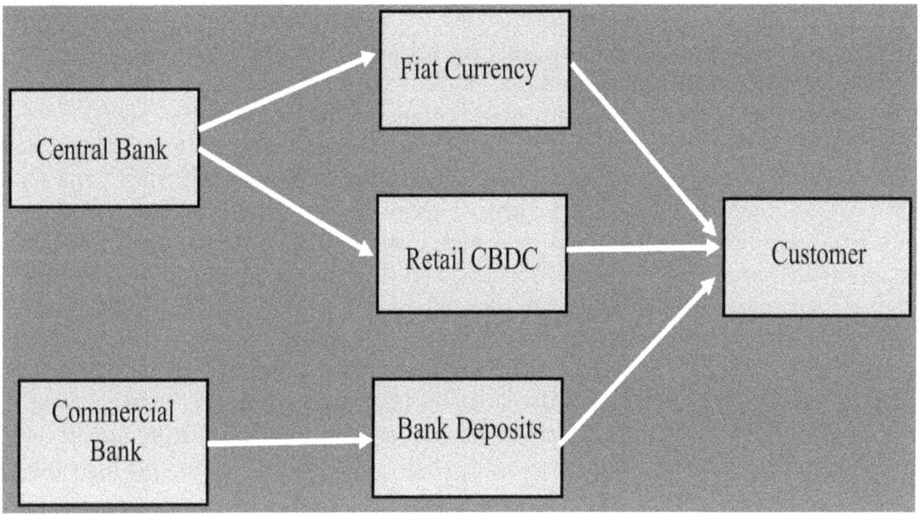

Figure 10.1 Working Model of CBDC

fiat currencies, the central bank establishes the monetary policy, sets the interest rate and regulates the money supply.

There are several ways to distribute CBDCs, such as via a digital wallet that the central bank, commercial banks or other suppliers offer. All citizens, residents and businesses are normally able to access CBDCs, and the central bank makes sure that everyone has equitable access to the digital currency.

Peer-to-peer transactions using CBDCs are quick and safe, negating the need for middlemen. A distributed ledger, like a blockchain, is used to record transactions, giving rise to an unchangeable and transparent record of all transactions. Real-time settlement makes it possible for parties to transfer money right away.

In contrast to conventional banking systems, CBDCs can provide a greater degree of privacy because transactions are recorded on a distributed ledger rather than in a centralized database. However, the CBDC's architecture and the central bank's regulations determine how anonymous a certain area is. While some CBDCs allow completely anonymous transactions, others may require users to submit personal information for transactions over a predetermined threshold.

Strong encryption and authentication procedures are built into CBDCs' architecture to safeguard user information and transactions. Using a DLT, like blockchain, makes the ledger resistant to tampering and attacks, making it a safe and dependable platform for transactions.

To facilitate smooth cross-border transactions and advance financial inclusion, CBDCs can be made to function internationally. CBDCs can be utilized across several nations and systems by achieving interoperability through the adoption of common standards and protocols, such as the ISO 20022 standard for payment messaging.

A general-purpose CBDC can be supported by one of two main architectural options: direct or two-tier. Individual CBDC customers and the central bank (or a central services provider operating on the central bank's behalf) can conduct transactions directly through a direct architecture.

Users of CBDCs are required to conduct transactions through payment service providers (PSP), such as commercial banks, due to the two-tier architecture. This frees up the private sector to concentrate on innovation and customer service while central banks concentrate on their core skills. Thus, we advise using the two-tiered strategy.

CBDC uses DLT to build a digital currency system that is safe, open and effective. The objectives, legal framework and technological considerations of the central bank putting the CBDC into practice determine the precise characteristics and configurations. The old monetary system has transformative potential thanks to the integration of DLT, which opens up new avenues for efficiency, security and financial inclusion.

To issue, maintain and enable transactions using digital currency, CBDC uses DLT, which makes use of blockchain or other decentralized ledger technologies. A distributed ledger is used by central banks to issue and track CBDC units. Using a permissioned blockchain or similar type of DLT, the ledger is kept up-to-date in a decentralized fashion. By automating the issuing process, smart contracts – self-executing contracts containing programmed terms – can guarantee that CBDC is produced and distributed in accordance with predetermined guidelines (Guo, Kreitem & Moser, 2022).

Real-time or almost real-time transaction settlement is possible with DLT. The distributed ledger lowers counterparty risks by facilitating prompt and secure settlement of CBDC transactions conducted by individuals or businesses. Consensus procedures are used by DLT to verify and approve the ledger's current state. This guarantees that every member of the network sees the CBDC transactions in the same, agreed-upon way. In the implementation of CBDC, consensus techniques such as proof-of-work (PoW) and proof-of-stake (PoS) are frequently chosen over proof-of-work mechanisms due to their energy-intensive nature and ability to preserve control and regulatory supervision.

User-friendly tools, including mobile apps or digital wallets, are often included in DLT-based CBDC systems to facilitate easy interaction between businesses and individuals with digital currency. By utilizing the advantages of DLT, central banks may keep control over the issuance and regulation of CBDC. The level of centralization is a design decision that strikes a balance between the benefits of decentralization and control. Implementations of CBDCs on DLT sometimes involve regulatory nodes or other organizations with the power to monitor and enforce adherence to financial regulations. This guarantees that the system complies with all applicable laws and regulations.

Scalability issues must be addressed in DLT implementations due to the possible volume of transactions in a national CBDC system. Sharding, layer 2 scaling solutions and other methods are possible options.

Cross-Border CBDC

Central banks issue and oversee CBDCs, which are digital renditions of a nation's fiat currency. They can be used for peer-to-peer transactions without the use of middlemen like banks and run on DLTs like blockchain (Themistocleous, Rupino da Cunha, Tabakis & Papadaki, 2023).

A central bank oversees the issuance and management of CBDCs and is in charge of the supply, circulation and general integrity of the virtual currency. As with traditional fiat currencies, the central bank establishes the monetary policy, sets the interest rate and regulates the money supply.

There are several ways to distribute CBDCs, such as via a digital wallet that the central bank, commercial banks or other suppliers offer. All citizens, residents and businesses are normally able to access CBDCs, and the central bank makes sure that everyone has equitable access to the digital currency.

Peer-to-peer transactions using CBDCs are quick and safe, negating the need for middlemen. A distributed ledger, like a blockchain, is used to record transactions, giving rise to an unchangeable and transparent record of all transactions. Real-time settlement makes it possible for parties to transfer money right away.

In contrast to conventional banking systems, CBDCs can provide a greater degree of privacy because transactions are recorded on a distributed ledger rather than in a centralized database. However, the CBDC's architecture and the central bank's regulations determine how anonymous a certain area is. While some CBDCs allow completely anonymous transactions, others may require users to submit personal information for transactions over a predetermined threshold.

Strong encryption and authentication procedures are built into CBDCs' architecture to safeguard user information and transactions. Using a DLT, like blockchain, makes the ledger resistant to tampering and attacks, making it a safe and dependable platform for transactions.

To facilitate smooth cross-border transactions and advance financial inclusion, CBDCs can be made to function internationally. CBDCs can be utilized across several nations and systems by achieving interoperability through the adoption of common standards and protocols, such as the ISO 20022 standard for payment messaging.

A general-purpose CBDC can be supported by one of two main architectural options: direct or two-tier. Individual CBDC customers and the central bank (or a central services provider operating on the central bank's behalf) can conduct transactions directly through a direct architecture.

Users of CBDCs are required to conduct transactions through PSP, such as commercial banks, due to the two-tier architecture. This frees up the private sector to concentrate on innovation and customer service while central banks concentrate on their core skills. Thus, we advise using the two-tiered strategy.

CBDC uses DLT to build a digital currency system that is safe, open and effective. The objectives, legal framework and technological considerations of the central bank putting the CBDC into practice determine the precise characteristics and configurations. The old monetary system has transformative potential thanks to the integration of DLT, which opens up new avenues for efficiency, security and financial inclusion.

To issue, maintain and enable transactions using digital currency, CBDC uses DLT, which makes use of blockchain or other decentralized ledger technologies. A distributed ledger is used by central banks to issue and track CBDC units. Using a permissioned blockchain or similar type of DLT, the ledger is kept up-to-date in a decentralized fashion. By automating the issuing process, smart contracts – self-executing contracts containing programmed terms – can guarantee that CBDC is produced and distributed in accordance with predetermined guidelines (He, Kokenyne, Griffoli, Miccoli, Olafsson, Soderberg & Tourpe, 2023).

Real-time or almost real-time transaction settlement is possible with DLT. The distributed ledger lowers counterparty risks by facilitating prompt and secure settlement of CBDC transactions conducted by individuals or businesses. Consensus procedures are used by DLT to verify and approve the ledger's current state. This guarantees that every member of the network sees the CBDC transactions in the same, agreed-upon way. In the implementation of consensus-based digital currency, consensus techniques such as PoW and PoS are frequently chosen over proof-of-work mechanisms due to their energy-intensive nature and ability to preserve control and regulatory supervision.

Table 10.1 Cross-Border CBDC Transaction

Sl No	*Project Name*	*Starting Year*	*Collaborating Countries*
1	mBridge	September 2021	Thailand, China, Hong Kong, UAE and BIS
2	Dunbar	March 2022	Australia, Singapore, Malaysia
3	Sela	June 2022	Israel, Hong Kong, BIS
4	Icebreaker	September 2022	Israel, Norway, Sweden, BIS
5	Mariana	November 2022	France, Switzerland, Singapore, BIS
6	Jura	June 2021	France and Switzerland
7	Onyx/Multiple wCBDC	July 2021	France and Singapore
8	Rosalind	June 2022	United Kingdom and BIS
9	Aurum	March 2021	Hong Kong and BIS
10	Helvetia	2020	Switzerland and BIS
11	Jasper	2017	Canada, United Kingdom and Singapore
12	Aber	2019	Saudi Arabia and UAE
13	Polaris	February 2023	Nordic Countries
14	Nexus	July 2021	Eurosystem, Malaysia, Singapore, Indonesia, Philippines, Thailand
15	Tourbillion	November 2022	BIS Swiss Centre
16	Cedar/Ubin	November 2021	USA and Singapore

Source: Bank of International Settlement (BIS).

Governments all throughout the world are pushing Fintech businesses with digital technology by introducing CBDC. The usage of CBDCs for cross-border transactions is known as "cross-border CBDC". This is the process of making overseas payments and transactions using digital renditions of national currencies, like the US dollar or the euro.

Currently, there are currently 12 cross-border wholesale CBDC projects. These projects are "Project mBridge, Dunbar, Sela, Icebreaker, Mariana, Jura, Onyx/Multiple wCBDC, Rosalind, Aurum, Helvetia, Jasper, Aber, Polaris, Nexus, Tourbillion and Cedar/Ubin" (BIS, 2023).

The details of the collaborations are given in Table 10.1.

Project mBridge

Four monetary authorities are working together on a multilateral collaboration called collaboration mBridge to provide the infrastructure needed to link CBDC. The Bank of Thailand, the PBOC, the Central Bank of the United Arab Emirates, Hong Kong's Monetary Authority (HKMA) and the Bank of International Settlements (BIS) are working together on the project. It seeks to use CBDCs to expedite and reduce the cost of international transactions. Project mBridge could provide a new payment architecture that is more adaptable in facilitating cross-border money movements to satisfy the four monetary authorities' complex and constantly changing connectivity requirements.

Central banks can impose quotas quickly in closed-loop systems or cross-border applications by having real-time transparency over how applicable quotas are being used thanks to a mBridge architecture. This lessens the amount of administrative labor and possible mistakes in the reporting that stakeholders submit.

The mBridge architecture enables the deployment of smart contracts that can be programmed to establish risk-adjusted and customized quotas. These contracts also have the ability to define a permissible product range at the client or wallet level, taking into account the suitability and profile of clients, such as retail, affluent and professional clients. Even if each investor possessed many wallets, regulatory bodies and central banks would have enhanced transparency and supervision tools to ensure enforcement.

Project Dunbar

The Reserve Bank of Australia, Central Bank of Malaysia, Monetary Authority of Singapore and Reserve Bank of South Africa are working together with the BIS Innovation Hub to take the lead in Project Dunbar. Project Dunbar aims to enhance the affordability, speed and security of cross-border payments by implementing a unified platform for several Central Bank Digital Currencies, known as multi-CBDCs. The report acknowledged the challenges of implementing a multi-CBDC platform that is jointly used by central banks and provided practical design solutions to address these challenges. The successful creation of technical prototypes on Corda and Partior validated these design methodologies and showcased the technical feasibility of the multi-CBDC concept.

The multi-CBDC shared platform developed by Project Dunbar has the capacity to substitute outdated payment systems and establish the foundation for a more efficient global settlement platform. The program aims to enhance public-private collaboration and streamline cross-border payments by combining the benefits of DLT with the efficiency of a common platform.

Project Sela

Project Sela, a collaborative experiment conducted by the BIS, the central banks of Israel and Hong Kong Special Administrative Region, has demonstrated the feasibility of a retail Central Bank Digital Currency (rCBDC) ecosystem. This ecosystem combines accessibility, competition and preventive cyber security, while preserving the key advantages of physical cash.

The HKMA has gained insights from Projects Aurum and e-Hong Kong dollar. The current project, led by the BIS Innovation Hub Hong Kong Center, incorporates the Bank of Israel's expertise in cyber security and their ongoing efforts on the digital shekel. It also incorporates other experiments conducted by the Innovation Hub on rCBDCs.

Sela's main policy objective was to establish a diverse and inclusive environment for rCBDC that fosters creativity, competition and easy accessibility for a wide range of use cases. Consequently, it aimed to decrease the barriers for service providers to enter and distribute the responsibilities related to rCBDC accounts among both public and private entities.

Achieving a digital payment method that maintains the benefits of cash, such as its lack of credit risk, accessibility, safety and value storage, as well as its ability to settle transactions instantly, operate at a low cost and protect end users' privacy, was another crucial objective. Because personal identifiers are obscured, the central bank of Sela is able to run the rCBDC ledger without jeopardizing end-user privacy. As a result, retail payments are immediately finalized and settled in a privacy-preserving way on the central bank's balance sheet.

Project Sela investigated the viability of a CBDC system in which the retail ledger is run by the central bank and access to the CBDC is expanded through a novel kind of intermediary known as an Access Enabler, which fosters competition and innovation. It demonstrated that this could be accomplished without jeopardizing end users' privacy or cyber security from the central bank.

Project Icebreaker

The BIS and the central banks of Sweden, Norway and Israel launched Project Icebreaker to investigate the possible advantages and difficulties of utilizing retail CBDC in cross-border transactions. Through the research, various experimental retail CBDC systems' ability to execute cross-border and cross-currency transactions was assessed for technological viability.

The goal of Project Icebreaker was to investigate a particular method of connecting home systems – referred to as a "hub-and-spoke solution". A foreign currency supplier that is engaged in both domestic systems breaks down a cross-border transaction into two domestic payments. Retail CBDCs never have to leave their own systems as a result.

Because it lacks control over the identity of the foreign exchange conversion provider, the payer in the majority of current cross-border payment systems is unable to choose the exchange rate. Several foreign exchange providers can submit bids to the system's hub in the model created by the Icebreaker project, and the hub will automatically choose the less expensive quote for the end customer.

The possibility of inadequate liquidity in the targeted currency pair, which can increase costs and possibly cause the transaction to be delayed, was reduced by this competitive setup. To encourage competition among foreign exchange providers, the Icebreaker system uses bridge currencies in the event that transactions between two particular end currencies are either unfavorable or unavailable.

The study also showed how the hub-and-spoke approach can execute cross-border transactions in a matter of seconds and lower counterparty and settlement risk by utilizing coordinated payments in central bank currency. The project offers a model for expanding CBDCs and innovative services into cross-border transactions for nations thinking about developing their own.

The results of Project Icebreaker gave central banks thinking about implementing retail CBDCs a better grasp of the technologies that are available and the technical and policy options that they can choose from. To connect domestic systems operating on various technologies – as was the case with the proofs-of-concept utilized by the three central banks – the project necessitates very minimal technical requirements. This promotes scalability, interoperability and simplicity.

Project Mariana

Project Mariana encompassed the participation of the central banks of France, Singapore, Switzerland and the BIS. The project investigated the application of innovative decentralized finance (DeFi) technologies on a public blockchain to facilitate cross-border trade and settlement of wholesale Central Bank Digital Currencies (wCBDCs) among financial institutions.

Project Mariana was developed through collaboration between three BIS Innovation Hub centers – the Swiss, Singapore and Eurosystem Hub Centers – and the Bank of France, the Monetary Authority of Singapore and the Swiss National Bank. The proof-of-concept for the project successfully tested the trading and settlement of simulated Swiss franc, Singapore dollar and euro wCBDCs between financial institutions across borders. The process was dependent on three components:

i. A common technical token standard provided by a public blockchain to facilitate exchange and interoperability between the different currencies.

ii. Bridges for the seamless transfer of wCBDCs between different networks.
iii. An Automated Market Maker (AMM), which is a specific type of decentralized exchange to trade and settle spot FX transactions automatically.

Project Mariana's AMM utilized sophisticated algorithms to merge the liquidity of theoretical euro, Singapore dollar and Swiss franc wCBDCs. This enabled the AMM to automatically determine prices and execute spot FX transactions with instant settlement. These protocols could be used by future financial market infrastructures to facilitate cross-border trading and settlement between financial institutions.

The architecture of Project Mariana seeks to achieve a harmonious equilibrium between the need for central banks to oversee and maintain independence within their own countries, and the demand of financial institutions to effectively hold, transfer and settle wCBDC on an international scale. This is achieved by using a standardized token on a public blockchain to ensure that wCBDC can be easily transferred and used across various local payment and settlement systems administered by participating central banks. Mariana offers some approaches for integrating an international element into ongoing wCBDC design inquiries.

Project Mariana introduced innovative technology for interbank foreign currency markets. The successful demonstration showed the possibility of exchanging wholesale CBDC across borders by utilizing innovative concepts like automated market makers. Success was achieved by assembling a varied team of software engineers, policy experts and FX specialists from three Innovation Hub centers and central banks.

Project Jura

The Project Jura examined the direct transmission of euro and Swiss franc wCBDCs between commercial banks in France and Switzerland on a unified DLT network overseen by a third party. Payment versus payment and delivery versus payment methods ensure secure and efficient resolution of asset and foreign exchange exchanges.

The experiment is conducted in a simulated setting that closely resembles reality, using genuine financial transactions and following established regulatory norms. The alliance comprises the Banque de France, the BIS Innovation Hub Swiss Centre, the Swiss National Bank and a consortium from the business sector.

Enabling the use of wCBDC on a third-party platform and granting non-resident financial institutions direct access to central bank money presents intricate legislative obstacles. Jura is conducting an inquiry into a new technique that involves using subnetworks and dual-notary signing. This method has the potential to provide reassurance to central banks, allowing them to distribute wCBDC on a third-party platform and offer non-resident financial firms access to wCBDC.

The project improves the existing G20 initiatives on international payments across borders. The proposed solution design not only addresses existing deficiencies but also has the capacity to bring novel approaches for conducting global financial transactions, including foreign exchange, securities and other financial instruments.

Project Jasper

Project Jasper is a joint research effort including both public and private sectors to explore the potential impact of DLT on the future of payments in Canada. The initiative was established in March 2016 by the central banks of Canada, the United Kingdom and Singapore. The project sought to investigate the feasibility of utilizing DLT for processing high-value interbank payments and to analyze the potential impact of DLT on the wholesale payments system.

Project Jasper is a noteworthy achievement in the payments industry since it was the first instance globally when a central bank collaborated with the private sector on a DLT project. The project consists of four phases, each dedicated to exploring various areas of the possible benefits of DLT.

The initial stage focused on exploring the application of DLT for processing high-value interbank payments. In the second phase, the platform was reconstructed using a different type of DLT to assess its effectiveness in processing high-value interbank payments for clearing and settlement. The third phase investigated the advantages of combining "cash on ledger" with other assets including foreign exchange and securities. The fourth step involves developing a cross-border, cross-currency settlement mechanism in collaboration with the Monetary Authority of Singapore and the Bank of England for the next stage of the experiment.

Project Nexus

Over 60 countries have implemented rapid payment systems, enabling individuals to transfer money to one another in a matter of seconds. Nevertheless, transferring money internationally frequently remains a time-consuming and costly process. Linking these national payment systems globally could enhance the efficiency, affordability and clarity of international payments.

Nexus is aimed to standardize the interconnection of these systems. Instead of creating individual connections for each new country, a payment system operator can establish a single connection to the Nexus platform. This singular link enables a rapid payment mechanism to access all other countries inside the network. The Nexus has the potential to greatly speed up the expansion of immediate cross-border payments.

In 2022, the team built a working prototype of Nexus and used it to connect the test systems of three established IPSs:

- The Eurozone's TARGET Instant Payment Settlement system, operated by Bank of Italy on behalf of the Eurosystem and overseen by the ECB
- Malaysia's Real-time Retail Payments Platform, operated by Payments Network Malaysia (PayNet) and overseen by Central Bank of Malaysia
- Singapore's Fast and Secure Transfers (FAST) payment system, operated by Banking Computer Services and overseen by the Monetary Authority of Singapore

In the next phase of work, the BISIH Singapore Centre is collaborating with the central banks of Indonesia, Malaysia, the Philippines, Singapore and Thailand as they work toward connecting their domestic payment systems.

Advantages and Challenges of Cross-Border CBDCs

Cross-border CBDCs have the ability to decrease the expenses and duration linked to conventional cross-border payment mechanisms like wire transfers and SWIFT transactions. Utilizing a centrally recognized and regulated digital currency can enhance the security and efficiency of cross-border transactions (Berry, Lund, Manyika, Singer & White, 2016).

Cross-border CBDCs have the potential to decrease dependence on the conventional banking system for global transactions. This can be especially advantageous for individuals and enterprises in countries with restricted access to conventional financial services.

Nevertheless, there are obstacles linked to the execution of cross-border CBDCs. One major obstacle is the requirement for coordination and cooperation among central banks, together with the necessity to guarantee widespread acceptance and usage of digital currency. Furthermore, there are worries regarding the potential consequences of cross-border CBDCs on financial stability and the capacity of central banks to regulate monetary policy.

CBDCs could alleviate existing challenges in international payments, especially if central banks incorporate an international perspective into the design of CBDCs from the beginning. Considering the preliminary stage, this research explores and analyzes the cross-border impacts of CBDCs in a scenario where they are extensively utilized. Domestic issuance of CBDC will undergo thorough economic and practical analysis before considering cross-border implementation (Das, Griffoli, Nakamura, Otten, Soderberg, Sole & Tan, 2023).

Cross-border CBDCs have the potential to transform international payments and transactions, but additional study and development are required to comprehensively grasp the advantages and obstacles linked to this technology.

Why Do Central Banks Need CBDC

A CBDC is a digital representation of a country's official currency, such as the dollar, euro, yuan or rupee, that is created and regulated by the central bank. The primary goal of CBDC is to provide a digital alternative to physical currency, facilitating faster and more efficient transactions within the digital economy (Soderberg, Kiff, Tourpe, Bechara, Forte, Kao & Yoshinaga, 2023)

The rise and progression of cryptocurrencies and blockchain technology have ignited heightened interest in civilizations that operate without physical currency and rely on digital forms of money. CBDCs have the capacity to improve financial inclusion and optimize the implementation of monetary and fiscal policy. Multiple countries are currently examining the potential ramifications of CBDCs on their economy, financial systems and stability.

CBDCs strive to provide companies and customers with the benefits of privacy, transferability, ease of use, accessibility and financial security. CBDCs can reduce the costs of managing a complex financial system, decrease cross-border transaction fees and provide more economical options for individuals compared to conventional money transfer methods. CBDCs would alleviate the risks associated with the use of digital currencies, such as cryptocurrencies, in their current form (Lannquist & Tan, 2023).

Why are central bankers so captivated by CBDC? They are concerned about the possible decrease in their control over monetary policy because of the growing popularity of digital currencies among young individuals. The emergence of cryptocurrencies has raised concerns over the stability of both monetary and financial systems. Cryptocurrencies have the potential to enable money laundering and bypass capital restrictions, essentially operating as a digital hawala channel. Market volatility can be intensified by financial hardship.

There are several potential benefits to CBDCs, including:

Increased financial inclusion: CBDCs have the potential to provide digital payment services to individuals who currently do not have access to traditional banking services or have limited access. CBDCs have the capacity to improve financial inclusion through several methods. CBDCs can be obtained using digital wallets or mobile devices, increasing accessibility for individuals who do not have traditional bank accounts. This can be particularly beneficial for individuals living in remote or secluded regions who may not have access to physical bank branches.

CBDCs have the potential to reduce transaction costs associated with traditional financial services, such as fees for fund transfers. This can be particularly beneficial for individuals with little financial resources who may be unable to afford these costs. CBDCs offer heightened security and safeguard against fraud and theft, beyond traditional cash or digital payment methods. This is particularly vital for individuals who may be vulnerable to financial fraud or theft. CBDCs provide greater privacy compared to traditional digital payment systems, which might be beneficial for individuals who are reluctant to share their financial information with financial institutions or government authorities.

Reduced Costs of Cash

CBDCs could offer digital payment services to individuals who are now without access to traditional banking services or have limited access. CBDCs have the potential to enhance financial inclusion through many means. CBDCs can be accessed via digital wallets or mobile devices, making them more accessible to persons without conventional bank accounts. This can be especially advantageous for persons residing in rural or isolated areas who may lack access to real bank branches.

CBDCs have the potential to decrease expenses associated with producing, moving and safeguarding paper currency. CBDCs have the ability to decrease the expenses associated with physical cash through many means. CBDCs offer a significant benefit by decreasing the reliance on physical currency, which incurs high expenses in terms of production, distribution and upkeep. CBDCs can lower expenses related to producing and transporting real currency by eliminating the necessity for cash.

CBDCs can lower the expenses linked to cash transactions for both businesses and people. Businesses that now use physical currency for transactions can benefit from reduced transaction expenses, such as counting and confirming cash and delivering cash to the bank. Individuals might also gain advantages from decreased transaction expenses, like the expenses associated with purchasing and selling currency, as well as the fees for using ATMs. CBDCs have the ability to decrease the expense of physical currency by eliminating its necessity, lowering cash handling expenses and cutting transaction costs for both enterprises and consumers.

Faster and Cheaper Payments

CBDCs have the potential to facilitate quicker and more cost-effective transactions, both within a country and beyond borders. CBDCs have the potential to transform payment methods. CBDCs facilitate transactions to be swiftly processed and finalized in real-time or near-real-time, resulting in expedited payments. CBDCs are digital and may be processed electronically, eliminating the necessity for intermediaries such as banks.

CBDCs might decrease transaction expenses by removing the requirement for middlemen, like banks, which usually impose charges for handling transactions. CBDCs can enhance payment accessibility by enabling individuals and businesses to conduct transactions without requiring a traditional bank account. This is crucial for individuals without access to conventional banking services, particularly unbanked populations.

CBDCs can lower expenses related to cash management, including transportation, security and processing of cash transactions. CBDCs can be held and exchanged electronically, eliminating the need for physical cash transit and lowering the danger of theft and loss.

CBDCs can lower the expenses linked to cash transactions for both businesses and people. Businesses that now use physical currency for transactions might save money by reducing transaction expenses, including counting and confirming cash and delivering cash to the bank. Individuals can also gain advantages from decreased transaction expenses, like the expenses associated with purchasing and selling currency, as well as the fees related to using ATMs. CBDCs have the potential to decrease the expense associated with physical cash by eliminating the need for it, lowering cash handling costs and cutting transaction costs for enterprises and people.

Improved Security

A primary benefit of a CBDC is enhancing security through the mitigation of fraud and counterfeiting risks. Every transaction with a CBDC is documented on a digital ledger managed by the central bank. Every transaction is traceable and easily validated, making it difficult for criminals to commit fraudulent operations like counterfeiting or money laundering.

A CBDC can enhance security by decreasing dependence on third-party intermediaries like banks. Individuals can conduct transactions directly with each other using a CBDC, eliminating the requirement for intermediaries. This minimizes the danger of intermediaries being hacked or exploited, thereby resulting in financial loss for people.

A CBDC can enhance the security of global transactions. International transactions with traditional fiat currency require numerous intermediaries and may take several days to finalize. A CBDC allows for rapid completion of international transactions, minimizing the possibility of delays or disruptions common with conventional fiat currencies.

A CBDC can enhance security by mitigating the danger of fraud and counterfeiting, decreasing dependence on third-party intermediaries and enhancing the security of international transactions.

Greater Financial Stability

CBDCs can mitigate systemic risk by offering a more secure option than physical cash and decreasing dependence on commercial banks. CBDCs enhance transparency by creating a digital ledger of transactions, facilitating the monitoring and deterrence of illicit activity.

New Opportunities for Innovation

CBDCs possess the capacity to generate novel opportunities for innovation in the domain of payments. CBDCs can enable the execution of smart contracts, which are contracts that automatically execute based on specified criteria. This can enhance operational efficiency and reduce the need for intermediaries in the Banking, Financial Services and

Insurance (BFSI) sector. Central banks can promote innovation in the BFSI industry by endorsing the development of novel technologies and services that leverage CBDCs, such as digital wallets, mobile payments and blockchain-based financial platforms. Central banks can optimize the efficacy of executing cutting-edge monetary policies by utilizing CBDC. Programmable currency has the potential to facilitate the implementation of negative interest rates or time-limited spending, providing new tools for monetary policy.

CBDC Implementation in the USA

The USA is at the exploratory stage of creating a CBDC. The Federal Reserve Board has been conducting a thorough examination and trial of CBDC to assess its benefits and limitations. The Federal Reserve has not made any determinations regarding the pursuit or execution of a CBDC. Nevertheless, they have published a discussion paper that examines the benefits and drawbacks of a potential US CBDC. This study examines the potential benefits of implementing a CBDC to improve the current safe and efficient US domestic payments system (Infante, Kim, Silva & Tetlow, 2022).

CBDC is commonly defined as a digital liability issued by a central bank that can be easily accessed by the general public. Federal Reserve notes are the only type of central bank currency available to the general public in the USA. A CBDC enables the general public to engage in digital transactions, like to other money types. A CBDC issued by the Federal Reserve would provide the highest level of security for the general public as a digital asset, without any hazards related to credit or liquidity.

Although the administration has not yet made a definitive choice regarding the implementation of a CBDC, the publication of the Comprehensive Framework for Responsible Development of Digital Assets by the White House on September 16, 2022, is perceived by certain individuals as a sign that a US CBDC is likely to be introduced in the future. The Clearing House has released a whitepaper that details significant choices in design and execution that might be taken in the USA. The document examines the potential outcomes of these choices and provides analysis on policy and legal considerations associated with the establishment of an American CBDC.

CBDC Implementation in Europe

The ECB launched the digital euro plan in 2020 to uphold the importance of central bank currency in the digital age. The digital euro project focuses on the development of a retail CBDC. In contrast, Project Jasper, which involves the Bank of Canada, Monetary Authority of Singapore, Bank of England, HSBC and KPMG UK, as well as Project Jura, which involves the BIS and the central banks of France and Switzerland, are both focused on the creation of a wholesale CBDC. A retail CBDC offers a universally recognized payment option for consumers and businesses, whereas a wholesale CBDC is restricted to interbank transactions and financial settlements (Passacantando, 2021).

The ECB focuses on three primary rationales for the digital euro project:

- Public funds may lose their function as the monetary stabilizer in Europe if the usage of physical currency keeps decreasing.
- Private suppliers are unable to fully imitate the function of central bank money. Lacking a robust monetary foundation could lead to ambiguity over the definition of money.

- The digital private sector is primarily controlled by a few providers based outside the European Union. This could increase the risk of non-European solutions and technologies dominating the European payments business.

For a digital euro to be accepted, it must offer a tangible advantage to users. Studies indicate that customers prioritize broad adoption, convenience of use, cheap cost, high speed, security and consumer protection. Merchants, on the other hand, seek low cost, ease of use and integration with current systems. Privacy protection should adhere to the highest quality, allowing users to select the amount of information they wish to reveal, while ensuring compliance with the law. Widespread distribution could help improve financial inclusion by providing access to financial services for those who previously had limited or no access to make and receive payments.

The ECB has been publishing an increasing number of articles on CBDC throughout the years. In 2020, 16 publications were released, followed by 26 in 2021 and an additional 14 in the first ten months of 2022. The ECB has consistently said in numerous publications that a digital euro will be designed to function similarly to cash, serving as a supplement rather than a replacement; be tied to the euro currency; be accessible to all individuals and businesses in the Eurozone.

The ECB is currently in the inquiry phase, which is expected to go until 2023. An investigation is now underway about the issuance of a CBDC known as the digital euro. The ECB has announced an implementation date set for around 2024. The digital euro is central bank money provided in digital format for citizens and companies to use in retail transactions.

The ECB has been releasing a range of publications on CBDCs, such as speeches, letters to Members of the European Parliament and legal documents. Piero Cipollone, a member of the Executive Board of the ECB, delivered a speech on the digital euro, focusing on its advantages and prospective economic effects. The ECB has also issued a statement regarding the digital euro. The ECB is scheduled to start its pilot for the digital euro, as reported by the Central Bank Digital Currency Tracker from Atlantic Council. More than 20 other countries are planning to start testing their CBDCs in 2023.

An implementation date of about 2024 was also announced. In the upcoming years, important architectural decisions will need to be taken. The goal of establishing a globally accepted payment mechanism for online and physical retailers in Europe implies a desire to utilize the current infrastructure, including the existing end-user interfaces and point-of-sale systems. The ECB disclosed its collaboration with five external companies, including Amazon, Nexi, Worldline, CaixaBank and the European Payments Initiative, to create a potential user interface. It appears that the ECB is choosing a hybrid structure in which commercial banks will play a substantial role in the CBDC ecosystem.

CBDC Implementation in Japan

Japan's adoption of CBDC began with the publication of a paper outlining its approach to CBDC in 2020. In December 2021, they initiated "Proof-of-Concept Phase 1" to evaluate fundamental features of CBDC such as issuance, distribution and redemption. In May 2022, the Bank of Japan carried out "Proof-of-Concept Phase 2" by conducting experiments on extra aspects of CBDC, such as offline capabilities. In May 2023, a pilot study was initiated to assess the technological feasibility of collaborating with private enterprises to develop a CBDC ecosystem. CBDC is anticipated to be fully implemented in Japan by 2026 (Kobayakawa, 2024).

CBDC Implementation in India

In 2022, the RBI introduced the Digital Rupee, which is India's CBDC and a digital representation of the country's official currency. The pilot effort began with a total of eight banks, namely the State Bank of India, Punjab National Bank, Bank of Baroda (BoB), HDFC Bank, ICICI Bank, Axis Bank, Kotak Mahindra Bank and Union Bank of India. Yes Bank, HSBC Bank and IDFC First Bank have since participated in the project (Kesavaraj, Jakhiya & Bhandari, 2022).

Upon its establishment, the central bank established two versions of the Digital Rupee: CBDC-Wholesale (CBDC-W) and CBDC-Retail (CBDC-R). CBDC-W is exclusively accessible to designated financial institutions, but CBDC-R is open to a broader spectrum of users, encompassing private sector organizations, non-financial customers and enterprises of various magnitudes.

The RBI is collaborating closely with financial institutions to introduce supplementary functionalities aimed at fostering the adoption of the e-rupee, the digital currency issued by the central bank. This initiative is a component of a broader campaign aimed at enhancing the use and integration of digital money inside the Indian financial system (Higginson, Hilal & Yugac, 2019).

The proposed features of the e-rupee include enabling offline digital transactions using the Indian unified payments interface (UPI). UPI is an instantaneous payment system that enables clients to transfer funds between several banks without disclosing their bank account details. The features are designed to enhance the convenience and accessibility of digital currency for consumers.

The RBI is asking banks to use a QR code system to facilitate seamless interchangeability between the e-rupee and UPI. This plan aims to streamline transactions and enhance the adoption of digital money by individuals and enterprises for diverse financial operations. Several renowned institutions, including the State Bank of India, have already integrated this interoperability capabilities.

Experts recommend that boosting the adoption of CBDC payments is crucial for facilitating wider usage, despite the fact that integrating with UPI will simplify transactions. Individuals and businesses using digital money may receive incentives in the form of rewards, discounts or other advantages. Offering incentives can effectively eliminate barriers to the adoption of CBDCs and incentivize a larger number of users to embrace them.

The retail e-rupee is available in various values, ranging from 50 paise to 200. In contrast, the wholesale e-rupee, as stated in the central bank's annual report for 2022–2023, does not specify specific denominations. The various denominations cater to the diverse financial needs and preferences of users inside the digital currency system.

Countries That Have Adopted CBDC

The countries of The Bahamas, Jamaica and Nigeria have successfully deployed CBDCs. The SandDollar, the world's first CBDC, was launched by The Bahamas in October 2022. The creation of SandDollar was the culmination of 20 years of efforts by The Bahamas Government to tackle the problem of financial exclusion (Ozili, 2023).

A number of Bahamian citizens live in remote locations. Transporting currency is expensive and inefficient, while establishing bank branches is not feasible due to the small population on most islands. Inhabitants of The Bahamas are vulnerable to severe weather phenomena. The occurrence of Hurricane Dorian in 2019 resulted in widespread flooding and significant destruction on isolated islands, leading to substantial interruptions in banking systems and limited access to cash. The surge in mobile phone usage in The Bahamas, together with the emergence of digital financial services, served as important catalysts for the creation of the SandDollar. A CBDC is perceived as the most all-encompassing, secure and convenient approach to offer payment services to all citizens in the nation, either without any fee or at a negligible expense.

The SandDollar is a digital representation of the Bahamian dollar that possesses equivalent legal standing to physical money and is designed for utilization on mobile wallet applications. The SandDollar is a legitimate kind of currency that is backed by foreign reserves, in contrast to cryptocurrencies which are digital assets used for storing value. Residents have the option to utilize their digital SandDollar-enabled wallet either on a mobile device or with a physical payment card, although the latter is less frequently employed.

Wallets can be classified into three distinct groups. Tier One wallets impose a maximum holding limit of $500 and a monthly transaction restriction of $1,500. Users are exempt from any consumer due diligence procedures. Wallets classified as premium (Tier Two) have a maximum balance limit of $8,000 and a monthly transaction limit of $10,000. Additionally, users are required to pass identity verification based on risk assessment. Tier Three Business wallets are designed exclusively for retailers and feature transaction restrictions that are defined on an individual basis.

Transactions are swiftly validated and consumers do not experience any fees or transaction charges. The payment system employs multi-factor authentication, sophisticated encryption mechanisms and enhanced KYC/AML regulations. Due to its utilization of blockchain technology, SandDollar ensures that every transaction is both unchangeable and traceable.

In The Bahamas, the current amount of currency in circulation is $1.4 million, representing a 30% growth compared to 2022. However, this amount still constitutes less than 1% of the total cash in circulation. There exist about 100,000 documented wallets, accounting for approximately 25% of the total population. There are a total of 1,800 merchants that have completed the registration process and have been officially authorized to use the SandDollar system. Additionally, there are nine financial institutions that have been granted approval to utilize SandDollar (Denecker, d'Estienne, Pierre-Matthieu & Sasia, 2022).

Jamaica has implemented "Jam-Dex" and has become the inaugural nation to legalize digital money. The Bank of Jamaica (BoJ) has formally authorized the adoption of CBDC as an additional alternative inside its cash-dependent economy. The BoJ has formally sanctioned the utilization of CBDC as an alternative to its cash-based economy, therefore removing prior ambiguities regarding its implementation.

Jam-Dex has been undergoing pilot testing since August 2022. In 2023, the Jamaican Senate granted authorization to the BoJ to establish Jam-Dex, sometimes referred to as the Jamaica Digital Exchange. Residential users can now access Jam-Dex. This can be employed to resolve any financial obligation in Jamaica. It serves as a means of trading and performs as the financial record-keeping system in Jamaica.

Nigeria has not successfully implemented a CBDC. In 2023, the Nigerian Government implemented eNaira, a CBDC that is legally supported and has full authority in Nigeria. It is issued by the Central Bank of Nigeria and serves as an official means of payment. The digital form of the Naira, known as electronic currency, is used in the same way as physical money. The eNaira wallet serves as a digital repository for storing the eNaira. The eNaira wallet is crucial for accessing, storing and utilizing eNaira. The eNaira functions as a means of measuring value, a means of storing wealth and a means of conducting transactions (Bijlsma, van der Cruijsen, Jonker & Reijerink, 2021).

Nigeria's efforts to introduce eNaira were unsuccessful as less than 0.5% of the population adopted it. This failure provides vital insights for Kenya and other developing nations contemplating the establishment of CBDCs. The Nigerian Government implemented cash withdrawal restrictions and currency modifications to encourage the adoption of CBDC, but these actions resulted in public backlash, sparking protests and discontent. CBDCs should be introduced inclusively, taking into account the community's needs and habits.

Difference between CBDC and Digital Currency

CBDC and digital currency are both forms of electronic money, but they have some key differences (Bindseil, 2019). Here are some of them.

Regulation

CBDCs are regulated and issued by the central bank, whereas digital currencies are decentralized and unregulated. CBDCs are government-backed and have legal tender status, unlike digital currencies.

Network

CBDCs operate on a controlled blockchain network that is permissioned, meaning participants need clearance from authorities to join. Digital currencies operate on a decentralized network, allowing public access without requiring authorization.

Value

CBDCs hold equivalent value to traditional physical fiat money and can be exchanged at a one-to-one ratio with the currency. Cryptocurrencies derive their value from market forces and can see substantial fluctuations.

Security

CBDCs provide enhanced security compared to other digital currencies due to the protection offered by the central bank and the inclusion of encryption technologies. Digital currencies are susceptible to hacking, theft and fraud because to their dependence on third-party wallets and systems.

Difference between CBDC and Cryptocurrency

CBDC and cryptocurrencies are both digital forms of currency, but they differ significantly in terms of their nature, issuance, underlying technology and regulatory framework (De Bode, Higginson & Niederkorn, 2021).

The following is a detailed note outlining the key differences between CBDC and cryptocurrencies:

Issuing Authority

CBDC: CBDC is issued and regulated by the central bank of a country. It is a digital version of a nation's fiat currency (e.g., the US dollar, euro) and is backed by the government.

Cryptocurrency: Cryptocurrencies are decentralized digital assets that operate on blockchain technology. They are not issued or controlled by any central authority, such as a government or central bank. Examples include Bitcoin, Ethereum and Ripple.

Centralization versus Decentralization

CBDC: Centralized by nature, CBDCs are controlled and regulated by the central authority or central bank. Transactions and issuance are monitored by the government.

Cryptocurrency: Cryptocurrencies are decentralized and operate on a peer-to-peer network. They rely on consensus mechanisms, such as proof-of-work or proof-of-stake, to validate transactions without the need for a central authority.

Technology

CBDC: CBDCs are typically built on centralized and permissioned ledger systems. The central bank has full control over the issuance, distribution and validation of transactions.

Cryptocurrency: Cryptocurrencies use decentralized and DLT, commonly blockchain. These ledgers are maintained by a network of nodes that reach consensus on the state of the ledger through cryptographic algorithms.

Legal Tender and Acceptance

CBDC: CBDCs are considered legal tender, and their acceptance is mandated by the government. They are designed to be used for everyday transactions, just like physical cash.

Cryptocurrency: Cryptocurrencies are not legal tender in most jurisdictions, and their acceptance is voluntary. They are often used as a store of value, a medium of exchange or a unit of account within their respective blockchain ecosystems.

Purpose and Use Cases

CBDC: CBDCs are primarily created to enhance the efficiency of the traditional financial system, reducing transaction costs and providing a digital alternative to physical cash. They can be used for everyday transactions, similar to traditional currency.

Cryptocurrency: Cryptocurrencies were initially conceived as an alternative to traditional currencies, providing a decentralized and borderless means of transferring value. They have various use cases, including cross-border payments, smart contracts, decentralized finance (DeFi) and as a hedge against inflation.

Regulation

CBDC: CBDCs are subject to strict government regulations, as they are directly issued by central banks. The regulatory framework is typically well-established and ensures compliance with financial laws.

Cryptocurrency: Cryptocurrencies often operate in a regulatory grey area. Governments around the world are working to establish frameworks to regulate and tax cryptocurrency transactions, but the regulatory environment varies widely.

In summary, while both CBDCs and cryptocurrencies are digital forms of currency, their fundamental differences lie in centralization, technology, legal status, purpose and regulatory framework. CBDCs are centralized, government-issued digital currencies, while cryptocurrencies are decentralized, often community-driven digital assets.

Potential Risks of CBDCs

There are also a number of potential risks associated with CBDCs, including:

Privacy concerns: CBDCs could raise privacy concerns, as central banks would have a record of all transactions.
Cybersecurity risks: CBDCs could be vulnerable to cyberattacks.
Potential for financial instability: CBDCs could pose a risk to financial stability if they are not properly designed and implemented.
Impact on the banking system: CBDCs could have a significant impact on the banking system, potentially reducing the demand for traditional banking services.
Technical complexity: CBDCs necessitate intricate infrastructure and advanced technology to guarantee their security, dependability and public accessibility.
Cybersecurity issues: Cyberattacks pose a threat to the security and stability of the financial system due to its vulnerability.
Potential disruption to financial intermediation: CBDCs could disrupt the role of banks and other financial intermediaries, leading to unknown impacts on financial stability.
Regulatory and legal frameworks: CBDCs pose several legal and regulatory challenges, such as governance and compliance with current financial laws.

It is essential to thoroughly study the advantages and obstacles of CBDCs to establish their suitability for a specific economy.

CBDCs offer tremendous advantages but also pose dangers that need to be carefully controlled to safeguard the stability and security of the financial system.

The Future of CBDCs

Worldwide, individuals are prepared to utilize cryptocurrency as a means of payment for purchasing products and services. Coinbase, a cryptocurrency exchange based in the USA, enables retailers to accept cryptocurrencies. PayPal, an online payment solutions provider, offers consumers the opportunity to pay with cryptocurrencies during checkout. Mastercard, a major player in the global card network, also facilitates the immediate settlement of cryptocurrencies.

In the near future, there will be payment systems allowing individuals who hold cryptocurrencies as investments to directly make payments to merchants. The merchant can choose to either sell the cryptocurrencies right away or retain them for savings or investment purposes. Stablecoins are becoming increasingly popular among shops for accepting crypto payments because they are tied to a fiat currency and maintain a stable value without fluctuations. Several applications facilitate the conversion of cryptocurrency to stablecoins. CBDC must compete with various forms of currency and payment methods to gain widespread acceptance (Berry, Lund, Manyika, Singer & White, 2016).

CBDCs could transform how individuals engage with money as financial institutions want to remain innovative in the constantly evolving financial environment. CBDCs function in a manner equivalent to withdrawing physical currency from an automated teller machine (ATM). Transactions are executed immediately and at lower costs as a result of the lack of intermediaries, such as financial institutions (Barquin, Vinayak & Shrikhande, 2018).

CBDC transactions are more secure than cash because they utilize advanced technology such as a digital certificate system, digital signature and encrypted storage. According to a PBOC White Paper, these technologies effectively mitigate problems such as double spending, illicit duplication, counterfeiting, transaction falsification and repudiation. CBDCs could enhance financial inclusion, streamline transactions and even address money laundering. Successful implementation of CBDC requires thoughtful consideration and collaboration among the government, financial institutions and the general public. To fully utilize CBDCs, important factors like digital infrastructure, regulatory frameworks and public trust need to be considered.

CBDCs offer several advantages, although they also have drawbacks. One concern is the risk of privacy loss due to CBDC transactions being recorded on a blockchain or distributed ledger. The implementation of CBDCs would need a significant overhaul of the financial system, perhaps leading to resistance from conventional financial institutions.

Despite the obstacles, the potential benefits of CBDCs make them a viable choice for India's currency in the future. It is crucial to investigate the potential impact of CBDCs on shaping India's financial sector in the upcoming years as the nation aims for advancement and economic growth.

The future of CBDCs remains unknown. The potential advantages of CBDCs are substantial, and they are expected to have a growing impact on the worldwide payment system in the future. CBDC has the capacity to revolutionize the future of financial transactions. It can be utilized to generate programmable currency that is restricted to specified expenditures. For instance, a government could implement a stimulus package that is earmarked for specific goods and services. This would guarantee that the funds be used as planned and thus decrease the likelihood of fraud. CBDC can enhance financial inclusion. Approximately 1.7 billion individuals lack access to fundamental financial services, as reported by the World Bank. CBDC can address this issue by offering a digital currency accessible to smartphone users without requiring a bank account.

CBDC has the potential to revolutionize the payment system. It will be intriguing to observe the market's development as more central banks delve into and implement this technology. It might transform the banking industry by offering a digital money that is more efficient, safe and transparent.

Questions for Discussion

1. Explain what you understand by CBDC. Why are governments across the world keen on implementing CBDC?
2. What are the different business models of implementation used for CBDC? What is the difference between account-based CBDC and token-based CBDC?
3. Explain the financial risks associated with CBDC.
4. What are the challenges faced in CBDC implementation?
5. Explain how you foresee the future of CBDC.

Case Study – CBDC Implementation in China

The digital yuan is a CBDC issued by the PBOC. This is equivalent in value to the standard renminbi (RMB). The digital representation of the physical Chinese currency, the RMB, is regarded as legal tender. CBDC transactions offer enhanced speed, greater cost efficiency and potentially heightened security compared to conventional methods such as e-payments or e-banking.

Since 2014, the People's Republic of China has been developing a digital currency called the digital yuan, also known as e-yuan, e-CNY, digital renminbi or digital RMB. This emerging technology provides numerous opportunities for monitoring China's extensive and intricate financial system, as well as the potential for economic influence on a global scale. The objective of the Chinese Communist Party is to establish the digital yuan as the predominant mode of payment for its population of 1.4 billion people and bolster China's technological prowess on a worldwide scale.

The USA has exerted substantial global economic influence as a result of the extensive utilization of the US dollar in commerce, foreign exchange reserves and international transactions. The introduction of China's digital yuan could potentially undermine the USA's ability to uphold trade partnerships, enforce sanctions and monitor financial transactions. The digital yuan raises cybersecurity risks related to data privacy, espionage and financial stability. While China makes progress in developing its digital currency, the USA falls behind, giving Beijing greater control over establishing the norms and regulations for this emerging technology, so diminishing Washington's competitive position.

CBDCs, such as the digital yuan, are distinct from cryptocurrencies. In 2017, China implemented a prohibition on cryptocurrency exchange activities, and, in 2021, they further barred transactions due to regulatory difficulties. Bitcoin and other cryptocurrencies operate using blockchain technology, which is a decentralized and immutable ledger designed to circumvent conventional financial institutions. CBDCs are considered as legal tender and are therefore subject to government oversight and control. The value of the digital yuan remains constant since it is tied to the same currency basket as the RMB, but the value of cryptocurrencies fluctuates owing to changing levels of supply and demand. Due to its centralized nature, China has a greater preference for a CBDC over a cryptocurrency.

Cryptocurrency transactions offer a high level of anonymity, which makes them well-suited for illicitly transferring funds. The primary objective of the digital yuan is to mitigate instances of financial crime and facilitate the identification of individuals responsible for such activities. This gives rise to apprehensions over surveillance and privacy. According to a press release from the PBOC, the digital yuan provides anonymity for little amounts and legal traceability for large amounts. Additionally, the central bank guarantees the adequate protection of personal information for the general public. The disclosure of users' data to government officials will only occur if mandated by laws and regulations, as explicitly stated in a PBOC White Paper (Xu, 2022). Article 28 of the Cybersecurity Law grants the government the authority to acquire data from any Chinese corporation using the pretext of "national security", so rendering anonymity highly unclear and contingent upon certain conditions.

In April 2020, China commenced testing programs for a CBDC, establishing itself as the first major economy to undertake such an initiative. The government implemented the currency exclusively in four cities: Shenzhen, Suzhou, Xiongan and Chengdu. Last autumn, the Vice President of the PBOC announced the expansion of the digital yuan pilot program to encompass 15 provinces and 23 cities. Chongqing and Guangzhou, both megacities, have recently introduced the digital yuan as a payment alternative, extending its availability to a total population of 98 million individuals residing in China's five largest cities. Furthermore, six cities in Zhejiang were incorporated as a result of the province being selected to host the 2023 Asian Games, and the PBOC wants to test the digital yuan with international participants.

In January 2022, the PBOC published a survey revealing that 261 million people have created a digital yuan wallet. This figure is equal to the whole populations of Russia, Germany and Canada combined, which is a notable achievement achieved in just two years of operation. Nevertheless, despite the fact that about 903.6 million people in China are utilizing mobile payments, a 28.89% usage rate is not particularly impressive. In addition, the possession of a wallet does not provide assurance that it contains funds, hence creating uncertainty on the successful utilization by the 261 million individuals.

Presumably, people created digital yuan wallets with the anticipation of obtaining free money. In 2022, 11 pilot cities, including Beijing and Shanghai, launched digital yuan lotteries, dispersing a combined sum of ¥340 million RMB ($50.47 million). In the summer of 2022, Meituan, a renowned e-commerce platform, organized a lottery with a prize pool of ¥30 million RMB. Additionally, Fuzhou's official app conducted a second lottery with a value of ¥20 million RMB. The digital yuan app offered a range of discounts, promotions and digital yuan red envelopes for gifting over the Lunar New Year, a season renowned for its extravagant spending in China.

While giveaways can initially motivate customers to use digital yuan, they do not guarantee sustained usage. For new technology to be effectively utilized, it is imperative that it seamlessly integrate with established traditions. In January 2022, the digital yuan application was introduced in 15 trial towns to facilitate the purchase of daily necessities by Chinese individuals through their cell phones. The subsequent action taken by the central bank involved partnering with renowned commerce platforms to gain access to their established consumer base. Tenpay, also known as WeChat Pay, and Alipay, owned by Ant Group, collectively control almost 93% of the mobile payment market in China. To maintain competitiveness, the digital yuan must get a comparable degree of extensive adoption.

Throughout the preceding summer, the Chinese authorities enforced rigorous COVID-19 restrictions, resulting in a widespread reliance on food delivery services and economic difficulties. Meituan and Shenzhen jointly conducted a digital yuan lottery, which encompassed 67,000 establishments and engaged 2.6 million patrons. Meituan collaborated with five banks to issue digital yuan vouchers worth ¥35.2 million RMB ($5.27 million) through a lottery system. This was a calculated endeavor to endorse the digital yuan and invigorate demand amid an economic downturn.

The Chinese Government created partnerships with e-commerce platforms to spread the acceptance of the digital yuan. JD.com, the largest e-commerce platform in China, announced that it successfully handled more than four million transactions, amounting to ¥900 million RMB ($133.5 million), after integrating digital yuan as a payment option in 2020. Ant Group incorporated the digital yuan into its platform in May 2021, while WeChat followed suit in March 2023. These improvements are essential as Ant Group previously exclusively accepted Alipay, whereas JD.com mainly utilized Tenpay.

The PBOC has delegated multiple responsibilities for the implementation of the digital yuan to the state-owned banks, which serve as the fundamental pillars of China's financial system. In its mobile banking app, the Industrial and Commercial Bank of China implemented a "smart exchange function" last year. This feature enables clients to automatically convert their CNY wallet balances into bank deposits. More than 40 employers in Hainan province availed themselves of Bank of

China's digital yuan service to disburse salaries. China Construction Bank has recently implemented the acceptance of digital yuan as a means of purchasing wealth management products. Agricultural Commerce Bank has announced the issuance of its first digital yuan loan, with a value of ¥500,000 RMB ($73,986). These banks wield substantial influence over a large number of individuals and organizations worldwide, positioning them as crucial actors in advancing the widespread adoption of the digital yuan.

Local authorities are integrating the digital yuan into standard public services. Starting in April 2022, residents of Zhejiang province will have the option to utilize digital yuan as a means of payment for taxes, stamps and social security. The digital yuan was utilized as a means of payment on 10 bus routes in Guangzhou and at 125 metro stations in Ningbo. Starting from April 2023, all government employees in Changshu City will get their salaries exclusively in digital yuan. Integrating the digital yuan into daily transportation and regular salaries is the strategic approach to establishing it as the principal payment mechanism in China.

The main target market for the digital yuan is local, while the PBOC is also exploring its possible use in international markets. Foreign athletes and tourists were allowed to use the digital yuan during the Beijing Winter Olympics in February 2022. As per a PBOC official, the daily expenditure of digital yuan during the Olympics was around two million dollars ($315,761).

The HKMA is participating in the mBridge project, an initiative aimed at establishing a bridge for CBDCs. Additionally, they are doing tests on the digital yuan. China, Hong Kong, Thailand, the United Arab Emirates and the BISs are working together to establish a comprehensive infrastructure that can facilitate several digital currencies and legal regulations. According to a news announcement from the HKMA, the banks carried out 160 payment and foreign currency transactions totaling more than HK$171 million, making it the most extensive cross-border CBDC pilot to date. If the pilots demonstrate efficacy, mBridge might potentially function as a viable substitute for SWIFT and associated sanctions.

The Belt and Road Initiative (BRI), an international development project aimed at enhancing connectivity in the Global South, provides further opportunities for globalizing the renminbi. Typically, a BRI project involves a foreign borrower signing a credit agreement with a Chinese bank to finance an implementation contract with a Chinese state-owned company. Chinese authorities may leverage these agreements by mandating that all individuals who incur debts, borrow money or engage in contractual agreements must make payments only using the digital yuan. As a condition for receiving a new power plant or transportation network, borrowers may be obligated to adopt the digital yuan. The requirement may be unnecessary or redundant. Many countries in the developing world lack the necessary financial infrastructure to sustain the dollar system, leading to costly and delayed money transfers. In the event that China was to implement the digital yuan as a component of the Digital Silk Road plan, nations involved in the Belt and Road plan might elect to decrease their reliance on the dollar and willingly accept the digital yuan.

The e-CNY in China serves as the most comprehensive and notable testing ground for evaluating the efficacy of a CBDC. The e-CNY system collaborates with commercial banks, payments providers, AI and big data suppliers, other central banks and international institutions. The pilot program is more sophisticated than the research phase of generating CBDC in many other countries. China's emphasis on the cross-border capabilities of the e-CNY and its advanced stage of development positions it strongly to set norms for the global advancement of CBDCs. There has been no official declaration addressing the complete implementation of the e-CNY, however it is possible that it may happen soon.

Case Study Questions

1. Explain how the CBDC is being implemented in China.
2. What were the enablers that helped CBDC to be implemented in China?
3. What are the factors causing resistance to CBDC implementation in China?

Further Reading

1. Mookerjee, A.S. (2021, October 15). What If Central Banks Issued Digital Currency? Harvard Business Review. https://hbr.org/2021/10/what-if-central-banks-issued-digital-currency
2. Mu, Y., & Mu, A. (2022). CBDC: Concepts, Benefits, Risks, Design, and Implications. Benefits, Risks, Design, and Implications (October 1, 2022).

References

Armelius, H., Claussen, C. A., & Hull, I. (2021). On the possibility of a cash-like CBDC. In *Sveriges Riksbank Staff Memo.*

Athanassiou, P. (2021). Wholesale Central Bank digital currencies: An overview of recent central bank initiatives and lessons learned. In *European Central Bank: European System of Central Banks Legal Conference* (Vol. 1, pp. 191–201).

Barquin, S., Vinayak, H. V., & Shrikhande, D. (2018). *Reaching Asia's digital banking customers.* McKinsey Quarterly.

Berry, C., Lund, S., Manyika, J., Singer, M., & White, O. (2016). *How Digital Finance Could Boost Growth in Emerging Economies.* McKinsey Global Institute.

Bijlsma, M., van der Cruijsen, C., Jonker, N., & Reijerink, J. (2021). What triggers consumer adoption of CBDC? *De Nederlandsche Bank Working Paper No. 709.* http://dx.doi.org/10.2139/ssrn.3836440

Bindseil, U. (2019). Central bank digital currency: Financial system implications and control. *International Journal of Political Economy*, 48(4), 303–335.

BIS. (2023). BIS Innovation Hub work on central bank digital currency (CBDC). *Bank of International Settlements.* www.bis.org/about/bisih/topics/cbdc.htm

Das, M. M., Griffoli, M. T. M., Nakamura, F., Otten, M. J., Soderberg, G., Sole, M. J., & Tan, B. (2023). *Implications of Central Bank Digital Currencies for Monetary Policy Transmission.* International Monetary Fund.

De Bode, I., Higginson, M., & Niederkorn, M. (2021). *CBDC and Stablecoins: Early Coexistence on an Uncertain Road.* McKinsey Quarterly.

Denecker, O., d'Estienne, A., Pierre-Matthieu, G., & Sasia, E. (2022). *Central Bank digital currencies: An active role for commercial banks.* McKinsey Quarterly.

Guo, S., Kreitem, J., & Moser, T. (2022). DLT options for CBDC. *Journal of Central Banking Theory and Practice*, 13(1), 57–88.

He, M. D., Kokenyne, A., Griffoli, M. T. M., Miccoli, M. M., Olafsson, M. T. T., Soderberg, G., & Tourpe, H. (2023). *Capital Flow Management Measures in the Digital Age: Design Choices for Central Bank Digital Currency.* International Monetary Fund.

Higginson, M., Hilal, A., & Yugac, E. (2019). *Blockchain and retail banking: Making the connection.* McKinsey Quarterly.

Infante, S., Kim, K., Silva, A. F., & Tetlow, R. J. (2022). The macroeconomic implications of CBDC: A review of the literature. *FEDS Working Paper No. 2022-76.* http://dx.doi.org/10.17016/FEDS.2022.076

Kesavaraj, S. V., Jakhiya, C. M., & Bhandari, C. N. (2022, October). A study on upcoming central bank digital currency: Opportunities, obstacles, and potential FinTech solutions using cryptography in the Indian scenario. In *2022 13th International Conference on Computing Communication and Networking Technologies (ICCCNT)* (pp. 1–10). IEEE.

Kobayakawa, S. (2024). Beyond Central Bank Digital Currencies: Lessons from Japan's experience. In *Digital assets and the law* (pp. 166–178). Routledge.

Kshetri, N. (2023). China's digital yuan: Motivations of the Chinese government and potential global effects. *Journal of Contemporary China*, 32(139), 87–105.

Lannquist, A., & Tan, B. (2023). Central Bank Digital Currency's role in promoting financial inclusion. *FinTech Notes, 2023(011).*

McKinsey. (2023). What is central bank digital currency (CBDC)? *McKinsey Quarterly*. www.mckinsey.com/featured-insights/mckinsey-explainers/what-is-central-bank-digital-currency-cbdc

Morales-Resendiz, R., Ponce, J., Picardo, P., Velasco, A., Chen, B., & Hodge, A. (2021). Implementing a retail CBDC: Lessons learned and key insights. *Latin American Journal of Central Banking*, 2(1), 100022.

Ozili, P. K. (2023). Central bank digital currency research around the world: A review of literature. *Journal of Money Laundering Control*, 26(2), 215–226.

Passacantando, F. (2021). The digital euro: Challenges and opportunities. Bilotta, N. & Botti, F. (ed.). *The (near) future of Central Bank digital currencies*. Istituto Affari Internazionali (IAI), Italy. pp. 113–130.

Soderberg, G., Kiff, M. J., Tourpe, H., Bechara, M. M., Forte, S., Kao, K., & Yoshinaga, A. (2023). *How Should Central Banks Explore Central Bank Digital Currency?* International Monetary Fund.

Themistocleous, M., Rupino da Cunha, P., Tabakis, E., & Papadaki, M. (2023). Towards cross-border CBDC interoperability: Insights from a multivocal literature review. *Journal of Enterprise Information Management*, 36(5), 1296–1318.

Tourpe, H., Lannquist, A., & Soderberg, G. (2023). A guide to Central Bank Digital Currency product development. *FinTech Notes, 2023(007).*

Tsai, W. T., Zhao, Z., Zhang, C., Yu, L., & Deng, E. (2018, September). A multi-chain model for CBDC. In *2018 5th International Conference on Dependable Systems and Their Applications (DSA)* (pp. 25–34). IEEE.

Xu, J. (2022). Developments and implications of central bank digital currency: The case of China e-CNY. *Asian Economic Policy Review*, 17(2), 235–250.

11 Application of Artificial Intelligence in Fintech

After reading this chapter you will:

- Know how artificial intelligence and machine learning is being used in the Fintech industry
- Know how automation is being done in the Fintech industry
- Understand how Fintech companies are getting competitive advantages by applying AIML
- Know how DevOps are being used to develop applications in the Fintech industry

Kabbage is a US-based Fintech startup that provides small businesses with online lending services. Kabbage uses AI to assess the creditworthiness of borrowers based on their real-time business data, such as bank accounts, accounting software, e-commerce platforms and social media. Kabbage can approve loans in minutes and provide funds in hours.

Kabbage's AI-powered platform collects data generated through business activity such as accounting data, online sales, shipping and dozens of other sources to understand performance and deliver fast, flexible funding in real time. Kabbage's AI algorithms analyze vast datasets to identify patterns, make predictions and improve over time.

Kabbage's AI-powered technologies help in analyzing customer data and behavior patterns, improving the decision-making process, ensuring rock-solid data security, forecasting future outcomes and trends, providing robust fraud detection, automating credit scoring and document analysis and reducing user support costs. Kabbage's AI-powered platform has enabled the company to compete with traditional banks by providing personalized services to consumers and streamlining processes.

Kabbage uses AI to offer small businesses access to credit and financial tools. The company's AI-powered platform can analyze data from various sources, including the business owner's online sales, social media activity and other data. This allows Kabbage to create a unique credit profile for each business, which is then used to determine the amount of credit the business is eligible for.

Kabbage's AI platform also helps the company automate the loan application process, making it faster and more convenient for small business owners to get the funding they need. Additionally, Kabbage's AI algorithms can monitor a business's financial activity in real time, allowing the company to identify potential issues and offer support before they become serious problems.

Overall, Kabbage's use of AI has helped the company to streamline its lending process, offer more personalized financing options to small businesses and provide valuable insights and support to its customers.

DOI: 10.4324/9781032699417-11

Introduction to AI

Artificial intelligence, also known as AI, gives the financial industry a unique opportunity to reduce costs, improve customer experience and increase operational efficiency, among other things. Financial companies can provide excellent financial services to their customers. Various features of AI are used by different Fintech companies around the world to make operations safer and more efficient. All these solutions have one important goal: they increase the productivity of Fintech companies. By using automation tools for data analysis and chatbots, companies can greatly reduce the workload of their staff (Zheng, Zhu, Li, Chen & Tan, 2019).

However, there is still often a lack of qualified AI developers. For this reason, banks are turning to specialized software development companies that have experienced engineers who are Fintech experts. Companies in the financial sector can use AI to analyze and manage data from multiple sources to gain valuable insights. These innovative results help banks address the challenges they face daily in delivering everyday services such as payment processing.

At present, AI is playing a crucial role. It is helping Fintech companies automate routine procedures and improve outcomes on a scale beyond human intelligence. The early application of AI enables Fintech companies to identify threats, prevent fraud, automate everyday tasks and enhance the quality of service. All these lead to improved efficiency and higher profits.

AI is increasingly being used in Fintech to improve various aspects of financial services. One way AI is being used is in fraud detection, where machine learning (ML) algorithms can quickly and accurately identify potentially fraudulent transactions. AI is also being used to improve customer service by providing chatbots that can quickly and accurately respond to customer inquiries. In addition, AI is being used to help companies make better investment decisions by analyzing large amounts of data and providing insights that would be difficult for humans to identify on their own. Finally, AI is being used to automate many routine tasks, such as loan approvals and credit scoring, allowing financial institutions to save time and money (Cao, 2022).

AI has been a transformative force in the financial services industry, revolutionizing how financial services are delivered and consumed. AI in Fintech, short for artificial intelligence in financial technology, refers to the application of artificial intelligence technologies in the financial services industry. This integration of AI in Fintech has been transformative, introducing innovative solutions that streamline processes, enhance decision-making and provide personalized services to consumers. The convergence of AI and Fintech has resulted in a wide range of applications across various segments of the financial sector (Binner, Kendall & Chen, 2004).

AI-powered technologies can help Fintech institutions in a variety of ways, including:

- Analyzing customer data and behavior patterns
- Improving decision-making process
- Ensuring rock-solid data security
- Forecasting future outcomes and trends
- Providing a robust fraud detection
- Automating credit scoring and document analysis
- Reducing user support costs

Here are some of the key aspects of AI in Fintech:

Machine learning (ML): ML algorithms analyze vast datasets to identify patterns, make predictions and improve over time. In Fintech, ML is used for credit scoring, fraud detection and personalized financial recommendations.

Natural language processing (NLP): NLP enables machines to understand, interpret and generate human-like language. In Fintech, NLP is used for chatbots, virtual assistants and sentiment analysis in financial news and social media.

Predictive analytics: Predictive analytics uses historical data and statistical algorithms to forecast future trends and behaviors. In Fintech, it aids in predicting market movements, customer behavior and credit risk.

Robotic process automation (RPA): RPA automates repetitive tasks and processes, reducing manual efforts and improving operational efficiency. In Fintech, RPA is employed for tasks like data entry, account reconciliation and compliance reporting.

Computer vision: Computer vision involves the use of AI to interpret and make decisions based on visual data. In Fintech, computer vision is utilized for tasks such as document verification, facial recognition for biometric authentication and fraud prevention.

AI in Fintech is a rapidly evolving field, and its role and impact are expected to grow in the coming years. The opportunities and use cases for AI in Fintech are vast, and it will be exciting to see how this technology continues to transform the financial services industry.

AI has significantly transformed the landscape of the financial technology (Fintech) industry, enhancing efficiency, accuracy and innovation across various financial services. The integration of AI in Fintech has led to the development of advanced applications, predictive analytics and automation, revolutionizing the way financial institutions operate.

What Do AI and Fintech Mean Exactly?

Fintech (financial technology) is technology-enabled innovation in the financial sector. This can range from managing financial transactions to fighting fraud, as we already wrote here. In recent years, the staggering rise of Fintech companies has offered consumers personalized ways to manage their hard-earned money in ways that were not possible a decade ago. AI-powered chatbots, for example, are being used by Fintech companies of all sizes, from customer service agents to salespeople (Zheng, Zhu, Li, Chen & Tan, 2019).

Indeed, the rise of financial technology has been significant in recent years. In fact, traditional banking has come to know of disruptive Fintech companies and their innovative solutions, introducing technologies that use AI and robotics to reduce costs and address consumer pain points.

The Benefits of AI for the Banking and Financial Services Industry

The similarities between AI and Fintech are enormous. Improved knowledge and social capabilities have pushed AI technology from the edge to the center of the debate. It brings back the personal touch to banking, which has been somewhat lost in recent decades due to the dominance of multinational banks. A description of how AI in the financial sector can improve banks' business processes follows (Sheth, Jain, Roy & Chakraborty, 2022).

Data Automation/Credit Risk Assessment

AI-based credit scores are perhaps the most promising and relevant. In short, credit scoring is an evaluation of how well a customer can pay and is willing to repay debts. AI decisions on credit scores are based on a lot of data, such as total income, credit history, transaction analyses and work experience. Credit scoring is a mathematical model based on statistical methods that consider a large amount of information. The result is that credit scores using AI provide sensitive, individual credit score assessments based on several additional real-time factors, potentially allowing more people with incomes to access finance (Moro, Cortez & Rita, 2016).

Detecting Banking Fraud

Data is analyzed using AI-based analytics tools to detect suspicious transactions that may indicate fraud. Through AI, users' behavior patterns can be monitored, and actions that deviate from the normal can be identified and could show fraud attempts or incidents. These cases are then passed on to human staff for consideration, saving them a great deal of time.

Another way AI data analysis can be used is for fraud detection and prevention. As mentioned earlier, AI and ML solutions can react in real time to the data presented to them, find patterns and connections and may be able to identify fraudulent activity. As one can imagine, this is hugely useful for the financial world, as an incredible number of digital transactions take place every hour, making increased cyber security and successful fraud detection a necessity. AI takes most of the work away from fraud analysts, allowing them to focus on higher-level issues, while AI works in the background to identify the smaller problems (Hassan, Aziz & Andriansyah, 2023).

One example of how AI can detect fraud is by detecting anomalies. In the bank scenario, someone may have tried to apply for ten identical loans in five minutes; a computer with AI could detect this as an anomaly and consider it suspicious. The computer has a basic sense of what is "normal" and when something deviates from this, it is able to identify and assess it.

Increasing Safety

AI in the financial world is the driving force behind many solutions to improve security. For example, banks offer apps that can only be accessed with face or fingerprint recognition. This is primarily made possible by AI.

AI in Fintech offers solutions based on behavior and could revolutionize the financial world. AI can monitor how a customer handles his transactions and determine his typical behavior. Suppose a customer tries to withdraw €5,000 from his account several times from somewhere-not-a-typical-location; artificial intelligence-driven learning can detect and block these activities as possible fraud (Bécue, Praça & Gama, 2021).

Automated Customer Service

Customer service and relationship management is another critical area where AI technologies provide tangible value. Fintech companies can use chatbots to quickly answer customer questions and improve customers' overall experience with their products and services. These chatbots allow customer service to be tailored to people and provide expert advice at a low cost (Sheth, Jain, Roy & Chakraborty, 2022).

In addition, chatbots can be available 24/7 and never take days off. Virtual assistants can also be augmented with AI to help the customer navigate the bank's offerings, enhance user data and provide personalized calls to action to increase targeted conversions. Virtual assistants and chatbots help Fintech companies save time and money on customer service. This will also help improve the quality of AI through its various capabilities.

Another application of AI is automated customer support. Nowadays, people are used to chatting boxes appearing at the bottom of the screen when they visit different websites, and these are of course chatbots with AI support ready to help. Companies can simply upload their most frequently asked questions and tell the chatbot which answers to give and also instruct it to refer the customer to someone else for more complex issues. Being able to answer frequently asked questions about the company or the product/service it provides ensures a better experience for the customer as he gets the answer to his question immediately. In addition, the company saves time and money by not having to employ someone to type out answers or by having an employee focus on something else.

Analyzing User Behavior

AI in Fintech can predict a user's behavior by using an interface to integrate various AI and ML techniques, allowing users to gain detailed insights into their data. These are also called AI APIs and can be used to the advantage of banks and Fintech companies (Königstorfer & Thalmann, 2020).

For example, the customer requests data on his expenses in the past month – a single request. The company uses AI to predict his follow-up request on the server side and provides this information in the same response. In this way, the company minimizes the number of requests and the burden on the business system. The customer also benefits, as the system works faster when the predictive analysis is correct.

Financial Forecasts

The use of AI in finance means that it can identify, analyze and adjust changes in data patterns on its own. Moreover, even if data quality is far from perfect, AI in Fintech can still come up with valuable insights into the exchange rates, investments and short- or long-term trend predictions (Cohen, 2022).

Even more impressive is the ability of AI to analyze unstructured data, which is essential for financial services. In Fintech, this can be applied in various ways, including predicting product suitability and adapting marketing strategy by analyzing customer behavior.

AI has several practical applications in the Fintech sector, throughout the financial world and even in the broader world beyond. The general essence of AI is that it solves problems; it enables companies to save both time and money.

In many cases, the practical use of AI has to do with data and enables companies to analyze that data efficiently and cost-effectively. Organizations, especially financial institutions, often have large amounts of data about their customers. Still, they do not usually do anything with it because it takes a lot of time to go through and analyze that data. This is where AI comes in, as artificial intelligence and ML effectively analyze large amounts of data in real time.

A specific example of applying AI with data is for banks to decide whether someone is creditworthy. Banks want to offer credit, but they also want to charge the right price.

They can avoid overcharging reliable customers and undercharging risky customers by looking at their credit scores. AI lets them look at their own customer data and draw conclusions. From these portfolios, AI can derive different kinds of connections. For example, job and address are obvious sources of information, but there is also the argument that even details such as what someone's email provider is could show more or less trustability (Sadok, Sakka & El Maknouzi, 2022).

Application of AI in Fintech

Here's a detailed note on how AI is used in Fintech:

Fraud Detection and Prevention

AI algorithms analyze vast amounts of transaction data to identify patterns and anomalies that may indicate fraudulent activities. ML models continuously learn from historical data, improving their ability to detect new and evolving fraud patterns in real time. Behavior analysis and biometric authentication contribute to robust security measures (Sheth, Jain, Roy & Chakraborty, 2022).

Credit Scoring and Risk Assessment

AI-powered credit scoring models leverage alternative data sources and non-traditional variables to assess the creditworthiness of individuals and businesses. ML algorithms predict default risks more accurately by considering a broader range of factors than traditional credit scoring models. Real-time risk assessment helps financial institutions make quicker and more informed lending decisions (Sadok, Sakka & El Maknouzi, 2022).

Customer Service and Chatbots

AI-driven chatbots and virtual assistants enhance customer service by providing instant responses to queries, handling routine tasks and offering personalized financial advice. NLP enables chatbots to understand and respond to user inquiries, improving the overall customer experience (Kediya, Dhote, Singh, Bidve, Pathan, Mohare & Suchak, 2023).

Algorithmic Trading

AI algorithms analyze market trends, historical data and news in real time to make informed trading decisions. ML models adapt to changing market conditions and optimize trading strategies, leading to improved returns and risk management (Tadoori & Guguloth, 2019).

Personalized Financial Planning

AI analyzes individual financial data, spending habits and investment preferences to offer personalized financial advice and investment strategies. Robo-advisors use AI to automate portfolio management, rebalancing and asset allocation based on the client's financial goals and risk tolerance (Sheth, Jain, Roy & Chakraborty, 2022).

Regulatory Compliance and Anti-Money Laundering

AI streamlines regulatory compliance by automating processes related to know-your-customer and anti-money laundering checks. NLP helps financial institutions sift through large volumes of legal and compliance documents, ensuring adherence to regulatory requirements (Han, Huang, Liu & Towey, 2020).

Data Analytics and Decision Support

AI enables Fintech companies to process and analyze vast amounts of data to derive meaningful insights. Predictive analytics assists in forecasting market trends, customer behavior and potential risks, facilitating better decision-making.

Blockchain and Cryptocurrency

AI enhances security and efficiency in blockchain transactions by identifying potential security threats and optimizing consensus algorithms. ML is utilized for price prediction in cryptocurrency markets, helping traders make more informed investment decisions.

Insurance Underwriting and Claims Processing

AI automates the underwriting process by analyzing customer data, assessing risk factors and determining appropriate premiums. Claim processing is expedited through AI algorithms that assess damage, validate claims and expedite payments.

Robotic Process Automation

AI-powered RPA automates routine and rule-based tasks, reducing operational costs and minimizing errors in processes such as data entry, reconciliation and report generation (Martínez-Rojas, Sánchez-Oliva, López-Carnicer & Jiménez-Ramírez, 2021).

In summary, the integration of AI in Fintech has led to significant advancements in fraud prevention, risk assessment, customer service, trading, compliance and various other aspects of financial services. The continuous evolution of AI technologies is likely to bring further innovation and efficiency to the Fintech industry, ultimately benefiting both financial institutions and consumers.

Use of DevOps in the Fintech Industry

DevOps, a combination of "development" and "operations", is an approach to software development that emphasizes collaboration and communication between software developers and IT professionals, aiming to automate the process of software delivery and infrastructure changes. In the Fintech industry, where agility, security and reliability are paramount, DevOps practices are increasingly being adopted to streamline development and operations processes (Zhou, 2022).

DevOps is a software development approach emphasizing collaboration, automation and continuous delivery to provide high-quality products to customers quickly and efficiently. DevOps breaks down silos between development and operations teams to enable seamless communication, faster time-to-market and improved customer

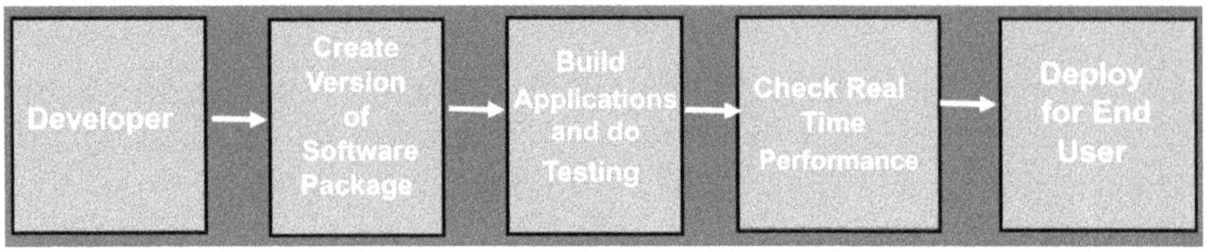

Figure 11.1 Process of DevOps

satisfaction. It allows a team to handle the complete application lifecycle, from development to testing, operations and deployment. It shows cooperation between development and operations groups to deploy code to production quickly in an automated and repeatable manner.

Every phase of the software development lifecycle, including planning, coding, testing, deployment and monitoring, is heavily automated in DevOps. This improves productivity, ensures consistency and lowers error rates in the development process. A culture of continuous improvement is also promoted by DevOps, where feedback loops are incorporated into the procedure to facilitate quicker iteration and better decision-making. Organizations can increase their agility, lower costs and speed up innovation by adopting DevOps.

The process of DevOps is given in Figure 11.1.

Here's how DevOps is being used in the Fintech industry:

Continuous Integration and Continuous Delivery

Continuous integration and continuous delivery (CI/CD) pipelines automate the building, testing and deployment of software, ensuring that changes are quickly and consistently integrated into the production environment. In Fintech, where rapid software delivery is crucial, CI/CD pipelines enable faster release cycles without compromising on quality, allowing financial institutions to respond quickly to market demands and regulatory changes (Van Merode, 2023).

Automation of Manual Processes

DevOps automation reduces manual intervention in various processes, including software testing, deployment and infrastructure provisioning. Fintech organizations leverage automation to minimize human errors, enhance efficiency and ensure that critical financial systems are always in a consistent and reliable state.

Collaboration and Communication

DevOps encourages collaboration between development, operations and other relevant teams, fostering better communication and understanding of each other's needs and constraints. Improved collaboration helps in aligning development efforts with business objectives and ensures that financial applications are developed and deployed with a holistic understanding of the business context.

Infrastructure as Code

Fintech organizations use infrastructure as code (IaC) to automate the provisioning and management of infrastructure components. Infrastructure changes are treated as version-controlled code, enabling organizations to replicate environments, maintain consistency and quickly scale infrastructure resources based on demand.

Security and Compliance

Security is a top priority in the Fintech industry, and DevOps practices include security measures from the early stages of development through to production. DevSecOps integrates security into the DevOps pipeline, incorporating security checks, code analysis and compliance measures to ensure that financial systems adhere to regulatory standards.

Monitoring and Incident Response

DevOps practices include the implementation of robust monitoring solutions to detect issues in real time. Automated incident response mechanisms help Fintech organizations address and resolve issues promptly, minimizing downtime and ensuring the continuous availability of financial services.

Microservices Architecture

DevOps aligns well with microservices architecture, allowing Fintech companies to build scalable and modular applications. Microservices enable the development of independent, deployable components, making it easier to update specific features without affecting the entire application.

Scalability and Resilience

DevOps practices facilitate the design and implementation of scalable and resilient systems. Fintech organizations can dynamically scale resources based on demand, ensuring that their applications can handle fluctuations in user activity without compromising performance.

Auditability and Traceability

DevOps tools and practices provide audit trails and traceability of changes, making it easier for Fintech organizations to track modifications to the codebase and infrastructure. This auditability is crucial for compliance purposes and helps in addressing any issues that may arise during regulatory audits.

In summary, DevOps in the Fintech industry is about combining development and operations practices to create a more efficient, collaborative and secure software delivery pipeline. By embracing DevOps principles, Fintech organizations can achieve faster time-to-market, improved reliability and enhanced security, ultimately delivering better financial services to their customers.

Benefits of Using DevOps in the Fintech Industry

The adoption of DevOps practices in the Fintech industry offers a range of benefits, aligning with the sector's need for agility, security and reliability (Zhou, 2022). Here are some key advantages of using DevOps in the Fintech industry:

Routine Operations Automation

DevOps principles and tools play a crucial role in automating routine operations in Fintech, enabling companies to deliver reliable, secure and scalable financial services while maintaining compliance with regulatory requirements. DevOps encourages the automation of the software development lifecycle, including building, testing and deploying code changes. In Fintech, where rapid updates and deployments are crucial, CI/CD pipelines ensure that changes are thoroughly tested and seamlessly deployed into production environments, reducing manual errors and speeding up the release process.

Fintech companies often deal with complex infrastructure setups to handle sensitive financial data securely. With IaC, infrastructure components such as servers, networks and databases are defined in code, enabling automated provisioning, configuration and management. This reduces the risk of configuration drift and ensures consistent environments across different stages of development and production.

Audit Facilitation

Fintech companies must adhere to various regulatory requirements and standards, such as GDPR, PCI-DSS and SOC2. DevOps practices can automate compliance checks and audits, ensuring that applications and infrastructure consistently meet regulatory standards. This reduces the burden on compliance teams and minimizes the risk of non-compliance. By adopting DevOps practices, Fintech companies can streamline audit processes, improve compliance posture and demonstrate a commitment to security and regulatory compliance. Automated documentation, compliance as code, continuous compliance checks, and robust logging and monitoring are key aspects of DevOps that contribute to audit facilitation in the Fintech industry.

DevOps pipelines can incorporate automated compliance checks and security scans into the CI/CD process. These checks verify that code changes adhere to regulatory standards and security best practices before being deployed into production. By integrating compliance checks into the development workflow, Fintech companies can proactively identify and address compliance issues, reducing the likelihood of audit findings.

Enhanced Collaboration

DevOps practices can greatly enhance collaboration within the Fintech industry by breaking down silos between development, operations, security and other teams, fostering a culture of communication, transparency and shared responsibility. DevOps fosters enhanced collaboration within the Fintech industry by promoting cross-functional teams, shared goals and objectives, automation and tooling, continuous feedback loops, a culture of learning and experimentation, CI/CD practices and security as code. By breaking down organizational barriers and fostering a collaborative culture, DevOps enables Fintech companies to deliver innovative and reliable financial services more effectively.

DevOps encourages the formation of cross-functional teams of members with diverse skill sets, including developers, operations engineers, security experts and business stakeholders. By working together in integrated teams, individuals gain a better understanding of each other's roles and responsibilities, leading to improved collaboration and faster problem-solving.

DevOps promotes the alignment of goals and objectives across different functional areas within the organization. Teams are encouraged to collaborate on defining common objectives, such as improving deployment frequency, enhancing system reliability or increasing security posture. Shared goals create a sense of unity and purpose, driving collaboration toward achieving common outcomes.

Transparency

DevOps practices promote transparency in the Fintech industry by encouraging open communication, visibility into processes and shared access to information across development, operations, security and other teams. By promoting open communication, shared visibility, transparent workflows, automated processes, IaC, audit trails, logging and collaborative decision-making, DevOps practices facilitate transparency in the Fintech industry. Transparency enables teams to work more effectively together, identify and address issues promptly and deliver high-quality financial services that meet the needs of customers and regulatory requirements.

DevOps promotes transparency in workflows by defining standardized processes and documenting workflows comprehensively. Teams follow clear, well-defined procedures for tasks such as code development, testing, deployment and incident response. Transparent workflows enable team members to understand their roles and responsibilities, identify bottlenecks and collaborate more effectively.

DevOps practices such as CI/CD promote transparency by automating the software delivery process and providing visibility into each stage of the pipeline. CI/CD pipelines enable teams to track the progress of code changes from development through testing to deployment. Automated tests, code reviews and deployment approvals ensure that changes are thoroughly validated and transparently communicated to stakeholders.

Security and Compliance

DevOps practices play a crucial role in ensuring security and compliance within the Fintech industry by integrating security measures into the software development and deployment process from the outset. DevOps promotes the concept of "security as code", where security controls, policies and best practices are codified alongside application code and infrastructure configurations. Security requirements are defined as code and automated security checks are integrated into the CI/CD pipeline. This ensures that security measures are consistently applied throughout the development lifecycle and can be automatically validated during deployments.

By integrating security into the software development lifecycle, automating security controls and compliance checks and promoting secure configuration management and access controls, DevOps practices help Fintech companies maintain a strong security posture and ensure compliance with regulatory requirements. This proactive approach to security and compliance reduces the risk of security breaches, protects sensitive data and enhances trust with customers and regulators.

Reduction in Downtime

The use of DevOps practices can lead to a reduction in downtime in the Fintech industry through several mechanisms that improve system reliability, fault tolerance and incident response. The adoption of DevOps practices enables Fintech companies to build more reliable, resilient and responsive systems that are less susceptible to downtime. By leveraging continuous monitoring, infrastructure automation, high availability architectures, incremental deployments, automated testing and incident response automation, DevOps helps organizations maintain high levels of service availability and minimize the impact of disruptions on their operations and customers.

DevOps emphasizes the implementation of robust monitoring and alerting systems that provide real-time visibility into the health and performance of applications and infrastructure components. Automated monitoring tools continuously track key performance indicators, such as response times, error rates and resource utilization. When anomalies or performance degradations are detected, alerts are triggered to notify operations teams, enabling them to respond promptly and prevent potential downtime.

DevOps encourages the automation of incident response processes to accelerate the detection, diagnosis and resolution of issues that may lead to downtime. Automated incident response playbooks define predefined response actions, escalation procedures and communication channels for different types of incidents. Incident response automation helps operations teams respond quickly to incidents, minimize downtime and restore service availability as soon as possible.

Better Forecasting

DevOps practices can aid Fintech companies in making better forecasts by providing more accurate data, improving collaboration between teams, enhancing agility in responding to market changes and increasing overall efficiency. The use of DevOps practices enables Fintech companies to make better forecasts by improving data quality and availability, increasing agility and responsiveness, promoting collaborative decision-making, incorporating continuous feedback loops, enhancing scalability and elasticity, mitigating risks and fostering a culture of continuous improvement. By leveraging DevOps principles and tools, Fintech companies can enhance their forecasting capabilities and make more informed decisions to drive business success.

DevOps practices incorporate continuous feedback loops throughout the software development lifecycle, enabling teams to learn from past experiences and make data-driven decisions. Automated testing, monitoring and incident response processes provide valuable insights into system performance and user behavior, which can inform forecasting models and strategies. By iteratively refining forecasts based on feedback, Fintech companies can adapt to changing market dynamics more effectively.

Accelerated Time-to-Market

DevOps practices, such as CI/CD, automate the software development lifecycle, allowing for faster and more frequent releases. Fintech companies can respond quickly to market demands, regulatory changes and customer feedback, gaining a competitive edge by delivering new features and updates more rapidly.

Improved Collaboration and Communication

DevOps fosters collaboration between development, operations and other relevant teams, breaking down silos and improving communication. Enhanced collaboration ensures that everyone involved in the software development process has a shared understanding of goals and requirements, leading to more effective and efficient workflows.

Enhanced Efficiency and Automation

Automation of repetitive tasks, such as testing, deployment and infrastructure provisioning, reduces manual errors and accelerates processes. Fintech organizations can achieve greater operational efficiency, freeing up resources to focus on innovation and addressing higher-value tasks.

Increased Reliability and Stability

DevOps practices emphasize IaC and automated testing, ensuring consistent and reliable deployment of applications and infrastructure. Financial systems benefit from improved stability, reduced downtime and fewer disruptions to services, contributing to a more reliable customer experience.

Scalability and Flexibility

DevOps enables Fintech organizations to design and build scalable architectures that can adapt to changes in user demand. The ability to scale infrastructure resources dynamically ensures that financial services can handle varying workloads without compromising performance.

Security Integration (DevSecOps)

DevOps practices incorporate security measures throughout the software development lifecycle, promoting a culture of security awareness. By integrating security into the DevOps pipeline (DevSecOps), Fintech companies can proactively address security vulnerabilities, comply with regulations and build robust, secure financial systems.

Cost Savings

Automation and efficiency improvements lead to cost savings by reducing manual labor, minimizing errors and optimizing resource utilization. Fintech organizations can allocate resources more effectively, improving cost management and focusing on strategic initiatives.

Auditability and Compliance

DevOps practices provide audit trails and traceability of changes, essential for compliance with regulatory requirements. Fintech companies can demonstrate adherence to industry regulations and standards through automated documentation and reporting.

Continuous Monitoring and Improvement

DevOps includes robust monitoring solutions that provide real-time visibility into the performance of applications and infrastructure. Continuous monitoring allows for prompt identification and resolution of issues, contributing to ongoing improvement and optimization of financial systems.

Innovation Enablement

DevOps encourages a culture of experimentation and innovation by providing a framework for rapid and iterative development. Fintech organizations can experiment with new features, technologies and business models, fostering innovation in the rapidly evolving financial services landscape.

In conclusion, the adoption of DevOps in the Fintech industry offers a comprehensive set of benefits, ranging from accelerated time-to-market and enhanced collaboration to improved reliability, security and cost-effectiveness. These advantages collectively contribute to the industry's ability to meet customer expectations, regulatory requirements and competitive challenges.

Case Study – How Stripes Uses DevOps

One example of a Fintech company that uses DevOps is Stripe. Stripe is a payment processing company that provides businesses with a suite of tools to accept and manage online payments. They use DevOps to streamline their development and deployment processes, ensuring that their services are reliable, secure and scalable.

DevOps is a set of practices that combines software development and IT operations to shorten the development life cycle and provide continuous delivery with high software quality.

Stripe's DevOps approach includes:

Continuous Integration (CI): Stripe uses CI to automatically build and test their code changes whenever a developer pushes code to their repository. This helps them to identify and fix any issues early in the development cycle, reducing the risk of errors and bugs in the final product.

Continuous Deployment (CD): Stripe uses CD to automate the deployment of their code changes to production. This helps them to quickly and efficiently deploy their software updates, improving their time-to-market and ensuring that their customers always have access to the latest features and improvements.

IaC: Stripe uses IaC to manage their infrastructure through code. This allows them to automate the provisioning and management of their servers, reducing the risk of human error and ensuring that their infrastructure is scalable, secure and reliable.

Monitoring and Feedback: Stripe uses monitoring and feedback tools to track the performance of their services and identify any issues or anomalies. This helps them to quickly identify and troubleshoot any problems and ensure that their services are always available and performing optimally.

Overall, Stripe's use of DevOps enables them to rapidly develop and deploy new features and improvements, while ensuring that their services are reliable, secure and scalable. By combining development and operations, they are able to streamline their processes, reduce errors and delays and improve their time-to-market, making them a leader in the Fintech industry.

Case Study Questions

1. What is DevOps? How is it used in the Fintech industry?
2. Explain how Stripes is using DevOps to streamline its functioning.
3. What are the advantages and disadvantages of using DevOps in Fintech? What should be the strategy for using DevOps in Fintech?

Further Reading

Townson, S. (2020). AI Can Make Bank Loans More Fair. Harvard Business Review. https://hbr.org/2020/11/ai-can-make-bank-loans-more-fair

Desai, M.A. (2023). What the Finance Industry Tells Us About the Future of AI. Harvard Business Review. https://hbr.org/2023/08/what-the-finance-industry-tells-us-about-the-future-of-AI

References

Bécue, A., Praça, I., & Gama, J. (2021). Artificial Intelligence, cyber-threats and Industry 4.0: Challenges and opportunities. *Artificial Intelligence Review*, 54(5), 3849–3886.

Binner, J. M., Kendall, G., & Chen, S. H. (2004). *Applications of Artificial Intelligence in finance and economics*. Emerald Group Publishing Limited.

Cao, L. (2022). AI in finance: Challenges, techniques, and opportunities. *ACM Computing Surveys (CSUR)*, 55(3), 1–38.

Cohen, G. (2022). Algorithmic trading and financial forecasting using advanced Artificial Intelligence methodologies. *Mathematics*, 10(18), 3302.

Han, J., Huang, Y., Liu, S., & Towey, K. (2020). Artificial Intelligence for anti-money laundering: A review and extension. *Digital Finance*, 2(3), 211–239.

Hassan, M., Aziz, L. A. R., & Andriansyah, Y. (2023). The role Artificial Intelligence in modern banking: An exploration of AI-driven approaches for enhanced fraud prevention, risk management, and regulatory compliance. *Reviews of Contemporary Business Analytics*, 6(1), 110–132.

Kediya, S. O., Dhote, S., Singh, D. K., Bidve, V. S., Pathan, S., Mohare, R. V., & Suchak, A. (2023). Are AI and chat bots services effects the psychology of users in banking services and financial sector. *Journal for ReAttach Therapy and Developmental Diversities*, 6(9s(2)), 191–197.

Königstorfer, F., & Thalmann, S. (2020). Applications of Artificial Intelligence in commercial banks – a research agenda for behavioral finance. *Journal of Behavioural and Experimental Finance*, 27, 100352.

Martínez-Rojas, A., Sánchez-Oliva, J., López-Carnicer, J. M., & Jiménez-Ramírez, A. (2021, August). Airpa: An architecture to support the execution and maintenance of AI-powered RPA robots. In *International Conference on Business Process Management* (pp. 38–48). Springer International Publishing, Cham.

Moro, S., Cortez, P., & Rita, P. (2016). An automated literature analysis on data mining applications to credit risk assessment. In *Artificial Intelligence in financial markets: Cutting edge applications for risk management, portfolio optimization and economics* (pp. 161–177). Palgrave Macmillan.

Sadok, H., Sakka, F., & El Maknouzi, M. E. H. (2022). Artificial Intelligence and bank credit analysis: A review. *Cogent Economics & Finance*, 10(1), 2023262.

Sheth, J. N., Jain, V., Roy, G., & Chakraborty, A. (2022). AI-driven banking services: The next frontier for a personalised experience in the emerging market. *International Journal of Bank Marketing*, 40(6), 1248–1271.

Tadoori, G., & Guguloth, Y. (2019, March). An introduction to quantamental investing. In *Two Day National Seminar on FinTech Adoption in the Indian BFSI Sector-Opportunities and Challenges* (pp. 19–20). Professional Book Publishers.

Van Merode, H. (2023). *Continuous Integration (CI) and Continuous Delivery (CD): A practical guide to designing and developing pipelines*. Apress LP.

Zheng, X. L., Zhu, M. Y., Li, Q. B., Chen, C. C., & Tan, Y. C. (2019). FinBrain: When finance meets AI 2.0. *Frontiers of Information Technology & Electronic Engineering*, 20(7), 914–924.

Zhou, J. (2022). DevOps: Speeding up financial applications delivery to the market. In *The future and FinTech: ABCDI and beyond* (pp. 391–422). World Scientific Publication.

12 The Future of Fintech Industry

After reading this chapter you will:

- Know how the Fintech industry is shaping up
- Know how the Fintech industry is facing the challenges of decentralized finance (DeFi)
- Understand how Fintech companies are applying technologies like artificial intelligence, machine learning and blockchain
- Know how the generative AI is going to influence financial transactions in the future
- Know how the Metaverse is going to influence financial transactions in the future

Apple Pay is a mobile payment and digital wallet service offered by Apple Inc. that allows users to make payments in person, through their various iOS apps and on the web. Apple Pay was launched in 2014 in the USA and has since expanded to other countries.

Apple Pay has become one of the biggest Fintech companies in the world due to its widespread adoption and integration with other Apple products and services. Apple Pay has over 500 million users worldwide. Apple Pay's success can be attributed to several factors, including its ease of use, security and convenience.

It offers a seamless and secure payment experience for users. With just a touch or a glance, users can make payments without the need for physical cards or cash. This convenience has made it a popular choice among consumers. Additionally, Apple Pay has partnered with various merchants and banks to expand its reach and availability. This has helped it gain a significant market share in the Fintech industry.

Furthermore, Apple Pay's integration with the iPhone's biometric authentication features, such as Touch ID and Face ID, adds an extra layer of security, making it even more appealing to users. Apple Pay also offers a range of features, such as the ability to store loyalty cards, boarding passes and tickets, making it a one-stop shop for all payment needs. Apple Pay has also partnered with several banks and financial institutions to offer additional services, such as credit cards and loans. Apple Pay's integration with other Apple products, such as the iPhone, Apple Watch and iPad, has also contributed to its success.

Overall, Apple Pay's combination of convenience, security and partnerships has contributed to its success and made it the biggest Fintech company in the world. Apple Pay has become a key player in the Fintech industry, and its success has inspired other tech giants to enter the space.

DOI: 10.4324/9781032699417-12

The Emerging Trends in the Global Fintech Industry

The Fintech sector has experienced significant growth in the past ten years, propelled by technological advancements and shifts in consumer behavior. As per report published by McKinsey, the Fintech companies have reached a market capitalization of $550 billion in 2023, representing a growth of more than 100% in the past five years. There are more than 272 Fintech Unicorns, whose total valuation is $936 billion (McKinsey, 2023).

Fintech companies are growing at an exponential growth rate. The mechanism of financial services is undergoing rapid transformation with the advent of technology. Digital payments have started replacing physical modes of financial transactions powered by PayTech companies like Apple Pay, Google Pay, Paytm, Alipay and Amazon Pay. Artificial intelligence (AI) and machine learning will have a substantial impact on the future of Fintech by enhancing fraud detection, risk assessment and customer service. The industry is poised to be significantly influenced by blockchain technology, which has the capacity to enhance the security and efficiency of financial transactions. In general, the outlook for Fintech appears promising, with numerous groundbreaking innovations that are expected to reshape the contours of the competitive landscape (KPMG, 2023).

The increasing complexity of regulatory requirements will drive the adoption of RegTech solutions. Fintech companies will leverage technology to streamline compliance processes, manage risks and ensure adherence to evolving regulatory standards. Automation and AI will play a crucial role in managing compliance efficiently, reducing costs and mitigating risks associated with regulatory changes (Anagnostopoulos, 2018).

The acceptance and adoption of cryptocurrencies, including Bitcoin and Ethereum, will continue to grow. Central banks worldwide are exploring the development of their digital currencies (CBDCs) to enhance financial stability and improve payment systems. Fintech companies will play a pivotal role in developing innovative solutions around digital currencies and blockchain-based financial infrastructure (Vigna & Casey, 2016).

Fintech will contribute to improved financial inclusion, especially in emerging markets where traditional banking services are less accessible. Mobile banking, digital wallets and innovative lending models will empower individuals and businesses in underserved regions, fostering economic growth (King, 2018).

The utilization of blockchain technology is anticipated to fundamentally transform the manner in which financial transactions are executed. Blockchain technology offers a means of conducting transactions that is both safe and transparent, resulting in increased efficiency. This eliminates the necessity for intermediaries and fosters more confidence among participants. The rise of blockchain and decentralized finance (DeFi) will challenge traditional banking models. DeFi platforms leverage blockchain to offer decentralized lending, borrowing and trading services without traditional intermediaries. Smart contracts and blockchain technology will play a pivotal role in creating transparent, efficient and secure financial ecosystems (Lightspeed, 2024).

PayTech is poised to gain more popularity in the coming days as customers cease to go to banks and use their mobile phones more frequently to make payments. Technologies like quick response code-based payments, near-field communication and unified payment interface (UPI)-based payments are going to grow in magnitude in days to come. These technologies will empower individuals to effectively and proficiently oversee their funds. The focus will now be on mechanisms to provide robust security to ensure that bank accounts and digital wallets are not hacked. Blockchain technology and tokenization of cards may provide the necessary protection against hacking and phishing activities. The implementation of open banking and application programming interface (API) integration would facilitate the collaboration between Fintech startups and traditional financial institutions, thereby offering consumers a wider range of comprehensive and integrated financial services (FinTech Times, 2023).

Open banking initiatives, facilitated by the use of APIs, will become more widespread. This trend fosters collaboration and data sharing between financial institutions, Fintech firms and third-party developers. Customers will have greater control over their financial data, allowing them to use diverse financial services seamlessly through integrated platforms. The rise of Neobanks will foster the growing demand for instant banking, where the customers will demand instant payments, instant loans, instant investments and on-demand insurance to cater to different needs. This will also see the popularity of innovative offerings like non-fungible tokens, smart contracts, buy now pay later (BNPL) schemes, algorithmic trading and pay-as-you-drive insurance schemes (Bhattacharjee, Chung & Singh, 2022).

AI and machine learning are anticipated to have a substantial impact on the future of Fintech. These technologies will empower Fintech companies to analyze immense quantities of data, enhance decision-making and offer tailored services to consumers. AI will continue to enhance customer experiences through personalized services. AI-driven chatbots and virtual assistants will become more sophisticated, providing tailored financial advice and assistance. Predictive analytics will empower Fintech companies to anticipate customer needs, enabling the development of personalized financial products and services (Arti, 2023).

With the increasing digitization of financial services, cybersecurity will be a top priority. Fintech companies will invest heavily in advanced cybersecurity measures to protect sensitive financial data and ensure customer trust. Privacy concerns will lead to the development of more secure and privacy-focused technologies, emphasizing user consent and data protection.

The Fintech industry will have to align with the growing emphasis on environmental, social and governance (ESG) considerations. Fintech firms will have to incorporate sustainable finance practices, providing customers with ESG-focused investment options and promoting responsible financial behavior. Fintech companies will also have to increasingly form ecosystems and collaborate with various stakeholders, including other Fintech firms, traditional banks, technology companies and regulators. Ecosystems will enable seamless integration of financial services, creating a holistic customer experience that goes beyond traditional banking boundaries (Wang, Peng, Tang & Wu, 2022).

These themes, along with others, are predicted to determine the future of the Fintech industry as companies in this sector continue to develop and disrupt the financial services industry. The future of the Fintech industry holds exciting possibilities driven by technological innovation, regulatory developments and changing consumer expectations. As Fintech continues to evolve, it will play a central role in shaping the future of finance, offering more inclusive, efficient and personalized financial services to individuals and businesses globally. The potential and applications for Fintech are extensive, and it will be fascinating to observe how this sector further revolutionizes the financial services business (McKinsey, 2023).

Growth of the Global Fintech Industry

Macroeconomic factors are driving the rise of Fintech companies and the wider financial services ecosystem. The prevalence of digital adoption has transitioned from being a mere inquiry to an undeniable fact. Currently, around 73% of global interactions with banks occur via digital means (McKinsey, 2023).

Furthermore, retail consumers worldwide now possess an equivalent degree of contentment and confidence in Fintech companies as they do in established banks. In 2021, McKinsey surveyed retail consumers and found that 41% of them expressed their intention to expand their usage of Fintech products. There is a greater demand and necessity for Fintech goods in developing economies. In 2022, Africa possessed almost 800 million mobile accounts, accounting for approximately 50% of the global total (McKinsey, 2023).

By 2030, the Fintech industry is estimated to reach a valuation of $1.5 trillion. Banking Fintechs are projected to make up around 25% of all banking valuations globally by 2030 (McKinsey, 2023). The growth in the Fintech Industry will be driven by innovation, technology adoption and financial inclusion (McKinsey, 2023).

In the last ten years, advancements and creativity in technology have propelled the Fintech industry from the outskirts to the leading position in financial services. The rise has been rapid and intense, driven by the strong expansion of the banking sector, swift digitization, evolving customer expectations and growing backing from investors and authorities. In recent years, Fintech companies have significantly transformed specific aspects of financial services through their inventive, unique and customer-focused offerings; cooperative corporate structures; and versatile and adaptable staff (Darshanbhai, 2023).

The growth in the Fintech sector is led by cryptocurrencies. After a downfall in 2022, the cryptocurrency market has recorded a sharp recovery in 2024. Bitcoin fell down by 42% in 2022, but rose from a level of $16,664 on February 1, 2023, to $72,831 on March 12, 2024, which is a whopping increase of 337%. This rise is attributed to the launch of Bitcoin exchange-traded funds (BTC-ETF) and the Bitcoin halving event that is expected to happen in April 2024. Ethereum (ETH) has also shown a spectacular rise from $1,500 in March 2023 to $4,024 on March 12, 2024, which is also a whopping increase of 337%. The cryptocurrencies are now all set to pose a tough challenge to Central Bank Digital Currency (CBDC), which many governments like China and India have launched to facilitate payments (Tambe & Jain, 2024).

With the rise of DeFi, the peer-to-peer (P2P) lending market has also seen a spectacular rise. The P2P lending business is growing with a compounded annual growth rate (CAGR) of 30%. The P2P lending companies are offering attractive returns of 12% to 16% to the investors which is much ahead of the return on investment offered by banks. For a borrower, P2P borrowing is attractive as it involves less paperwork and the processing time is much faster. The P2P lending companies in India are managing investments of more than $500 million, while globally the turnover is more than $90 billion (Precedence Research, 2023).

Wealth Management has gone through a drastic overhaul with the advent of WealthTech. Investors who had lost faith in personal finance managers are now taking the services of bots, algorithm-based trading and robotic process advisors for investing their money. The automated processes are delivering more swiftness, accuracy and 24/7 support in comparison to their human counterparts (Botha, 2023). The rise of WealthTech has been phenomenal, transforming the way investors oversee and enhance their wealth. By harnessing technology, WealthTech platforms have made wealth management services more accessible, personalized and user-friendly. The sector's exponential growth is a testament to the growing demand for innovative financial solutions and the disruptive potential of technology in the financial industry. As the sector progresses, it holds the potential to democratize wealth (Hasan, Al-Okaily, Choudhury & Kayani, 2023).

The insurance sector has traditionally carried the stigma of doing push marketing and dumping the wrong insurance products on gullible customers to earn attractive commissions. Now the insurance sector has become more customer-friendly and offers insurance-on-demand and pay-as-you-drive insurance schemes. The collection of information for enrolling in insurance and claim processing has become very fast with the use of big data, AI and blockchain technology. The global on-demand insurance market is expected to grow at a compound annual growth rate of 21.2% from 2023 to 2030 to reach US$ 4.33 billion by 2030 (Grand View Research, 2023).

To take advantage of this demand, Fintech companies will need to stay updated with rapidly changing rules and ensure they have sufficient resources and capability to adhere to them. Several European Union member states, including Ireland, are subjecting BNPL firms to financial regulation. Simultaneously, the US Consumer Financial Protection Bureau intends to release a proposed regulation regarding open banking this year. This regulation would mandate that financial firms reveal consumer data when requested by consumers. Fintechs must ensure they possess the requisite resources and capability to address these needs. This phenomenon is contributing to the growing demand for RegTech services, which is growing at a stupendous pace. The global RegTech market size was valued at $10.47 billion in 2022. The market is projected to grow from $12.82 billion in 2023 to $60.77 billion by 2030, growing at a CAGR of 24.9% (Fortune Business Insights, 2023).

In 2022, the banking industry produced over $6.5 trillion in revenues, experiencing growth in both volume and revenue margins compared to the previous year. Considering the dynamics of the Fintech business, it can be inferred that there is still ample opportunity for additional expansion in both public and private markets.

A significant portion of this revenue growth will be driven by emerging markets. Last year, Fintech revenues in Africa, Asia-Pacific (excluding China), Latin America and the Middle East accounted for 15% of worldwide Fintech revenues. According to McKinsey experts, the aggregate percentage is projected to climb to 29% by 2028. Conversely, North America, which presently represents 48% of global Fintech sales, is projected to reduce its share to 41% by 2028 (Barquin, Vinayak & Shrikhande, 2018).

Although Fintech penetration in emerging nations is currently the highest globally, its growing potential is emphasized by several factors. A significant number of these economies suffer from a lack of access to conventional banking services and have a substantial proportion of their population that is underbanked. Fintech companies have seen some success in addressing these unfulfilled requirements. According to reports, the adult population of Brazil has seen a significant increase in the usage of Nubank, a Fintech bank in Latin America. It is estimated that 46% of adults in Brazil already use Nubank, which is twice the percentage recorded two years ago (Sirota & Fratini, 2018).

Furthermore, although the market capitalization of private Fintech companies has experienced significant growth in the past ten years, their presence on the public market is still limited. From 2014 to October 2022, a total of 44 contemporary Fintech companies (established in 1999 or after) conducted an initial public offering (IPO), resulting in a collective market capitalization of $0.3 trillion. By comparison, within the same time frame, there existed over 2,500 traditional public financial institutions (established on average in 1926) with a total market capitalization of $11.1 trillion (McKinsey, 2023).

According to McKinsey's study, Fintechs represented 5% (equivalent to $150 billion to $205 billion) of the net revenue generated by the worldwide banking system in 2022. Projections suggest that this portion might surge to over $400 billion by 2028, indicating a yearly growth rate of 15% in Fintech income between 2022 and 2028. This is three times higher than the approximately 6% growth rate of the whole banking business (McKinsey, 2023).

Generative AI and the Future of Banking

To maintain their competitive edge, Fintech companies must persist in their pursuit of innovation. There is always some imminent and significant agent of disruption on the horizon. Generative AI technologies are expected to profoundly transform the competitive environment of the banking industry in the coming decade (Polishchuk, 2023).

The scarcity of available labor has also increased the difficulty for Fintech companies to attract and recruit skilled technology professionals. According to a Fintech executive headquartered in Europe, Fintechs are currently less appealing due to the increased recognition that it is a high-risk profession compared to traditional banks. Conversely, significant Fintech companies are reducing their workforce, which can result in the availability of a fresh talent pool to entice (Vaganova, Bykanova, Gordya & Evdokimov, 2021).

Within this context, Fintech companies must strive to enhance their organizational culture and mission and, as a result, refine their approach to recruitment. For instance, a particular European payment Fintech company has implemented distinct techniques that are tailored to the specific requirements of different job positions.

The Fintech business is experiencing a significant transformation, requiring its participants to adapt to ensure their survival. The approaches will differ based on the Fintech's level of development and its specific industry and geographical focus. Quantified expansion will be derived from a consistent foundation. The necessity will be to prioritize the establishment of a robust and secure core business with a well-defined and validated market fit before pursuing expansion, instead of attempting to simultaneously develop and reinforce the core (Ünsal, Öztekin, Çavuş & Özdemir, 2020).

Fintech Landscape in India

The worldwide financial services business has been greatly revolutionized by Fintech, which has been made possible by the use of developing technologies and innovative solutions. India is currently at the forefront of the Fintech adoption race, boasting an acceptance rate of 87%, which is far higher than the global average of 64%. By 2030, it is projected that the Indian Fintech market will achieve assets under management worth $1 trillion and generate revenue of $200 billion. The Indian Fintech ecosystem has established itself as a powerful global presence and is consistently expanding to become one of the largest Fintech marketplaces worldwide (Stobdan & Kumar, 2024).

The expansion of the Indian Fintech sector is supported by various initiatives implemented by the government and regulators, a favorable funding environment and a robust venture capital ecosystem. Additionally, the significant demographic opportunities, widespread adoption of Fintech and availability of technology and talent contribute to the growth of entrepreneurs targeting the emerging Indian market. There are a few other considerations. The challenges encompassed in this statement are potential risks to data security and privacy in partnership situations, uneven adoption of digital financial services among different demographic groups, a lack of financial knowledge and awareness, underperformance of IPOs, geopolitical and macroeconomic events that make institutional investors hesitant to make significant investments (which is evident in the funding trends of the first half of 2022) and the rapid changes in regulations that keep Fintech companies alert and responsive.

Despite the hurdles, the Fintech industry offers significant opportunities. The government continues to prioritize financial inclusion due to the limited presence of traditional financial services providers in rural areas, among the aging population, in unorganized sectors and among gig workers. Fintech companies have the opportunity to capitalize on improved client experiences and the demand for specialized products, such as innovative Neobanking models. Insurance and wealth have experienced a promising increase, although their market penetration is still low. The Fintech business has experienced significant growth due to favorable market conditions and proactive regulatory bodies. Fintech companies have successfully attracted highly skilled individuals from other industries, which will continue to contribute to their ongoing success (Haralayya, 2021).

India's Fintech sector has witnessed a remarkable increase in funding in recent years, drawing substantial investment from prominent venture capital and private equity organizations. Fintech companies leveraged the increasing need for the digitalization of financial services during the COVID-19 pandemic. The Indian Fintech market attracted a total investment of $8 billion in 2021, resulting in the emergence of more than 15 Fintech unicorns during the year.

The Way Forward

Financial inclusion and education will be propelled by the deployment of digital technology in the financial services sector. The objective of digitalization and the growing prevalence of Fintech is to extend financial services to the underserved population.

Banking institutions and financial technology (Fintech) companies are expected to collaborate to develop highly personalized products. Banks will leverage their existing customer base and regulatory expertise, while also taking advantage of Fintech's agility and customer-centric approach to deliver innovative and customer-focused offerings.

Ecosystem business models are expected to undergo transformation. Ecosystem business models involve the creation of products and services through collaboration, targeting a shared consumer base. This approach generates additional value and enhances the overall customer experience (FinTech Times, 2023).

The potential for further expansion in the InsurTech industry is immense. The integration of technology into insurance processes will lead to greater customization and transparency, which in turn will decrease apprehension and increase the need for insurance. The utilization of bundling with other services is anticipated to be a significant means of accessing client demand for insurance and enhancing both awareness and sales of insurance products.

The evolving rules will prioritize both the expansion of the market and the establishment of secure trading environments. In most of the countries, the regulatory framework has been designed to promote the adoption of Fintech by implementing standards and laws that are interactive and flexible. These policies are continuously evolving to keep up with the changing market conditions and prioritize the needs of the customers. The regulations in the Indian Fintech sector prioritize general growth and the establishment of secure marketplaces, while also following an iterative approach.

The increasing development of the Fintech ecosystem has combined the consolidation of the digital experience of financial services within one of the largest marketplaces. This demonstrates self-assurance and fosters confidence in international markets regarding the proficiency of the Fintech industry. The implementation of an account aggregator has the potential to greatly influence the lending and other financial services sector, potentially leading to a huge breakthrough in the Fintech industry, similar to the impact of the UPI.

Case Study – Banking and Financial Services in Metaverse

The Metaverse is a digital universe that exists parallel to the physical world, accessible through virtual reality (VR), augmented reality (AR) and the Internet. It is essentially a collective virtual shared space where users can interact with each other, digital objects and the computer-generated environment in real time. The Metaverse has the potential to revolutionize various industries and banking and financial services are no exception.

The Metaverse is an innovative way for people to interact with emerging technologies, including but not limited to VR and AR. It has led to the creation of a digital economy, where goods can be created and acquired virtually. The Metaverse has the potential to permeate traditional sectors, including finance.

In the Metaverse, users may utilize digital wallets to store both traditional and digital assets, including cryptocurrencies. Cryptocurrencies like Bitcoin and Ethereum might play a significant role in Metaverse transactions. Traditional banks or new entities could establish a virtual presence in the Metaverse.

Virtual banks might offer a range of financial services, including virtual account management, lending and investment opportunities. Smart contracts could facilitate automated and secure financial transactions within the Metaverse. DeFi platforms might offer services such as lending, borrowing and trading of digital assets.

Metaverse could host virtual stock exchanges and trading platforms where users can buy and sell virtual assets. These platforms might integrate real-time market data and allow users to execute trades in a simulated environment. Virtual assets and properties within the Metaverse may require insurance coverage. Companies could offer virtual insurance products for virtual assets and liabilities.

Virtual real estate within the Metaverse may become a significant asset class. Financial institutions could facilitate investments in virtual properties, generating income and potential capital gains for investors. The Metaverse could simplify cross-border transactions, allowing users to transfer digital assets seamlessly across borders. Blockchain and cryptocurrency technologies might facilitate faster and more cost-effective international transactions.

As with any digital space, ensuring the security and privacy of financial transactions and user data is crucial. Developing a regulatory framework for financial activities within the Metaverse is essential to protect users and ensure compliance with existing financial regulations. Bridging the Metaverse with the physical world's financial infrastructure and regulatory frameworks may pose challenges.

The success of banking and financial services in the Metaverse depends on user adoption and their willingness to trust and use virtual financial platforms. The development of banking and financial services within the Metaverse is an evolving landscape, and it's crucial to stay updated on the latest developments in technology, regulation and user behavior to understand its full potential and impact.

Banking and financial services in the Metaverse are a rapidly developing area that offers new opportunities and challenges for the financial industry. The Metaverse is a virtual world that is becoming increasingly popular, and it is expected to have a significant impact on the way we live, work and interact with each other.

One of the key opportunities for banking and financial services in the Metaverse is the ability to offer new and innovative products and services to customers. For example, virtual banks can offer virtual accounts, virtual credit cards and virtual loans to users, allowing them to manage their finances in a completely virtual environment.

Another opportunity is the ability to provide a more seamless and convenient customer experience. In the Metaverse, users can interact with banks and financial institutions in real time, using avatars and virtual environments to access and manage their accounts. This can reduce the need for customers to visit physical branches, saving them time and money.

However, there are also challenges that the financial industry must address when providing services in the Metaverse. One of the biggest challenges is ensuring the security and privacy of user data. As virtual transactions become more common, it is essential to ensure that sensitive information is protected from hackers and other cybercriminals.

Another challenge is ensuring compliance with regulatory requirements. Financial institutions must ensure that they comply with all applicable laws and regulations when providing services in the Metaverse. This may require significant investments in legal and compliance teams to ensure that the institution is meeting all requirements.

Overall, the Metaverse presents both opportunities and challenges for the banking and financial services industry. As the Metaverse continues to grow and evolve, it is likely that financial institutions will need to adapt and develop new strategies to remain competitive and provide the best possible service to their customers.

Metaverse technology enables banks to establish virtual branches where customers can interact with banking services, staff and advisors in immersive virtual environments. These virtual branches offer services ranging from account management and loan applications to financial consultations, all within the Metaverse. The employment of VR and AR during COVID-19 and remote work conditions enabled greater collaboration in teleconferencing where professionals used annotating, chatting and screen-sharing features, allowing them to work efficiently while not in the same physical space 1. VR and AR can also be used by financiers in individual capacities, particularly with data visualization, aiding them in analyzing financial risks and providing more precise services to customers.

The Metaverse's ability to create virtual environments for people to connect may severely impact the financial industry. Virtual environments can be used in consumer-oriented manners. The creation of digital shopping environments in the Metaverse acts as a hub for companies to reach a wider range of consumers without geographical constraints, allowing for greater exposure. Such virtual shopping hubs can employ digital payment means so that transactions take place entirely within the realm of the Metaverse. Through digital means, financial advisors can provision for greater convenience, signifying a shift in the industry and broadening the scope of the services clients can be provided with, such as AR being used to simulate different financial scenarios so that customers can visualize them with ease.

The Metaverse is an exciting new frontier for the banking industry, providing a platform for digital identity management, virtual investments and financial education. By leveraging the power of the Metaverse, banks can transform the way customers interact with financial services and create new revenue streams in the process. However, there are several questions to address before *exploring the Metaverse's potential to permeate traditional sectors including finance. Firstly, will the Metaverse enhance existing customer experiences where it is implemented, or will it lead to the creation of new ones? Will it be swiftly adopted by customers, or will its imposition cause friction? Has market research been conducted to ascertain this? Finally, considering that the imposition of more technology is not always the answer, can the Metaverse's impact on business outcomes be quantified compared to existing technological infrastructure?*

Case Study Questions

1. Explain how Metaverse is impacting and reshaping the banking and financial services industry (BFSI) sector.
2. What are the innovative strategies required to make the BFSI sector successful in the Metaverse? Explain.
3. What do you think is the future of the Fintech Industry in the context of rapid technological advancement? Explain.

Further Reading

"Fintechs: A new paradigm of growth" – A McKinsey Report by Lindsay Anan, Alexis Krivkovich, Marie-Claude Nadeau, Diego Castellanos Isaza, Fernando Figueiredo, Tunde Olanrewaju, Max Flötotto, André Jerenz, Zaccaria Orlando and Alessia Vassallo.
www.mckinsey.com/industries/financial-services/our-insights/fintechs-a-new-paradigm-of-growth
"Seven key trends shaping the future of FinTech industry" An E&Y Report by Nilesh Naker, www.ey.com/en_in/consulting/seven-key-trends-shaping-the-future-of-fintech-industry

References

Arti. (2023). Top 10 AI applications in FinTech industry. *Analytics Insight*. www.analyticsinsight.net/top-10-ai-applications-in-fintech-industry

Barquin, S., Vinayak, H. V., & Shrikhande, D. (2018). *Reaching Asia's Digital Banking Customers*. McKinsey Quarterly.

Bhattacharjee, A., Chung, V., & Singh, S. (2022). Building a winning AI Neobank. *McKinsey*. www.mckinsey.com/industries/financial-services/our-insights/building-a-winning-ai-neobank

Botha, F. (2023). Growth and investment into family office WealthTech. *Forbes*. www.forbes.com/sites/francoisbotha/2023/11/17/growth-and-investment-into-family-office-wealthtech/?

Darshanbhai, P. N. (2023). FinTech as a driver of the financial market's creative growth, *International Journal of Law Management and Humanities*, 6, 396.

FinTech Times. (2023). PayTech in 2024. *FinTech Times*. https://thefintechtimes.com/2024-paytech-predictions-with-intix-brite-ppro-emerchantpay-valopa-bottomline-primer

Fortune Business Insights. (2023). RegTech market size, share & Covid19 impact analysis. *Fortune Business Insights*. www.fortunebusinessinsights.com/regtech-market-108305

Grand View Research. (2023). On-demand insurance market size, share & trends analysis report by coverage. *Grand View Research*. www.grandviewresearch.com/industry-analysis/on-demand-insurance-market-report

Haralayya, B. (2021). How digital banking has brought innovative products and services to India. *Journal of Advanced Research in Quality Control and Management*, 6(1), 16–18.

Hasan, F., Al-Okaily, M., Choudhury, T., & Kayani, U. (2023). A comparative analysis between FinTech and traditional stock markets: Using Russia and Ukraine war data. *Electronic Commerce Research*, 1–26.

King, B. (2018). *Bank 4.0: Banking everywhere, never at a bank*. John Wiley & Sons.
KPMG. (2023). Pulse of FinTech – 2023. *KPMG*. https://kpmg.com/xx/en/home/industries/financial-services/pulse-of-fintech.
Lightspeed. (2024). FinTech 2024: Innovation meets consolidation. *Lightspeed*. https://lsvp.com/stories/fintech-2024-innovation-meets-consolidation
McKinsey. (2023). FinTechs: A new paradigm of growth. *McKinsey Quarterly*. www.mckinsey.com/industries/financial-services/our-insights/fintechs-a-new-paradigm-of-growth
Polishchuk, Y. (2023). FinTech future trends. In *The European digital economy* (p. 204). Taylor and Francis.
Precedence Research. (2023). Peer-to-Peer (P2P) lending market. *Precedence Research*. www.precedenceresearch.com/peer-to-peer-lending-market
Sirota, F., & Fratini, G. (2018). *A Case about Nubank: The Story of an Innovative FinTech in Brazil*. Scuola di Ingegneria Industriale e dell'Informazione.
Stobdan, J., & Kumar, S. (2024). Advancements in the Indian FinTech landscape. In *Exploring global FinTech advancement and applications* (pp. 109–120). IGI Global.
Tambe, N., & Jain, A. (2024). Why is the crypto market rising today? *Forbes*. www.forbes.com/advisor/in/investing/cryptocurrency/why-is-crypto-going-up
Ünsal, E., Öztekin, B., Çavuş, M., & Özdemir, S. (2020, October). Building a FinTech ecosystem: Design and development of a FinTech API gateway. In *2020 International Symposium on Networks, Computers and Communications (ISNCC)* (pp. 1–5). IEEE.
Vaganova, O., Bykanova, N., Gordya, D., & Evdokimov, D. (2021). Growth points of Fintech industry in the perception of financial market transformation. In *Finance, entrepreneurship and technologies in digital economy*, edited by N. Lomakin (Vol. 103, pp. 435–441). European Publisher.
Vigna, P., & Casey, M. J. (2016). *The age of cryptocurrency: How bitcoin and the blockchain are challenging the global economic order*. Picador Publisher.
Wang, D., Peng, K., Tang, K., & Wu, Y. (2022). Does FinTech development enhance corporate ESG performance? Evidence from an emerging market. *Sustainability*, 14(24), 16597.

Index

Page numbers in *italic* indicate a figure and page numbers in **bold** indicate a table on the corresponding page.

Accel Partners 143
account-based CBDC 211
Acko 5, 143
AI *see* artificial intelligence (AI)
AIG 35
AIML *see* artificial intelligence and machine learning (AIML)
Airtel 6
Alameda Research 28
algorithmic trading 109; working mechanism of 110–111, *110*
AlgoTrader 120–121
Alibaba 55
Alipay 3, 55, 67
Alonzo 19
Alteryx 165–166
Amareos 5
Amazon 6, 35
Amazon Pay 7
AML *see* anti-money laundering (AML)
AMLD *see* Anti-Money Laundering Directive (AMLD)
Andresen, G. 14
Ant Group (Ant Financial) 4, 56, 67
anti-money laundering (AML) 85, 159, 164, 168–171; regulations 160; Screening and Monitoring Software 169
Anti-Money Laundering Directive (AMLD) 160
ANZ 30–31
API *see* application program interface (API)
Appian 163
Apple Inc. 6, 63
Apple Pay 63–65, 253
application program interface (API) 60–62, *61*; benefits of using 62–63
application-specific integrated circuits (ASICs) 16, 17, 24
artificial intelligence (AI): AI-based claims processing 145–146; applications in Fintech 237–251; automated customer service 240–241; for data automation/credit risk assessment 240; definition of 239; for detecting banking fraud 240; DevOps 243–250, *244*; financial forecasts 241–242; Fintech applications of 242–243; generative 258; innovation enablement 250; safety, increasing 240; user behavior analysis 241
artificial intelligence and machine learning (AIML) 83, 129, 146, 169; applications in RegTech 175
ASICs *see* application-specific integrated circuits (ASICs)
Aspiration 5
assets under management (AUM) 106, 121, 124
ATM *see* automated teller machines (ATM)
Attia, T. 151
AUM *see* assets under management (AUM)
automated customer service 240–241
automated teller machines (ATM) 55
Auxmoney 95–96
Avant 4
AXAXL 143
AxiomSL 164

Bagri, V. 201
BankBazaar 4
Banking, Financial Services and Insurance (BFSI) 6, 35, 39, 49
banking fraud detection, using AI 240
Bankman-Fried, S. 27, 28
Bansal, A. 152
Bansal, I. 106, 120
Barron, J. S. 55
Bear Sterns 11

Betterment 114
BFSI *see* Banking, Financial Services and Insurance (BFSI)
Bharat Bill Payment System 49
Bharat Interface for Money (BHIM) 4, 6, 47, 62, 68–69
BharatQR 49
Bhatt, B. 117
Bhatt, P. 125
BHIM *see* Bharat Interface for Money (BHIM)
big data analytics: RegTech 175; underwriting 144–145
BigID Inc. 178–179
Binance 26; Binance Chain 19; Binance Coin 19
Bisht, V. 201
"Bitcoin: A Peer-to-Peer Electronic Cash System" (Nakamoto) 12, 14, 32, 35
Bitcoin (BTC) 11, 12, 46; mining process 15–17, *16*; reward for **17**; rise of 14–15
Bitcoin Foundation 14
Bit Gold 12
Bitstamp 26
BitTorrent 78
blockchain 14, 30–52; advantages of 46–48; applications in RegTech 176; applications of 39–40; in banking, challenges of adopting 50–52; blocks in *33*; database *vs.* 34, **34**; definition of 33; disadvantages of 48; functionality of 38–39; future outlook of 49–50; history of 34–35; implementation of 48–49; origin of 32–33; types of 35–38
B-Money 12
BNPL *see* Buy Now Pay Later (BNPL)
Bogle, J. C. 114
Bombay Stock Exchange (BSE) 7
BSE *see* Bombay Stock Exchange (BSE)
BTC *see* Bitcoin (BTC)
Buterin, V. 17
Buy Now Pay Later (BNPL) 88–90, 99–100

Cabbage 4
CAGR *see* compounded annual growth rate (CAGR)
CAN-SPAM 160
Capgemini 39
Cardano 12, 19–20
Carroll, D. 121
Catamaran Ventures 143
CBDC *see* Central Bank Digital Currency (CBDC)
Central Bank Digital Currency (CBDC) 5–6, 206–235, 254; adoption of 226–228; advantages of 220–221; challenges of 220–221; cross-border 214–220, **216**; *vs.* cryptocurrency 228–230; development of 212; digital currency *vs.* 228; faster and cheaper payments 222–223; financial stability 223; future of 230–231; implementation in China 232–235; implementation in Europe 224–225; implementation in India 226; implementation in Japan 225; implementation in the USA 224; improved security 223; innovation, new opportunities for 223–224; need of 221–224; potential risks of 230; reduced costs of cash 222; types of 209–212; working model of 212–214, *213*
Central Bank of China 90
centralized exchanges (CEX) 25
CEX *see* centralized exchanges (CEX)
CFPB Regulation E 160
CFPB *see* Consumer Financial Protection Bureau (CFPB)
CFT *see* combating financial terrorism (CFT)
Chainalysis 180, 181
Chari, R. 71
Charles Schwab Corporation 115–116
chatbots 146–147
Chaum, D. L. 11
Cheque Truncation System 49
Chime 4, 5, 198
China, CDBC implementation in 232–235
CIBIL *see* Credit Information Bureau (India) Limited (CIBIL)
Coinbase 26
CoinDCX 26
Coinswitch 26
Collison, J. 65
Collison, P. 65
combating financial terrorism (CFT) 168, 172–173
commercial insurance 132
Compliance.ai 164
ComplyAdvantage 180
compounded annual growth rate (CAGR) 256, 257
comprehensive robo-advisors (CRA) 107, 109
computer vision 239
concessional loans 82–83
consortium blockchain 37–38
Consumer Financial Protection Bureau (CFPB) 90
counterterrorism financing (CTF) 172
COVID-19 pandemic 6, 27
CRA *see* comprehensive robo-advisors (CRA)
Credit Information Bureau (India) Limited (CIBIL) 76, 77, 168
credit risk assessment, AI for 240
Creditstar Group 92

Kumar, Raghu 119
Kumar, Ravi 119
Kuvera 124–125
KYC *see* know your customer (KYC)
KyoLab 5

Lakhani, K. R. 33
Laplanche, R. 91, 92
Lee, C. 24
legacy planning 104
legal expenditures 132
Lehman Brothers 11
Lemonade 5, 148
Lendbox 86
LenDen 39
Lendermarket 92–93
LendingClub 84, 85, 91–92
Lendingkart 4, 39, 86, 97–98
LendInvest 96–97
LendTech 2, 4, 39, 76–100, *83*; Buy Now Pay Later 88–90, 99–100; companies 91–98; concerns and debates of 90; invoice financing 86–87; P2P lending 84–86; sector, future of 91; Trade Receivable Discounting System 87–88
letter-of-credit (LoC) 48, 49
life insurance 131
Lightning Network 24
Linux Foundation 43, 44
Litecoin (LTC) 12, 24, 36
loans 77–78; concessional 82–83; demand 81–82; schemes, types of 80–83, *80*; secured 81; subsidized 82; unsecured 81
Loantap 4
LoC *see* letter-of-credit (LoC)

machine learning (ML) 239
Mallaya, V. 78
Markets in Financial Instruments Directive II (MiFID II) 161
Markus, B. 21
McNamara, F. 55
Mehta, R. 63
mempool 16
Merkle Trees 35
Metaverse, banking and financial services in 260–262
MetricStream 164
Mexican Central Bank 90
micro-investment services (MISs) 113
MiFID II *see* Markets in Financial Instruments Directive II (MiFID II)
Ministry of Finance, India 169
MISs *see* micro-investment services (MISs)
Mist 38
ML *see* machine learning (ML)
Mobikwik 7
Modi, N. 48–49, 78
Monese 5
Monetary Authority of Singapore 79
Moneytap 4
Monzo 5, 199
M-Pesa 69–70
mProfit 125
Musk, E. 22

Nadal, S. 42
Nakamoto, S. 6, 12–14, 27, 46; "Bitcoin: A Peer-to-Peer Electronic Cash System" 12, 14, 32, 35
Namecoin 12
National Automated Clearing House 49
National Payment Corporation of India (NPCI) 3, 6, 49, 68
National Security Agency: "How to Make a Mint: The Cryptography of Anonymous Electronic Cash" 11
National Stock Exchange (NSE) 7
natural language processing (NLP) 239
near-field communication (NFC) 60
Neobanking 2, 5, 185–204; account aggregation 188; advantages of 186; architecture *195*; banking-as-a-service 190; customized financial products 188; definition of 185–187; digital banks *vs.* 191–192; disadvantages of 186–187; features of 187–188; as flexible and scalable tech platforms 190; future of 202–203; hassle-free account creation 191; importance of 195–198, *196*; instant bank account 187; international payments 187, 191; marketing as strategic differentiator 190–191; mobile banking 188; operating model of 192–195; process flow diagram *194*; quick credit, loans and mortgages 188; remittances 187; smart reporting 191; spend management 188; traditional banks *vs.* 188–191, **189**; user-friendly interface 191; in world 198–202
NFC *see* near-field communication (NFC)
NFTs *see* non-fungible tokens (NFTs)
NICE Actimize 164
Nigam, S. 71
Nintex 163
Nirjar, A. 152
Niyo Neo 201
NLP *see* natural language processing (NLP)
Nominated PoS (NPoS) 23
Nonce 40
non-fungible tokens (NFTs) 18, 23, 38, 39, 45–46; commercial applications of 46
non-life insurance 131
NPCI *see* National Payment Corporation of India (NPCI)

NPoS *see* Nominated PoS (NPoS)
NSE *see* National Stock Exchange (NSE)
N26 200
Nutmeg 122–123

on-demand coverage 142–143
over-the-counter (OTC) exchanges 26

Palmer, J. 21
PAN *see* permanent account number (PAN)
Payment and Settlement Systems Act (2007) 161
payment business, evolution of 55–56
Payment Card Industry Data Security Standard 58
payment gateways 58, *59*
PayPal 3, 7
PayTech 2–3, 54–75; companies 63–72; future of 72
Paytm 3, 7–8, 47, 56, 67–68
Peercoin 12
peer-to-peer (P2P): insurance 142; lending 84–86; networks, history of 78
permanent account number (PAN) 76, 77
permissioned blockchains 36
personal identification number (PIN) 55
PhonePe 7, 47, 71–72
PIN *see* personal identification number (PIN)
PoH *see* proof of history (PoH)
Policybazaar 5, 152–153
Polkadot 19, 23
PoS *see* proof-of-stake (PoS)
PoW *see* proof-of-work (PoW)
PPBL *see* prohibit Paytm payments bank (PPBL)
PPI *see* prepaid instruments (PPI)
predictive analytics 239
prepaid instruments (PPI) 90
Prevention of Money Laundering Act (2002) 161
private blockchain 36–37
Procter & Gamble 35
professional liability insurance 132
prohibit Paytm payments bank (PPBL) 8
Project Dunbar 217
Project Icebreaker 218
Project Jasper 219–220
Project Jura 219
Project Mariana 218–219
Project mBridge 216–217
Project Nexus 220
Project Sela 217
proof of history (PoH) 22
proof-of-stake (PoS) 12, 19, 36, 40–42, **41**
proof-of-work (PoW) 12–14, *14*, 16, 17, 32, 36, 39–42, *41*, **41**; definition of 40
property insurance 132

Prosper 84, 85
public blockchain 36

QR (quick response) code 59–60, *60*
Quantemplate 5

Rachleff, A. 121
RapidMiner 165
RASs *see* robo-advisory services (RASs)
Rastogi, G. 124
Razorpay 3, 5; Loyalty Wallet 74; MagicX 73–74; Payment Gateway 3.0 73–75; Razorpay AI-Nucleus 74; Razorpay Magic Konnect 74
RBA *see* risk-based authentication (RBA)
RBI *see* Reserve Bank of India (RBI)
Reg-Room 5
RegTech 2, 5, 6, 39, 134, 155–183; AIML applications in 175; AML and KYC compliance 159; applications 170–174; banking and financial transactions 170; benefits of 177–178; big data analytics, application of 175; blockchain applications in 176; capital adequacy 160; companies 178–181; consumer protection 159; cross-border regulations 160–161; crowdfunding regulations 159; cybersecurity 159; data protection and privacy 159; definition of 156–157; ecosystem 174, *174*; financial terrorism, combating 172–173; history of 157–158; identity management 173; IoT applications in 177; licensing and regulation 159–161; money laundering, prevention of 170–171; need of 168–170; payment services regulations 159; phases of 161–166, **162**; process flow 166–168, *166*; prudential standards 160; regulatory reporting 174; risk-based authentication 171–172; risk management 173–174; RPA applications in 176–177; rules governing Fintech industries 158–159; transaction management 173
regulatory reporting 136, 162–164, 167, 174, 175, 178
Reiss, J. 179
Reitwiessner, C. 43
Reserve Bank of India (RBI) 8, 49, 79, 90, 169
retail CBDC 211–212
Revolut 4, 5, 199
Ripple 20–21
Ripple Labs 20
risk-based authentication (RBA) 171–172
risk management 129–153, 173–174
Rivest Shamir Adleman (RSA) 35
Robinhood 118
Robinson, J. 179